Google AdWords™ For Dummies®, 2nd Edition

W9-AWM-479

Sheet

AdWords Terms

Ad position: The placement of an ad on the Google search results pages. Position #1 is at the top of the first page.

Bid price: The maximum amount of money an advertiser is willing to pay for a click from a given keyword.

Call to action: Directions within an ad or a Web page for the reader to take an action.

Conversion: A desirable action by a Web-site visitor, including joining a mailing list, buying a product, calling a phone number, or downloading a file.

CPC (cost per click): The amount an advertiser is charged for a single click. Different keywords cost different amounts, depending on competition.

CTR (click-through rate): The number of clicks an ad receives divided by the number of impressions. The higher the CTR, the more effective Google considers the ad.

Impression: The display of an ad on a Web page.

Landing page: The first Web page shown after an ad is clicked. The page is constructed to appeal to the same desire as the ad.

PPC (pay per click): The advertising model that charges advertisers only when their specific ads are clicked.

Split test: Test that divides online traffic randomly between two or more creative approaches (ad, Web site, e-mail, and so on) and measures which one generates more conversions.

Traffic: The number of visitors to your Web site.

Visitor value: How much money, on average, a single visitor to your Web site is worth.

Landing Page Elements to Test

- **Headline:** Use the results from your ad split tests to inform different headlines. Proclaim a big benefit, ask a question, start telling a story, make a scary prediction, and so on.
- **Offer:** Do your visitors prefer an e-book, a newsletter, a minicourse, a sales quote, a CD, a return phone call, a cheat sheet, or a suitcase filled with unmarked $100 bills? (Just kidding about the suitcase.)
- **Location of opt-in form:** Try the opt-in form on the right or the left, above the scroll, every four paragraphs, and so on.
- **Graphics:** Test different photos of the product. Add shadow. Make the pictures bigger or smaller. Experiment with removing the header graphic. Try different colors and fonts for text and hyperlinks.
- **Background color:** Try lighter or darker colors, warmer or cooler, with or without repeating background graphics.
- **Multimedia:** Test adding audio or video to your page to orient, instruct, and win over your visitor.

Wiley, the Wiley Publishing logo, For Dummies, the Dummies Man logo, the For Dummies Bestselling Book Series logo and all related trade dress are trademarks or registered trademarks of John Wiley & Sons, Inc. and/or its affiliates. All other trademarks are property of their respective owners.

For Dummies: Bestselling Book Series for Beginners

Google AdWords™ For Dummies, 2nd Edition

Cheat Sheet

Campaign-Optimization Tips

- **Separate Google, Search Partners, and Content Network traffic into different campaigns.** Keep your traffic streams separate so you can track the visitor value from each stream individually; optimize your sales funnel for each group.

- **Create tightly focused ad groups with closely related keywords.** Avoid sloppy ad groups with thousands of words all pointing to some loosely related ad. Group common desires and mindsets; send each to a targeted landing page.

- **Place underperforming keywords in new ad groups and optimize the ads for those keywords.** If one of your top traffic keywords in an ad group is getting a significantly lower CTR than the rest, move it to its own ad group and write an ad with that keyword in the headline (and perhaps in the URL).

- **Build ad groups with enough traffic to split-test in a timely fashion.** Don't take too long to declare split-test winners.

- **Add long-tail keywords to decrease CPC and increase traffic.** Three- and four-word phrases tend to have less competition and represent buyers rather than lookers.

- **Focus your energy on the changes that will make the biggest difference.** Before managing and optimizing your account, sort campaigns, ad groups, and keyword lists by impressions. Start where the most traffic is so your improvements lead to increased or more qualified visitor flow.

Free AdWords Resources

AdWords Home Page: `https://adwords.google.com` to sign up for AdWords and to log in to your account.

AdWords Help Center: `https://adwords.google.com/support` for answers to frequently (and not-so-frequently) asked questions.

AdWords Learning Center: `http://www.google.com/adwords/learningcenter` for text and multimedia AdWords lessons. You can watch short videos, take quizzes, and even become a Qualified Google Advertising Professional.

AdWords Editorial Guidelines: `https://adwords.google.com/select/guidelines.html` reminds you what not to put in your ads.

Google Group for AdWords Help: `http://www.google.com/support/forum/p/AdWords` to connect with over 11,000 AdWords users to ask questions and receive answers from Google-approved experts (free registration required).

Free Split Tester: `http://www.askhowie.com/freesplit` allows you to enter statistics for two ads and determine whether you have a winner.

Companion Web Site for This Book: `http://www.askhowie.com` includes updates, an AdWords tips newsletter, free teleseminars, video tutorials, and information about AdWords consulting, coaching, and campaign management.

Copyright © 2009 Wiley Publishing, Inc. All rights reserved. Item 5577-7.
For more information about Wiley Publishing, call 1-877-762-2974.

For Dummies: Bestselling Book Series for Beginners

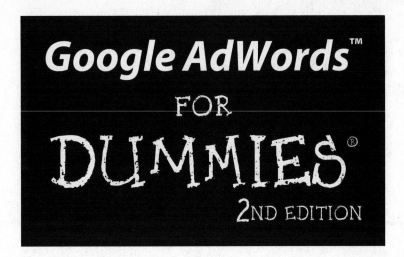

Google AdWords™
FOR
DUMMIES®
2ND EDITION

by Howie Jacobson, PhD

WILEY

Wiley Publishing, Inc.

Google AdWords™ For Dummies®, 2nd Edition

Published by
Wiley Publishing, Inc.
111 River Street
Hoboken, NJ 07030-5774

www.wiley.com

Copyright © 2009 by Wiley Publishing, Inc., Indianapolis, Indiana

Published by Wiley Publishing, Inc., Indianapolis, Indiana

Published simultaneously in Canada

No part of this publication may be reproduced, stored in a retrieval system or transmitted in any form or by any means, electronic, mechanical, photocopying, recording, scanning or otherwise, except as permitted under Sections 107 or 108 of the 1976 United States Copyright Act, without either the prior written permission of the Publisher, or authorization through payment of the appropriate per-copy fee to the Copyright Clearance Center, 222 Rosewood Drive, Danvers, MA 01923, (978) 750-8400, fax (978) 646-8600. Requests to the Publisher for permission should be addressed to the Permissions Department, John Wiley & Sons, Inc., 111 River Street, Hoboken, NJ 07030, (201) 748-6011, fax (201) 748-6008, or online at http://www.wiley.com/go/permissions.

Trademarks: Wiley, the Wiley Publishing logo, For Dummies, the Dummies Man logo, A Reference for the Rest of Us!, The Dummies Way, Dummies Daily, The Fun and Easy Way, Dummies.com, Making Everything Easier, and related trade dress are trademarks or registered trademarks of John Wiley & Sons, Inc. and/or its affiliates in the United States and other countries, and may not be used without written permission. Google AdWords is a trademark of Google, Inc. All other trademarks are the property of their respective owners. Wiley Publishing, Inc., is not associated with any product or vendor mentioned in this book.

LIMIT OF LIABILITY/DISCLAIMER OF WARRANTY: THE PUBLISHER AND THE AUTHOR MAKE NO REPRESENTATIONS OR WARRANTIES WITH RESPECT TO THE ACCURACY OR COMPLETENESS OF THE CONTENTS OF THIS WORK AND SPECIFICALLY DISCLAIM ALL WARRANTIES, INCLUDING WITHOUT LIMITATION WARRANTIES OF FITNESS FOR A PARTICULAR PURPOSE. NO WARRANTY MAY BE CREATED OR EXTENDED BY SALES OR PROMOTIONAL MATERIALS. THE ADVICE AND STRATEGIES CONTAINED HEREIN MAY NOT BE SUITABLE FOR EVERY SITUATION. THIS WORK IS SOLD WITH THE UNDERSTANDING THAT THE PUBLISHER IS NOT ENGAGED IN RENDERING LEGAL, ACCOUNTING, OR OTHER PROFESSIONAL SERVICES. IF PROFESSIONAL ASSISTANCE IS REQUIRED, THE SERVICES OF A COMPETENT PROFESSIONAL PERSON SHOULD BE SOUGHT. NEITHER THE PUBLISHER NOR THE AUTHOR SHALL BE LIABLE FOR DAMAGES ARISING HEREFROM. THE FACT THAT AN ORGANIZATION OR WEBSITE IS REFERRED TO IN THIS WORK AS A CITATION AND/OR A POTENTIAL SOURCE OF FURTHER INFORMATION DOES NOT MEAN THAT THE AUTHOR OR THE PUBLISHER ENDORSES THE INFORMATION THE ORGANIZATION OR WEBSITE MAY PROVIDE OR RECOMMENDATIONS IT MAY MAKE. FURTHER, READERS SHOULD BE AWARE THAT INTERNET WEBSITES LISTED IN THIS WORK MAY HAVE CHANGED OR DISAPPEARED BETWEEN WHEN THIS WORK WAS WRITTEN AND WHEN IT IS READ.

For general information on our other products and services, please contact our Customer Care Department within the U.S. at 877-762-2974, outside the U.S. at 317-572-3993, or fax 317-572-4002.

For technical support, please visit www.wiley.com/techsupport.

Wiley also publishes its books in a variety of electronic formats. Some content that appears in print may not be available in electronic books.

Library of Congress Control Number: 2009929466

ISBN: 978-0-470-45577-7

Manufactured in the United States of America

10 9 8 7 6 5 4 3 2 1

WILEY

About the Author

Howie Jacobson, PhD, has been an Internet marketing strategist since 1999. He specializes in helping clients use Google AdWords to grow their businesses. Because he was forced to study statistical methods in graduate school, Jacobson took to direct marketing as soon as he tripped over it in 2001.

He is the creator of the AdWords Ball, AdWords Checkmate, and Traffic Surge programs. He also runs the Ring of Fire AdWords coaching club.

Jacobson has presented at several System Seminar events, at Perry Marshall's AdWords Seminar, Agora's Early to Rise conferences, and at workshops and seminars around the world. He is a regular contributor to HorsesMouth.com, a performance-improvement site for financial advisors, as well as a former writer for Vault.com. He leads telephone seminars on beginner and advanced AdWords topics and provides online coaching and support at his Web site, www.askhowie.com.

Jacobson also runs www.loweryourbidprice.com, a company that produces software tools that help AdWords advertisers and AdWords consultants save time, reduce costs, and increase profits.

Luckily for you, Jacobson began his career as a schoolteacher. Through trial by fire, he learned how to be engaging, clear, and entertaining while providing value and motivating results. He is also a business coach and trainer, skilled in turning learning into action, helping his own clients and a horde of others in association with Bregman Partners, Inc., and The Avoca Group.

Jacobson combines his marketing expertise with his background in and passion for health and fitness at FitFam.com, a resource for parents struggling to raise fit and healthy kids in a crazy-busy world.

He lives in Durham, North Carolina, with his wife, two kids, big, goofy dog, and three-legged rat. His lifelong ambition is to bring about world peace through marketing — and after that's accomplished, to play Ultimate Frisbee in the 2044 Olympics in Maui.

Dedication

This book is dedicated to the people I annoyed and ignored the most during the writing of it: my children, Yael and Elan, and my wife. Mia, I love you more than any of my favorite song lyrics can say. Yael, continue to strive for justice and keep making the world a more beautiful and unpredictable place. Elan, keep growing strong and true, and share your belly laugh and music with everyone you meet.

I also dedicate this book to my mother, Lucie Jacobson, whose example reminds me to give generously and live big, and the memory of my father, Joel R. Jacobson, a courageous man with a kind heart and a great squash serve.

Author's Acknowledgments

If I were to properly acknowledge on one page all the help I received while writing this book, I'd be using Times New Roman 0.01-point font and you'd be reading this with an electron microscope.

My wonderful editors at Wiley Publishing: Amy Fandrei, Chris Morris, Brian Walls, and Jennifer Riggs. They have been patient with my whining, accepting of nothing but my best, and always ready with advice and reassurance. And Jim Kelly, tech editor extraordinaire, keeps me honest and entertained at the same time.

My technical advisors at Google, Devin Sandoz, Gopi Kallayil, Jason Rose, Fred Vallaeys, and Emily Harris, answered my frequent volleys of questions with celerity and grace. We haven't met, but I like to think of them riding their Segways from the office to the gourmet lunchrooms at the Googleplex.

Big hugs to the many AdWords experts who shared their wisdom, stories, and sometimes, even keywords. Perry Marshall is such a fine AdWords teacher, business associate, and friend that I wonder what good deeds I performed in my previous life to deserve him. Kristie McDonald and David Rothwell are my "ears to the ground" AdWords practitioners who always seem to know what Google is up to before anybody else. David Bullock and Glenn Livingston shared their best stuff with me freely and often — I apologize to their clients and spouses for all the time I monopolized while asking them questions. David even agreed, in a moment of weakness, to become the technical editor for the first edition of this book. Luckily, I asked and he agreed just before he was featured in Black Enterprise Magazine and became the most sought-after Taguchi expert in the country.

Sean D'Souza has rocked my world with the quality of his thinking, teaching, and heart. He and my coach, Christian Mickelsen, have shown me the way to a sustainable, joyous online business.

Timothy Seward, my neighbor in North Carolina, has taught me more about Analytics than I thought there was to know. If I'd been paying for his time, he'd be retired by now. The fabulous Joy Milkowski shared her methodologies with me and helped me rewrite the chapter about creating compelling ads. The friendship we developed during this project has been an added bonus. Don Crowther, one of the cleverest and under-the-radar marketers on this or any other planet, shared more cool ideas with me than I could ever have hoped. And Dan Hollings, the man behind the online success of "The Secret," reached out to me in an Amazon.com review of the first edition of *AdWords For Dummies* and has been blowing my mind with his crazy-brilliant online strategies ever since.

Bryan Todd and I have argued and philosophized about metrics more than either of us cares to admit. Kelly Muldoon shared her experience with geographic targeting and always has the right amount of sympathy and chocolate for any situation. Michael Katz, the world's expert on e-newsletters, was so helpful during this project that I almost forgive him for being funnier than I am. Joe Chapuis generously shared his knowledge about the cutting edge of online video, while Ari Galper enlightened me about the marketing potential of live chat and allowed me to reveal his strategies and show his screen shots. Thanks also to my many clients who shared case studies with me — sorry about all the ones I couldn't use.

Rob Goyette, Steve Goyette, and Erik Wickstrom were never more than a cell phone call away whenever I had a question about PHP, HTML, or the MLB MVP. Working with these talented programmers and marketers is like having three genie-filled lamps.

Elizabeth Edmiston, the other half of my business brain (and that's an understatement), keeps me on track, keeps clients and customers delighted, and creates the most amazing software. Head on over to www.magic adwordsbutton.com if you don't believe me.

Ken McCarthy is, quite simply, the source. He understood the potential of the Internet long before the dot.com craze, and he has been quietly creating business leaders and success stories for over 15 years. The combination of masterful teacher and brilliant business strategist is a rare one; throw in loyal friend and passionate righter of wrongs and you have Ken.

Brad Hill believed in me enough to get this whole adventure in motion, and he has encouraged me to become the writer my elementary school teachers always said I'd become. Danny Warshay has been a business and life mentor since we met as roommates in Jerusalem in 1986. And Peter Bregman gave me my introduction to the business world when I was a naïve, befuddled PhD freshly minted from grad school. He always encouraged me to ask questions, no matter how stupid, and except for that time when I asked the HR Director from American Express what exactly she meant by "P&L," it all worked out. Without Peter's guidance and wicked humor, my life would be unimaginably less rich.

Publisher's Acknowledgments

We're proud of this book; please send us your comments through our online registration form located at http://dummies.custhelp.com. For other comments, please contact our Customer Care Department within the U.S. at 877-762-2974, outside the U.S. at 317-572-3993, or fax 317-572-4002.

Some of the people who helped bring this book to market include the following:

Acquisitions, Editorial

Senior Project Editor: Christopher Morris

Acquisitions Editor: Amy Fandrei

Copy Editors: Brian Walls, Jennifer Riggs

Technical Editor: James Kelly

Editorial Manager: Kevin Kirschner

Media Development Project Manager: Laura Moss-Hollister

Media Development Assistant Project Manager: Jenny Swisher

Media Development Assistant Producers: Angela Denny, Josh Frank, Shawn Patrick

Editorial Assistant: Amanda Foxworth

Sr. Editorial Assistant: Cherie Case

Cartoons: Rich Tennant (www.the5thwave.com)

Composition Services

Project Coordinator: Kristie Rees

Layout and Graphics: Christin Swinford, Ronald Terry, Christine Williams

Proofreader: ConText Editorial Services, Inc.

Indexer: Joan Griffitts

Publishing and Editorial for Technology Dummies

> **Richard Swadley,** Vice President and Executive Group Publisher

> **Andy Cummings,** Vice President and Publisher

> **Mary Bednarek,** Executive Acquisitions Director

> **Mary C. Corder,** Editorial Director

Publishing for Consumer Dummies

> **Diane Graves Steele,** Vice President and Publisher

Composition Services

> **Debbie Stailey,** Director of Composition Services

Contents at a Glance

Table of Contents

Introduction

Most business owners I meet have never heard of Google AdWords. My prediction: If you aren't advertising your business in Google within two years, you're not going to stay in business. The age of the Yellow Pages is ending, and online advertising — led by AdWords — is taking over.

For those who take the time to master this new advertising medium, it's an exciting time. AdWords represents a revolution in the advertising world. For the first time ever, businesses large and small can show their ads to qualified prospects anywhere in the world, when those prospects are hungriest for the business' products and services. AdWords allows fine geographic targeting, like a Yellow Pages ad, but (unlike the Yellow Pages) *also* allows advertisers to edit, pause, or delete their Google ads any time they like, in real time.

Unlike a traditional advertisement, Google ads cost money only when they are clicked — that is, when a live prospect clicks the ad to visit your site. And perhaps most important, AdWords enables advertisers to test multiple ads simultaneously and to track the return on investment of every ad and every keyword they employ.

Since a click can cost as little as a penny and each click can be tracked to a business outcome, even small, cash-strapped businesses can find AdWords an effective way to grow without betting the farm on untested marketing messages. Google's ads reach across the entire Internet. In addition to the 200 million Google searches per day (almost 60 percent of all Internet searches), Google provides search results for AOL, EarthLink, Netscape, and other big Internet service providers. And through its AdSense program, Google's ads appear on sites all across the Internet — in thousands of newspaper Web sites and hundreds of thousands of blogs, as well as on Gmail pages.

Yet few small businesses have ever advertised through AdWords. The pay-per-click technology, combined with the unfamiliar form of direct-response marketing, has so far kept most small businesses away from the potential benefits of AdWords. If few businesses are using it, even fewer are using it wisely. Marketing executives at large companies have been slow to embrace the direct-response model, having been trained in brand advertising that has little place in a results-accountable medium like AdWords.

About This Book

I've consulted with hundreds of AdWords clients over the past several years, working with everyone from complete beginners who didn't know how to set up their account to power users spending more than a million dollars a month in clicks. Nothing in this book is theoretical — every concept and strategy has been tested under fire in some of the most competitive markets on Earth. When you play the AdWords game, you don't have much room to spin failure into success. You either make money or lose money, and the numbers tell the story.

This book strives to explain clearly, in layperson's terms, the AdWords mechanics and best practices for businesses large and small. You will discover how to build smart and elegant campaigns based on an understanding of the direct marketing principles.

This book isn't meant to be read from front to back. (I didn't even write it from front to back.) It's more like a reference. Each chapter is divided into sections, so you can jump in anywhere and find out how to accomplish a specific AdWords task.

You don't have to remember anything in this book. Nothing is worth memorizing, except the mantra, "Thank you, Howie." The information here is what you need to know to create and manage successful AdWords campaigns — and nothing more. And wherever I mention a new term, I explain it in plain English. When the movie comes out (I'm thinking Kevin Spacey plays me, although Daniel Day Lewis would also be a good choice), these explanations will be in bold subtitles. I rarely get geeky on you, because AdWords is largely a user-friendly interface. Occasionally, I do show off by explaining a technical phrase — feel free to skip those sections unless you're preparing for a big game of Trivial Pursuit — Cyber Edition.

Conventions Used in This Book

I know that doing something the same way over and over again can be boring (the opening credits of *The Brady Bunch* comes to mind), but sometimes consistency can be a good thing. For one thing, it makes stuff easier to understand. In this book, those consistent elements are *conventions.* In fact, I use italics to identify and define the new terms. I also put search terms and keywords in italics.

Whenever you have to type something, I put the stuff you need to type in **bold** type so it's easy to see.

When I type URLs (Web addresses) within a paragraph, for the rare snippets of code I show you, and for keywords, I use a monospace font that looks like this: `www.dummies.com`.

What You Don't Have to Read

This is the hardest part of the book for me because each word I wrote is my baby, and they're all wonderful. Nevertheless, I am contractually obligated to let you off the hook at least a little, so here goes.

You can skip all the paragraphs marked with the Technical Stuff icon. I just put that in because I like the icon, and to give you confidence that I know what I'm talking about. The sidebars aren't crucial to the plot either, although many of them feature tips and examples from very sharp AdWords users.

If you already have an AdWords account, you can actually skip Chapter 2, which shows you how to set up an AdWords account.

Foolish Assumptions

As I gaze into my polycarbonate ball (crystal balls are breakable, and I can be clumsy), I see you as clearly as if you were sitting here with me in this hotel lobby in Wisconsin at 5:30 in the morning. You have a barely noticeable scar just above your right elbow where you cut yourself against a pool wall when you were eleven, and you are wearing a plaid watchband.

The foolish assumptions that informed my writing include the guess that the main market for your ads reads and speaks English. If not, no big deal: Just substitute Spanish or Russian or Azerbaijani for English as you read (although the reference to Azerbaijani muffins may confuse you).

I'm also assuming that your AdWords goal is business-related, especially in the way I talk about the desired outcomes of your campaigns — that is, leads, sales, profits, and so on. If you're advertising on behalf of a nonprofit, you can easily substitute your own desired outcomes, including signatures on an online petition, additions to your mailing list, or attendance at an event. Your outcomes can be nonmeasurable as well, such as convincing Web site visitors to reduce their energy consumption, support a political candidate or position, eat healthier food, and so on.

I make several foolish assumptions about your level of computer savvy. I assume you can make your way around a Web site, including clicking, typing in Web addresses, completing forms, and so on. I assume you have access to a working credit card (no, you can't borrow mine) so you can sign up and pay for AdWords.

I don't assume that you're using a PC or a Mac. You can benefit from this book whatever computer platform you use: Mac, PC, Linux, Hairball (all right, I made that last one up). Some third-party software works on Windows PCs only, but you can accomplish 99 percent of the tasks in this book using just a Web browser and text editor.

I also assume you can get Web pages created. You don't have to create them yourself, but either through your efforts or someone else's, you can design, upload, name, and edit simple HTML Web pages.

How This Book Is Organized

I sent my editor an unabridged dictionary and told him all the words from the book are in it, and he could decide which ones go where (that's his job, after all). It turns out I was wrong: Google wasn't even in the dictionary (the one I got for my college graduation in 1987), so it was back to the drawing board.

On my next try, I divided this book into parts, which I organized by topic. Google AdWords is the big topic, but much of the book focuses on what you have to do before and after AdWords in order to be successful. You don't have to read it in order. In fact, every time I wrote, "As you saw in Chapter 4," my editor sent a slight electric shock through the Internet into my keyboard. So start anywhere you like, and go anywhere you like. If you're looking for information on a specific AdWords topic, check the headings in the Table of Contents or skim the Index.

By design, this book enables you to get as much (or as little) information as you need at any particular moment. Having gotten through college English by reading the jacket blurbs of great novels (this was before Google appeared in the dictionary), I understand the value of strategic skimming. By design, *Google AdWords For Dummies* is a reference that you reach for again and again whenever you encounter a new situation or need a fresh poke of inspiration.

Part I: Becoming a Google Advertiser

Before you drive your AdWords vehicle to success, let's get you pointed in the right direction. Forget everything you learned about marketing in business school, and understand that AdWords is fundamentally a direct marketing medium. You discover what that means, and how it differs from the brand advertising that we see all around us, and how to play the direct marketing game to win.

Once you're oriented and pointed toward success, I show you how to start your engine and drive around the block safely before going to the races.

Part II: Launching Your AdWords Campaign

Before you activate your first campaign, I introduce you to the single most important element of AdWords (actually, of just about all online marketing): choosing the right keywords. I show you how to do this through various online research tools and methods, most of which are quick, free, and easy.

Next, you master the ads themselves. Because AdWords is the most competitive advertising space in existence (slapping your ad in the middle of 20 others offering more or less the same thing), you must deploy advanced strategies for creating compelling, action-triggering ads. Otherwise no Web traffic, no leads, no money. I focus on text ads because they are the most common and (in their simplicity) provide the best opportunity to illustrate direct marketing principles. I also cover image ads, video ads, and local business ads connected to Google Maps.

Part III: Managing Your AdWords Campaigns

The two bricks of your AdWords campaign are keywords and ads. If you hired me to build you a house and I just dropped a dump truck full of bricks on your empty lot, you wouldn't be happy. The chapters in this part give you the blueprints to turn your bricks into a sound and effective structure, and the tools to build and maintain it. You learn how to structure campaigns and ad groups, manage keyword bids, and target the right traffic.

Part IV: Converting Clicks to Clink

This is my favorite part of the whole book, the part where my family dragged me away from my keyboard as I kicked and screamed, "Wait, I haven't told them about Crazy Egg yet." After you set up your campaigns and paid for visitors to your Web site, you learn how to use lead-generating magnets to collect contact information from visitors — and to use e-mail to stay in touch and build a relationship. I also cover Web site strategies to extract maximum value from each visitor.

Part V: Testing Your Strategies and Tracking Your Results

Actually, this is my favorite part of the whole book (okay, my other favorite) because I show you how to fail your way to success inexpensively, quickly, and predictably. When you test multiple approaches, one is almost always better than the other. As long as you keep testing properly and paying attention to the results, you can't help but achieve constant incremental (and sometimes enormous) improvement in your profitability.

Part VI: The Part of Tens

Part of my hazing in the *For Dummies* fraternity included creating top-ten lists that, alas, will never make their way onto Letterman. They include beginners' mistakes you want your competitors to make instead of you, and case studies that bring the principles of the book to life. The Part of Tens is a resource you can use whenever you're stuck, except for wedding toasts and term papers about the causes of World War I.

Be sure to check out www.dummies.com/go/adwords to see this book's two bonus chapters as PDF files. These two bonus chapters provide you with top-ten lists of the best AdWords tools available and tips for writing great ads.

Icons Used in This Book

Unfortunately, I could not convince my editor to let me use an icon of a sumo wrestler wearing a tutu hurtling toward you on ice skates to indicate, "This paragraph makes absolutely no sense, but you should pay close attention to it anyway." So I stuck with the standard *For Dummies* icons:

I hope my tips don't hurt as much as the one in the icon, but are just as sharp. I use this bull's-eye to flag concepts that can cut months from your AdWords learning curve.

I use this icon to remind you to remove the string that's cutting off the circulation to your index finger. (What were you thinking?) Also, this icon highlights points and items that should be on your AdWords To-Do list. Little tasks that can prevent big problems later.

I've heard too many stories of AdWords beginners turning on their campaigns, going to bed, and waking up to $16,000 craters in their credit cards. I use the bomb icon when a little mistake can have big and nasty consequences.

I'm probably less geeky than you are. I've learned enough code writing to be dangerous (ask my Webmaster, who probably has installed a one-click backup for my sites by now), but not enough to be useful. So I use this icon only to impress you with my knowledge of certain geeky terms and when I share a snippet of code that your Webmaster can deal with if you don't want to.

I've created a companion Web site to this book at `www.askhowie.com`. Many of the processes you implement can be hard to describe on paper, but simple to show in a video tutorial. (If you're not sure what I mean, try describing to someone how to tie his shoes.) I include video footage of my own computer screen so you can see and hear exactly how to do what I tell you to. Also, the Web addresses of articles, resources, and tools change from time to time. When I suspect that the current URL won't be valid by the time you read this, I send you to my site, which will either automatically redirect you to the right location, or provide an even better resource that wasn't available when I was writing the chapter.

Where to Go from Here

I'm thinking that a nice bowl of gazpacho would be nice right about now. Fresh Roma tomatoes, cilantro, onions, some cumin, and maybe a few chunks of cucumber, sweet corn, and avocado floating on top. Wanna join me?

You can start reading wherever you want, but I'd like to point out a couple of fundamental chapters that you will want to understand fully before spending money on AdWords. Chapter 1 gives you the direct marketing mindset you need to use AdWords effectively, and Chapter 4 guides you to a deep understanding of your market. Skim Chapters 10 and 11 before turning on the traffic to your Web site.

When you have the lay of the land, you may want to implement the tracking described in Chapter 14 as soon as you set up your account (explained in Chapter 2). Knowing the profitability of each element of your AdWords campaign makes everything easier and more fun.

The companion Web site www.askhowie.com is a good place to go for more information, detailed video tutorials, updates, and an e-mail newsletter on AdWords tips and strategies. If you encounter something online that is different from the book, check the www.askhowie.com/readers site for updates. You can also check out www.dummies.com/go/adwords2e for other updates.

If you're aching to tell me how much you love this book and how you'd like to fly me, first-class, to Cape Town, Fiji, or Maui to teach a workshop, give a keynote, or just enjoy a well-deserved vacation, feel free to e-mail me at support@askhowie.com.

Part I

Becoming a Google Advertiser

The 5th Wave   By Rich Tennant

"Look—you can't just list an extraterrestrial embryo on AdWords without using some catchy phrases or power words to make it seem interesting and unique."

In this part . . .

This part introduces Google AdWords and shows you how to get started. Almost everyone is familiar with the Google search engine; however, few people understand how easy it is to pay to display your ad listing on the coveted first page of search results — and how challenging it can be to do so profitably.

Chapter 1 discusses online search as a revolution in advertising and reveals the marketing-mindset shifts required for success. You discover how to get into your customers' minds and see through their eyes so your advertising will be customer-centric and effective.

Chapter 2 takes you through the mechanics of creating — and immediately pausing — a single campaign. (Patience, grasshopper.) Chapter 3 shows you step by step how to populate that account correctly with keywords, ads, placements, and bids. These chapters provide the foundation upon which your AdWords success is built — customized campaigns with settings that support the achievement of your goals.

Chapter 1

Profiting from the Pay-Per-Click Revolution

*H*ave you ever bought an ad in the Yellow Pages? I remember my first time — I was terrified. I didn't know what to write. I didn't know how big an ad to buy. I wasn't sure which phonebooks to advertise in. I had no idea what headings to list under. I had to pay thousands of dollars for an ad I wouldn't be able to change for the next 12 months. And I had recurring nightmares that I mistyped the phone number and some baffled florist in Poughkeepsie got thousands of calls from my customers.

Why am I telling you this? (Aside from the fact that my therapist encourages me to release negative emotions?) Because I want you to appreciate the significance of Google AdWords as a revolution in advertising.

You can set up an AdWords account in about five minutes for five dollars. Your ads can be seen by thousands of people searching specifically for what you have, and you don't pay a cent until a searcher clicks your ad to visit your Web site. You can change your ad copy any time you want. You can cancel unprofitable ads with the click of a mouse. You can run multiple ads simultaneously and figure out to the penny which ad makes you the most money.

You can even send customers to specific aisles and shelves of your store, depending on what they're searching for. And you can get smarter and smarter over time, writing better ads, showing under more appropriate headings, choosing certain geographic markets and avoiding others. When your ads do well, you can even get Google to serve them as online newspaper and magazine ads, put them next to Google Maps locations, and broadcast them to cell phones — automatically.

AdWords gives you the ability to conduct hundreds of thousands of dollars of market research for less than the cost of a one-way ticket from Chapel Hill to Madison. And in less time than it takes me to do five one-arm pushups (okay, so that's not saying much).

AdWords can help you test and improve your Web site and e-mail strategy to squeeze additional profits out of every step in your sales process. It can provide a steady stream of qualified leads for predictable costs. But AdWords can also be a huge sinkhole of cash for the advertiser who doesn't understand it. I've written this book to arm you with the mindsets, strategies, and tactics to keep you from ever becoming an AdWords victim.

Introducing AdWords

The Google search engine, found at www.google.com, processes hundreds of millions of searches per day. Every one of those searches represents a human being trying to solve a problem or satisfy an itch through finding the right information on the World Wide Web. The AdWords program allows advertisers to purchase text and links on the Google results page (the page the searcher sees after entering a word or phrase and clicking the Google Search button).

You pay for the ad only when someone clicks it and visits your Web site. The amount you pay for each visitor can be as low as one penny, or as high as $80, depending on the quality of your ad, your Web site, and the competitiveness of the market defined by the word or phrase (known as a *keyword*, even though it may be several words long) typed by the visitor.

Each text ad on the results page consists of four lines and up to 130 characters (see Figure 1-1 for an example ad):

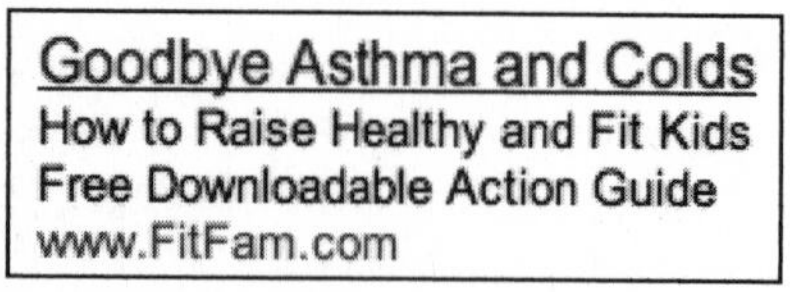

Figure 1-1:
This AdWords ad targets parents whose children suffer from asthma.

<u>Goodbye Asthma and Colds</u>
How to Raise Healthy and Fit Kids
Free Downloadable Action Guide
www.FitFam.com

✔ **Line 1:** Blue underlined hyperlinked headline of up to 25 characters

✔ **Line 2:** Description line 1 of up to 35 characters

✔ **Line 3:** Description line 2 of up to 35 characters

✔ **Line 4:** Green display URL (URL stands for Uniform Resource Locator, the way the Internet assigns addresses to Web sites) of up to 35 characters

The fourth line, the display URL, can differ from the Web page your visitor actually lands on. I cover this in detail in Chapter 6.

Where and When the Ads Show

You can choose to show your ads to the entire world, or limit their exposure by country, region, state, and even city. You can (for example) let them run 24/7 or turn them off nights and weekends. You also get to choose from AdWords' three tiers of exposure, described in the following sections.

Google results

When someone searches for a particular keyword, your ad displays on the Google results page if you've selected that keyword (or a close variation) as a trigger for your ad. For the ad shown in Figure 1-1, if someone enters `kids asthma prevention` in Google, they can view the ad somewhere on the top or right of the results page (see Figure 1-2).

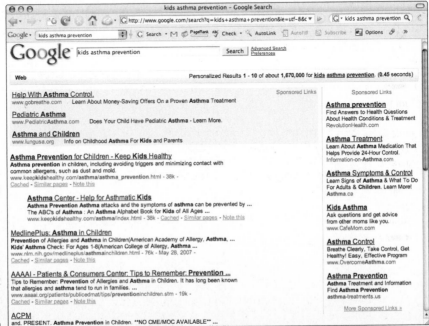

Figure 1-2: AdWords results are labeled Sponsored Links at the top and right.

Search partners results

Your ads can also show on Google's search partners' network. Companies such as AOL and EarthLink incorporate Google's results into their search pages, as in Figure 1-3.

A partial list of Google search partners includes

- ✔ **American Online (AOL):** www.aol.com
- ✔ **Ask.com:** www.ask.com
- ✔ **CompuServe:** http://webcenters.netscape.compuserve.com/menu
- ✔ **EarthLink:** www.earthlink.net
- ✔ **Netscape Netcenter:** www.netscape.com
- ✔ **Shopping.com:** www.shopping.com

AdSense sites and Gmail

Additionally, hundreds of thousands of Web sites show AdWords ads on their pages as part of the AdSense program, which pays Web site owners to show AdWords ads on their sites. (See Figure 1-4 for an example.) Think of an online version of a newspaper or magazine, with ads next to the editorial content. The content of the page determines which ads are shown. On sites devoted to weightlifting, for example, Google shows ads for workout programs and muscle-building supplements, rather than knitting and quilting supplies. Google lets you choose whether to show your ads on this Content network, or just stick to the search networks.

Although anyone with a Web site can use the AdSense program, Google has a special relationship with some of the most popular content sites on the Web, including

- ✔ **About:** www.about.com
- ✔ **business.com:** www.business.com
- ✔ **Food Network:** www.foodnetwork.com
- ✔ **HGTV:** www.hgtv.com
- ✔ **HowStuffWorks:** www.howstuffworks.com
- ✔ **InfoSpace:** www.infospace.com
- ✔ **Lycos:** www.lycos.com
- ✔ **The New York Times:** www.nytimes.com
- ✔ **Reed Business:** www.reedbusiness.com

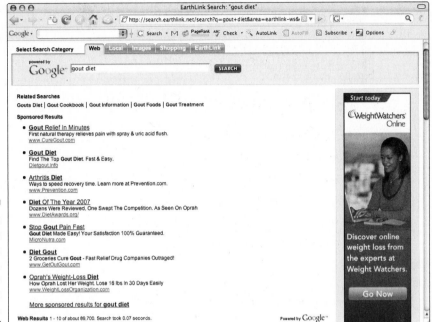

Figure 1-3:
AdWords
ads shown
by EarthLink,
a Google
search
partner.

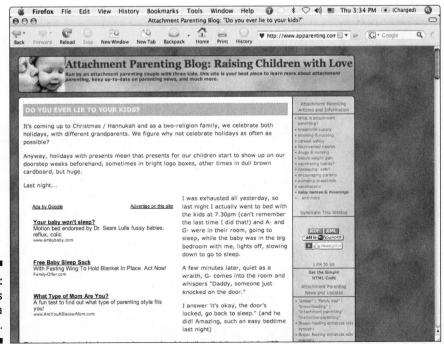

Figure 1-4:
AdWords
ads on a
Web page.

Gmail is Google's Web mail service. It displays AdWords results to the right of the e-mail you receive. If you choose to syndicate your ads, your prospects who use Gmail may see them if the text of the e-mail is deemed relevant to your offer. For example, Figure 1-5 shows an e-mail that I (almost) sent to the MacArthur Foundation, humbly explaining why I should receive one of their "genius grants." To the right, you can see ads for small business grants, a Cow Ringtone, triggered by my mention of a self-esteem program for cows, and two resources for college grant-seekers.

Figure 1-5: Google's AdSense program places AdWords ads to the right of a Gmail e-mail.

AdWords in the Total Google Context

Google rose from nothing to become the world's most popular search engine in just a few months because it did one thing faster and better than all the rest: help Internet searchers find what they were looking for. I don't want to overload you with the details of Google's search algorithm (especially because it's such a secret that if I told you, I'd have to kill you, and I would have to understand words like *eigenvector* and *stochastic* in order to explain it), but you will become a better Google advertiser when you get the basic principles. The most important word in Google's universe is *relevance*.

When you type a word or phrase into Google, the search engine asks the World Wide Web for the best page to show you. The big innovations Google uses are a couple of calculations: One, called PageRank, is basically a measure of the popularity of a particular page, based on how many other Web pages link to that page and how popular *those* pages are. (Sort of like high school — the definition of a popular kid is one who is friends with other popular kids.) The other calculation is known as Page Reputation, which answers the question, "Okay, this page may be popular, but for which topic?" The Page Reputation of a Web page determines whether it will appear in a given search; the PageRank determines whether it will be the first listing, the third, or the four million and eleventh.

The entire Google empire is based on this ability to match the right Web pages, in the right priority order, with a given search phrase. The day Google starts showing irrelevant results is the day *after* you should have sold all your Google stock.

When Google started, it only showed the results of its own calculations. These results are known as *organic listings.* Organic listings appear on the left side of the Google results page (see Figure 1-6, which includes organic listings only and no AdWords entries).

In the early days of AdWords, your ad was shown based on a combination of two numbers: your *bid price,* or how much you were willing to pay for a click (that is, someone clicking your ad and visiting your Web page), and a very important metric called Click-Through Rate (CTR), which is the percentage of searchers who click your ad after seeing it. Now, Google also takes into account the quality of the fit between the ad and your Web site. If searchers exit your site so fast that they leave skid marks, Google figures that they didn't find what they were looking for, and you're penalized for irrelevance.

Figure 1-6: Google's organic listings appear on the left of the results page.

A really short history lesson

The first pay per click (PPC) search engine, goto.com (whose name changed to Overture and now is known as Yahoo! Search Marketing), ran on a straight auction basis. Whoever wanted to show an ad in the top position simply bid more per click than everyone else for a given keyword. Google rose to preeminence in the PPC world because it figured out that letting badly written, unappealing ads rise to the top just because an advertiser was willing to spend a lot of cash was bad for everyone. Bad for the search engine, because the search engine doesn't get paid unless a Web visitor likes the ad enough to click it. Bad for the advertiser, because unappealing ads usually come from the same lazy or confused thinking that produces unappealing and unprofitable Web sites. And most important, bad for the search engine user, who was now getting unappealing and irrelevant listings muddying the results page, and would therefore start searching for a better search engine.

AdWords elegantly solved this problem by rewarding advertisers whose ads were popular with searchers. If your ad was twice as popular as a competitor's (meaning it was clicked twice as often), your cost per click (the amount of money you paid Google when a searcher clicked your ad and visited your Web site) was half what your competitor was paying for the same position on the page.

For example, suppose you and your competitor both bid $1.00 on the keyword elephant ride, and 1,000 people see each ad. Forty people click your ad, and 20 people click your competitor's. Your ad would appear *above* your competitor's for a cost per click of around $0.51 — if it's twice as popular, it costs half as much.

Highly relevant and compelling ads rose to the top of the page, while unappealing ads faded away as they proved unprofitable. Google also began AdWords with a cutoff on CTR: If your ad couldn't compel at least 5 out of the first 1,000 viewers to click it, Google would disable it and make you rewrite it before it could be shown again. They also instituted a three-strikes-and-you're-out rule — after the third disablement, you had to pay $5.00 to resuscitate your ad.

Over the years, Google has been tweaking the AdWords program to provide more and more relevant search results to its users. This book contains the very latest updates as I write, but please realize that Google never stops moving. While it's impossible to predict the exact changes Google will implement, you can be sure that it's always moving in the direction of greater relevance for its users. If your ads and Web pages always provide real value to real people, and don't exist just to "game" the AdWords machine, you're probably going to be just fine no matter what Google dreams up next.

Pay Per Click: Your Online Gumball Machine

AdWords is a PPC (pay per click) advertising medium. Unlike other forms of advertising, with PPC you pay only for results: live visitors to your Web site.

AdWords allows you as the advertiser to decide how much you're willing to pay for a visitor searching on a given keyword. For example, if you sell vintage sports trading cards, you can bid more for `Babe Ruth rookie card` than `John Gochnaur card` if you can make more money selling the Babe Ruth card.

For many businesses, advertising is like a slot machine: You put in your money, pull the handle, and see what happens. Sometimes you do well; sometimes you don't. Either way, you don't learn much that will help you predict the results of your next pull. PPC has changed all that for businesses with the patience and discipline to track online metrics. Just as a gumball machine reliably gives you a gumball every time you drop a quarter, PPC can reliably deliver a customer to your Web site for a predictable amount of money. Once you run your numbers (explained in Part V), you know exactly how much, on average, a visitor is worth from a particular keyword. You may find that you make $70 in profit for every 100 visitors from AdWords who searched for `biodegradable wedding dress`. Therefore, you can spend up to $0.70 for each click from this keyword and still break even or better on the first sale.

The Direct Marketing Difference: Getting Your Prospects to Do Something

Direct marketing differs from "brand" marketing, the kind we're used to on TV and radio and newspapers, in several important ways. AdWords represents direct marketing at its purest, so it's important to forget everything you thought you knew about advertising before throwing money at Google.

Direct marketers set one goal for their ads: to compel a measurable response in their prospects. Unlike brand marketers, you won't spend money to give people warm and fuzzy feelings when they think about your furniture coasters or ringtones or South Carolina resort rentals. Instead, you run your ad to get hot prospects to your Web site. On the *landing page* (the first page your prospect sees after leaving Google), you direct your prospect to take some other measurable action — fill out a form, call a phone number, initiate a live chat, drop everything, race to the airport and hop on the first plane to Hilton Head, and so on.

On the Web, you can track each visitor from the AdWords click through each intermediate step straight through to the first sale and all subsequent sales. So at each step of the sales cycle, on each Web page, in each e-mail, with each ad, you ask your prospect to take a specific action right now.

Brand advertisers rarely have the luxury of asking for immediate action. The company that advertises home gyms during reruns of *Gilligan's Island* has no illusion that 8,000 viewers are going to TiVo the rest of the episode and drive, tires squealing, to the nearest fitness store to purchase the GalactiMuscle 5000. They count on repetition to eventually lead to sales.

Contrast that approach with infomercials, which have one goal: to get you to pick up the phone NOW because they realize that once you get distracted, they've lost their chance of selling to you.

The Internet outdoes the immediacy and convenience of the infomercial by maintaining the same channel of communication. Instead of jumping from TV to phone, AdWords and your Web site function together as a seamless information-gathering experience.

You can measure your results

Because your prospects are doing what you want them to do (or not), you can measure the effectiveness of each call to action. For example, say you sell juggling equipment to left-handed people. You show your ad to 30,000 people in one week. Your ad attracts 450 prospects to your Web site, at an average CPC of $0.40. Your landing page offers a 5% off coupon in exchange for a valid e-mail address, and by the end of the week, your mailing list has 90 leads — 20% of all visitors. You follow up with an e-mail offer that compels 10 sales totaling $600.00.

The following table shows an example of an AdWords ad campaign's overall metrics.

Metric	Total cost or percentage
Total advertising cost	$180 (450 × $0.40)
Sales total	$600
Return on investment (ROI)	333% ($600 ÷ $180)
AdWords ad CTR	1.5% (450 ÷ 30,000)
Landing page lead conversion	20% (90 ÷ 450)
E-mail sales conversion	11% (10 ÷ 90)
Cost per visitor	$0.40
Average visitor value	$1.33 ($600 ÷ 450)
Cost per lead	$2.00 ($180 ÷ 90)
Average value of a lead	$6.67 ($600 ÷ 90)
Cost per sale	$18.00 ($180 ÷ 10)
Average value of a sale	$60 ($600 ÷ 10)

What does this horrific flashback to SAT prep mean to your business? These numbers give you control over your advertising spending, allow you to predict cash flow (just play a game of Monopoly with my daughter if you don't appreciate the value of positive cash flow!), and enable you to assess additional market opportunities by comparing them to this pipeline. (If you're not rubbing your hands together and going, "Muahahaha" like a cartoon villain, I still have some explaining to do.)

In this hypothetical case, you have found a gumball machine that gives you $1.33 every time you drop 40 cents into the machine. You've set it up once, and it happens automatically as long as Google likes your credit card. ROI is a metric that simply converts your input amount to a single dollar, so you can easily compare ROI for different campaigns and markets. ROI answers the question, if you put a dollar into this machine, how much comes out? ROI of 333% means that you get $3.33 out for every dollar you put in. If you found a gumball machine that managed that trick, you'd never go back to slot machines again.

Now suppose the market becomes more competitive, and your CPC rises. If you were advertising in your local newspaper and the ad rep told you that prices were going up by 25 percent, what would you do? Would you keep advertising at the same level, cut back, or stop showing your ads in that paper completely? Unless you're measuring the ROI of your ads, you have no way to make a rational decision.

Say your AdWords CPC from the example shown in the preceding table increases by 25 percent. Now your cost per visitor is 50 cents. Do you keep advertising? Of course — you're still paying less for a lead than the value of that lead — 83 cents less. Your ROI is down from 333% to a still respectable 267% (total advertising cost is now $450 \times \$0.50 = \$225$, and $\$600 \div \$225 = 267\%$).

But wait — there's more! (Did I mention how much I enjoy a good infomercial?) AdWords makes it simple not only to see your metrics but also to improve your profitability by conducting tests. The ability to test different elements of your sales process is the next important element of direct marketing.

Keep improving your marketing

So far in this chapter, I've only discussed inputs (how much you pay to advertise and how many Web site visitors) and outputs (how much you receive in sales). But it's really the intermediate metrics (called *throughputs* by people like me who sometimes find it useful to pretend we went to business school) that give us an opportunity to make huge improvements in our profitability.

For example, imagine you improve the CTR of your ad from 1.5% to 2.2% without lowering the quality of your leads. Big whoop, right? An improvement of 0.7% — who cares? Actually, it's an improvement of 68% — for the same $180 advertising spend, you now get 660 visitors instead of 450. If everything else stays the same, your visitor value of $1.33 means your sales increase to $880, for an ROI of 489%.

But wait — there's more! What's to stop you from improving your landing page by 20 percent by testing different versions? Instead of getting 20 leads out of 100, you're now collecting 24. Six hundred sixty visitors now translate into 158 leads. If 11 percent of them make a purchase from your e-mail offer, that's 17 sales. At an average of $60 per sale, you've now made $1,020.

But wait — there's more! How about testing your e-mail offer too? Let's say you get a 36 percent improvement, and now 15 percent of e-mail recipients make a $60 purchase. That's 23 sales at $60, for a new total of $1,380.

Thanks to the miracle of compounding, the three improvements ($68\% \times 20\% \times 36\%$) give you a total improvement of 230%. This isn't pie-in-the-sky math, either — when you test the elements of your sales process scientifically, it's hard not to make significant improvements. See Chapter 13 for the stunningly simple explanation of how to do it. And Chapter 14 shows you how to consistently improve the ability of your Web site to turn visitors into paying customers.

It's dating, not a shotgun wedding

In case you got a little lost in the numbers in the previous section, I want to make sure you got the moral of that direct marketing story: It's a process of multiple steps. Seth Godin (marketing guru and author) compares direct marketing to dating. You wouldn't walk up to a stranger in a museum and propose marriage. (If you did, and you're happily married 17 years later, please don't take offense; I'm not talking about you.) In fact, there are a lot of things you wouldn't suggest to a stranger in a museum that you might very well suggest to someone who knew you a little better. (If you're not sure what these are, check out Dr. Ruth's contribution to the *For Dummies* series.)

Direct marketing operates on the premise that you have to earn your prospects' trust before they become your customers. As with dating, you demonstrate your trustworthiness and likeability by asking for small commitments with low-downside risk. Your ad, the first step in the AdWords dating game, makes a promise of some sort while posing no risk. Your visitor can click away from your Web site with no hassle or hard feelings. AdWords' Editorial Guidelines commit you to playing nice on your landing page: an accurate display URL, no pop-ups, and a working Back button so your visitors can hightail it back to their search results if they don't like your site.

Your landing page makes a second offer that involves getting permission from your prospects to communicate with them. Here's the deal you're offering: "I'll give you something of value if you let me contact you. And any time you want me to stop contacting you, just let me know and I'll stop. And I'll never share your contact information with anybody else who might try to contact you."

Sometimes you can go right for the sale on the landing page, and sometimes it's better to focus on turning your visitor into a *lead* — someone with whom you can follow up later. Chapter 10 offers guidelines for creating an effective landing page.

When your prospect gets to know you and trusts you, you increase the value you provide while asking for larger and larger commitments. Depending on your business, your sales/dating process could consist of surveys, reports, free samples, try-before-you-buy promotions, teleseminars, e-mails, live chat, software downloads, and more. When you ask for the sale, you in effect, are proposing marriage — or a long-term relationship, anyway.

Following up with your best prospects

Direct marketing focuses on prospects — people who raise their hands and tell you they're interested in what you have. When folks click your AdWords ad, they've just identified themselves to you as someone worth developing a relationship with. Returning to the dating analogy, this is like a stranger smiling at you at the museum. You respond by striking up a conversation about the artwork you're both looking at ("Do you think the green splotch in the upper-left-hand corner represents a rebirth of hope or an exploding drummer?") If the two of you hit it off, you don't want to leave the building without getting a phone number.

In dating, the phone number is the litmus test of interest. If you can't get the phone number, or if you call it and discover you've really been given the number for the West Orange Morgue (now why are you assuming that actually happened to me?), you know that relationship has no future.

Your prospect has the online attention span of a guppy. When we go online, we typically multitask, we have multiple windows open, we're checking e-mail, IMing, watching videos, listening to MP3s, and searching and browsing and surfing. Not to mention answering the phone, opening the mail, eating and drinking, and dealing with other people. How many times have you visited a Web page, been distracted, and never found it again? How many times have you bookmarked a Web page, intending to visit again, and haven't gotten around to it?

Get the prospect's e-mail address as soon as you can. Before they get distracted. Before they browse back to Google and click one of your competitors' ads. Before they spill a cappuccino latte all over the keyboard.

With their e-mail address and permission to follow up, you've done all you can to inoculate yourself from the short Internet attention span. You now have a chance of continuing the conversation until it leads to a sale.

How to Think Like Your Prospect

I began this chapter with a pathetic rant about my experiences as a Yellow Pages advertiser. Now let's look at the Yellow Pages from the point of view of the user — the person searching for a solution to a problem. But I'm done whining, so I'm not going to complain about figuring out which heading to look under, deciding which listing to call, dealing with voice mail (no, really, I'm done whining). Instead, imagine a totally new experience: the Magic Yellow Pages.

In the Magic Yellow Pages, you don't have to flip through hundreds of pages. In fact, the book doesn't *have* any pages — just a blank cover. You write down what you're looking for on the cover, and then — Poof! — the listings appear. The most relevant listings, according to the Magic Yellow Pages, appear on the cover. Subsequent pages contain more listings, in order of decreasing relevance.

But wait — there's more! The listings in the Magic Yellow Pages don't have phone numbers. Instead, touch the listing and you're magically transported to the business itself. Don't like what you see? Snap your fingers and you're back in front of the Magic Yellow Pages, ready to touch another listing or type another query.

This is how AdWords functions from the point of view of your prospects: They have all the power. They conjure entire shopping centers full of competing shops by typing words — and they window-shop until they find what they want or give up.

Their search term represents an itch that they want to scratch at that very moment — some unsolved problem. They are looking for the shortest distance between their itch and a good scratch. Maybe they want information. Maybe they want a product. Maybe they want to be entertained. Maybe they want to be told that their problem isn't so bad.

It's your job to figure out what they really want (based on the keyword they type) and give it to them quicker and more obviously than your competitors. In the Magic Yellow Pages, the rules are, "Give the prospect what she wants and nobody gets hurt." Winning the game of AdWords comes down to figuring out what your prospect — the person you can help — is thinking and feeling as they type their search. When you understand this, you bid on the right keywords, you show compelling ads, and you present clear and irresistible offers on your Web site. See Chapter 4 to discover how to conduct quick and easy keyword research, so you can become the champion itch-scratcher in your market.

Chapter 2

Setting Up Your AdWords Account

*Y*ou're about to set up a fully functioning AdWords account! I congratulate you on this momentous step in your online advertising career. I'm so glad I'm here to share it with you.

In this chapter, I walk you through setting up your account. If you already have an existing account, you can skip ahead to the next chapter "Managing Your AdWords Account," where you explore three basic account features: campaign management, keyword selection, and ad writing.

Opening a New AdWords Account

Fortunately, Google has greatly simplified the process for opening a new AdWords account:

1. **Open your Web browser and go to http://adwords.google.com.**

2. **(Optional) Choose a language other than English (US) from the drop-down list at the top right, and Google will translate the page into that language.**

3. **Click the Start Now button at the top right.**

    (Sometimes the button is labeled Click to Begin or Let's Get Started. I've never seen it read Drink Me, but I'm hopeful . . . .)

4. **Select Standard Edition and click the Continue button.**

This step may no longer be part of the process because the Starter Edition is headed toward retirement. So if you don't see this option, relax, remember that AdWords continues to evolve, and skip to Step 5. If you wish to learn more about the Starter Edition or already have a Starter Edition account, you may want to check out the Starter Edition bonus chapter, which is available online at www.askhowie.com/starter.

5. **Select the type of e-mail you want to use with your AdWords account. If you chose an existing Google Account, enter your Google Account information, and then click the Continue button. Otherwise, type your e-mail address, new password (twice), and the Visual Verification text, and then click the Create Account button.**

An AdWords account can be created with any e-mail address combined with an AdWords–specific password. If you already have a Google Account for Gmail or other Google services, you can use it for your AdWords account. If you are a Gmail junkie, for example, you'll want to connect the accounts so you don't sign yourself out of AdWords every time you check your mail. If you don't have a Google Account, you're prompted to create one using an existing e-mail account. Watch out for the Visual Verification text that Google uses. It took me only three tries to get it right.

6. **Select your currency from the drop-down list and click the Continue button.**

Your AdWords account is now created. If you used an existing Google Account, your account is now active. You will receive an activation e-mail with a link to the AdWords start page. Click that link and skip to Step 9. If you did not use an existing Google Account, then a verification e-mail is sent to the e-mail address you used in Step 5.

7. **Check your e-mail and click the verification link in the Google AdWords Account Verification e-mail.**

Your AdWords account is now activated.

8. **Click the Click Here to Continue link.**

This takes you to the AdWords start page in Step 1.

9. **Log in to your new AdWords account (upper-right side) by typing the e-mail and password you used in Step 5 and clicking Sign In.**

Are you in? Congratulations! You are now ready to create your first campaign.

Creating Your First Campaign

Google has made creating your first campaign as easy as possible. Here's all you have to do:

1. **Click the Create your first campaign button.**

2. **(Optional) Select one or more languages from the list box.**

   If you're advertising exclusively in English, do nothing. To choose multiple languages, hold down the Ctrl key while you click (for PC users) or the ⌘ key (for Mac users).

3. **(Optional) Click the Change Targeting link to change the country or countries where you want your ads to be seen:**

   a. A pop-up window with lots of options appears, but to keep it simple for now, try to ignore the map and click the Browse tab. In the upper box (left side), click the appropriate check box to select each country in which you want your ads to be shown. The selected locations appear in the lower box. You can target your ads with flashlight-like (not really laser-like) precision. I show you how to do this in Chapter 7.

   b. To remove a country, just click its check box to unselect it.

   c. When you're done, click the Done button to close the pop-up window.

4. **Click the Continue button.**

5. **Fill in the text boxes to create an ad; click the Continue button when you're finished.**

   Now Google wants you to create your first ad. What, you're not ready to whip out a masterpiece of persuasive prose at the drop of a cursor? No worries. Type pretty much anything here — you won't show it to the world for a while. The following list provides guidance on what to enter in those text boxes:

   • In the Headline text box, type the problem or opportunity.

   • In the Description Line 1 text box, enter a short description of big benefit.

   • In the Description Line 2 text box, write a short description of your product/service.

   • In the Display URL text box, type your Web site's name.

   • In the Destination URL text box, enter the URL of the exact Web page you want customers to visit first (called the *landing page*).

The display URL is what your prospect sees in the ad itself. It must be "real" enough to go somewhere relevant if they were to type it, but it doesn't have to be the same as the actual destination URL. Think of the display URL as the name of your online store; would you rather buy a CN Netcom amplifying phone headset from www.StuffThatSitsOnYourDesk.com or www.PhoneSupplies.com/Netcom-Headsets? You can use the destination URL to track your Web site's traffic and to show different pages to different markets.

See Figure 2-1 for an example. But please don't sweat it at this point. Just write something that doesn't violate Google's editorial or content guidelines (see the section, "When nobody can see your ad," later in this chapter) and move on.

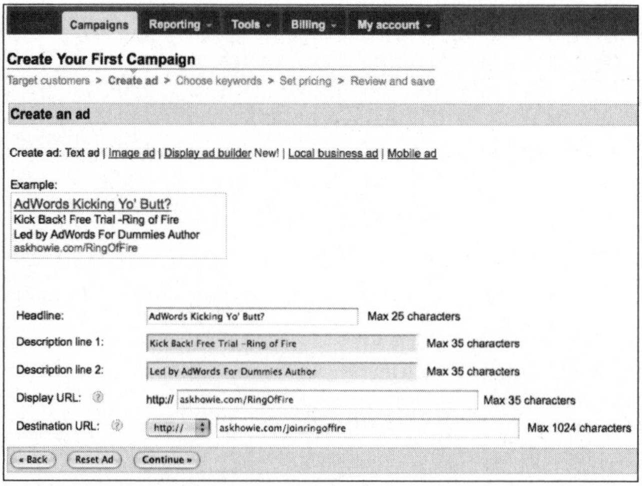

Figure 2-1: Write your first ad.

6. **Type your chosen keywords into the text box and click the Continue button when you're finished.**

   For now, choose a single keyword that someone searching for your business might type. For example:

   ```
   used cars
   glow in the dark poker chips
   functional fitness training
   ```

   You should also use two variations of this keyword that represent phrase and exact matches. For a phrase match, enclose the keyword in quotes; for an exact match, enclose the keyword in brackets. These variations are described in detail in Chapter 5. If your keyword is gout recipes, then the two variations would be "gout recipes" and [gout recipes].

Type your keyword along with its two variations into the keyword text box, one keyword per line. (See Figure 2-2.)

Just above the Continue button, Google asks whether you want to look for more keywords. For now, ignore the invitation. In Chapters 4 and 5, you discover how to find keyword variations to your heart's delight.

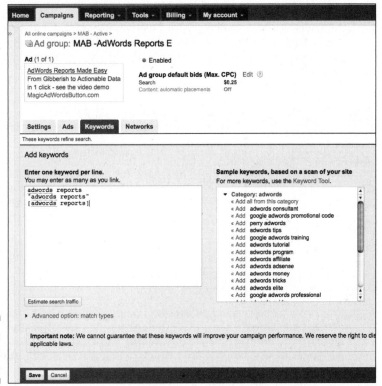

Figure 2-2:
Adding
keywords.

Google is, at its core, a very large data processor. By tracking the behavior of searchers, it gets smarter all the time — and can offer better suggestions to advertisers and better search results to shoppers. Google notices, for example, how long a person stays away after clicking an ad or free listing. Say you click my ad, look at my Web page for 3 seconds, and then click back to Google for another search; that tells Google you didn't think much of my site. Enough data like that, and my bid prices will increase to penalize me for not giving Google's users what they want.

The keyword-suggestion tool can be helpful, but don't use it right now. Until you understand how to create tightly focused ad groups, the tool will create a messy and unfocused campaign. Use the tool later to refine your campaigns. Right now, just pick one or two closely related terms, if you like, and continue.

7. **Type how much you're willing to spend in the Enter Your Daily Budget and the Enter Your Maximum CPC text boxes.**

   Ready to have some fun? It's trial-and-error time, thanks to Google's Traffic Estimator. Enter any numbers you like for daily budget and maximum CPC and then click the View Traffic Estimator link. It shows you estimated CPC, the position of your ad, the likely number of clicks per day, and your daily cost. An ad position of 1 puts you at the top of the first page, 9–10 put you at or near the bottom of the first search-results page or top of the second page, and 11+ puts your ad squarely on page 2, or worse.

   Typically, an ad on page 2 gets one-tenth the impressions of the same ad on page 1, so (unless the clicks are ridiculously expensive on the first page), page 1 is where you want to be.

   To view the maximum traffic you could possibly expect from that keyword, enter a maximum CPC of $100 and a daily budget of $10,000.

   Make sure you change these back before continuing!

   Google shows you the most you'll pay for a click if your ad is in the top position and the maximum number of clicks each keyword will generate in a day. Keep in mind, your ad may outperform or underperform this estimate, depending on how well it connects with your prospects.

   Settle on a CPC you can live with financially that puts your ad somewhere on the first page. You can make adjustments when you have actual results to base them on.

8. **Click the Continue button.**

9. **Review your selections on the next page, decide whether you want e-mail from Google about AdWords strategies and tips, choose an appropriate answer from the How Did You First Hear about Google AdWords drop-down list, and finally, click the I'll Set Up Billing Later button.**

Managing Your Account

The two right-most tabs at the top enable you to manage the business side of your AdWords Account: Billing and My Account. The Billing tab allows you to keep track of your spending and update credit cards. Click the tab and you see two items in a drop-down list: Billing Summary and Billing Preferences.

Billing Preferences is where you go to set up your payment options. Don't forget to use the AdWords Gift Card code included with this book when you are providing your other billing details.

The My Account tab (see Figure 2-3) allows you to update your login information, set your e-mail notification preferences, and enable access to your account by other users. It also has two subtabs: Account Preferences and Account Access. Explore them at your leisure — they're pretty self-explanatory.

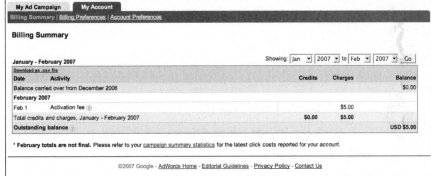

Figure 2-3:
The My
Account
tab.

If you run an online pharmacy, you'll need a PharmacyCheckerID before Google will let you advertise. Go to the Account Preferences subtab, find the PharmacyCheckerID section, and click the Edit link. On the page that appears, click the Read Our FAQ link to find out how to apply.

Activating your account

Your ads won't show up on-screen until you activate your account by giving Google five bucks and a working credit card number (you get $25 in prepaid clicks when you use the gift card in the back of this book). You can do this by clicking the link in the warning box with the reddish-pink background and following the account activation wizard, or take the tour first and pay later. Even if you activate now, you can pause your campaigns so you aren't charged for a lot of traffic before you know what you're doing. After you complete your account setup, wait 15 minutes, and then browse to www. google.com and do a search on your keyword. (See Figure 2-4.)

My Ad Campaign	My Account

Billing Summary | Billing Preferences | Account Preferences

Account Setup

Select location > Choose form of payment > Agree to terms > Provide billing details

1. Select the country or territory where your billing address is located.
This choice may affect the payment options you'll have in the next step.

United States ▾

2. Select a permanent time zone for your account.
This will be the time zone for all your account reporting and billing.

> **Please choose your time zone carefully. Once you finish setting up your billing account you won't be able to change time zone again.** Learn more.

Time zone country or territory: United States ▾

Time zone: (GMT−05:00) Eastern Time ▾

3. If you have a promotional code, enter it here (optional).
Promotional code:

Continue »

Figure 2-4:
Activating
your
account.

To activate your account, follow these steps:

1. **Click the Billing tab and then click Billing Preferences.**

2. **Use the drop-down list to select your billing country.**

   The most common choices are at the top, followed by a long list of just about every country there is.

3. **Select your country from the Time Zone Country or Territory drop-down list, and then select your time zone from the Time Zone drop-down list.**

   Google won't let you change your time zone after you set it, so be careful here. No second chances!

4. **Click the Continue button.**

5. **Choose a payment method.**

   You can choose between Postpay Billing (to be charged when clicks come in) and Prepay Billing (having the cost of clicks deducted from a prepaid balance). For Postpay, you can choose between Direct Debit from a bank account and a charge to a credit card, such as American Express, JCB, MasterCard, or Visa. For Prepay, your only option is a credit card.

   Dave Jabas of www.myemailassistant.com recommends using a dedicated low-limit credit card just for your AdWords billing. Although Google includes circuit breakers like budgets and maximum click costs, sometimes things go wrong. If you limit your exposure to a few hundred or a few thousand dollars, you won't wake up one morning with a giant Google bill and no earthly idea how it happened.

6. **(Optional) Click the Understanding AdWords link.**

   This is where Google explains that Google does not pay you to write ads; you pay Google.

7. **Click Continue.**

   You're taken to a screen where you fill out billing information. If you've ever bought anything online, the process is straightforward and simple.

   Google's preferred phone-number format includes dashes, but no parentheses or periods:

   ```
   919-555-3167
   ```

   not

   ```
   (919) 555-3167
   ```

   Don't forget to click the Click Here link next to "Do you have a promotional code" if you own this book and aren't reading it in the bookstore café with a latte on your lap. Then enter the promotional code, printed on the big green coupon in the front of the book, in the text box. The promotional code provides you with $25.00 worth of AdWords clicks, and covers your $5.00 activation fee.

   After you complete the form, your account is live — and your ad should start showing on the right side of the Google search results page for the keywords you selected.

After you complete your account setup, wait 15 minutes, and then browse to www.google.com and do a search on your keyword.

Look at the top and the right of the search results page. If you don't see your ad, scroll down and click the More Sponsored Links link. Keep going through the pages until you see your ad or you get to the end of the listings. This exercise gives you an idea of the competitiveness of your market. If you see a lot of competitors, don't get discouraged. It means a lot of people think they can make money here. The information in this book will put you way ahead of most of them. Seeing no or few competitors for a keyword may indicate a market that's too small or too unresponsive.

When nobody can see your ad

If your ad doesn't appear in the right column within 30 minutes of account activation, you may have a problem. Usually, correcting it is simple — once you figure out what it is.

If your ad isn't receiving any impressions (indicated by a 0 in the last row of the Impressions column), you may be a victim of one of the following:

✔ **Editorial disapproval:** Have you violated Google's editorial guidelines? If you throw exclamation points around like crazy, promise "the best" or "the cheapest" stuff, capitalize like you're screaming in a chat room, use copyrighted terms, offer cheap drugs from Canada or $25 Rolexes or nuclear-weapon-making instructions, or commit any of a dozen other infractions, your ad won't show.

Google lays out their rules here:

- *Editorial Guidelines:* `https://adwords.google.com/select/ guidelines.html`

- *Content Guidelines:* `https://adwords.google.com/select/ contentpolicy.html`

✔ **Low ad rank:** Based on your monthly budget (which you set when you create the account) and your choice of a maximum bid price (which you can edit at any time), your ad may be relegated to page 19 of search results. That is the equivalent of scribbling it onto the back of a gas station receipt in yellow crayon and tossing it into a dumpster.

You can see exactly in what positions your ads show. At this point, you can try raising your minimum bid — and monthly budget — to see if that gets you onto the first page of search results.

✔ **Poor keyword performance:** If your keyword is `pink slippers big enough to fit an African elephant` or some other phrase that few or no people would ever search for, you could wait a long time before seeing a single click. In Chapter 5, I introduce you to the spy tools that help you find exactly what people are typing into their online searches.

✔ **Poor keyword Quality Score:** Google assigns each keyword in your account a Quality Score, based partly on the match between the keyword, the ad, and the landing page of the Web site, and partly on the historical performance of that keyword in other AdWords accounts. If Google thinks that a keyword you've chosen isn't going to make them money (because it won't generate AdWords clicks) or will give searchers a poor quality experience if they select your ad, your ad will appear far away from the first page of search results. Google forces you to improve the quality score (see Chapter 5) or place a really high bid to show your ad.

When just you can't see your ad

Sometimes your ad is receiving impressions, but try as you might, you can't find it yourself. Before you start humming the *Twilight Zone* theme, consider the possibilities described in the following subsections.

Google thinks you're searching outside your geo-targeting

When you first set up your account, you had to choose a geographic location within which to advertise. Google may be interpreting the information it's reading on your computer (specifically, its Internet Protocol [IP] address), to mean you yourself are outside of your targeted area. IP addresses are loosely connected to different parts of the world.

To find out where the Internet thinks you are, go to www.ipligence.com and scroll down until you can see the map at the bottom right, shown in Figure 2-5.

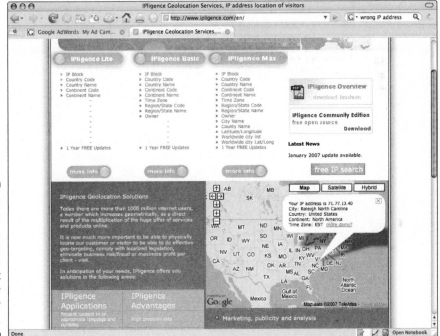

Figure 2-5: Here ipligence. com shows me where the Internet thinks my computer resides.

There are many reasons why Google could get confused about where in the world you are. First, IP addresses aren't exact — they're not like zip codes or postal codes. Second, if you're connecting to the Internet through a service that's somewhere other than where you are, Google can be misled. Third, little green aliens from outer space sometimes take over my fingers when I'm typing stuff I really don't know anything about so that the paragraphs look long enough to be authoritative.

Every machine connected to the Internet has a unique IP address, a string of four numbers separated by dots. Google's IP address, for example, is 216.239.51.100. The IP address is the "real" Internet address. We humans give Web sites names, like Google and WalletEmptyingJunk.com, so we can find them more easily. The Internet machines map these names onto the numbers to send our browsers and e-mails to the right places.

Confused? Try this experiment: Open a Web browser, type **216.239.51.100** into the address bar, and press Enter. If you enter the numbers and dots correctly, you should arrive at Google's home page.

Your IP address may be unique to your computer, shared by other computers on your network, or even shared by many of the computers served by your Internet service provider (ISP).

You chose a different language

If you choose to advertise in Spanish (for example), you may not be able to find your ad if your Google searching preference is set for English. To change it (you can always change it back), go to www.google.com and click Preferences next to the search box. Click the Search Only for Pages Written in These Language(s) radio button and put a check next to the relevant language. Click Save Preferences to return to your search.

Chapter 3

Managing Your AdWords Account

After you set up your AdWords account, it's time to explore Mission Control. In this chapter, I focus on the three basic AdWords tasks: campaign management, keyword selection, and ad writing.

Running Mission Control with the Campaign Management Tab

The first screen you see when you go to `http://google.com/adwords` and enter your user name and password is the Account Snapshot screen (shown in Figure 3-1). The snapshot screen shows the summary statistics of all the campaigns in the account: total cost, total number of clicks, total impressions, and overall CTR. If you prefer to go straight to the Campaign Summary page when you log in, scroll to the bottom of the Account Snapshot page and click the Make Campaign Summary My Starting Page link.

You spend the majority of your AdWords time in the Campaigns tab. After this chapter, most of the book shows you how to improve your online advertising by using various features within this tab. For right now, I show you the cockpit without asking you to go for a test flight.

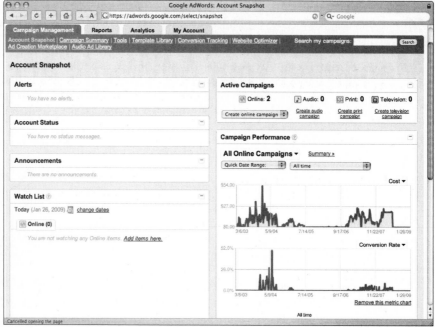

Figure 3-1:
The
Account
Snapshot
page gives
you an
overview of
your entire
account.

You can view your account from three levels that range from overview to granular. The All Online Campaigns view lists your campaigns and gives you basic metrics on each one. The individual campaign view provides the same level of detail about the different ad groups in a particular campaign. The ad group view shows you the finest details about every ad and every keyword in that ad group. This last view is where you spend most of your time. Use the other two views to help you prioritize which ad group will give you the biggest return for time spent.

All Online Campaigns view

The All Online Campaigns view gives you another set of tabs: Campaign, Ad Groups, Settings, Ads, Keywords, and Networks. This page lists your campaigns and gives summary data about each of them. The column headings (Campaign, Budget, Status, and so on) are clickable, so you can sort your campaigns in various ways. For example, you probably want the campaigns that cost the most to be in your face more; click the Cost heading to sort from most to least costly. Click Cost again to reverse the order.

By default, Google shows all your campaigns as folders on the left of your screen, with a Help section just below. When you click a folder or campaign name, you enter that campaign, and can access individual ad groups as sub-folders. I often hide this section of the page by clicking the double chevron button at the top right of the section, especially when I want to see all the data for a campaign or ad group without having to scroll left to right. You can always get the folder view and Help section back by mousing over the left margin, or by clicking the double chevron button (now pointing the other direction).

Campaign

By default, AdWords assigns your campaign exciting and informative names like Campaign #1 and Campaign #2. For your own sanity, please replace these generic names with descriptions that will make sense when you're running dozens of campaigns at once. You can change the name of a campaign by placing your cursor over the name and then clicking the Edit icon (looks like a pencil) to the right of your cursor. Replace Campaign #1 with a more useful name and click the Save button.

Budget

Google shows you the daily budget you set for each campaign. It's grayed and bracketed in paused and deleted campaigns. You can change your daily budget for any campaign by clicking the budget amount ($20/day, for example), changing it in the text within the yellow pop-up, and then clicking Save.

Current Status

Campaigns can be active, paused, or deleted. You change the status of a campaign by clicking the little icon to the left of the campaign name. You can choose a green dot for active, two vertical lines for paused, or a red x for deleted.

- ✔ **Active:** Active campaigns display your ads to searchers. They cost you money and bring visitors to your Web site.

- ✔ **Paused:** Paused campaigns are on hold, but can be reactivated by placing a check next to the campaign and clicking the Resume button above the list of campaign names. Pausing a campaign automatically pauses all the ad groups in that campaign. No impressions, no clicks, no visitors.

- ✔ **Deleted:** Deleted campaigns can also be reactivated by a single click. So what's the difference between pausing and deleting a campaign? Beats me. If you delete a campaign, you can't actually make it go away. You can hide it by clicking the All but Deleted link (just above the Cost column).

This can be helpful if you don't want to clutter your screen with old campaigns, but still want to see active and paused campaigns. Also, it's helpful to delete campaigns if you're writing *AdWords For Dummies* and you don't want the world to see every detail of your AdWords account in your screen shots. (See Figure 3-2.)

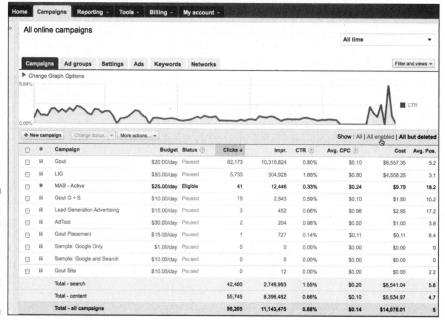

Figure 3-2:
You can hide paused or deleted campaigns to simplify your screen.

Clicks

A *click* represents one person clicking your ad and arriving on your landing page. Google doesn't count multiple clicks from the same computer on the same day (or tries very hard not to) — that's so your competitors can't sit behind their desks and develop carpal tunnel syndrome trying to bankrupt you by clicking your ad repeatedly. Two clicks equal two unique visitors to your site.

Clicks are good, right? The more clicks, the more visitors to your Web site. Well, not so fast. Clicks cost you money, remember? You make back that investment only when the visitor buys something from you. The goal of your ad is twofold:

✔ To get all the people who will eventually buy from you to click your ad

✔ To discourage all the people who will never buy from you from clicking your ad

Obviously, you can't know beforehand who will buy and who won't. However, you can make some pretty good guesses until you implement conversion tracking (see Chapter 14).

For example, if you're advertising a ponytail holder worn by Paris Hilton and you mention Paris Hilton in your ad and select `Paris Hilton` as a keyword, chances are you'll find a lot of visitors who have no interest in your hair accessory but a lot of interest in, shall we say, a multimedia Paris Hilton experience.

When you gain AdWords experience, you'll learn how to turn the prospect tap wider or narrower to maximize profits.

Impr.

Impr. is short for *impressions*. Technically, an *impression* is a single instance of a search results page that contains your ad. It doesn't mean the searcher saw the ad; he saw a search results page with your ad on it. If the searcher has a small screen with high resolution and your ad appears below the scroll (meaning he'd have to scroll down to view it), it's still counted as an impression. So, if he clicks the first listing, before he look at yours, it still counts.

Impressions can indicate the potential size of your AdWords market. If you're bidding on popular keywords, you can expect lots of impressions. But if your bidding strategy places your ad very low in the ad rankings, and it shows up on page four, you'll see very few impressions — even though the market itself may be huge — because few searchers will actually go to page four of the search results.

CTR

CTR (Click-Through Rate) is the ratio of clicks to impressions, expressed as a percentage. It's one of your most important AdWords numbers, so if you're confused, take a little time to get clear on the concept. You can calculate CTR by dividing clicks by impressions. For example, if 200 people see your ad, and 12 of them click it, here's the math:

```
12 ÷ 200 = .06 = 6.00%
```

You'd then brag at the AdWords Saloon, "My CTR is 6 percent." And everyone would understand that your ad was so compelling, 6 out of every 100 people who saw it ended up on your Web site.

Avg. CPC

The Avg. CPC *(cost per click)* column tells you how much, on average, you pay Google to get a visitor to your Web site. You may have different average CPCs by campaign, ad-group, keyword, and ad. A big part of AdWords management is deleting or improving elements of your advertising that cost you more than you make back, so your average click cost is an important metric.

Cost

Your *cost* is simply all the money you spend on clicks. On this screen, cost is broken down by campaign. When you drill deeper, you can see how much each ad and each individual keyword costs you. (After you set up conversion tracking, described in Chapter 14, you can also track how much each ad makes you.)

Note: Some of the screen shots in this chapter include six columns you won't see until you set up conversion tracking: Conv. rate, Cost/conv., and Conversions, each with two variations, One Per Click and Many Per Click. (See Chapter 14 for more on conversion tracking. Oh, the fun that awaits you!)

You can change the date range in the All Campaigns (or any other) view. Select one of the presets in the drop-down list at the top right of your screen, just below the green band that includes the top navigation, or select the first item in that list, Custom Date Range, input any two dates, and click the Go button. For some reason, Google insists that your start date be before your end date (that's a little un-quantum-physics, don't you think?). Get into the habit of first checking your date range when you work on campaign management. Otherwise, you panic when you see only six clicks and the cause isn't a broken campaign, but a view set to Today instead of This Month.

Individual campaign view

Click your campaign name to see an overview of the ad groups within that campaign. You see all your ad groups' statistics, including several new columns: Max. CPC (up to three different types), Avg. Pos, and Avg. CPM.

- **Search Max. CPC:** This is the maximum cost per click (CPC) you select for clicks generated on the Google search results page when you create the account. You can change this bid for specific campaigns, the ad groups, or even individual keywords. In Chapter 7, you discover smart strategies for bidding different amounts on different keywords.

- **Content Managed Max. CPC:** This is the maximum you will pay for a click from content sites that you specify. You see this column only after you create managed placements; that is, you choose sites on the content network where you want your ads to appear.

- ✔ **Content Auto Max. CPC:** This is the most you're willing to pay for a click from the content network when Google chooses the pages based on your keywords.

- ✔ **Avg. Pos:** The average position of your ad refers to where it appears in relation to all other ads showing for the same keyword. At the ad group level, an average position of 5.7 means that on average, your ad shows most often in position 6, less often in position 5, and occasionally higher or lower. If your average position is greater than 8, your ads are not showing nearly as much as they might — only very determined searchers ever go to the second page of Google results.

- ✔ **Avg. CPM:** If your ads are showing on the content network, you will see this column, which tells you how much on average you are paying for 1,000 impressions.

Even though Google uses a pay-per-click model, it's useful to think of buying ad space on a pay-per-impression basis. Google is trying to maximize its own profit per impression (that's why Google rewards high CTR with lower bid prices), so you should also aim to make as much money as possible per impression. Plus, after you've had considerable experience in the content network, you may want to change your bidding method from CPC to CPM. But don't even think of CPM bidding until you really know what you're doing in the content network. Otherwise, you may wake up to a painfully large bill and no visitors to your site.

You can see some trends, even with extremely small numbers. For example, my Gout diet ad group (in Figure 3-3) has received 27,052 clicks out of 2,876,166 impressions, for a decent 0.94% CTR. This CTR translates into 94 visitors to my Web site for every thousand people who view the ad in the Gout diet ad group. Each click costs me $0.11 on average, so I can expect to pay $10.34 for those 94 visitors.

Just because Google gives you lots of data to look at, you don't have to rush out and buy a 30-inch monitor just so you can see it all without scrolling. You can hide columns: Click the Filter and Views button to the upper-right of the ad groups table, select Customize Columns from the drop-down list, and then remove the checks next to the columns you don't need to see. You can also reorder columns by dragging and dropping them. When you finish, click the Save button to return to a more manageable dashboard.

Don't make any assumptions or decisions based on numbers as low as I describe here. Generally, you want to see at least 30 total clicks before ascribing validity to the data. I know of one business owner who drove his business into the ground making knee-jerk changes based on tiny numbers. See Chapter 13 for more than you ever want to know about statistical significance.

When you have more than one ad group in a campaign, the column headers become clickable and sortable.

Individual ad group view

In the Individual Campaign view, click the name of an ad group to drill down to the most detailed and powerful view, the individual ad group (see Figure 3-3).

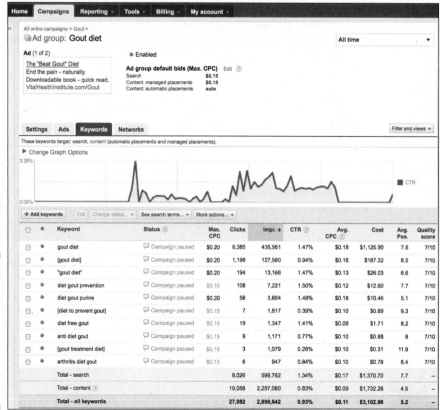

Figure 3-3:
Clicking an ad group's name takes you into the powerful Individual ad-group view.

Keywords tab

The Keywords tab is the first thing you see when you enter an individual ad group. It shows you several things at a glance:

✔ Look above the ad at the top left to see how many ads are competing in this group. At first, you see 1 of 1. I'll want to create another ad — you almost always want to run multiple ads simultaneously to find the most effective one (I show you how to do this in Chapter 13). For now, you'll see 1 of 1.

✔ Check the date range at the top right, just below the green header bar. You can change it by clicking the down arrow to the right of the current date range.

✔ Check how each of your keywords is doing. In addition to the columns you see at the campaign and ad group levels, you now see the Quality Score of each keyword. After you set up conversion tracking, you may also see several columns of conversion statistics (*conversion* is a fancy marketing word for "the visitor did something good at my Web site"). In Chapter 5, you discover the power of this screen — and learn to drive it like a pro.

Networks

To the right of the Keywords tab is the Networks tab. Click it to view and manage content network campaigns to determine where to show your ads (see Chapter 7).

Ads

To the left of the Keywords tab is the Ads tab. Click it to view your ad. You see how that ad is doing and the networks it's showing on. (To give you a taste of what's in store, Figure 3-4 shows an ad group with two ads running simultaneously.)

Click the ad headline to go to your landing page. Mouse over the ad to see the Edit icon to the right (looks like a pencil). Click the pencil to change the ad. Delete it by marking the check box to its left and clicking the Change Status button (just above the ad) and then selecting Delete from the drop-down list.

By default, Google displays only your root URL — that is, only up to the `.com` or `.org` or `.whatever` — in the fourth line of the ad. Use your display URL to attract visitors to your Web site. For example, if you sell red staplers and are advertising on the keyword `red stapler`, the second URL below would be more attractive to prospects:

```
www.StaplerHeaven.com
www.StaplerHeaven.com/Red-Staplers
```

Change the URL by clicking the Edit link next to the fourth text box (the one with your Web site name in green) near the bottom of the page. Your display URL (the one that shows in your ad) doesn't have to be identical to your landing URL (the page your visitors go after clicking). See Figure 3-5 for an example.

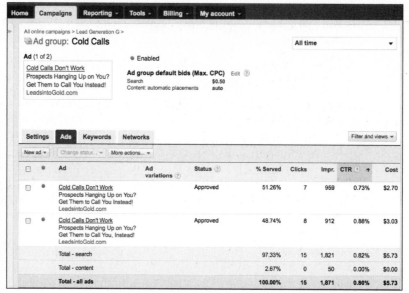

Figure 3-4:
You can compare two ads' performance and replace ineffective ads with new challengers.

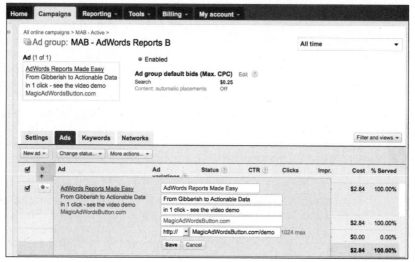

Figure 3-5:
The landing URL and the display URL are different, but both point to the same Web site (www.magicadwordsbutton.com).

Writing a second ad

I will repeat it until you're sick of hearing it; the key to success in Internet marketing is ongoing split-testing. *Split-testing* is creating two variations (in this case, of your ad), sending half your traffic to each, and seeing which one generates a better response. Not only that, the key to success in Internet marketing is ongoing split-testing. (I told you I'd repeat it.) AdWords gives you the ability to create a second ad to run alongside the first by following these steps:

1. **On the Ad Group page, click the New Ad button (to the left of the Change Status button) and select Text Ad from the drop-down list.**

2. **Create a new ad and then click the Save Ad button in the lower left of your new ad.**

   You immediately notice a second ad in your ad group. Now you can monitor the difference between your two ads by counting clicks. One of the ads will probably receive more clicks than the other ad. When your ads have accrued enough clicks to make a statistician happy, you can replace the "losing" ad with another challenger. For the full sermon on split-testing, please turn in your hymnal to Chapter 13.

Content network

Below your keyword list are three rows: Total – Search, Total – Content, and Total – All Ad Groups. These rows break down your results by source of traffic — Search refers to visitors who enter a keyword in the Google search engine; Content includes visitors who click your ad after seeing it on some Web page.

You can let the content network run for a bit just for curiosity's sake, but a best practice is to turn it off for now. Here's why: You may get a lot more content searches than keyword searches, which can overwhelm your monitoring. Keyword searches, because they're tied to specific words, give you much better market data than impressions and clicks from a bunch of Web sites that are unknown to you.

Turn off the content network by following these steps:

1. **Click the Settings tab and then click the Change Campaign Settings link.**

2. **In the Networks, Devices, and Extensions section, click the Edit link to the right of the list of networks and devices.**

3. **Click the radio button next to Let Me Choose and then remove the check from the box next to Content Network.**

4. **Ignore Google's drop-down warning, click OK, and then click the Save button.**

When your campaigns based on keywords are humming, see Chapter 7 to find out how to set up content network campaigns that won't muddy your reporting.

Part II
Launching Your AdWords Campaign

The 5th Wave   By Rich Tennant

"Maybe your keyword search, 'legal secretary, love, fame, fortune,' needs to be refined."

In this part . . .

This part is dedicated to finding and counting your prospects, so you can determine whether you have a business that can benefit from AdWords (or any other online-traffic-generation program), and then connecting with your prospects on an emotional level so they see your ads and Web site and immediately get the urge to reach for their wallets. The biggest business mistake is ignoring your market and trying to sell what you have, regardless of whether anybody needs or wants it.

Chapter 4 introduces you to the underground world of online market research. You see how to assess the profitability of a market in an afternoon, so your online adventures can be close to risk-free.

You explore the heart and soul of online marketing in Chapter 5: keywords. Keywords are the words and phrases that people type into search engines, YouTube, and eBay when they're looking for something to read, watch, or buy. When you understand the keywords your prospects use to find you, and the hidden desires represented by those keywords, you'll be successful.

Chapter 6 builds on the keyword foundation and shows you how to write ads that inflame the desires represented by keywords. It covers fundamentals and clever variations to make your ads more compelling and profitable.

Chapter 4

Discovering Your Online Market

- -

- -

*T*he Internet is the ultimate spy tool — (ahem) I mean, *market-research opportunity.* If you know where to look (and you will by the end of this chapter), you can determine pretty precisely how many people are looking for your product, how much they're willing to pay for it, and how much money your competitors are making from those people. You can also see how your competitors are marketing — their ads, Web sites, e-mails, promotions, pricing, customer service — and learn a lot about what works and what doesn't. On the Internet, we're all marketing naked. In this chapter, you'll discover how to become a peeping tom of prospects and competitors. Enjoy the view!

Assessing Market Profitability (Don't Dive into an Empty Pool)

In the movie *Field of Dreams,* the Ray Kinsella character builds a baseball diamond in his Iowa cornfield based on a voice that mysteriously repeats, "If you build it, he will come." That philosophy made for a great movie, but I don't recommend it as a customer-acquisition strategy. If you build it, you'll probably end up with a garage full of it — unless you take the time to figure out whether anybody's going to want it enough to pay for it.

Ken McCarthy, creator of The System Seminar for Online Marketing (www. thesystemseminar.com), once asked during a lecture, "If you were an Olympic diver, what would be the most important skill you could possess?" The answers varied — the ability to hold a triple gainer, strong core alignment, powerful legs, and so on — but Ken kept shaking his head no to each try. Finally, when we were getting really frustrated, he shared his answer: "The ability to tell if there's enough water in the pool before diving."

In other words, find out whether there's a market before you commit large amounts of time and money to creating a business or a product (or to learning fancy marketing tricks to attract buyers). As Perry Marshall points out, amateur marketers create a product and then look for people to sell it to — whereas professional marketers *find customers* and then look for something to sell them.

Whether you're starting a new venture online or you have an existing business that you're looking to expand online through AdWords, don't spend any time writing ads, creating Web sites, sourcing products, setting up factories, hiring employees, or printing letterhead *until* you've looked into the pool and determined that you can dive without hitting the concrete floor at 60 miles per hour.

In the old days of business, that sort of market research was a drag. Labor-intensive, expensive, imprecise, and slow. But if you want to sell online through paid search, you can save yourself months of agony and thousands of dollars in less time than it takes to fly from Bath, New York to Bath, England.

Glenn Livingston, a former consultant to Fortune 100 companies, has been doing online market research on a do-it-yourself budget with impressive results: He's entered 12 online markets and achieved profitability quickly in all 12. That's quite a batting average, considering that 78.6 percent of all new businesses fail within six months. (See *Conveniently Making Up Statistics For Dummies* for a full explanation of this calculation.) Considering that Glenn offers seven hours of free audio training on his state-of-the-art market-research techniques at www.ultimateadwordsresearch.com (which you should take advantage of), I'm glad he could boil down those techniques to five critical factors for inclusion in this book:

"Traditional marketing wisdom says you make your money when you choose your market. Any fisherman will tell you that the best rod and bait in the world won't do you any good in a mud puddle, so let's talk about how to find the best fishing holes.

"While there are literally dozens of factors to consider when choosing a market, here are four of the absolute most important things to know before you go fishing . . .

"How big is your market? (Market Size)

"How much is the average visitor worth? (Average Spend)

"What's the total dollar volume? (Market Size x Average Spend)

"How stable is the market? (Market Stability & Trends)"

"Are you willing to do what it takes to get into THIS market?"

"Look at your competitors. How much personal contact are they offering? Do they only offer an e-book with electronic download and no live-chat or 800#, or are they offering done-for-you services with personalized account reps and a massage for every customer? As a market gets more competitive, it moves from the former to the latter, and you have to be willing to jump in at an equal or better level of service than your competitors, or you'll drown. Similarly, if everyone else in the market is providing a high end, $1,000 product with a 50 percent margin, it's going to be nearly impossible for you to get in with a $97 information product. Even if you're the world's most efficient and creative AdWords advertiser, they'll be able to outspend, and therefore out-market you."

Glenn boils down initial market research into one key question: "Are other people making money there?" Because the Internet is so decentralized, nobody knows exactly how big and juicy a given market is. And, as the diet ads say, individual results may vary. Glenn created some guidelines that allowed him to evaluate a market on a lazy Sunday afternoon, and have a very good idea of the potential profitability of the market by dinnertime.

Remember when your high school Social Studies teacher got mad at you for skipping all the comments on your essay and just flipping to the letter grade on the last page? You're about to discover why — in the case of PPC (pay-per-click) marketing, the *letter grade* — the potential profitability of the market — can get you into a lot of trouble if you don't understand the data behind it. For example, certain markets can be profitable for advanced marketers and not beginners. Some markets can produce good results with a dozen keywords, while others require tens of thousands. No tool can ever replace your own judgment.

Determining market size by spying on searches

Want to know how many times people searched for keywords related to your business last month? How about which keywords were the most popular? And suppose you could do it in about 20 seconds — are you willing to spend the time before setting up your AdWords campaigns?

The number of searches is a critical number if you plan to make AdWords a significant part of your business acquisition strategy. Think Yellow Pages — if no one is looking for the listing *Unicycles,* a unicycle shop that relies on the Yellow Pages is going to have trouble paying the rent. Of course, many items and services are sold that aren't searched for — just not with AdWords. For example, lots of people buy CDs with guided meditations. But very few people searched for them (about four per day), so you could reasonably expect one sale every one to two months from AdWords traffic if your ad and Web site were very good. And with that tiny trickle of traffic, your testing of alternate ads (see Chapter 13) and landing pages (Chapter 15) will provide conclusive results some time around the next ice age.

Use Google's Keyword Tool (here's a shortcut: `www.askhowie.com/kwtool`) to discover the popularity of the search terms in your market. When you navigate to the Keyword Tool shortcut, here's all you have to do:

1. **Tell Google what language and geographic location you're curious about by clicking Edit link next to the default options.**

2. **Make sure the Descriptive Words or Phrases radio button is selected.**

3. **Type your main keyword into the search box.**

4. **Deselect the Use Synonyms option.**

   You'll want to include synonyms as you build your keyword empire, but right now, focus on the main keyword family.

5. **Type the squiggly characters into the box below to prove you're a human.**

6. **Click the Get Keyword Ideas button.**

Google gives you a list of the top keywords that include the words you typed, as shown in Figure 4-1. In the last column, Match Type, choose Exact from the drop-down list. You see the number of times each keyword phrase is searched on Google, during the previous full month and on average. Click the Approx Avg Search Volume header to sort by average monthly search volume, from greatest to least.

Scroll down to the end of the list (but before Additional Keywords to Consider) and download all the keywords by clicking the text, the `.csv` (for Excel), or `.csv` link. (If you have Excel on your computer, choose the Excel option.) A download window appears, allowing you to open the file directly or save it to your hard drive. When you open the spreadsheet, you see a column of keywords and three additional columns: Advertiser Competition, Approx Search Volume: *December* (or whatever the last month was), and Approx Avg Search Volume. The last column is the one you're most interested in right now. For later searches, you'll include data on average cost per click and estimated ad position by selecting those columns from the Choose Columns drop-down list above the keyword list.

Quickly scan the keywords and delete any rows unrelated to your market. For example, if you sell books and supplies to rabbit owners, remove irrelevant terms, such as Velveteen Rabbit and Who Framed Roger Rabbit, from the list. Examine the remaining keywords, paying attention to several things:

- ✔ Which keywords are more popular (higher on the list) than others?
- ✔ Are there just a few keywords that result in the vast majority of searches?
- ✔ Do some of the keywords represent sub-markets within the main market (for example, rabbits for hobbyists versus rabbits for commercial purposes — pets or meat)?

Figure 4-1: Quickly find out how many people are searching for your keywords with the free Google Keyword Tool.

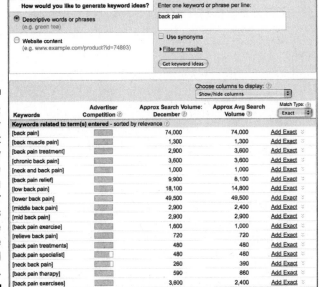

Figure 4-1 shows that people searched for back pain 74,000 times the previous month. The top related terms include lower back pain (49,500), low back pain (14,800), and back pain relief (9,900). This information is helpful — not just now, while you're assessing the potential risks and rewards of entering the market, but later on, when you choose keywords and write sales copy. For example, more than three times as many people searched for lower back pain than low back pain. If you're writing the headline of a Google ad promising relief from back pain, that information would lead you to choose lower back pain as the term that mirrors the language of your market. You'd also use that information to create the copy on your Web site, and in offline marketing materials such as brochures, print ads, business cards, and so on.

The total number of searches for these keywords, which you can calculate in Excel by selecting the cell below the final entry in the Approx Avg Search Column and hitting the Autosum button (∑) in the Standard toolbar, is a good indication of whether it's a good market to enter.

You can calculate how much traffic you need to be profitable with the Search Volume Profitability Calculator at www.askhowie.com/profcalc.

Estimating profitability by snooping on your competitors' keyword bids

Most smart businesses will spend money on customer acquisition until they reach the break-even point. If you know that every time a Google user visits your Web page, you make 35 cents (on average, not for every single visitor) and you have the ability to sell additional products and services to that customer in the future, you'd probably be willing to pay 35 cents to get the Google user to visit. That is, you're willing to break even on the first sale to gain a valuable business asset: a customer with whom you can build a relationship. (Chapter 14 celebrates the break-even concept to your heart's content.)

If you're selling a product that promises customers will save or make money by using it, you can usually charge more for it than if the product doesn't promise financial reward. It's hard to translate money into happiness. It's easy to compare the price of the product (say, a $750 AdWords telephone consultation with me) with the thousands of dollars you'll save on your AdWords campaigns. That's why marketing consultants make more than life coaches. Keep this distinction in mind as you explore your markets.

If the average bid is under a dime, you can assume that very few people have figured out how to sell high-ticket or high-margin products or services. For example, about 75,000 people search for home remedies each month, yet the average bid hovers around 10 cents. Home remedy seekers are do-it-yourselfers, looking for cheap and ingenious tips rather than expensive do-it-for-me solutions. Compare that to starting a business, which goes for over two dollars per click. This comparison points out an important distinction between markets: the buying-dollars-for-dimes market versus everything else.

In some markets, bid prices bear little relation to the value of a visitor. *Big* companies (which I define as any organization where the person in charge of AdWords campaigns isn't using a personal credit card to pay) tend to overbid. Some businesses are so good at earning money from visitors that they can afford to lose money to acquire a customer. But in general, the average bid price for a keyword gives you a good idea how much a click is worth, on average, to your competitors.

Google doesn't share its bid prices publicly, but you can estimate them using either the Keyword Tool or the Traffic Estimator tool in your AdWords control panel. Both tools are erratic in their ability to predict your actual bid prices, but as long as you're using them to compare markets in a very preliminary "Is this worth my time?" sort of way, you needn't worry about pinpoint accuracy.

Sizing up the entire market by tallying total advertising spent

By doing a little keyword research and entering your results into the MPG calculator that you can download from www.askhowie.com/mpg, you can assess the Total Market Health (TMH) — man, am I a fabulous acronym builder (FAB) or what? — of your market by combining the total number of bids with a weighted average of bid prices. This gives you a rough estimate of how much money is being spent in the market by PPC advertisers.

The process takes you fewer than ten minutes per market (I've done it so often I can do it in under five minutes), and it looks more complicated than it is. If you've never used a spreadsheet program before, you may want to have an Excel jockey friend on hand to help you the first time. Here's all you need to do:

1. **Go to www.askhowie.com/mpg and download the MPG Calculator. (I ask for your name and e-mail address in exchange — see Chapter 11 to discover my strategy.)**

   You'll need Microsoft Excel or the free spreadsheet Calc available at www.openoffice.org to open the MPG.

2. **After you've downloaded and opened the MPG, enter the keyword you searched using the free Keyword Tool.**

   I describe this tool in the "Determining market size by spying on searches" section, earlier in this chapter.

3. **Enter the total monthly search volume from the spreadsheet with the top 100 keywords into the MSV column of the MPG.**

4. **Log in to your account at `http://google.com/adwords`.**

5. **Click the Tools link and choose Traffic Estimator from the Optimize Your Ads section.**

6. **From the keyword spreadsheet, select and copy the entire column containing the keywords.**

   Do not include the search volume numbers, just the keywords themselves.

7. **Paste those keywords into the box at the top of the Traffic Estimator.**

8. **Leave Max CPC and Daily Budget blank, select the language and location targeting based on the market you're going after, and click Continue.**

9. **Sort the results by Search Volume by clicking the Search Volume column header. Look at the Average CPC for the most searched keywords.**

   This is Google's estimate of the cost of showing your ad in positions 1–3.

10. **Divide the Average CPC in half and enter that number in the Maximum CPC field. Click Get New Estimates.**

11. **Again, sort the keyword list by Search Volume. Keep reducing your Maximum CPC until the Estimated Ad Positions are 4–6 for the majority of your highest volume keywords.**

    (Keep sorting by Search Volume after each iteration.)

12. **Now take the Average CPC estimated by Google and paste it into the CPC column of the MPG.**

The MPG calculates the TMH for the market defined by that broad keyword. TMH is a number between 0 and 5,000 (some markets may top out above 5,000, but that's rare). Try this exercise with different markets, and especially with different variations of your main keywords. Which appears more profitable: car insurance or auto insurance? Back pain or back ache? Beekeeper or apiarist?

What sort of TMH are you looking for? The longer you do this, the better your feel will become, but for right now, you can follow Glenn's rule of thumb: AdWords beginners should enter niche markets with TMHs between 100 and 200. At 200, the markets become more competitive, and below 100, there's not enough money to go around. One exception to this rule is the dollars-for-dimes market. If you're helping people make or save money, you can probably make a go of it with a TMH between 50 and 200.

Don't get freaked out if Google's Traffic Estimator tool initially predicts very high CPCs — those numbers are the bid prices for the top positions, which you probably don't want, and reflect the "ignorance tax" Google imposes on advertisers who don't follow the strategies you're learning here. (See the "Bid persistence: Will you still love me tomorrow?" section, later in this chapter.)

Giving your market a stress test to determine future health

If Oprah ever reads my hilarious yet touching and wise essay, "Manifesto of an Average Ultimate Frisbee Player," surely she'll invite me to be a guest on her show. For several weeks after this, many people will search online for `Oprah Frisbee guy` and a few variations. But would it be wise to build a business based on that keyword family? Probably not, because my fame (and it is coming, I tell you) is likely to be fleeting. If your business success depends on short-lived trends or fads, you'll never turn your AdWords campaigns into business assets. They won't be reliable. Similarly, if your market is trending downward (Ken McCarthy discovered that very few people in the 21st century are searching for `buggy whips` anymore, even though they had been all the rage 100 years earlier), you can't rely on past data.

Luckily, Google publicly shares a tool that allows you to view trends in your market to help you decide whether it's stable, growing, or declining.

Visit Google Trends (`www.google.com/trends`) and search for the major keywords in your market. Is the traffic stable over the past few years? Trending upward? Good. If it's trending downward, beware. You'll see seasonal cycles in the Google Trends graphs, as shown in Figure 4-2. Don't worry about dips that occur regularly each year. Be worried if the overall graph trends downward.

Aside from being fascinating and addictive (at least for people who subscribe to *American Demographics* magazine), Google Trends gives you a longer-term picture of your market. Why, for example, did searches on `back pain` spike in July 2005? I don't know, but I'll bet some chiropractic market analyst has an answer. The Cities, Regions, and Languages tabs provide more useful information. For instance, the Regions tab reveals that 9 of the 10 countries ranked for most `back pain` searches were part of the British Empire at one point in their history. Coincidence? Maybe.

Sometimes, Google superimposes news headlines on the graph, as shown in Figure 4-3. William Shatner's hospitalization for back pain in October 2005 (point B on the graph) appears to have triggered little additional interest, but the December 2006 ABC news report on lower back pain and yoga (point C) either anticipated or sparked another explosion of interest going into the new year. I don't know what any of this means, but if I were selling products to help your aching back, I'd spend a lot of time looking at graphs like these. And whatever your market, I recommend you do the same.

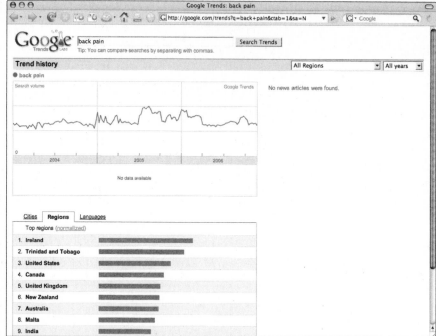

Figure 4-2:
Google
Trends
alerts you
to stable,
blossoming,
and dying
markets.

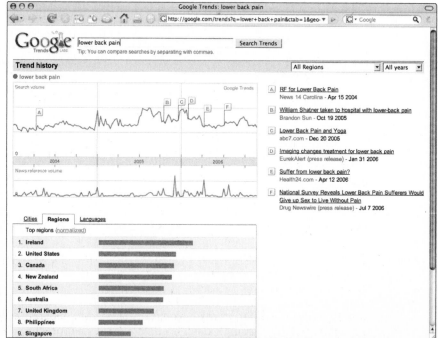

Figure 4-3:
Google
Trends
showing
when news
stories
related
to your
keyword
occurred.

Taking the Temperature of Your Market — Advanced Methods

The search data described in the preceding section represents the demand side of your market. The following sections look at the supply side — information about the businesses selling in that market, and how much they're making.

To continue paying homage to Ken McCarthy's swimming-pool metaphor, it's not enough for the Olympic diver to be able to tell that the pool contains 660,253.09 gallons of water. If the water is frozen solid, diving in isn't a good idea. If the market consists of hundreds of thousands of monthly searches *but no buyers,* you're diving in a frozen market — and it won't feel good when you land on your head (or your empty wallet).

The average bid price, which I describe earlier in this chapter, is one indicator of the responsiveness of a market. But this issue is so important that you should take some time and corroborate your first impression with several other data sources.

Number of advertisers on Google

In the popular imagination, entrepreneurs get rich by creating products and services that nobody else has ever thought of. In real life, that rarely happens. Truly original products and services often languish for years until they catch on. Rather than celebrating when you discover that no one else is selling what you want to sell, you should become somber and a little nervous. Then take a deep breath, relax your shoulders, and continue with your day. (I didn't want to leave you all nervous and tense — you might get back pain, and I'm not selling anything in that market. Much better for me if you get gout.)

Go to www.google.com, search for your keyword, and count the number of sponsored listings. You can do this by clicking More Sponsored Links just below the column of AdWords ads on the right (see Figure 4-4). The first ten listings appear on that page. Click the Next button at the bottom to bring up listings 11–20. Keep clicking Next on each subsequent page until you run out of Next links to click. Figure 4-5 shows the end of the long line of ads for the keyword lower back pain. Seven ads on result page 9 translate to 87 ads.

For some reason, Google doesn't always display the More Sponsored Links link the first time you search. Refresh the page until that link appears by choosing View⇨Refresh or View⇨Reload in your browser.

You'll see slightly different results depending on your geographic location — a number of listings in my example were for local chiropractors — but the general trend will be clear.

Glenn Livingston (www.ultimateadwordsresearch.com) cautions AdWords beginners to avoid competing on keywords with more than 25 competitors. After you've cut your teeth in less competitive markets, you can begin to assault the lofty domains of high profit. After all, if someone's doing well there, why not you?

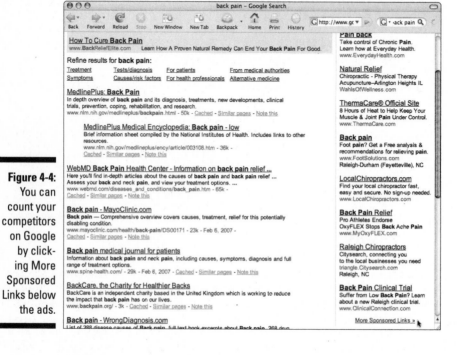

Figure 4-4:
You can count your competitors on Google by clicking More Sponsored Links below the ads.

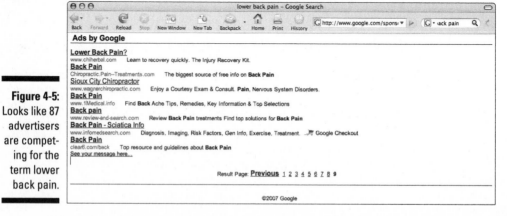

Figure 4-5:
Looks like 87 advertisers are competing for the term lower back pain.

Bid persistence: Will you still love me tomorrow?

Beware of markets full of here-today-gone-tomorrow advertisers. After all, advertisers are trying new things all the time, thanks to Google's no-commitment, low-cost model. Just because you can gather more market data on a Sunday afternoon than Procter & Gamble could amass during the entire Carter administration doesn't mean the data is stable. Bids especially are vulnerable to sudden change because each bid represents not an entire market segment but one merchant's decision that day.

A simple way to establish bid persistence is to print the first two pages of the sponsored listings and then print the listings again at least three weeks later. To reduce your risk as much as possible, repeat this exercise again three weeks after that. If you see that the listings are stable over those six weeks, these folks are either very careless or they're making money.

Going deeper with the AdWords Keyword Tool

Earlier in this chapter, I describe how to use the Keyword Tool and Traffic Estimator to assess Total Market Health. Now I show you how to use the Keyword Tool to figure out whether you can afford to use AdWords to test your initial sales process. Google is famous for being wildly inaccurate in predicting your actual bid prices because your actual bid depends on the quality of your Web site (as well as on the invisible hand of capitalism). The Keyword Tool, like the Traffic Estimator, gives you a dollar amount based on the history your competitors have amassed, which makes it more, not less, valuable at this point in your research.

To use the AdWords Keyword Tool within your account, follow these steps:

1. **Log in to your AdWords account, click the Tools tab, and then select Keyword tool from the drop-down list.**

2. **Enter your main keyword and enter click the Get Keyword Ideas button.**

3. **In the Choose Columns to Display drop-down menu, select Show Estimated Avg. CPC and Show Estimated Ad Position.**

Figure 4-6 shows the estimated CPC for `back pain` and — hundreds of related keywords — as well as the position you can expect for that CPC. If your default CPC for that ad group is too low, enter a higher Max CPC in the box and click the Recalculate button. You can also enter smaller CPCs and recalculate to find out how little you can expect to pay for various positions. The lower the CPC, the less profitable it's been in the past for other AdWords advertisers. You're looking for a sweet spot, where the Max CPC is low enough that you can afford to pay for enough clicks to test and improve — and high enough that you can be sure others are making money in this market.

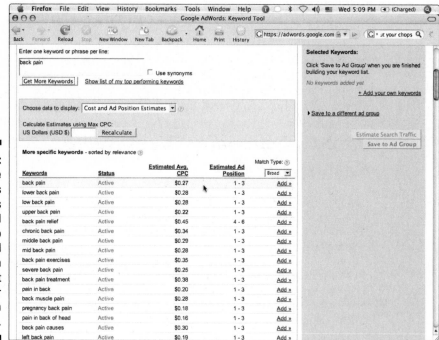

Figure 4-6:
Google estimates that bids of around one to two dollars will get you on the first page for back pain keywords.

Discovering buying trends at online stores

Another source of Internet market data are the popular online stores. To different degrees, they reveal what their merchants are selling and/or what their patrons are buying.

PayPal

Many online merchants conduct business using PayPal as their Web host and merchant account. PayPal graciously provides you with revealing glimpses of their bloomers by listing the sales numbers each shop has made (which is one reason not to use PayPal shops if you're in a competitive market).

To score this data, go to www.askhowie.com/paypalshops, enter a keyword and search for shops, or browse the category listings on the left, just below the search box (see Figure 4-7). In most cases, the category listings are too broad to help you assess the strength of a niche market. You can see 16 pages of PayPal shops — at 25 listings per page, that's a minimum of 376 merchants selling products related to back pain.

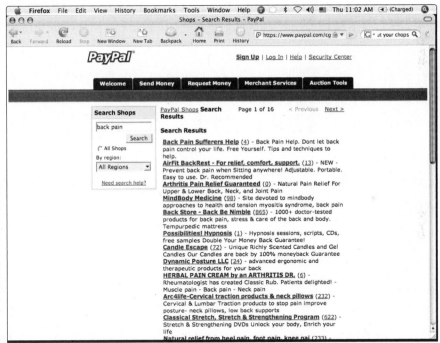

Figure 4-7: PayPal shows you exactly how many sales its PayPal Shops merchants have made.

Spend some time looking at which merchants are making the most — and fewest — sales. Mattresses and magnetic wraps (passive devices) seem to be more popular than hypnosis products and advice (products that require active participation). Save yourself the grief of creating another failing online store by making sure that at least a few people are making sales of products similar to yours.

Amazon

Remember way back when Amazon.com was just a bookstore? Now it sells electronics, kitchen gadgets, outdoor furniture, clothes, shoes, musical instruments, groceries, jewelry, sporting goods, toys, and pretty much everything else that can be put in a box and sent by UPS. Amazon has succeeded partly because it analyzes every bit of customer data it collects. If you've shopped at Amazon before and you have its cookie on your computer, it'll show you a home page calculated to vacuum the maximum amount of money from your wallet, based on what it thinks you'll want to buy next.

You want to search Amazon anonymously — so if you, too, get a personal greeting from Amazon (and you thought you were special, huh?) — so click the link at the top that says `If you're not Jack Bauer, click here`. On the sign-up page that follows, don't fill in anything. Instead, click the Amazon.com tab at the top left to re-enter the site as a stranger. Now, when you search, Amazon won't filter the results based on your shopping history. Instead, it'll serve you the most profitable products in each category.

A *cookie* is a tiny piece of code that a Web site stores in your computer so the Web site will recognize you in future visits. Amazon always greets me by name when I log on and shows me the items I looked at last, along with new recommendations. If I delete all my cookies in my Web browser Options or Preferences menu, the next time I show up, Amazon will treat me like a new customer, about whom it knows nothing.

As in PayPal Shops, you can type in a search term or just browse by category. A category search of Exercise & Fitness (see Figure 4-8) shows the three most profitable products front and center: a stationary bicycle, a treadmill, and an elliptical trainer. On the right, it offers a low-cost item (a yoga mat) and a slightly higher-priced step system.

Drill down into categories and subcategories to see what Amazon knows it can sell in each market niche. You can also search by keyword; a search for `back pain` on the entire Amazon.com site (as shown in Figure 4-9) displays, on the left, 28,000 books, 1,436 products in Health & Personal Care, 211 items in Sports & Outdoors, 88 in Home & Garden, and so on. Click each category to find the bestselling items within it.

I want to see what's hot in Health & Personal Care related to back pain. When I click that category, Amazon shows me the most popular items it or its partner stores carry (see Figure 4-10). In this case, it's a Spine-Worx Back Realignment Device, a Body Back Buddy — which presumably can double as a coat rack — and lumbar support for the cheap desk chair your company buys because ergonomically sound chairs cost too much.

Figure 4-8:
Shopping anonymously at Amazon.com puts millions of dollars of market research at your fingertips.

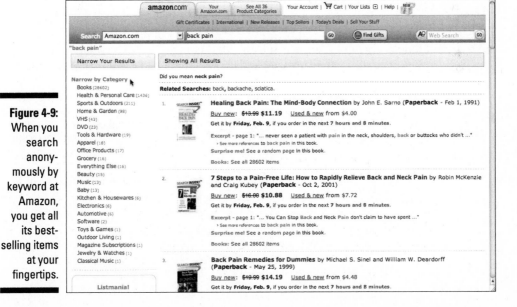

Figure 4-9:
When you search anonymously by keyword at Amazon, you get all its best-selling items at your fingertips.

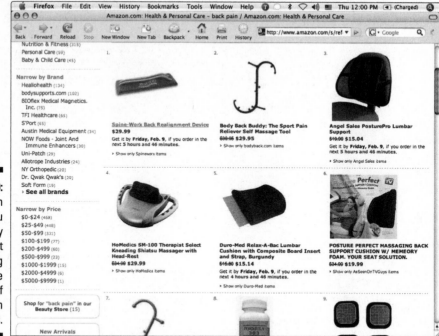

Figure 4-10:
Amazon tells you exactly what's hot by putting it on the first page of the search results.

You might be tempted to throw in the towel if you see the product you want to sell, or a very similar one, listed on Amazon for 30 percent less than you can buy it for. Don't worry — you have a huge competitive advantage over Amazon if you've chosen a specific market niche. Amazon will bid on AdWords, but your ads will be better. Your campaigns will be more efficient and more tightly targeted, and you will understand your customers' fears and desires better than Amazon does.

The bottom line of all your research is to answer the question, "Are people making money online in this market using PPC?" If the answer is no, let go of this market for now and repeat the research process with a different market.

If the search volume is high enough and the customers are ready to spend money, you're ready to go to a higher and more intensive level of research to find out what your prospects want — and what drives them crazy about their current situation.

Eavesdropping at the Watering Hole

The size and temperature of your market tell you whether to enter that market. Knowing how many people are searching and buying doesn't help you market to them yet. You just know they're out there, poking around and buying stuff from your competitors. The next three research questions guide you to develop the right product and sell it using the right concepts.

Your future customers will tell you what they want to buy, how they want to buy it, what color and size and shape it should be, what kind of delivery options they prefer, and how much you should charge for it. They'll talk for hours about what bugs them about other options and what the perfect solution to their problems would be. All you have to do is find out where the conversations are happening, sit down, and start listening.

Remember those nature specials on public television that show all the animals gathered around the watering hole in the savannah? They're all hanging out, drinking, socializing, eating some grass, and sharing the day's gossip. Your market has a watering hole where your buyers gather, too. If you want to find out what to sell to your market and how to sell it, you have to hang out at the watering hole.

Your market's watering hole is where your prospects come to gather information and develop relationships that will help them in their business. The offline component of a watering hole includes lunches, golf meetings, conferences, phone calls, trade journals, water cooler gossip (a literal watering hole!), and the daily routines of business. The online component has two big parts: online groups and the *Blogosphere* (a cool word meaning *the world of blogs*).

Online groups

The two big providers of free groups are Yahoo! and Google. Spend some time on each site, searching for groups related to your keywords and your market. Join the most active groups, read the message archives, and follow the daily threads. Verify that the people in the groups are your prospects.

Resist the urge to do any selling in these groups. You're at their watering hole, remember? If you start pitching your product or services, or contribute comments that are off-base or self-serving or unhelpful, you've just identified yourself not as a zebra, giraffe, springbok, or wildebeest, but as a crocodile! If you want to come back and sell to these groups later, after you've mastered their jargon and understood their concerns, they'll freeze you out if you pushed too hard at the beginning.

Yahoo! Groups

Begin at http://groups.yahoo.com. To join Yahoo! Groups, you need a free Yahoo! account. If you don't yet have one, you'll be prompted to create one. You can start searching for groups without an account, but you'll need to create an account before you can join a group. If you have a Yahoo! account, log in and start searching. You can apply to join groups right away.

After you've done some searching, you'll discover why Google, not Yahoo!, is the preferred search engine. Yahoo! focuses exclusively on keywords, and ignores meaning and context. When I typed **Juggling** into the Groups search box, the first two groups listed (as shown in Figure 4-11) were a support group for work-at-home moms and another for Christian homeschoolers with more than two children. They were in the top positions not for relevance, but because they were the two largest groups that had the word *juggling* in their description. Both groups, of course, used the term *juggling* metaphorically. So neither is a particularly useful watering hole to learn about your prospects' views on replaceable wicks for juggling torches or the proper weight of a silicon stage ball. The next three groups, however, are closer to the mark: a group dedicated to Contact Juggling, a group of Christian clowns, and the main Yahoo! juggling group. The Contact Juggling group's archives are public, whereas the other four groups require membership.

In addition to the keyword search, Yahoo! also gives you a directory of categories that may be more useful. At the top of Figure 4-11, you can see the categories Hobbies & Crafts > Hobbies > Juggling. Click Juggling to view 192 different juggling-related groups. The first two groups look familiar. When you click Juggling2, you're taken to the group's home page, where you can read a description of the group, see how active the members are (by viewing the message-history chart), and decide whether it's worth your time to join this group. To join, click Join This Group! on the right. On the next page, select the e-mail address you want linked to this group, choose how you want to receive messages (individual e-mail, daily digest, or Web only), select the e-mail format, copy some text to prove you're a human and not a software program, and click Join. I recommend choosing the daily digest over individual e-mails — if it's an active group, you could easily spend your entire day dealing with off-topic threads about whether other threads are off-topic and nonsense like that. You can always change your preferences after you've joined, and you can also quit any group easily.

After you join, you can read through the archives and view profiles of group members. Figure 4-12 shows posts in the Juggling2 group.

If you wanted to launch a competing product to the Dube Airflight Clubs, you could gain valuable insight into what people like and don't like about them. The posts shown in Figure 4-12 indicate that clubs striking in midair is a problem for some jugglers.

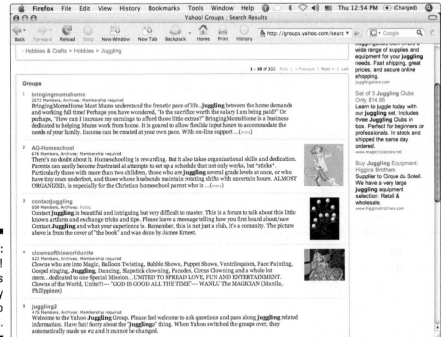

Figure 4-11:
Yahoo!
Groups
supposedly
related to
juggling.

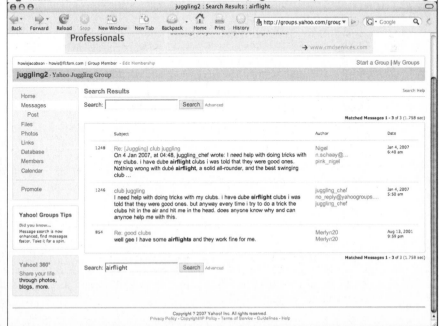

Figure 4-12:
Members
of the
Juggling2
Yahoo!
Group
discussing
a particular
brand of
clubs.

If you wanted to (say) sell against Airflight, you could create thinner clubs less likely to bang into each other, or softer clubs that wouldn't hurt so much if they hit people in the head. And you'd save this post in an idea file for when you started writing AdWords ads. You might come up with an ad that targets the problem you found:

```
Clubs hitting in midair?
Tired of getting bonked on the head?
Try Thin and Soft Juggling Clubs
www.SoftThinClubs.com
```

Google Groups

To search Google Groups, go to `http://groups.google.com`. Google Groups hasn't been around as long as Yahoo! Groups, so you won't find Google communities as established as the Yahoo! ones. But Google Groups gets direct feeds from many of the independent *Usenet* groups that have existed since the late 1980s, and so provide much more comprehensive coverage of the market. When you search Google Groups for `juggling`, you don't get the irrelevant listings that Yahoo! served up. The first groups Google shows you are a unicycling group, a non-Google group dubbed rec.juggling (which I talk about in a minute), and a discussion list for the Vancouver Juggling Club (as shown in Figure 4-13).

To join a Google Group, click Apply for Group Membership on the right. If you're logged in to your Google account, you're taken to a sign-up page where you choose your e-mail delivery schedule, provide a nickname, and apply.

After you've been approved for membership, you can read and reply to messages, search the message archive by keyword, and post new questions. Google formats its group messages on the Gmail template — meaning that replies are kept next to the original message in chronological order.

Other free and paid subscription groups

The Yahoo! Juggling Group moderator sent a welcome e-mail informing me that the group doesn't get much activity these days, and if I wanted to be in the thick of the juggling watering hole, I should try `www.jugglingdb.com/news`, a portal to *rec.juggling,* a forum independent of Yahoo! or Google. In fact, I already saw a link to this group for the Google Groups search results.

The first page of messages on that forum is shown in Figure 4-14.

Even before joining this group, you can read all the posts, search for members by country (useful for figuring out geographic ad targeting in AdWords), and look at the Juggling FAQs and lists of current vendors. If you're starting or expanding an online business, this sort of homework is required if you prefer making money to gambling. And it's so cheap, easy, and quick, I hereby grant you no excuses for not doing it.

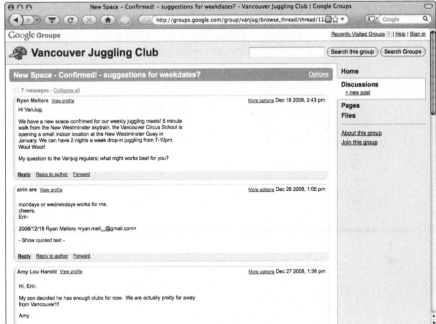

Figure 4-13:
The home
page of
a Google
Group, with
a list of
recent
messages.

Figure 4-14:
This
hopping
Juggling
forum
received
six posts
already
today.

Search for your keyword as you would normally on Google. When the results page comes up, click the Show Options link near the top of the page, just below the search box. Google gives you several options for refining your search. Click the Forums link on the left to view forum discussions about your topic. For example, in the top image in Figure 4-15, a forum search for mcat prep turns up some spirited discussions from College Confidential on the best way to study for the medical school entrance exams. The second link brings you to the discussion shown in the lower image in Figure 4-15. If you were selling in this market, these unfiltered discussions would be incredibly valuable in reading the minds of your prospects and marketing effectively to them.

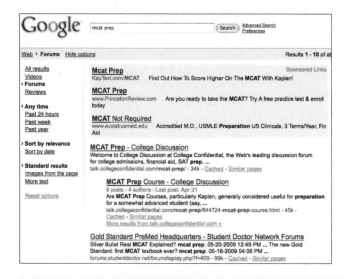

Figure 4-15: Forum discussions are great places to hear the unfiltered opinions and pressing questions in your market.

The Blogosphere ("World of Blogs")

Blogs are great places to learn about your customers because, for some reason, people write blogs like online diaries — little held back, little left to the imagination. When they rant about a vendor or a product they don't like, they go all out. Also, bloggers love to link to and comment on one another's blogs in a particular market space, so true conversations develop. Arguments, discussions, reviews, comparisons — read influential bloggers' posts and you'll quickly feel the pulse of a market segment's desires.

How do you find the blogs and blog posts relevant to your business using? Technorati is the most useful search engine for blogs.

Technorati

Go to www.technorati.com, and enter your keyword phrase in the search box at the top, and hit Return. Then filter the results on the next page by selecting "A Lot of Authority" from the drop-down list.

This search often returns a list of often-influential blogs that deal with your market. The list in Figure 4-16 shows several blogs that write about home gym equipment. If you're selling home gym equipment, go visit them (by clicking their URL) and find out what they're ranting about and what's tickling their fancy. Pay attention to visitor comments, if any (few comments probably means few readers and not much influence), and follow the *blogroll* — the list of blogs that this blog thinks is important.

The third listing for Home Gym Equipment is a post called "6 Ways to Create a Great Home Gym For Less." Technorati assigns an authority score of 925 to this blog, which means something only in comparison to other blogs ranked by Technorati.

You should filter the results by authority (a measure of how many other blogs link to that blog) to weed out insignificant blogs. Because the Blogosphere represents a network, you can usually find your way to the center of that network just by observing who's quoting whom. Blogging expert Dave Taylor (of www.askdavetaylor.com) likens the Blogosphere to a giant party. The person in the middle of the room surrounded by gaping hangers-on is probably the most influential person. Sidle over to that group and you'll learn a lot about your market. On the other hand, you can also find blogs that don't link to other blogs, that just try to sell you stuff, that rant and rave but have no influence whatsoever. That's like a person loudly talking at a party, but no one is listening.

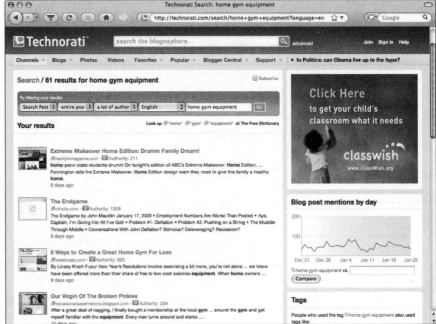

Figure 4-16: Technorati blog search results can help you find the pulse and the opinion makers in your market.

Loitering on Web sites

Your competitors' Web sites are great places to learn what to do and what not to do. When I talked about bid persistence earlier in this chapter, I advised you to print a list of the top AdWords advertisers in your market three times over six weeks. Grab those printouts now and circle the Web sites that appear on all three pages — both the sponsored and organic listings. It's time to hang out with successful businesses and see what they're up to.

First, look at your competitor's Web site as if you're a potential customer. Can you find what you're looking for? Does the site confuse or bore you? Is it easy to contact the site owner and ask questions? Do you trust the site? Can you order easily?

Remember that the home page may not be the landing page you get to by clicking its ad. Check out its landing page and see how it draws you in — or not. Pay attention to how that landing page connects to the rest of the site. Does it try to make a sale or to capture your contact information? What are the featured products? What are its shipping and return policies?

Also, do other sites link to your competitor's Web site? Google loves sites with a lot of *inbound links*. You can find out who's linking to a Web site by typing **link:** and then the URL at `www.yahoo.com` (for some reason, Yahoo does a much better job of reporting links than Google). The link: search takes you to Yahoo's very useful Site Explorer. In Figure 14-17, for example, `link:www.monkeybargym.com` returns 1392 linking pages A high number of inbound links helps increase their organic Google traffic — as well as decrease their PPC bid prices by increasing quality score.

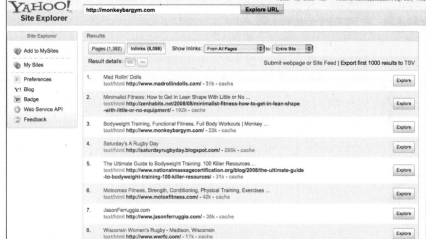

Figure 4-17:
Use Yahoo's Site Explorer to find out how many sites are linking to a given site.

Sleeping with the enemy

But wait, there's more! Don't just float around on your competitors' sites — if you can afford it, become their customer. Get into their sales funnel. Discover how they treat their customers, and whether (and how) they try to grow the relationship. You may discover that their initial sale is a *loss leader* — that is, they lose money on the front end because they have an effective system for selling additional products on the back end.

Do they send e-mail offers for additional products? Do they give coupon codes for dollars off? Do they request feedback? Do they ship promptly? Does the merchandise do what they say it does?

So what do you do if your competitors do everything right? Here's a little online marketing secret: Your competitors are also your best potential business partners. If you can figure out how to share customers, everyone can increase profits by promoting different offers to different market segments. You can play nice with competitors only when you can figure out ways to differentiate yourself from them.

Cutting Through the Clutter with Positioning

You know how big your potential market is. You know how hungry they are. You've discovered what they care about — and what frustrates them about the existing situation and options. You've figured out what kind of pricing structure and market response you need to be profitable. And you've scoped out the competition to see what needs are not yet being filled.

Armed with this information, you're now ready to construct the most important sentence in the life of your business: your positioning statement.

Marketing master Ken McCarthy (TheSystemSeminar.com) explains positioning this way:

> *Successful marketing is a multi-dimensional process. What do I mean by that? Remember the three-dimensional chess board featured on Star Trek? Instead of one board and two dimensions, there were multiple boards on different levels and pieces could move up and down in space as well as backwards and forwards.*

> *Many advertisers obsess about THEIR product and THEIR advertising. That's all well and good, but what these business owners fail to include in their calculations is the total space of the market they hope to enter. Rarely do prospects see only your product and your advertising. They're usually aware of other offers that — on the surface — appear similar to yours. Further, because we're all so busy and have so many things on our minds, we don't have a lot of extra processing power to think deeply about any company's offer.*

> *Here's the key: You can't expect your prospects to do any heavy mental lifting. If it's not crystal clear why your offer is unique, it will be added to the rummage sale pile in their minds where all the other products go that they don't quite understand and will probably never buy.*

Your goal as a business is very simple: You want your offer to occupy a completely unique place in the cubbyhole system of your prospect's mind and you want to figure out how to telegraph that unique value in seconds.

Better marketing and advertising is not just about building a better mouse-trap (or creating a better ad), it's about figuring out where your offer fits in the market space and why you're uniquely qualified to hold a place in it, then communicating that message simply and powerfully, over and over again.

Let me give you two examples of how this works. The ultimate romantic city destination for lovers — what place pops into your mind? Probably Paris.

An innovative computer hardware company that's especially friendly to creative types — which company is already there staking out that space? Probably Apple.

A good rule of thumb is that there's probably only one space per category in everyone's mind. Second place is the same as last place.

Your mission as a smart marketer is to go boldly where few marketers tread and figure out what place your offer can own and then make sure every ad you run reinforces that message. Positioning is the thing that separates the marketers who are standing on the winner's platform from the ones who are perennially treading water.

Your ad copy, your Web site, your e-mails, the way you answer your telephone — all these marketing elements must flow out of your positioning. The easiest way to establish top positioning is to carve a market segment that no one else has claimed. For example, there are many competing merchants in the fitness space. That niche is far too big to attack with limited resources. What about home gym equipment? Also big — and full of established competitors. What about home gym equipment for parents with young children? Indoor playgrounds the size of a home gym that both parents and toddlers can enjoy safely — and that parents can use for a real workout while watching their kids? No company I've ever heard of has told *that* story before. If your research tells you that parents with young children are frustrated about their exercise options, you may stake your fitness-industry positioning on catering to that market. You may find that your initial idea doesn't fly — they don't have enough room in their house for a gym that big, or they doubt that it's safe for kids. But as you watch the market, you'll discover things they *will* search for and buy. And your positioning, based on those discoveries, will make you the obvious choice when they see your Google ad.

Ken McCarthy likens online market research to sitting next to a busy road and watching the cars go by. First you find the potholes, by seeing what people want and aren't getting. Then you create products and marketing messages to fill those potholes.

Chapter 5

Choosing the Right Keywords

● ●

In This Chapter

▶ Understanding the importance of keywords

▶ Reading your prospects' minds through their search behavior

▶ Discovering tools for keyword research

▶ Mastering keyword formats and variations

▶ Sorting your keywords into ad groups

▶ Discouraging the "wrong" people from visiting your site

▶ Increasing traffic by discovering new keywords

● ●

You're in control of most parts of your online marketing. You write your ads. You design and create your Web site. You write checks for advertising. You set your prices, hours of operation, and policies. But one of the most important elements of your online strategy isn't created by you at all, but by your prospects: the keywords they use to search for your solution to their problem. Your job isn't to invent keywords, but to identify the keywords they're already typing. If you can't find those keywords, the AdWords game is over before it starts. No keywords means no impressions, no clicks, no leads, no sales.

After you've discovered those keywords, however, your job isn't over. Now you have to figure out "the want behind the word." Each keyword represents a different mindset — a different set of assumptions about how to fulfill a need, and a different state of buying readiness. For example, the singular and plural keywords can imply huge differences. Someone searching for used car is probably closer to buying than someone who types **used cars**. The plural searchers typically are at the early stages of their quest, whereas the singular searchers have, in their minds, a picture of one item that they'll buy when they find it.

I use the singular/plural example because it's surprising, perhaps, that one letter can make such a big difference. Other keyword variations, such as synonyms, are equally significant:

- ✔ car **versus** auto
- ✔ used **versus** pre-owned

If you've ever received high-quality sales training, you know to pay attention to prospect cues and clues before making your pitch. You might steer one prospect to a 1958 MG convertible, a second to a 2001 Odyssey minivan, and a third to a 2009 Toyota Prius. With AdWords, your prospects' keywords are your only initial clues to their innermost desires. Different keywords trigger different ads, take prospects to different landing pages, and make them different offers.

This chapter shows you how to interpret keywords to help you read your prospects' minds. Armed with this fundamental understanding, you discover how to conduct keyword research to find the words and phrases that will bring you qualified search traffic. You discover how to manage your keyword lists in AdWords, separating them into ad groups and using the positive and negative keyword formats to get as many good prospects as possible while discouraging nonbuyers from seeing and clicking your ads.

Decoding Keywords to Read Your Prospects' Minds

The golden rule of marketing, in my book (hey, this *is* my book — cool!), was first articulated by Robert Collier in his 1934 book, *The Robert Collier Letter Book:* "Join the conversation already going on in your prospects' mind." His example: If you want to sell a winter coat to a man walking down the street talking with a friend, don't jump out and interrupt him with a statement about what a great winter coat you have here. Instead, start walking along with the pair, listening and nodding at their conversation. Here and there ask a question, offer a relevant comment, and watch for an opening. When talk comes around to vacations, steer it gently to trips to cold climates. When your prospect is primed, you can show him your coat. (Please remember that's a metaphor, not a suggestion to lurk in doorways and stalk strangers!)

Because Google has not (yet) hooked up electrodes to our brains while we browse the Web, the keyword is your best guide to the conversation already going on in your prospects' heads.

Perry Marshall of www.perrymarshall.com is fond of saying that every keyword represents an unscratched itch. You search to solve a problem. Maybe you literally itch and are looking for an ointment. Maybe you're bored and are looking for excitement. Maybe you're worried and looking for peace of mind. Maybe you accidentally dropped your cell phone in a cup of coffee. Maybe you want to find a summer camp for your kid. Whatever it is, the fact that you're searching means you don't have enough information to take action immediately. A gap exists between what you know and what you need to know in order to make a decision.

A nifty Web portal created by Seth Godin, www.squidoo.com, says it well:

> *We believe that when you go online, you don't search. You don't even find. Instead, you are usually on a quest to make sense.*
>
> *That's the goal of most visits to Google or Yahoo! or blogs or Wikipedia. How do you make sense of the noise that's coming at you from all directions?*
>
> *You won't take action, you won't buy something, book something, hire someone, or take a position on a political issue until you've made sense of your options.*
>
> *Searching online should really be called poking online. Because that's what you do. You poke around. You poke in Google and you poke at some ads. After looking at a bunch of links and pages, then, finally, you get it. You understand enough to take action — to buy something or make a decision.*

Your mission as an AdWords advertiser is to help your prospects make sense of their options. And to do it faster and more completely than anyone else. The word *client* comes from the Middle Ages, where it originally meant, "person seeking the protection or influence of someone powerful." Think of yourself as the expert in your market, the protector of the hordes of confused seekers, the one who will take your prospects by the hand and guide them through the hype and confusion and lies, and take them to the promised land of clarity and truth.

Squidoo's description suggests that "poking" is often inefficient because the searchers encounter lots of false starts and dead ends, confusion, frustration, and mistrust. What if you could figure out, just by the keywords they used, where your prospects are and what paths they need to follow to achieve understanding? Then you become their protector, and they become your clients — trusting you to show them the next piece of information they need to make a decision and act on it. That's the ultimate goal of your AdWords strategy — to show each prospect that you understand him or her, and can give them what they want each step of the way — including the part where they pull out a credit card and pay you for it. You achieve this goal by finding out how to interpret keywords. Your best teachers are Google, your own practice of empathy, and the data you collect.

Learn from Google

Google won the search-engine wars, in part, because it got very good at figuring out what people were looking for based on what they were typing. And the more data Google collects, the smarter it gets. Every time you perform a Google search and click a link, Google follows you and adds your actions to its database. It knows which sites you visit as part of your search. It knows how long you stay and how many pages you browse. If the advertiser has installed Google Analytics, conversion tracking, or a Web site optimizer, Google knows whether you've signed up for a mailing list, or bought something, and even how much you spent. The next time someone searches on that or a similar keyword, Google tweaks the search results to reflect what you told Google through your actions.

To fully appreciate the differences that Google has discovered, try this experiment: Perform a search on any keyword and print the first page of search results. Then search for a synonym and print *that* page. Compare the two pages — what percentage of the listings has changed? For example, try searching for `vermiculture` and then its synonym `worm farming`.

If you take the time to visit the landing pages on each results page, you'll discover something of what Google knows about the mindset difference between `vermiculture` and `worm farming`. Perhaps one group is professional, whereas the other is made up of amateurs. Maybe vermiculturists are just worm farmers with more education and higher credit limits. Could be that vermiculturists are into composting, whereas worm farmers are into selling fish bait. (If I didn't have 12 more chapters to write — and had some worm-farming supplies to sell — I might spend the time to find out.)

If you're preparing to advertise your business on Google, researching the keyword differences in your market will significantly increase your chances for success.

Decision mindset

Perform Google searches for the top keywords in your market and scan the results for clues. In particular, look for clues about what values will dominate their decision-making process. What data will they consider before making a decision, and how will they evaluate and prioritize that data? What's the first question they need answered to alleviate feelings of impatience, confusion, or frustration?

The following subsections help you determine your potential customers' mindsets.

Buyer or tirekicker

Are they serious about buying or just fantasizing? `Big mansion` sounds like a dream, whereas `9 BR Colonial Princeton NJ` looks like a serious quest.

Market-savvy or innocent beginner

Are they familiar with standard industry terms or new to the industry? For example, whenever I go to the home-improvement store, I have to describe the tool or part I'm looking for with lots of hand gestures, analogies, and facial contortions because I don't know the name of anything in the store except for *hammer, Snickers bar,* and *toilet-bowl flange* (please excuse me as I process this flashback). Whether I walk out with a frown or a ratcheting 11mm box wrench depends on the patience, empathy, and experience of the clerk I manage to find hiding in Aisle 53. (Do they hide from you, too, or it is just me?)

For example, someone who wants to make their own beer might search for `beer making` or `homebrew`. The very fact that some folks are familiar with the "insider" term *homebrew* suggests they're at least somewhat market-savvy. The savvier the prospect, the more knowledgeable *you* must appear about the market and the product choices. Even experts are looking for leadership.

Discretionary or nondiscretionary purchase

How badly does your prospect want or need what you have? How hard do you have to work to convince that person to buy? Imagine a long sales letter, an e-mail follow-up course, a video demonstration, and an hour of audio testimonials for . . . a box of large paper clips. Overkill. Paper clips are an office necessity, needed when they're needed. Compare that to motivational posters for the office, a product that didn't even exist until some entrepreneur figured out that managers are lousy at motivating employees and would pay money to get a picture to do it for them.

Problem-conscious or solution-conscious

For example, `get more clients` represents the problem (not enough clients), whereas `CRM software` (*CRM* stands for *Customer Relationship Management*) is one solution to that problem. Your ads can focus on problems (empathizing, agitating) or solutions (describing, proving, advocating). Remember: Join the conversation already going on in your prospect's mind.

Suppose that every prospect is searching for a solution, and you have a competing solution to the same problem. In that case, start by talking about the solution they're already thinking of. My Leads into Gold campaign does this with prospects searching for `cold calling scripts`. One ad headline reads, "Stop cold calling." Another: "Cold Calling Doesn't Work." You can also raise questions about the solution: "Does Cold Calling Work?" Or position yourself as an expert above the fray: "Cold calling scripts compared."

Solution-conscious shoppers think they know what they need but are often wrong. To the extent that your ads and Web site can educate them through a consultative approach, you can shift them away from preconceptions that are limiting their thinking. Problem-conscious shoppers typically open their minds to a broader array of solutions.

Price shopping or feature shopping

If someone searches for `Canon PowerShot SX10 IS 10 MP 20X Zoom` you can bet they're looking for a price, shipping info, and a store they can trust. Compare that to a search for `10 MP SLR digital camera` — which indicates more of an interest in general camera types (and possibly price *ranges*) than in specific brands and features.

Need it now or planning for future need

Your prospects' time frame is important because you always have a choice to send them to a "buy now" page, or a "sign up for my 56-day e-mail course" page. Don't pitch a course on avoiding plumbing emergencies to someone with a busted pipe flooding their basement. And don't try, on the landing page, to sell a luxury beachfront property in Tasmania to someone searching for `retirement property`.

Sale or information

As I mention earlier in this chapter (unless you're reading it backward, in which case "retpahc siht ni retal noitnem I sa"), singular and plural keywords often point to big differences in desired outcome. Someone ready to buy a pet cockatiel, for example, would probably begin with `cockatiel` rather than with `cockatiels`. Someone just doing research on longevity, tricks, and annoying habits would be more likely to begin with the plural.

Practice thinking like your prospect

Following the Google trail is a start. The next step is to put yourself into your prospect's head, walk a mile in his moccasins, see through his eyes, and feel through his kidneys (or whatever), for all of them and each of them.

Why did they type those particular search terms at that moment? What went through their minds during the seven seconds prior to the search? What were the triggers? How long have they been thinking about this problem? What tasks did they just interrupt to conduct this search? What environmental distractions are competing for their attention right now?

Who are they? What do they care about? What are their hopes, fears, dreams? What are their deepest, most secret desires? Can I stop writing romance-novel back-cover teaser questions?

The practice of market empathy is one of the hardest marketing tasks you'll ever have to accomplish. Before you can pretend to be someone else, you first have to pretend you aren't you. You, after all, are a very small but very loud market sample, and the more you listen to yourself, the less room you have in your brain for thinking about others. When you think your prospect is the same as you, the "Market to Yourself Syndrome" follows: You speak in industry jargon, you assume everyone knows the purpose, history, and significance of your product, and you believe everyone can see the dramatic differences between your product and the competition. Because it's obvious you're talking to yourself, your prospects politely ignore you.

The more words in the keyword phrase, the more information you have about your prospect. Look at the following four-word keywords, each including the words `treatment for gout`. What differences might exist in the minds of the three different searchers?

- ✔ `natural treatment for gout`
- ✔ `alternative treatment for gout`
- ✔ `symptom treatment for gout`

I'm intrigued by the difference between *natural* and *alternative* — the two terms overlap a lot. I feel the alternative seeker is more desperate than the natural seeker. *Natural* implies high standards, whereas *alternative* tells me that conventional treatments haven't worked. *Symptom* may be a quick-fix tell, a searcher who wants immediate relief rather than to address the root causes.

What can you do with this information? If my livelihood depended on selling as much stuff as I could to these three people, I might craft my ad pitches accordingly:

Keywords	*Ad Pitch*
`natural treatment for gout`	Natural Gout Treatment — no side effects
`alternative treatment for gout`	Gout Treatment Your Doctor Doesn't Know
`symptom treatment for gout`	Quick Relief from Gout Pain

My landing page would immediately indicate that I understand them. For example:

Keywords	*Landing-Page Text*
natural treatment for gout	"Are you worried about the side effects from the pills your doctor prescribed for your gout flare-ups? Want to be drug-free? Want to prevent future attacks naturally?"
alternative treatment for gout	"You've tried the drugs, and they didn't work. You wonder whether Western medicine really knows how to treat gout. Your doctor just keeps prescribing higher doses of the same stuff. Want to get off the drug treadmill completely and discover a treatment that attacks the causes of gout, not just the symptoms?"
symptom treatment for gout	"You live in fear of a sudden onset of painful symptoms, and you're always wondering when your next attack will occur. Instead of treating the symptoms when you're already in agony, want to learn how to prevent flare-ups in the future?"

Mastering the Three Positive Keyword Formats

You can't possibly guess all the variations of keywords your prospects will type when they're trying to find you. Fortunately, Google doesn't force you to be specific, although it allows you to be. AdWords lets you input *positive* keywords (that is, keywords that trigger your ad, as opposed to *negative* keywords that prevent your ad from showing) three different ways: broad match, phrase match, and exact match. They look like this:

- **Broad match:** Buddha statue
- **Phrase match:** "Buddha statue"
- **Exact match:** [Buddha statue]

Broad match

Broad match keywords show your ad when the actual keyword is similar to yours. `Buddha statue` shows for the following actual searches (note the differences in spelling and capitalization):

- ✔ `Buddha statue`
- ✔ `statue of the Buddha`
- ✔ `Buddah statue`
- ✔ `Korean statue of buddha`
- ✔ `Buddhist statues`

Broad-match keywords are useful when you don't know what people are searching for, and you want to make sure you capture all relevant searches. The downsides of broad matching are the inability to match ad copy to the keyword, as well as lower CTR (click-through rates) and higher bid prices.

Phrase match

Putting the broad match in double quotes converts it to *phrase match,* meaning the characters between the quotes must appear exactly as they are somewhere in the actual search. `"Buddha statue"` matches the following searches:

- ✔ `Buddha statue`
- ✔ `"Buddha Statue"`
- ✔ `Chinese Buddha statue`
- ✔ `grinning Buddha statue`

Phrase matches generally have higher CTR and lower CPC (cost-per-click) than broad matches because they eliminate synonyms and changes in tense, number, and order. The most accurate matching occurs with the third syntax: exact matching.

Exact match

You indicate an exact match with square brackets, generally found to the right of the P key on your keyboard. `[Buddha statue]` will show only for the following searches:

✔ `Buddha statue`

✔ `buddha Statue`

✔ `"Buddha statue"`

Exact-match keywords are the most precise. You know exactly what the searcher typed when you register an exact match impression.

If you include the broad, phrase, and exact matches of the same keyword in your ad group, phrase trumps broad — and exact trumps both. In other words, if your keyword list includes

✔ `Buddha statue`

✔ `"Buddha statue"`

✔ `[Buddha statue]`

and someone searches for `life-sized Buddha statue`, that searcher triggers the phrase match (in quotes), but not the broad or exact match. And `Buddha statue` triggers the exact match.

The goal: From vague to specific

Exact match is a powerful way to exclude searches you don't want to attract. But it's a double-edged sword — exact match can also eliminate searches you do want, but haven't thought of yet. In a perfect AdWorld, the vast majority of your traffic comes from exact matches (because you know what your prospects are thinking and typing) and you still capture other relevant searches. When you start advertising on AdWords, you may not have enough traffic for your exact matches, so you'll have to use broad- and phrase-match keywords for a while. If you keep track of the actual search terms people use to get to your Web site (see the later section, "Using your server log to get smarter"), you can replace broad-match keywords with the exact keywords that triggered your ads.

Over time, you replace keyword guesswork with precise knowledge. For example, Kerry Nesbit offers logos for veterinary practices at `www.veterinary logos.com`. Her main keywords, when she began the campaign, were veterinary logos and veterinarian logos. She soon discovered, via the logs on her Web server, that Google was showing her ads to people searching with similar intent, but different language:

- ✔ animal hospital logos
- ✔ veterinary clinic logos
- ✔ vet hospital logos
- ✔ dvm logos

After you start seeing these searches in your server log or Search Query Report (see Chapter 14), you add them as broad-match and exact-match keywords. The number of impressions for veterinary logos goes down as these keywords pick up the slack. Eventually, you may be able to retire your broad-match keywords entirely.

"Why would I want to retire my broad-match keywords?" I hear you ask. Kerry found that Google's broad match was often, er, a bit too broad. Her ads were also being shown for such searches as:

- ✔ animal symbols
- ✔ medical emblem
- ✔ veterinary marquee
- ✔ Vietnam vet burn signs
- ✔ signs of canine pregnancy

Yikes! Obviously, none of these searches represents a serious prospect for graphic design for a veterinary practice. If you were Kerry, would you want to show your ad to people who want to know whether their dog is expecting? If not, you're attracting the wrong prospects — and needlessly lowering your CTR and quality score, and increasing your bid price for clicks. So how can you turn off your ad for these searchers? One solution, which I cover later in this chapter, is the use of negative keywords. You can add -pregnancy to your keyword list to tell Google, "Hide my ad if *pregnancy* is in the keyword."

By monitoring the actual phrases that trigger visits to your site (via the Search Query Report), you eventually can eliminate many irrelevant searches by choosing only the keywords that *qualified* prospects are typing.

I show you how to move from vague to specific keywords later in this chapter, in the "Sorting Keywords into Ad Groups" section.

Researching Keywords: Strategies and Tools

In the perfect AdWords campaign, every click leads to a sale and you don't miss any clicks that *could* have led to a sale. In real life, of course, such a perfect campaign is impossible. But it's the goal of everything you're doing. Your keyword selection represents a balancing act between hyper-aggressive and hyper-conservative:

- ✔ **Hyper-aggressive:** If you choose every keyword in the universe, you won't miss anybody, but your CTR will be microscopic and your bid prices will be astronomical.

- ✔ **Hyper-conservative:** If you bid only on the very obvious keywords, you'll miss a lot of sales from prospects who approach the search process differently from you.

The ideal balance point is the one that maximizes your business goals, whatever they are. If you're advertising a for-profit business, your goal may simply be the highest possible profits. You may sacrifice some profits for quality of life and go for the highest ROI. If you're building a company to sell, you may prefer to build a huge subscriber base to earning profits up front.

Whatever the goal, the same three-part strategy applies:

1. Start with the obvious keywords.

   Make a list of the keywords you'd search if you were your customer.

2. From there, go laterally into synonyms and related searches.

   Conduct the research described in Chapter 4, use the Google Keyword Tool, and one or more of the tools described a little later in this chapter.

3. Tweak or fire underperforming keywords — and keep looking for new ones.

Part III shows you how to manage your AdWords campaigns to continually improve your results.

Eventually, you'll have a stable of reliably profitable keywords pointing to the appropriate ads, taking visitors to effective Web sites.

The Google Keyword Tool

You can use the Google Keyword Tool (which I mention in Chapter 4 in the section on the size and health of your online market) at www.askhowie.com/kwtool to generate related search terms. Simply type the main keyword in the box (this time keeping the Use Synonyms option selected) and click the Get Keyword Ideas button to receive a list of related terms. For example, a search for `used cars` produced synonyms, such as `used suvs` and `secondhand cars` among dozens of others. You can explore the keyword landscape and download keywords to your computer in a file that you can open in a spreadsheet program, such as Microsoft Excel or Google Spreadsheets.

Another use for the Google Keyword Tool is to search Web sites for keyword ideas. At the top, select the Website Content radio button and enter the URL of a site related to your keyword. For example, `edmunds.com` returned the following keyword families: `used car` (31 variations), `new car` (23), `car price` (7), `invoice price` (9), `car dealer` (6), `for sale` (6), `car` (51), `dealer` (14), and `auto` (17).

Google has a Search-based Keyword Tool (see Chapter 9 for the scoop on all the free Google tools in your account) specifically designed to give you keyword ideas from your Web site, but it doesn't work very well yet. Stick to the main Keyword Tool until you hear differently from me.

Thesaurus tools

Remember the frantic high-school-essay writer's best friend, *Roget's Thesaurus?* It got you through some pretty rough papers by giving you 12 ways to say *accomplish* and 19 ways to say *want.* (Although my history teacher thought *hanker* too colloquial and *prefer* too wishy-washy.) Well, the old thesaurus is now online, in two free incarnations, and can lead you to keywords you'd otherwise miss.

Online Thesaurus

Go to `http://thesaurus.reference.com` to access the online version of *Roget's New Millennium™ Thesaurus*. Type your keyword (one word, generally) into the text box near the top of the page and click the Search button.

For example, when you type the keyword **insurance**, one of the synonyms, `coverage`, can open a huge new set of keywords. Just about anywhere you can use `insurance`, you can now use `coverage`:

- ✔ `health insurance` and its synonym `health coverage`
- ✔ `automobile insurance Omaha Nebraska` and its synonym `automobile coverage Omaha Nebraska`

Every synonym in the online thesaurus is hyperlinked to a list of its synonyms. Clicking `coverage` takes you to another set of results for `compensation`.

For your purposes, the majority of thesaurus results are irrelevant. Look for words that jog your brain into thinking, "Oh, *that's* a good keyword, too."

Quintura.com

Quintura.com is a visual thesaurus that shows you, at a glance, the major themes in a market. Figure 5-1 shows the search themes related to veterinary logos in a *word cloud* on the left, whereas the Yahoo! search results appear on the right. The cloud immediately suggests a couple of additional keyword groups, veterinary clinic logos and veterinary practice logos, as well as phrases with `brochure` and `design`.

If you sell logo design services to veterinarians, several of the results of this Quintura search will point you in promising directions (`clinic` and `prac-tice`, for example), whereas others will help you brainstorm negative keywords (see the later section, "Deploying Negative Keywords").

Figure 5-1:
Veterinary logos are related to several additional sets of keywords; some relevant, some not.

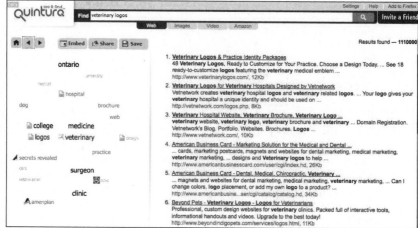

Google's Wonder Wheel

Google's Wonder Wheel is a visual representation of related searches that shows you, at a glance, the major themes in a market. Access the Wonder Wheel by performing a regular Google search, then clicking the Show Options link just below the search box. From the left navigation, select Wonder Wheel. Figure 5-2 shows the search themes related to mcat prep in a hub and spokes pattern on the left, with the search results corresponding to the center term bon the right.

Click any of the underlined keywords to further explore the subcategories of your market. Again, you'll discover keywords to add and exclude.

Google's Related Searches

While you're showing the search options, also take a few minutes to explore Google's Related Searches feature. At the top of the page, Google shows you a list of searches that relate to your keyword. Many include your keyword within them, but others are semantically related (that is, they are connected by meaning, not by words). For example, a related search for The Beatles returns the names of the Fab Four, Bob Dylan, Across the Universe, the Beach Boys, and the Doors. Google is revealing what people who searched for The Beatles also searched for within the same session.

Figure 5-2:
The Wonder Wheel shows connections among keywords in a visual and interactive way.

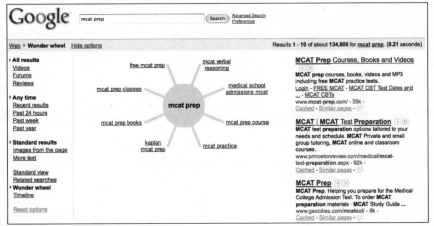

KeywordSpy.com

If you're serious about using AdWords, KeywordSpy.com is one of several paid tools I recommend highly. Go to www.keywordspy.com, type a keyword in the search box, and click the Search button. In the Paid Keywords tab of results, you're shown to a list of Web sites bidding on that keyword, as shown in Figure 5-3. Click any of the Web site links to see a long list of *their* other keywords.

In other words, if your competitor has done a good job of researching keywords, you can use this sneaky tool to take advantage of all their hours of hard work. If you need to compete against established competitors in an AdWords market, this tool is a no-brainer.

Using your server log to get smarter

Quietly, uncomplainingly, your Web site has been storing a gold mine of visitor data, patiently waiting for you to realize its value. If your Web site has been welcoming visitors for any length of time and you haven't perused your server log yet, you're in for a treat. Among lots of other useful data, your server log will tell you exactly what search terms visitors typed to land on your site. All the tools I've talked about in this section are useful as idea generators — but your server log tells you exactly what keywords are *already* getting people to your site. (Once you start driving AdWords traffic, you can run search query reports to find out the exact search phrases entered by your visitors.)

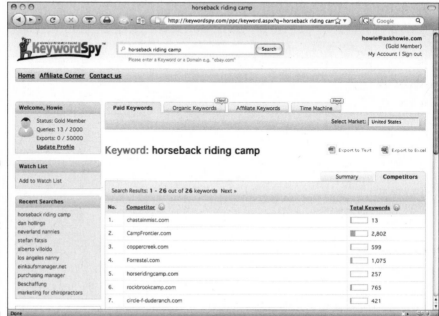

Figure 5-3:
Keyword
Spy.com
returns a list
of Web sites
currently
bidding on
the same
keyword.

Because Web servers differ significantly, unfortunately I can't tell you exactly how to find and read your own server logs. If you're technically savvy about your Web site, you already know where to find the server log. If you're not sure how to view your server logs, contact your hosting provider.

What you want to look for in your server logs are the key phrases and keywords that people typed into a search engine just *before* visiting your site. You want to select a reporting period that makes sense (last month, last year, and so on). Figure 5-4 shows the server logs for key phrases and keywords that lead visitors to my site, www.leadsintogold.com, for one year. Most of the keywords you find this way are "long-tail" — lots of rarely searched variations (see the next paragraph). Occasionally you can discover a high-traffic keyword this way. Mostly, I use this information to add negative keywords — words that disqualify the searcher as a prospect — and thereby save money by avoiding unprofitable clicks.

Figure 5-4:
My server
log shows
me rarely
searched
keywords
that have
brought visi-
tors to my
Web site.

gold calling leads	6	0.7 %
cold prospecting	6	0.7 %
gold calling scripts	5	0.6 %
cold calling alternative	5	0.6 %
cold calling scripts	5	0.6 %
end cold calls forever	4	0.4 %
bernie heer	4	0.4 %
cold call alternatives	4	0.4 %
cold calling doctors	4	0.4 %
cold calling stats	3	0.3 %
leads to gold	3	0.3 %
cold calling template spreadsheet	3	0.3 %
www.leadsintogold.com	3	0.3 %
gold calling system	3	0.3 %
gold leads	3	0.3 %
keyword variant generator	3	0.3 %
leadsintogold	3	0.3 %
forex-edge.com	3	0.3 %
end cold calling forever	3	0.3 %
leadsintogold.com	3	0.3 %
cold calling for an internet provider	2	0.2 %
cold calling specialist	2	0.2 %
gold calling success	2	0.2 %
m howard jacobson	2	0.2 %
leads for cold calling	2	0.2 %
cold call statistics	2	0.2 %
www	2	0.2 %
cold walking prospecting	2	0.2 %
howard jacobson durham	2	0.2 %
end cold calling	2	0.2 %
cold calling procedure	2	0.2 %
attract marketing leads	2	0.2 %
howard jacobson	2	0.2 %
never cold call again reviews	2	0.2 %
advertising cold calling	2	0.2 %
script for calling old leads	2	0.2 %

Long-tail keywords refer to phrases that are rarely typed and will therefore
bring you very few visitors, but collectively can generate many sales. The
concept of the long tail (the phrase itself refers to the shape of the graph of
the statistical distribution of events) was popularized in the book *The Long
Tail,* by Chris Anderson, who argued that in a digital world with no production or shipping costs, the combined profits generated by long-tail products
can be greater than the profits from the blockbuster bestsellers. Amazon.
com, for example, can be more profitable than brick and mortar bookstores
because such a large proportion of Amazon's sales come from obscure books
that physical stores wouldn't be able to stock due to shelf space limits.

Before 2009, one way to win the AdWords game was to add as many long-tail
keywords as possible. The long-tail keywords were often cheaper, with less
competition. Google changed the game, however, by disqualifying keywords
with low search volume. Now, if you want your ad to appear when someone
searches for red canon camera that takes great pictures of lorikeets, you just
bid on "red canon camera" in phrase match and hope Google takes care of
the rest.

Finding Sneaky Variations for Fun and Profit

So far you've been looking at semantic variations — keywords with similar but slightly different meanings. Now you can explore the wide world of sneaky variations — slight keyword tweaks that can mean the difference between lackluster and sizzling campaigns.

Some quick ways to vary keywords

For openers, here are a couple of simple sources of keyword variation — geographic location and human typographical error:

- **Geography:** As you saw in the `used Toyota trucks` example, keywords sometimes include geographical terms. If you ship home gym equipment anywhere in the U.S., you want to capture searches for `home gym Alaska` to `home gym Vermont`. You may even want to get more granular than the state level: `home gym Chicago` and `Chicago home gym`.

- **Misspellings:** Let's face it — everyone couldn't win the spelling bee in elementary school. And people often type so quickly, they mess up wodrs and phraess (oops) while they search. Don't take my word for it — check out this hilarious page, courtesy of Google, that lists the misspelled searches for Britney Spears over a three-month period:

      www.google.com/jobs/britney.html

If you bid on misspellings that your competitors ignore, you have a twofold advantage:

- **Significantly decreased competition:** When I search for `low cholesterol recipes` in Google, I find eight sponsored listings. When I enter `low cholesterol recipies` I see only one. Ten advertisers, including heavyweight Lipitor.com (a Pfizer Web site about its cholesterol medication), did not think to show their ad for a common misspelling. You have a much higher chance of compelling a click if you're in a beauty pageant against only one or two other competitors.

- **Lower CPC:** With less competition, you don't have to bid as much to appear on the coveted first page. In the `low cholesterol recipies` example, the misspelled keyword costs about half as much as the correctly spelled term.

Misspellings won't generate huge search traffic. The Britney Spears example shows the correct spelling receiving almost half a million searches, and the most popular misspelling (*britanny*) getting 10 percent of that. Most of the misspelled keywords (have you ever noticed how the word *misspelled* just doesn't look right?) occurred four times or fewer. The goal in using misspellings isn't to double your traffic. Instead, it's to *lower your average cost of customer acquisition.* The goal of the AdWords game — as with a lot of business — is to turn cheap raw materials (in this case, clicks) into valuable products (in this case, hungry customers with working credit cards). You can use misspellings to lower your average CPC slightly and increase your traffic slightly, which gives you slightly more money to spend on advertising and slightly more traffic to run through your split testing machine (see Chapter 13) — and become slightly better at turning visitors into customers. The cumulative effect of all these slight advantages is enough to snowball into market dominance.

Different versions

If you sell different versions of the same basic product, you'll improve your CTR by including specific search terms. A business selling light bulbs might bid on the following general terms:

- ✔ fluorescent light bulb
- ✔ compact fluorescent light bulb
- ✔ flood light
- ✔ floodlight
- ✔ lightbulb
- ✔ flourescent bulb

Their customers may be searching for much more specific items:

- ✔ 36" fluorescent light bulb
- ✔ dimmable compact fluorescent light bulb
- ✔ 14 watt compact fluorescent light bulb
- ✔ red 150 watt flood light
- ✔ green 150 watt flood light

If you sell 20 different colors or shapes or sizes or types of a product, be sure to include *all* those variables in your keyword list. Google may disqualify some or even most of the longer, more specific keywords, but any you can keep will increase your relevance and lower your average cost per click.

Different points of view

A realtor may advertise for the keyword `real estate Carrboro NC` and miss the following keywords that include the perspective of different searchers:

- ✔ `buy real estate Carrboro NC`
- ✔ `buying real estate Carrboro NC`
- ✔ `sell real estate Carrboro NC`
- ✔ `selling real estate Carrboro NC`
- ✔ `looking for real estate Carrboro NC`
- ✔ `shopping for real estate Carrboro NC`
- ✔ `house hunting real estate Carrboro NC`

A regular verb and a gerund (the verb with *-ing* at the end) can signify completely different mindsets. Until you're sure you don't want the customer with a particular mindset, include them all.

Singular and plural

The difference between a singular and plural word can mean a lot of things. Sometimes, people looking for information type the plural (`digital cameras`), whereas more serious shoppers use the singular (`digital camera`). If the plural keyword is significantly cheaper to bid on than the singular, you know that other advertisers have found it harder to make money from the less-expensive keyword. If you optimize your sales process to bring the information-seeker to the point of purchase, you can take advantage of the cheap, plentiful "pre-transaction" keywords such as general plural terms.

.com

Every year, the number of Internet users grows. Because a steady stream of Web newbies are searching for your products, you can profit by knowing the search "mistakes" they often make. Web neophytes can confuse the Google Search box with the *address bar* (where you type the URL of the Web site). So if you sell red flood lights, you can snag some inexpensive traffic by bidding on (say) `redfloodlights.com`.

LowerYourBidPrice.com — sneaky keywords made easy

I've developed a keyword-manipulation tool, the AdTool, which makes it easy to generate thousands of "sneaky" keyword variations from a single keyword. You can add U.S. cities and states before and after all your keywords, you can substitute synonyms with the click of a button, you can add hundreds of mis-spellings, convert singular to plural and vice versa, add `.com` to the end of your keyword, and add quotes and brackets automatically (if you're as bad a typist as I am, this one feature will save you hours).

Let's say you've brainstormed 1,000 keywords that all contain `mortgage`. Now you discover that 5 percent of searchers spell *mortgage* without a "t" as *morgage*. The AdTool lets you replace `mortgage` with `morgage` in all 1,000 keywords — and add *those* new 1,000 keywords to your campaigns.

You can also use it to generate hundreds of keyword phrases with the phrase combiner. For example, someone who sells collegiate team clothing might sell 20 different items (hats, jerseys, sweatshirts, and so on) related to 12 different sports (baseball, basketball, lacrosse, and so on) for 150 colleges and universities (Duke, UNC, Princeton, and so on):

$$20 \times 12 \times 150 = 36{,}000 \text{ keywords}$$

In Figure 5-5, I've included four colleges, five sports, and five items. The AdTool instantly generated 209 variations, including two-word phrases like `Duke hat` and `Princeton sweatshirt`.

The AdTool is available for a full-featured 21-day trial for $3.95 at `www.lower yourbidprice.com`. It includes many other features that I don't want to hurt your brain with right now. But because I developed it for my own personal use, it's grown to do just about everything I recommend in this book.

Figure 5-5:
The AdTool combiner feature generates hundreds or thousands of keywords based on the elements you input.

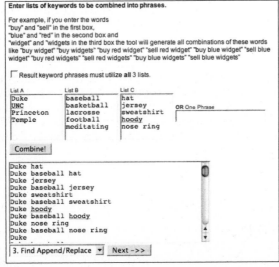

Sorting Keywords into Ad Groups

After you've generated your keywords, your next step is to organize them into ad groups. Your mission, should you choose not to waste money and time, is to match your ad closely with the keywords in that group. In the first part of this chapter, I emphasize that each keyword has a mindset that goes with it. The *mindset* represents what the searcher wants and how she or he wants it; if you put all your keywords into a single ad group, you can't write an ad that will appeal to all those different mindsets. I'll give you seven reasons to organize your keywords into coherent groups:

✔ **You can scratch the right itch:** Perry Marshall puts it this way: "Think of a group of keywords as a bundle of desires. Some desires go together better than others. Some are alike and some are very different. Each ad group must clump together the most similar desires, so the ad can mimic and inflame those desires. You want every one of the people who views your ad to say, 'Yeah, that's for me.'"

Say you run an online golf store, selling clubs, balls, bags, shoes, instructional books and videos, training aids, and so on. You can bid on thousands of keywords and send them all to your home page, www. jimsgolfemporium.com. The keywords could include

- golf
- golf clubs
- putters
- golf shoes
- improve your golf swing
- improve your golf game
- correcting a slice in golf

and many others. Each of these keywords represents an "itch." The search results page is nothing other than a race among all the listings to scratch that itch first. If your ad is a generic golf ad, you can't compete with an ad that names the itch and promises to scratch it good.

If you had typed **left-handed titanium drivers**, which headline would catch your eye — Golf Clubs and Clothing or Lefty Titanium Drivers?

The big reason to separate similar keywords into ad groups — to show an ad that scratches the itch — is supported by other reasons:

✔ **Google bolds keywords in the search results:** Type any word or phrase into Google and look at the results page. Every keyword you typed (except for *a, an, the, for,* and suchlike) appears in bold in every listing, whether sponsored or organic. Bold text catches the searcher's eye.

✔ **The Quality Score of each keyword depends, in part, on how well it matches the ad:** Google assigns a Quality Score to each keyword in your account, based on click-through rate and how well your ad and landing page match the keyword. A poor Quality Score will raise your bid prices and make it difficult for you to compete. If you have dozens or hundreds of keywords pointing to the same ad, you can't make them all relevant to that ad.

✔ **Talk to your prospects in their language:** If your prospect is searching for `foods that prevent gout` and you put that exact phrase in the headline, you've scored an empathy point. The way they search is the way they talk to themselves. Tap into their lingo and you demonstrate understanding.

✔ **Improve your ads by split testing:** If you don't segment your market, you're missing key split test data. Maybe you have two ads running neck and neck (see Chapter 13 for the details on split testing), with a CTR of 1.4. In actuality, Ad #1 has a CTR of 3.6 with people who typed **tiger woods putter** and only 0.03 with people who typed **golf shoes**.

✔ **Show visitors the right landing page:** The golfer searching for left-handed titanium drivers doesn't want to land on your home page and have to play hide-and-seek with your site navigation. Google has made us impatient and lazy — your visitors will go back to Google before trying to make their way through a confusing site. With a tight ad group, you can send all the traffic to a perfectly matched landing page — either for a selection of left-handed titanium drivers, or the best-selling men's and women's drivers, or an article on how to choose a left-handed titanium driver. The easier you make it for your visitors, the more likely they are to follow your lead.

✔ **Easy campaign management:** Managing different ad groups is easier than handling one larger group. If your AdWords campaign consists of 1,000 keywords, all in one ad group, you'll have a miserable time trying to manage that campaign. You'll have trouble comparing keyword performance because you'll have too much data to look at. You may end up spending time inputting keywords you already have but can't find.

Divide keywords into concepts

Separating the list of golf keywords into concepts, or "bundles of desires," you get big groups and smaller groups within the big groups. The big buckets are

✔ Clubs

✔ Accessories

✔ Clothing

✔ Instruction

You can divide, say, Clubs into the following categories:

- ✔ Left-handed and right-handed
- ✔ Men's, women's, and juniors'
- ✔ Putters, drivers, fairway woods, irons, and wedges
- ✔ Power and accuracy
- ✔ Different brands

The combination of these splits could be the ad groups:

- ✔ Left-handed men's putters
- ✔ Right-handed women's drivers
- ✔ Junior fairway woods

For accessories, a big subcategory is "golf balls." Your ad groups are probably named for the brands. Pay special attention to the most-searched brands.

Don't get paralyzed here, looking for the one right way to organize your keywords. You can't know for sure at this point. Your data will help you optimize your campaign over time — right now, take your best guesses (the market research described in Chapter 4 helps here), and create ad groups that are tight enough to be coherent and not so numerous as to defy effective management.

Spend more time on the high-traffic keywords than the long tails. Think of the high-traffic keywords as your prize pumpkins, the ones that can win you a gold medal at the state fair. The low-traffic keywords are the apples on the trees in the orchard — collectively, they're valuable, but you couldn't spend ten minutes a day on each apple.

Organizing your keywords

I manage keywords for my AdWords campaigns with three tools: a text editor, the AdTool (from www.loweryourbidprice.com), and Microsoft Excel.

Step 1: Collect keywords with a text editor

As I'm doing my initial market research, I just copy and paste all my keywords into a text file. Your PC or Mac almost certainly comes with a text editor. Notepad is bundled with PCs and can be accessed by choosing Start⇨ All Programs⇨Accessories⇨Notepad. On the Mac, the default editor is

TextEdit and can most easily be found by typing **textedit** into the Spotlight search box at the top right and choosing the TextEdit application. I prefer a simple text editor to a complicated word processing program like Microsoft Word because the word processors sometimes add funny stuff (formatting commands, invisible characters, whatever) to the text. With plain text, what you see is what you get.

If you're so familiar with Word that you can't bear the thought of learning another program, just save the Word file as `.txt` instead of `.doc` in the drop-down menu in the Save screen. Don't forget to save the text file somewhere you can find it easily — and remember: Word won't show you files that end in extensions other than `.doc` unless you specifically ask it to.

Step 2: Input the words into the AdTool and generate new ones

Copy the keywords list in your text editor and paste them into the AdTool. You can then peel and stick the keywords into individual Excel sheets by ad group.

One of the AdTool's tabs is called *Peel & Stick*. This phrase entered the AdWords landscape courtesy of Perry Marshall, who used it initially to describe the process of removing a single keyword from an ad group and building a new ad group around that one key keyword. More broadly, *peeling and sticking* refers to tightening ad groups by moving keywords into new ad groups — and writing ads that more specifically target those keywords.

The AdTool's peel and stick function allows you to peel keywords out of your giant keyword bucket according to common words or letters.

After you've generated all your keywords, go to the Peel & Stick tab. Choose a word that's contained by all the keywords you want to peel out of the big group. For example, suppose I peel keywords containing `course` for the golf ad campaign and then e-mail them to myself. I can then stick them straight into AdWords, edit them further, or save them for future work. For that matter, instead of e-mailing the list, I could copy it to my Clipboard and paste it into a text or spreadsheet file.

Step 3: Sort the keywords with Excel

I use Excel to help me view my keywords as sorted by ad group. The first sheet is my summary sheet. It includes the names of all my ad groups and the search volume for each group. Figure 5-6 shows a very neat division of ad groups in the Golf Lesson market, courtesy of Glenn Livingston of www.ultimateadwordsresearch.com.

Each subsequent sheet shows the keyword list for that ad group, as in Figure 5-7.

A spreadsheet laid out this neatly makes it a breeze to input the keywords into AdWords. Just select column A by clicking the A at the top of the column, copy the entire column, and paste it into the AdWords Add Keywords tool.

	A	B	C	D
282	Golf Lesson	60113		
283	Golf Lesson Local Search	10420		
284	Online Golf Lesson	7533		
285	Free Golf Lesson	2889		
286	Golf Lesson Video	2405		
287	Golf Lesson Tips	1895		
288	Golf Swing Lesson	1771		
289	Golf Lesson Plans	1252		
290	Child Golf Lesson	1251		
291	Golf Lesson International	1139		
292	Golf Lesson Las Vegas	879		
293	Golf Lesson Florida	853		
294	Golf Lesson Atlanta	757		
295	Golf Lesson San Diego	739		
296	Golf Lesson Beginner	734		
297	Golf Lesson New York	706		
298	Golf Lesson Chicago	705		
299	Golf Lesson Instruction	702		
300	Golf Lesson LA	627		
301	Golf Lesson Putting	620		
302	Golf Lesson Grip	569		
303	Golf Lesson California	528		
304	Golf Lesson Arizona	493		
305	Austin Golf Lesson	480		
306	How To Play Golf Lesson	438		
307	Golf Lesson Boston	432		

Summary ⟋ Golf ⟋ Golf Instruction Beginners ⟋ Golf Instruction ⟋ DVD Golf ⟋ Golf Instructio

Figure 5-6:
The summary sheet of the spreadsheet includes every ad group with a search count.

Go to www.askhowie.com/keywords5 for a video demonstration of using Excel for keyword management.

Use each keyword only once in your AdWords account. If you include the same keyword in two different ad groups, or campaigns, Google will show only one ad, based on the keyword's quality score. Google won't let you compete against yourself by showing both ads. Also, when you have duplicate keywords, your campaign management becomes a mess. You can't be sure how much traffic your keywords are getting because the traffic is divided among your ad groups. If you want to delete a nonperforming keyword, you have to hunt for it in more than one place. So begin your account with a clean structure; you'll find it easy to follow through with best practices later on.

◇	A	B
1	arizona and golf and fitness lesson	10
2	arizona golf in lesson	14
3	arizona golf lesson	436
4	arizona golf lesson 20	5
5	arizona+golf+lesson	1
6	golf lesson arizona	3
7	golf lesson in arizona	3
8	golf lesson mesa arizona	1
9	golf warehouse golf car golf lesson arizona golf	4
10	phoenix scottsdale arizona golf lesson	16
11		
12		
13		493
14		
15		
16		
17		
18		

Figure 5-7:
This ad group, called Golf Lesson Arizona, contains just 10 keywords.

Deploying Negative Keywords

In the movie *The Verdict,* Paul Newman plays Frank Galvin, an outgunned lawyer representing an injured client in a medical malpractice lawsuit. When Galvin realizes that the defendant is hiding incriminating evidence, he requests delivery of the damning documents. The defendant delivers the evidence in a way that ensures (he hopes) it won't be found before trial — buried somewhere in truckloads of meaningless paper. Your AdWords traffic is the same — there are a few gems (your future customers and referrers) buried in a giant stream of nonbuyers. Negative keywords are your first line of defense, a filtration system that keeps the wrong folks away while letting the right folks see your ad.

Let's say you sell wooden kits for building bat houses. You bid on the keywords bat and bats and discover that, for some reason, you're getting large numbers of impressions but very low CTRs. What's going on? Are your ads ineffective? Maybe. But the first problem you have to solve is related to keywords, not ads.

Who else might be searching for bat or bats? Go to www.lexfn.com and type **bat** in the Word 1 search box. Click the Submit Query button, as shown in Figure 5-8.

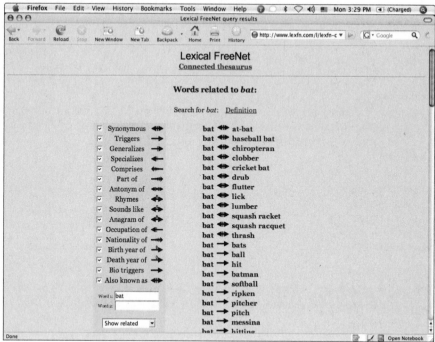

Figure 5-8:
The term *bat* occurs in many contexts other than flying mammals that can echolocate their prey and (allegedly) turn into vampires.

Baseball, cricket, and squash fans are also typing **bat** into Google, without the remotest interest in attracting mosquito-eating flying mammals by building houses for them. The actual search numbers for the top 10 bat-related keywords, according to LowerYourBidPrice.com, are shown in Table 5-1.

Table 5-1	Searches for Top 10 Bat-Related Keywords over a 12-Month Period
Search Term	*Number of Hits*
baseball bat	420,784
softball bat	380,614
bat	147,129
the bat	73,019
easton baseball bat	35,204
bat softball	24,984
milken softball bat	22,484
bat house	22,297
easton bat	19,159

If you're bidding on `bat` as a broad match, you're going to show your ad to a lot of the wrong people. If they don't click, they don't cost you money directly, but by lowering your CTR, they have a negative impact on your quality score. The lower your quality score, the more you need to bid to remain in a desirable position. Fortunately, Google provides a solution to help you filter out traffic you don't want: negative keywords.

Negative keywords are words and phrases that automatically disqualify your ad from showing should they appear in a search. In the `bat house` example, you'd designate the following negative keywords:

- ✔ `baseball`
- ✔ `softball`
- ✔ `ball`
- ✔ `easton`
- ✔ `milken`

You don't need to include `base ball` or `soft ball` because `ball` already takes care of all variations in which `ball` is a separate word.

Brainstorming negative keywords

You should spend some serious time finding negative keywords. One of the most common and costly AdWords mistakes is focusing all your attention on positive keywords. Positive keywords *bring* you traffic, whereas negative keywords *filter* it for you so only the quality searchers ever get to your ad. A comprehensive list of negative keywords increases the quality of your traffic and improves your CTR significantly. Several sources of negative keywords are discussed in the following subsections.

Thinking about who isn't your customer

No database or tool can replace your own insight and common sense. For example, `bath house` may be a reasonable typo of `bat house` — you may want to include the negative keyword `bath`. Consider other searches that may be triggered by your broad-match keywords. Do you want to show your ad to people concerned about bat bites, for example? They may be searching for an exterminator or a medical Web site, but perhaps you can entice them with an ad like this:

```
Bat Problems?
Don't kill them - Help them move!
Bat House Kits - vs. Yard Pests.
www.BatHouseKits.com
```

If your best efforts at selling to `bite` keywords fail, turn `bite` into a negative keyword and move on.

Running the Search Query Report to build your negative keyword list

The Search Query Report (which I discuss more fully in Chapter 14) shows you the exact keyword phrases that got searchers to your Web site. If you're bidding on `bat problems` as broad match, this report will show you that one of the visitors to your site triggered that keyword match by typing **bat problems in the dugout**. Aha! You've just found another negative keyword — `dugout` — to add to your list.

Searching Google for negative keywords

For example, a Google search on `bat` brings up the following concepts, all unrelated to flying mammals:

- British American Tobacco (BAT) company
- The BAT! Email Client
- Balanced Audio Technology
- Infogrip BAT Keyboard
- Brockton Area Transit (BAT) Authority
- BATch files

Finding negative keywords with the AdWords Keyword Tool

First, go to the ad group you're working on by logging in to your account and choosing the campaign and ad group from the Campaign Summary screen. From within that ad group, click the Keywords Tab and select the Keyword Tool. Enter your keyword, making sure the Use Synonyms check box is selected, and click the Get More Keywords button. (See Figure 5-9.)

In this example, the suggestion tool yields several more negatives:

- `file`
- `glove`
- `gloves`
- `command`

What about `guano` and `vampire`? Both terms relate to your kind of bat, but may bring you high school students looking for articles to rip off for term papers (or, for that matter, *Twilight* or *Buffy* fans). Can you turn them into customers? Perhaps — but you'll want to keep these traffic streams separate from the others so you can send them to the appropriate landing pages (and then track your success).

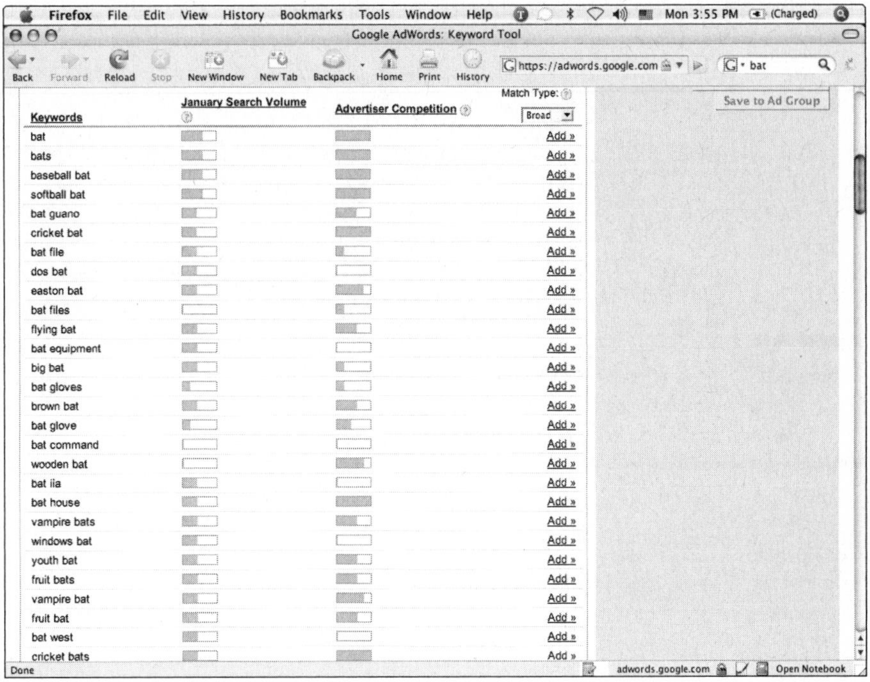

Figure 5-9:
Some of
Google's
keyword
sugges-
tions make
excellent
negative
keywords.

Adding negative keywords

Add negative keywords quickly to your keyword list by clicking the Keywords tab from within an ad group, and then selecting Quick Add, just below the date range. You add negatives to your keyword list by typing a hyphen before the word or phrase, as shown in Figure 5-10.

Adding, Deleting, and Editing Keywords

All these keywords won't do you any good until you place them in your ad groups. If you've opened up an AdWords account, you have at least one keyword in each ad group. Here's a look at how to add, subtract, edit, and manage keywords in the individual ad-group interface.

Log in to your AdWords account and navigate to an individual ad group. Click the Keywords tab at the right to view the list of all your keywords, as shown in Figure 5-11.

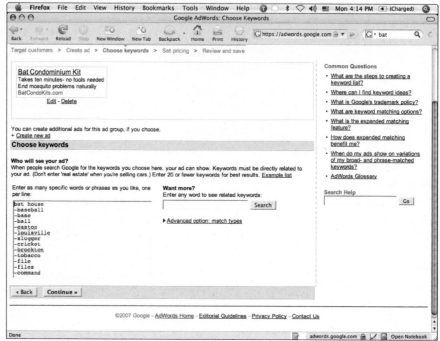

Figure 5-10:
Put a hyphen before your negative keywords when adding them to your keyword list.

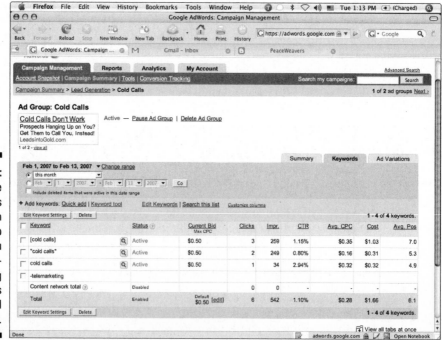

Figure 5-11:
The Keywords tab within an ad group shows you each keyword along with its status and history.

Growing your keyword list

In your AdWords account, you can add keywords to your ad group in two ways:

✔ **Add Keywords: From within an ad group, select the Keywords tab.**
Add keywords by clicking the Add Keywords button, just above the keyword list. Google gives you a text box into which you can type or paste keywords, one word or phrase per line, as shown in Figure 5-12. You can add them straightaway by clicking the Save button, or you can see how much traffic Google expects to give you for each of them by clicking the Estimate Search Traffic button.

Don't worry about adding a keyword that you already have in your ad group — Google kindly filters out duplicates for you.

✔ **Keyword Tool:** The Keyword Tool, accessible from the Tools tab at the top of the page, allows you to type or paste keywords or let Google do it for you.

I strongly recommend using Google's vast keyword capabilities *before* you get to this point. Don't let Google add words directly into your account. Instead, use this tool to generate lots of keywords, and then manipulate and filter them in a text file or spreadsheet.

Figure 5-12:
I add two phrase match and three negative keywords to my existing list.

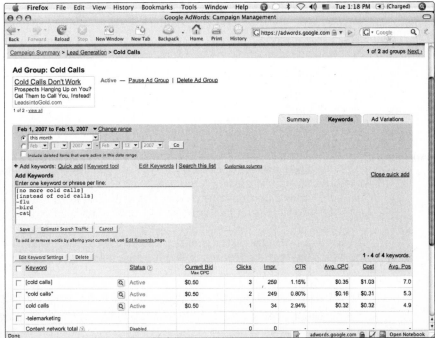

Editing your keywords

Click the Edit Keywords link (next to the Keyword Tool link) to bring up your entire list in a text box. Here you can remove, add, and change keywords, as well as change your *default bid* (the amount you'll pay for a click unless you set specific maximum CPCs for individual keywords). Note that negative keywords do not trigger bids, so you don't need to worry about bid prices for them.

Below the Save Changes button, Google instructs you on changing cost-per-click bids and destination URLs manually. That's right — each non-negative keyword can have its own bid *and* its own landing page.

Individual CPC bids

Use Google's syntax `keyword**0.55` to override your default bid for a specific keyword (see Figure 5-13 for an example). You can accomplish the same task much faster, with less possibility of typing or syntax error, through the Edit Keywords interface on the main ad group page.

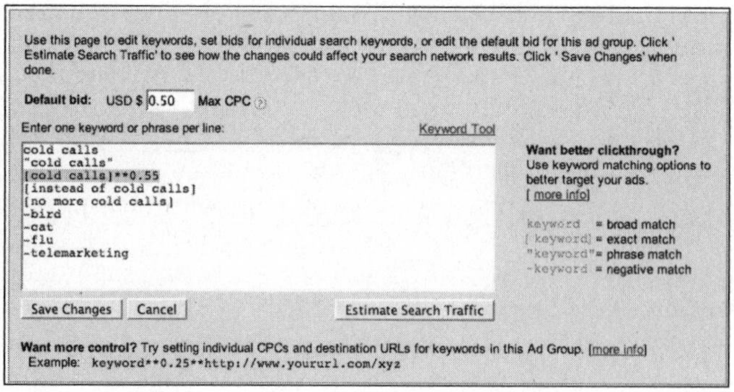

Figure 5-13:
The exact match [cold calls] now has a bid of $0.55 instead of the ad group default of $0.50.

Use this page to edit keywords, set bids for individual search keywords, or edit the default bid for this ad group. Click ' Estimate Search Traffic' to see how the changes could affect your search network results. Click ' Save Changes' when done.

Default bid: USD $ `0.50`   Max CPC ⓘ

Enter one keyword or phrase per line: Keyword Tool

```
cold calls
"cold calls"
[cold calls]**0.55
[instead of cold calls]
[no more cold calls]
-bird
-cat
-flu
-telemarketing
```

Want better clickthrough?
Use keyword matching options to better target your ads.
[more info]

keyword = broad match
[keyword] = exact match
"keyword" = phrase match
-keyword = negative match

Save Changes   Cancel   Estimate Search Traffic

Want more control? Try setting individual CPCs and destination URLs for keywords in this Ad Group. [more info]
Example: `keyword**0.25**http://www.yoururl.com/xyz`

To change bids easily and safely, select the keyword or keywords you want to re-bid by clicking the check box to the left of each keyword. To select all the keywords, select the Keyword check box at the top of the column. Now click the Edit Keyword Settings button just above the keyword column to find a page like the one shown in Figure 5-14.

Change bids by replacing the number next to the currency sign. Google tells you which bids are too low to show on page 1, marking each one with a V icon.

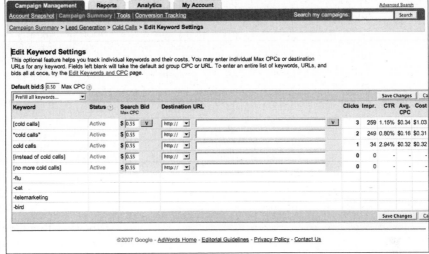

Figure 5-14:
You can
change
maximum
CPCs and
destination
URLs with
Google's
Edit
Keyword
Settings
page.

Individual landing pages

You can change *destination URLs* (landing pages) for each keyword as well. Because each keyword represents a slightly different mindset — and buying readiness — the perfect AdWords campaign would send each visitor to a landing page tailored specifically to his or her keyword. In a perfect world, however, you'd have so much money you wouldn't be reading this book (and I'd be playing Ultimate Frisbee instead of writing this book), so don't get carried away by fantasies of unlimited resources. Fact is, you have a certain amount of time to spend on AdWords, and no more. Creating individual landing pages for low-traffic keywords isn't the best way to spend your precious AdWords minutes.

At this point, you may be wondering why Google bothers you about different landing pages at the same time you set your bids. It's because the fit among your keyword, ad, and landing page helps determine your ad's Quality Score — which determines your minimum CPC for Google and the search network. In other words, if your ad isn't showing on the first page of search results, your only option isn't to raise your bid. You can also improve your ad, improve your landing page, and find a better keyword. Raising your bid is simply the quickest and least time- and energy-consuming way to get back onto the first page.

In the old days (pre-2004), Google would disable keywords that didn't achieve a minimum 0.5 percent CTR. Now they impose a lazy-tax (in the form of a poor Quality Score) on advertisers who show uncompelling ads that invite searchers to unhelpful and irrelevant landing pages. So instead of being disabled, your keywords now require exorbitant bids to show on the first page of search results. Like a *maitre d'* angling for a tip to get you a table at a "full" restaurant, Google holds out its palm and says, "You wanna show your ad to my people? That'll be 10 bucks a click."

In the Edit Keywords tool, you can change the URL after a keyword, like so:

```
keyword**http://www.yoururl.com/xyz
```

In Figure 5-15, I've added two keywords whose traffic I'm sending to www.leadsintogold.com/fa, a Web page I set up specifically for financial advisors who work for big houses such as Smith Barney and Morgan Stanley.

Figure 5-15:
Those searching for "financial advisor cold calling" (and alternate spellings) are taken to a different Web page.

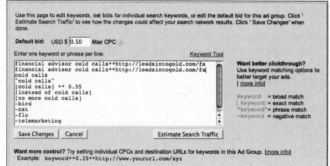

In the Edit Keyword Settings screen, change destination URLs by typing the new URL in the long text box next to http://.

Chapter 6

Writing Magnetic Ads

. . . .

. . . .

*T*his sentence contains the same number of characters — 130, including spaces — that Google allows you in an ad.

You get four lines of 25, 35, 35, and 35 characters to tell enough of your story to compel the right people to choose your ad over all the other ads and organic listings on the Google search page. If you're advertising on the content network, your ad is competing with articles, videos, games, and more. I've heard professional copywriters say that the Google ad is the most challenging form of salesmanship-in-print they've ever attempted.

Depressed? Don't be. Writing effective ads is hard for everyone, not just you. Spend some time preparing, practicing, and (especially) testing your ads, and you'll quickly rise to the top of your industry. As business philosopher Jim Rohn says, "Don't wish it were easier — wish you were better."

This chapter helps you stop wishing and start improving. First, I explain the three-pronged goal of your ad. Most advertisers focus on one prong only, to their detriment. You discover how to balance the first two goals for maximum profits by bringing in the right kind of traffic (not just the maximum possible traffic), and how to reach the third goal of setting visitor expectations so your prospects are primed for your Web site. Next, you discover how to tune your ad to your prospect's radio station, WII-FM (What's In It For Me?), based on the keyword. I share with you the missing link between your ad and your Web site — the call to action. I cover some basic strategies for effective ad writing, as well as a few top-secret (until now!) "black belt" techniques that you'll need if you're playing in a hyper-competitive market. Finally, I introduce you to some alternatives to the standard text ad: image, mobile text, local business, and video ads.

Understanding the Three Goals of Your Ad

A good ad attracts the right people — your best prospects — to your Web site. Your ad has three goals:

- Generating clicks from qualified visitors
- Discouraging the people who are unlikely to become your customers from clicking your ad
- Setting your prospects' expectations so that your Web site satisfies (and possibly even delights) them

The following sections discuss these three goals in detail.

Attracting the right prospects while discouraging the wrong people

The AdWords medium encourages a stepladder approach. The job of the ad is to deliver drooling prospects to your Web site. They don't even have to be drooling over what you want to sell them, just over what you're offering them in the ad. Sometimes the ad offer and the first sale are identical — selling a product they're searching for by name and model. Other times, you're dangling a magnet that will attract the quarters and ignore the wooden nickel. (I talk more about lead-generating magnets in Chapter 10.)

Your four-line ad can't make a sale, any more than a door-to-door salesperson can ring the doorbell, utter one sentence, and sell a $1,000 vacuum cleaner. The first sentence is meant to make the prospect listen to the second sentence. Likewise, the Google ad isn't long enough to capture the prospects' attention, pique their interest, stroke their desire, and make them pull out their credit card. Let your Web site, e-mails, and phone calls accomplish the heavy lifting. Craft your ad to make or imply a promise that your landing page can keep.

The rest of this chapter shows you how to write an attractive ad. Right now, though, I'm going to tell you how to make your ad unattractive. After all, a click means you just paid Google. Clicks from the wrong people can cost you a lot of money without putting any of it back in your pocket.

You may remember magazine ads that featured a huge red headline of the word *sex*, with the subhead, "Now that I've got your attention . . ." The ad would go on to sell some product totally unrelated to the headline. Similarly, many people use names of celebrities (Britney Spears and Paris Hilton, for example) in their ads to grab attention. Don't try that with AdWords. In cyberspace, folks are serious about their searches. If they feel misled by your ad, they'll cost you a click and never visit you again. For example:

```
Free Britney Spears Pics
Hundreds of exclusive photos
and videos - all completely free!
www.BootzRus.com/BritneyGoesWild
```

If your site actually sells custom inserts for cowboy boots, this ad will almost certainly achieve a higher CTR (click through rate) than the more traditional ad that follows:

```
Custom Cowboy Boot Inserts
Instant relief of bunions and corns
Cures athlete's foot - free shipping.
www.BootzRus.com/CowboyBootInserts
```

But how qualified is the traffic from the first ad? Aside from their anger at being duped when they arrive at a site featuring cowboys with corns and not the celebrity gossip or racy pictures they expected, how likely would they have been to *want* boot inserts in the first place?

The Britney mistake doesn't usually look that stark and ridiculous, but I see it all the time in my clients' campaigns. Big promises are great, but when they're too vague, they attract the wrong people. For example, NovaMind. com sells mind mapping software to help writers and others brainstorm creatively and efficiently. Here's an ad I made up that would probably beat all their other ads' CTRs, but wouldn't lead to many sales:

```
Be More Creative
Amazing Technique Helps You
Brainstorm Brilliant Ideas
www.NovaMind.com
```

This ad promises a big benefit — one that the software theoretically can deliver on — but doesn't qualify the benefit with any information that would allow someone to say, "Oh, that's not for me."

Here's one of their real ads:

```
Mind Map Software
Organize your Creative Thoughts and
Mind. Download a Free Trial now!
www.NovaMind.com
```

The headline states what the product is and by implication disqualifies people who don't own, like, or use computers. The free trial offer is appealing, but suggests that the product itself isn't free. *Free* is a powerful word and must be used cautiously in AdWords. People who have no desire to pay for something will still take one if it's free. If the ad had promised a free download without qualifying it as a *trial,* they would have increased CTR at the expense of the traffic quality.

Writing a personals ad

Think of your ad like a personals ad. If you're putting personals ads in local papers or Match.com, your goal isn't to attract every bozo in the county. Instead, you want to weed out the incompatibles and make every date a potential winner. Personals ads achieve this qualification by stating who should not apply:

> *Divorced White Male, 53, in good health, seeks Single White Female, non-smoker, under 45; no cats or whistling cockroaches; must not be allergic to peanuts or mangos; must like Berlioz, Bartok, and organic kohlrabi.*

Negative qualifiers not only weed out the wrong folks; they also attract the right folks: ("He's right — I could never live with a whistling cockroach. We're a lot alike. I wonder what he looks like. . . .")

Your ad can qualify based on location (Roslindale IT Consultant), price (Downloadable Book — $17.77), limited options (Red and Gold Only), platform (Not Mac-Compatible), profession (For Teachers), personality (No Whiners!), and many other characteristics. Brainstorm a list of qualifiers by answering the question, "Who shouldn't buy from me?" If you sell a stand-alone version and a prospect is searching for an enterprise edition, don't even waste a nickel of your cash or a minute of their time. If your negative keywords didn't turn them away (see Chapter 5), let your ad do it before they cost you money.

Which side do you want to err on?

Every ad has to choose between Mistake #1 and Mistake #2. Mistake #1 is the false positive: Someone clicks who isn't your customer. You've just wasted the click price. Mistake #2 is the false negative: You send away someone who would have bought from you.

Which mistake is worse depends on how much each mistake costs you and how often it occurs. If your clicks cost 5 cents and your average sale is $800, you can afford a lot of false positives ($800 \times 20 = 16,000$ to be exact) for each sale. On the other hand, if clicks cost $32 each, your campaign will hemorrhage cash if you aren't very particular about whom, exactly, you invite to your site.

Ultimately, the decision to widen or narrow the ad comes down to the value of a visitor from that ad to your Web site. One ad will simply make you more money (after subtracting your advertising spend) than all the others. Your mission is to keep writing ads until you find that one.

Telling your visitors what to expect

The third goal of your ad is to *manage expectations.* If your ad conveys playfulness, don't send your visitor to a dry and hyper-professional-looking landing page. If you advertise a free download, make it easy to find that download. If you highlight a benefit, focus the landing page on that benefit. Show your prospect that you keep your promises, even the little ones you make in your ads. Think of the ad as the headline of your landing page — make sure it signals the precise benefit someone will get when she clicks through to your site.

Tuning Your Ad to the Keyword

Imagine that your goal is to sell a photocopier to Al Schmendrick, a local business owner. Which ad headline has the best chance of success?

A. Big Sale on Business Machines This Week

B. Are You Tired of Clearing Paper Jams from Your Old Copier?

C. Hey, Al Schmendrick: Are You Tired of Clearing Paper Jams from Your Old Copier?

If my kids' college tuition depended on the sale, I'd choose headline C in a heartbeat. Why? It's all about the prospect, and it's very likely to get his attention. In fact, if Al Schmendrick doesn't read the paper that day or skips the page that contains my ad, I'd bet that one of Al's friends will tell him about it.

The meta-message of your ad to your best prospect is, *"This ad is all about you."* Marketing consultant Dan Kennedy talks about the message-to-market match. The keyword defines the market — who they are and what they want. Your ad is the message that must address their self-identity and desires. As I talk about in Chapter 5, the tighter your ad groups, the more precisely your tone, message, and offer can match what each market will respond to.

Marching to a Different Drummer

AdWords is arguably the most competitive advertising real estate on earth. Where else can you find dozens of competitors crammed sardine-like into the same space, vying for eyeballs and actions? If you said "the Yellow Pages," you're almost right. AdWords functions like the Yellow Pages, except in four important respects that make AdWords far more competitive:

✔ In the Yellow Pages, customers might find your ad on the third page of listings, but it could be the very first ad they see. Position is less important than size and look. An AdWords ad on page 8 is essentially invisible.

✔ The Yellow Pages separates the free and paid listings into white and yellow pages. Google shows both on the same page. I've heard from AdWords clients who also have first-page organic rankings who tell me that their organic listing generates three times as many clicks as their ad.

✔ Because AdWords is a *results-accountable medium* (meaning, you can tell when your ad works and when it doesn't), many AdWords competitors have become proficient through trial and error. Most Yellow Pages ads are just plain awful because businesses haven't discovered the direct-marketing principles that allow for continuous improvement. (For more on this, visit my Web site www.leadsintogold.com.)

✔ In the Yellow Pages, you don't pay less or move to a better position if your ad is more effective than a competitor's. The Yellow Pages is like golf: Your score doesn't directly affect your competitor's score. AdWords rewards relevance with lower prices and higher position, making it more like tennis.

The most important rule when trying to stand out in a crowd is, "When they zig, you zag." As you compose your ad, keep your prospect's big question in mind: "Why should I click your ad instead of all the other ads and organic listings on this page, instead of typing a different search term — and instead of blowing off this search entirely and logging on to Facebook for three hours?"

Studying your competition

Search for your top 5–10 keywords and print the results pages. Study these sheets — they may represent hundreds of hours and tens of thousands of dollars of market research and testing. Get a notebook and jot down your observations about each of the ads:

✔ What's the big promise?

✔ What's the tone?

✔ What's the emotional appeal?

✔ What's the logical appeal?

✔ How does each ad position itself as different from the rest?

✔ What features are highlighted?

✔ What proof is offered?

✔ What is the call to action?

Positioning your offer

Different isn't enough — your ad must be better. Your goal is to write an ad that sets you apart from the other ads in a way that connects you with your market. For example, say you sell industrial fans. You check out the AdWords competition and discover that the keyword `industrial fan` brings up ads that focus on models, features, and price. You can differentiate your company by writing an ad citing benefits and ROI.

You can position your offer as unique in many ways. Your market research (detailed in Chapter 4) can give you ideas about what your market wants and what the competition is currently providing and talking about. Now you can write ads that address unmet needs.

When most businesspeople think of competition, they think first of price. If you can produce your goods and services more efficiently than others, you can compete on price. After all, Wal-Mart does it. But being the cheapest isn't usually the most compelling sales argument. Do you want the cheapest flooring in your living room? Do you want to drive the cheapest car? Do you want the cheapest heart surgeon operating on you? Besides, price wars often end up as a damaging race to the bottom for all involved, including the customer who finds that the business can't deliver quality at the price quoted.

If a segment of your market is searching for a particular model, like the Lifeline USA Power Wheel or the Canon PowerShot SX10IS, they may have decided on that particular model already and are now comparison-shopping for the best deal. In that case, an ad that mentions price can be effective.

Two fundamental ways to position your ad

One way to position your ad is to *slice the niche differently.*

For example, if you sell martial arts training videos, books, and equipment, you might assume that the entire world of martial arts students and enthusiasts is your market. If you claim a slice of that market and speak to them specifically — for example, college-age women, senior citizens, bouncers —

you can position yourself as their supplier of choice. Each of those niches might be small, but you can own them all if they self-identify with their keywords.

The second way to position your ad is to *make a better first offer.*

Even though the goal of the ad is to make a first sale, you can offer other things that your prospects may want or need before they buy. Reviews, free samples (physical, informational, or software), advice, video demonstration, discussion, and so on can be dangled in front of prospects who haven't yet made up their minds. As long as the "magnet" attracts your prospects and leaves nonprospects cold, you can generate the right clicks by offering an intermediate step of value.

No matter what you sell, you can always position yourself as an expert in the field. Search, by definition, implies some gap between your customers' desires and the information they have about how to fulfill those desires. If your ad offers to guide and educate, rather than simply to sell, your offer can stand out.

Motivating Action in Four Lines

Everyone makes decisions rationally, right? People weigh the pros and cons, consider their values and priorities, and maximize benefits while minimizing costs. People balance risks and rewards, and get better over time as they learn from their experiences.

That doesn't sound like anybody I know.

The truth is, all people make decisions emotionally, in their guts. They justify those decisions using logic, but the part of the brain that can handle matrices and cost-benefit analyses is just slower than the part that acts out of fear and greed. Before they consciously ponder, that old reptile brain decides instantly whether someone is friend or foe, prey or predator.

The AdWords ad heightens the emotional aspect of decision making because the rational brain has very little to go on: three lines of text and a Web address. Marketing consultant David Bullock, of www.davidbullock.com, puts it this way:

> *How do you connect to the "right" click?*
>
> *One second is all that you have to get the attention of your online visitor. That's it.*
>
> *The fastest way to meet your revenue goal is to figure out what to say, write, or display in this little 1-inch space to get, hold, and motivate the viewer to click your AdWords ad.*

Simply, the idea is to develop a stunning emotional appeal that gets the "right" click.

By definition, emotional appeal is the mental state that arises spontaneously rather than through conscious effort and is often accompanied by physiological changes; a feeling: the emotions of joy, sorrow, reverence, hate, and love.

As you boil it down, most of the decisions people make are based on fear and desire. All emotional states arise from one of these two states. We are either moving toward something or away from some situation.

Your ad has to hit the visitor/searcher right between the eyes, make an instantaneous connection and move the visitor to spontaneously gravitate towards your offer. It is not a matter of logic. Your visitor has no time to think about not *clicking your AdWords ad. Your goal is to get them to your landing page and move forward in your customer-acquisition process.*

Either you hit the mark or you are off. You either get the click or you don't. Period. End of story.

Your four lines must focus on emotions first and logic second. Your prospect will use logic to construct a search strategy (choosing keywords, searching for information, refining the search to longer and most specific keywords, and so on), but moves toward and away from search results and Web sites based on a subconscious emotional response.

To write effective ads, you have to understand the conversation that just took place inside the head of your prospect as he typed the keyword that brought him ad to them. What is his story? What is he telling himself about his situation and how to improve it?

And I mean *story* quite literally. Go check out a book of fairy tales, or rent a couple of Disney movies to remind yourself what a story contains: a hero (that's them), a problem, a trigger to action, obstacles and villains, and a happy ending. If your ad can connect to the right place in their story, you can grab their attention and lead them the rest of the way.

Figure 6-1 shows the top ten ads for the keyword home based business. Which ads plug into compelling stories?

Home-based business offers tap into the business opportunity market, which is actually several different markets, each with its own set of motivations and internal stories. Examine the first four ads to identify what they're up to:

- ✔ **Home Business:** A no-nonsense ad that uses words like *legitimate* and *serious* to emphasize the soberness of this opportunity. The syntax implies that the entrepreneur in question is already doing this, making it by definition *do-able*. The ad connects with the prospect whose story is, "I don't believe in something for nothing. If I want to be successful, I have to be willing to work for it. (But not too hard, I hope.)"

✔ **I Was Scammed 37 Times:** This ad allows the reader to bond with Danny over his misfortunes, and to feel superior to him even as they take his advice. The word *scammed* appears three times, tying into the cynicism of the serial opportunity seeker who too has felt scammed yet keeps hoping that the perfect business opportunity is just around the corner. The word *absolute* is a powerful emotional trigger, making the tone one of righteous indignation. Prospects who subconsciously want a protector will be drawn to this ad.

✔ **Home Based Business — Free:** The emotionally laden phrase in this ad is, "You won't get rich." The word *realistic* and the modest income claims support the notion that this opportunity, unlike others, is achievably modest. It's designed to give hope to those who have been burned or turned off by big promises. This ad connects with the story, "If something's too good to be true, it probably is." The URL reflects the theme of realistic expectations by calling it a project and promising a payday rather than a windfall.

✔ **Don't Lose $49 Bucks:** This ad is similar to the second one, but speaks directly to the prospect's fear of loss by concretizing and quantifying the risk. Even without knowing how they might lose this $49, the prospect for this ad is suspicious enough to want to find out. The ad appeals to "cautious risk-takers" who believe that having inside information can make them safe. Their story goes like this: "The world is a dangerous place for suckers, but I will be rewarded for my educated boldness."

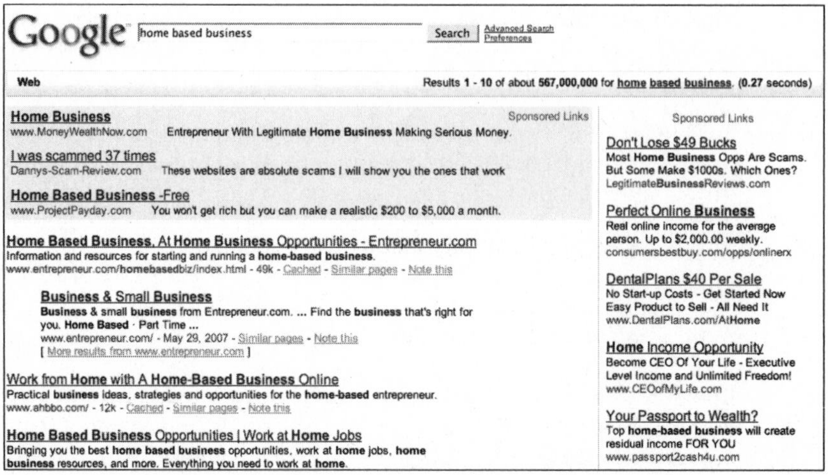

Figure 6-1: Each ad addresses a different story the searcher may be narrating to her- or himself.

The two ads at the bottom of the right column (Home Income Opportunity and Your Passport to Wealth?) are interesting because of their choices of emotionally laden words. *CEO* implies power and status, and speaks to a frustrated employee of a large company who envies and probably resents the CEO. The word *passport* attracts prospects who view exotic travel as market of success. They crave movement and excitement over security.

An old marketing acronym, AIDA, names the four states that have to occur, in order, in your prospect before you can make a sale:

- ✔ **Attention:** Attention is compelled by a headline that names the prospects or their pain, or connects with one of the big three motivators: greed, fear, or curiosity.

- ✔ **Interest:** Interest is raised by naming features and benefits (price, free shipping, options, works in zero gravity, you know the drill).

- ✔ **Desire:** The desire is the happy ending, or a promised step in that direction. (They can't slay the dragon until they find the enchanted sword.)

- ✔ **Action:** The action is the click, to go from the Google results page to your landing page.

All this highfalutin' theory is great, but time to get down to business. You have four lines to accomplish these marketing tasks. The following sections break down the task of each line so you can begin to create magnetic ads.

Grabbing them with the headline

The goal of the headline is to get your prospects' attention while leaving everyone else unimpressed. Classic headline gambits include the following:

- ✔ **Name Them:**
  - Considering a Unicycle
  - Mind Maps for Teachers
  - Actor's Disability Insur.

- ✔ **Mirror Their Itch:**
  - Suffering from Gout?
  - Rotten-Egg Water Odors?
  - Disorganized?

- ✔ **Pick Their Scab with a Provocative Question:**
  - Suffering IBS for Years?
  - Do You Hate Filing?
  - Got a Jerk for a Boss?

✔ **Arouse Curiosity:**

- Are You Right-Brained?
- Are You a Slacker Mom?
- Copywriting Secret #19

✔ **Warn Them:**

- I was scammed 37 times
- Howie Jacobson Exposed
- Biodiesel Scandal

✔ **Make a Big Promise:**

- Write and Publish a Book
- The "Beat Gout" Diet
- Jump Higher in 14 Days

✔ **Offer Unbiased Information:**

- 8 Shower Filters Tested
- Flat-Panel TV Reviews
- Compare Autoresponders

Use the keyword if appropriate

If you include the keyword in your headline, you can almost always increase your ad CTR. For example, an ad with the headline "Homebrew for Beginners" achieved a 3.88 percent CTR for the keyword [homebrew] but pulled only 1.01 percent for [home brew].

Matching the ad to the exact keyword tells your prospects that you understand them (even if you don't). NLP (Neuro-Linguistic Programming) experts tell you that people build rapport by using the same words as others rather than paraphrasing. Also, Google bolds keywords on its results page. If you search for healthy recipe, you'll see several advertisers who take advantage of this fact, whereas others offer healthy recipes and don't get the benefit of bolding.

If your competitors are all using the keywords in their headlines (or, in the case of keywords of 20–25 characters, as their headlines), you'll want to choose a different strategy to stand out. But it's a rare ad that won't benefit from inclusion of keywords somewhere in the headline, description, or URL.

Develop a swipe file

A *swipe file* is a collection of successful advertising pieces from which you can draw inspiration. Professional copywriters rarely invent headlines and bullets from thin air; instead, they modify old standards. For example, John

Caples famously (among direct marketing geeks, anyway) sold a piano home study course with the headline, "They laughed when I sat down at the piano but when I started to play . . . !" Today, copywriters model this formula in selling everything from baking magazines ("They laughed when I got up to bake") to dog training ("They laughed when I issued my $10,000 dog-trainer challenge . . .").

Perry Marshall recommends building your own AdWords swipe file quickly and inexpensively by visiting your local library or supermarket and copying the text on the covers of popular magazines. If you prefer to stay at home, go to `www.magazines.com` to view covers of current issues. Here are some headline formulas from this week's issues of *Cosmo, O, Woman's Day,* and *Vogue,* followed in parentheses by possible AdWords adaptations:

- ✔ 19 dresses that show who's boss (7 skateboards that show who's boss)

- ✔ The season's hottest styles (The season's hottest cameras)

- ✔ Weird male behavior decoded (Weird dog behavior decoded)

- ✔ Break your bad food habits (Break your bad skiing habits)

- ✔ Shhh! We've got a big secret to less stress (Shh! A big packaging secret)

Using the description lines to make them an offer they can't refuse

AdWords consultant Joy Milkowski (`getmoreaccess`) has put together a menu of ad elements you can deploy in your two description lines. She recommends choosing two, plus a call to action. (See the "Sending Out a Call to Action" section for more information.)

Take some time and brainstorm a few elements for your ad for each of the following menu items. Don't worry yet about fitting your copy into the AdWords space restrictions. Just get the concepts first and whittle away the extra words later.

Your menu of ad elements

I'm going to find examples of Joy's ad elements in phrases from real ads for a single keyword: `data recovery`.

- ✔ **Address a Pain Point:** If your customers are searching because they want to prevent or alleviate a problem, you can stoke their interest and build rapport by showing them you understand their situation.

    - Lost data?

    - No Need to Panic

✔ **Offer a Solution:** It's a marketing cliché that people buy holes, not drills, yet businesses routinely neglect to advertise the solutions they provide. One way to get at the solution your customers want is to fill in the blanks, "We provide _____ to _____ and what this means to you is _____." What you wrote in the last blank is the solution. The solutions listed as follows are tame. I would enliven them by adding a "what this means to you" phrase (in parentheses following each solution).

- Restore Lost or Deleted Data (so you can keep billing your customers)

- Fast data recovery for SQL Server (so you can keep your business running)

✔ **List Features:** If your product or service is significantly different from your competitors' offerings, list the differentiating features. Banks that are open on Sunday and late on weekdays, environmentally friendly dry cleaners, and single-volume print-on-demand presses are all examples of companies seeking an advantage by doing things a little differently.

- HD, RAID, Tape, CD/DVD, Memory Card

- 24/7 Support

- On-Site Clean Room

✔ **Short Value Proposition:** A value proposition is the answer to the question, "What do you do that makes you the best choice for me?" The first example is a no-quibble guarantee, whereas the second sets out a specific performance goal.

- No Data, No Cost

- We Recover Most Data in 24 Hours

✔ **Differentiator:** You can compare your business favorably to others, either overtly or by implication. Google generally frowns upon superlatives *(best, cheapest, biggest)*, but usually is okay with qualifiers such as *better, cheaper, bigger.* Two of the following examples trash the competition by implication: "We actually do it" implies that others don't, whereas "no junk fees" suggests that competitors tack on extra charges to pad their margins.

- Others say $379, we actually do it!

- Fastest Turnaround Time

- No Junk Fees

✔ **Price:** In a price-sensitive market, you can signal that you're the best deal by naming a specific price, by telling your prospect that you have low prices, or by offering free shipping. For some reason, free shipping is a very popular online feature. People will pay $20 for the product if they can avoid a $7.95 shipping fee (not consciously, but it happens all the time).

- $379

- Low Flat Rates

- Free Shipping

✔ **Sale/Promotion:** Do you have anything free or on sale? Can you offer two for the price of one? What about throwing in a copy of *AdWords For Dummies* with every purchase? (Just a thought.) Retail stores have attracted customers with sales since Grog drew a crowd by offering a free club with every spear.

- Free Evaluation!

- Free Consulting

- Free Trial

✔ **Credentializer:** You can mention any awards you've received, well-known clients, certifications, media mentions. For example, when I searched for diet tips, the phrase "As Seen on Oprah" appeared twice in the first eight sponsored listings.

- Since 1980

- Industry-Leading 90% Success Rate

- 12 Yrs. Crashed Hard Drive Recovery

- Experts on RAID

Benefits before features

No one formula for effective ad writing exists, and you have to make sure the elements you combine make sense together and all pull in the same direction. In general, though, you won't go wrong by putting the big benefit on the first line and the differentiating feature on the second line. The second line will also contain the other crucial element of your ad: the call to action.

Sending Out a Call to Action

You usually want your prospects to click your ad. (In some cases, you may prefer that they phone; if so, include your phone number in the ad. Several of the data-recovery ads had phone numbers, probably on the assumption that someone typing data recovery is in a state of near-hysteria and wants to contact a real person ASAP.) Joy Milkowski suggests two tactics to compel the click: Offer something in exchange for action and create a sense of urgency.

Making an offer with action words

When you offer something, use action words. Your prospect is searching with a "gatherer" mentality. Offer something bright and shiny to shift them into "hunter" mode. Active action words include

 ✔ *Get, buy,* or *purchase*
 ✔ *Order, call,* or *sign up*
 ✔ *Try* or *download*

More passive action words help the prospect make a decision:

 ✔ *See, learn, compare,* or *discover*
 ✔ *View, listen,* or *watch*

The following examples are from ads that appeared when I searched for the keyword `data recovery`. Note how they all begin with action words.

 ✔ Get a Quote Today
 ✔ Call 1-800-555-1212 for Free Analysis
 ✔ Discover reliable data recovery.
 ✔ View demo — whitepaper

Fanning desire with urgency qualifiers

Nothing stokes desire as much as unattainability. If you can't have it, you want it all the more. Joy uses urgency words to compel immediate action:

 ✔ Now
 ✔ Today
 ✔ By (date)
 ✔ While it lasts (in conjunction with a sale price)

Mastering the Medium and Voice at Haiku U.

Once you've chosen your approach and selected elements that will compel action from the right prospects, you have to fit that content elegantly into 135 characters. Joy Milkowski calls this step, "Sell to me in ten words or less."

Stop thinking *sales pitch* and start thinking *haiku* — the Japanese poetic art that paints a compelling mental picture in 17 syllables.

First, forget everything your high-school English teachers taught you about grammar. Your ad must read like a conversation, not an essay. Notice that Joy didn't use the more grammatically correct construction, "Sell to me in ten words or fewer." Write like you talk — or better yet, write like your *market* talks.

Apple Computer is running very effective ads featuring two actors portraying a Mac and a PC. The Mac actor is a hip young dude, whereas the PC actor is a pocket-protector–wearing nerd who awkwardly stumbles and bumbles through life. If huge multinational companies develop personalities in the minds of consumers, your business too needs a voice. Your ads are the first words in this voice that your prospects will hear.

The best business personalities are slightly exaggerated but basically accurate extensions of the business owner or leader. Start adopting that voice in your ads. An Internet marketer calling himself "The Rich Jerk" used the following ad when the name of another Internet marketer (whose name I've omitted) was typed as a keyword:

```
I'm Rich. You're Not.
How much money did [name] make?
Who cares? I make millions.
therichjerk.com
```

This ad works both to attract a certain type of person and to strongly repel everyone else. In some markets (like Internet marketing, for example), your tone can be brash. In others, you must come across as professional and no-nonsense. You can be caring, efficient, funny, angry, matter-of-fact, exasperated, excited, clinical, or poetic. Test different voices to find out which one connects best with your market. But your best voice will most often be your genuine voice — just smoothed and amped a bit to cut through the clutter of Timid Timmies and Me-Too Mollies. Your prospects are looking for authenticity in a world full of fakeness. Connect to them as your unique self and you're already cutting through the clutter.

Almost everything about your business can be copied, except for you. No one else has your thoughts, your experiences, your unique point of view. Most businesspeople hide this aspect of themselves to appear professional. It's possible to do both — be real *and* be professional. Take advantage of your only true differentiator and be yourself whenever possible.

AdWords consultant Garrett Todd of www.impresscallers.com cautions against rampant creativity. Extensive testing has shown him that classic direct-marketing approaches outperform offbeat, creative ads. He shared his top two formulas with me:

✔ **Who Else Wants to . . .**

```
Music On Hold
Who Else Wants to Reduce Hang-Ups
and Impress On-Hold Callers?
www.Impress-Callers.com
```

✔ **If . . . Then . . .**

```
Music On Hold
If You Want to Reduce Hang-Ups
Then Try Custom Music On Hold.
www.Impress-Callers.com
```

Garrett reports that the first ad generates an impressive 11.02 percent CTR. Note that his display URL includes a hyphen; he found that separating the two words increased CTR. The www prefix also improved CTR.

Rob Goyette of `www.howtomarketbetter.com`, another crackerjack AdWords user, found that his most successful problem headline was

```
Got [problem]?
```

For example:

```
Got Gout?
```

Naming Your Online Store Effectively

Many advertisers spend dozens of hours brainstorming and agonizing over their headline and two description lines, and never play with their URLs. That's a big mistake; your URL makes up 25 percent of your entire ad and is often the most important line. Your URL is the name of your store; it conveys lots of meta-information about who you are and whom you serve.

For example, I used to funnel some `cold calling` traffic to `Free-Lead-Generation-Course.com`, which offered a 7-day e-mail course instead of a sales-letter Web site. My CTR was comparable to ads that sent traffic to `LeadsintoGold.com`, but the free course generated about half as many sales.

Buying more domain names

Even if you have one main Web site, you can buy other URLs and use them in your ads. Domain names cost about $8.00 a year these days (I use `www.get goingonline.com`).

Glenn Livingston offers the examples shown in Figure 6-2 of huge differences in CTR due solely to changes in the display URL.

Microwave Oven Mania
If You're Looking For A Microwave
Oven This Is For You!
www-Microwave.com
129 Clicks | 10.9% CTR | $0.49 CPC
Served - 31.2% [more info]
Edit - Delete

Microwave Oven Mania
If You're Looking For A Microwave
Oven This Is For You!
www.SharpUSA.com
64 Clicks | 6.2% CTR | $0.73 CPC
Served - 27.3% [more info]
Edit - Delete

Buying A Piano?
Please Don't Buy Your Piano Before
You Take A Serious Look At This.
www-Piano.com
46 Clicks | 6.7% CTR | $0.52 CPC
Served - 52.9% [more info]
Edit - Delete

Buying A Piano?
Please Don't Buy Your Piano Before
You Take A Serious Look At This.
www.PianosByRosch.com
20 Clicks | 3.3% CTR | $0.68 CPC
Served - 47.1% [more info]
Edit - Delete

Figure 6-2:
Different
display
URLs can
double CTR.

The domain suffixes also tell a story. The business-focused `.com` sometimes can be beaten by the nonprofit `.org`, and even `.org` domains can in fact front for-profit businesses. If you offer reviews or comparisons, `TheAntiWrinkleInstitute.org` may pull better than `JanesWrinkleBustingCream.com`.

Google doesn't allow you to use more than one domain name per ad group and insists that the domain in the display URL be the same as the domain of the actual landing page, so you can't split-test display URLs to the same extent as the other three visible lines of your ad.

You can use Glenn's clever method of testing URLs as headlines. Say you're curious about which URL will produce better results: `RealDogLovers.com` or `HelpSavetheDogs.com`. Test those URLs as headlines: `Real Dog Lovers` versus `Help Save the Dogs`. After you have a winner, buy that domain name and use it as the display URL and the domain of your landing page.

Adding subdomains and subdirectories

Joy Milkowski improved her die-cutting client's CTR by changing the display URL from `www.MyClient.com` to `www.MyClient.com/die-cut`. (Her client's URL wasn't actually `myclient.com` — most successful AdWords advertisers view their ads and keywords as maps to secret fishing holes, kept close to the chest and never shared with potential competitors. And with AdWords' low barrier to entry, pretty much everyone is your potential competitor.)

In the preceding example, `/die-cut` is a subdirectory, or folder, within the Web site. You can also test subdomains, which look like this:

```
die-cut.myclient.com
```

If you're not sure how to create subdomains or subdirectories, ask your Webmaster.

Testing capitalization and the www prefix

Check out the two ads shown in Figure 6-3. The top ad received 4.64 percent CTR, compared to only 2.22 percent CTR for the second ad. The only difference was the URL.

Figure 6-3: Two ads with differ- ent CTRs.

Get started Beekeeping.
Set up hives, harvest honey - be safe and have fun! Family activity.
www.Beekeeping-Secrets.com

Get started Beekeeping.
Set up hives, harvest honey - be safe and have fun! Family activity.
beekeeping-secrets.com

The top ad included the www and capitalized the first letter of each keyword — and attracted more than twice as many clicks per impression as the lower ad.

Wielding "Black Belt" Techniques for Hyper-Competitive Markets

I know you bought this book to figure out the basics of AdWords, to get into the game. But if your market is highly competitive, you have to start at the Big Leagues level just to get any impressions on your keywords. If your keywords are expensive, you may need one of more of the following three techniques just to stay solvent while you crack the AdWords code:

- ✔ **The "fake" www domain** is easy enough to try, as long as someone else in your market hasn't thought of it already. (Hey, here's an idea: Buy up every copy of this book you can find, just to make sure your competition doesn't know this technique.)

- ✔ **Dynamic keyword insertion** is almost a Google secret. For good reason — do it wrong and you're looking at an AdWords bill that could fund a flight to Mars. So read carefully — and don't even consider using it until you've installed and mastered conversion tracking and analytics on your Web site.

- ✔ **Subdomain redirects** were pioneered by Perry Marshall, who has many happy clients using it for all their domains. It's a way to test hundreds of URLs without having to buy them. This technique is a little complicated, but worth it in many cases.

The fake www-domain technique

You may have noticed the trick that Glenn Livingston of `www.ultimate adwordsresearch.com` used in creating his winning display URLs earlier in this chapter. He added `www-` to a popular keyword and showed that to searchers.

This technique works because it tricks the eye into seeing your domain as the *main* Web site in the category. Someone searching for `digital cameras` will view `www.DigitalCameras.com` as the most relevant and authoritative domain to visit. Glenn bought the domain `http://www.www-digital cameras.com` and simply omitted the "real" `www` from the display URL. The searcher sees `www-DigitalCameras.com` and can easily confuse it for `www. DigitalCameras.com`.

This technique is a cheap trick, but it's possibly worth the price of several cases of this book.

Dynamic keyword insertion

Do you ever wonder how eBay and Amazon manage to bid on practically every keyword in existence and show those keywords in their ads? They don't have thousands of employees creating millions of different ads. Instead, they use a special format to stick the keyword right into a generic ad, as shown in Figure 6-4. And now you can do it too!

Figure 6-4: These ads dynamically insert the keyword.

David Broza at Amazon.com
Low prices on new & used music.
Qualified orders over $25 ship free
Amazon.com/music

CD's, DVD by **David Broza**
Large selection of Israeli CD's
Listen Online before You Buy!
www.orlysbookstore.com

David Broza
Looking for **David Broza**?
Find exactly what you want today.
www.eBay.com

To use dynamic keyword insertion, first make friends with the squiggly brackets. On most keyboards, you can find them by using the Shift key with the square bracket keys, just below the - and = keys near the top right. They look like this:

{ left squiggly bracket

} right squiggly bracket

Dynamic keyword insertion requires two decisions:

- How you want to handle capitalization of keywords?
- What do you want to appear on-screen in case the keyword is too long to fit into the ad?

Say you sell mobile phone ringtones and you know lots of people are searching by typing their favorite performer, composer, or type of music followed by `ringtone`. The list of potential keywords could be enormous. Without dynamic keywords insertion, you'd either spend hundreds of hours creating tightly focused ad groups (see Chapter 5), like `Mozart ringtone`, `Beethoven ringtone`, `Bach ringtone`, `Beyonce ringtone`, and so on or you'd have a few big ad groups with thousands of those keywords and very vague ads with headlines like these:

- Classical Music Ringtones
- R&B Ringtones
- Hip-Hop Ringtones

To use dynamic keyword insertion, create medium-sized ad group buckets:

- Classical Music
- Pop Music
- Country Music
- Rap Music

and so on. Put all your classical music terms — `Beethoven`, `Hilary Hahn`, `violin concerto`, `Leonard Bernstein`, `Philharmonic` — in the Classical Music ad group. Then create the following headline:

```
{KeyWord:Classical Music Ringtones}
```

Note that the colon is not followed by a space!

Now if someone searches for one of your keywords, she'll see that keyword in the headline if it contains 25 characters or fewer:

- `Hilary Hahn Ringtones`
- `Bach Requiem Ringtone`
- `Missa Solemnis ring tone`

If the keyword is too long (`Alicia de Larrocha Mozart piano sonata in C ringtone`), she'll see the default keyword `Classical Music Ringtones` instead.

To capitalize every word of the keyword, capitalize the K and W in `KeyWord`:

```
{KeyWord:Alternate Text}
```

Capitalize just the first word by capitalizing the K only:

```
{Keyword:Alternate Text}
```

If you want the keyword to appear in all lowercase, don't capitalize any letters:

```
{keyword:Alternate Text}
```

If her keyword doesn't fit, the alternate text will appear exactly as you've typed it — capitalized or not.

If you're careless about your keyword list, you could end up spending a lot of money that you won't make back. An extreme example to make the point: Say my friend Battery Bob accidentally includes `Paris Hilton` in the keyword list for his cell phone battery ad group.

Without dynamic keyword insertion, the worst that happens is a million teenagers looking for gossip or racy photos see and ignore the following ad:

```
Cell Phone Batteries
All Makes and Models
Low Prices - Same Day Shipping
www.BatteryBob.com
```

But with dynamic keyword insertion, here's what they might see:

```
Paris Hilton Videos
All Makes and Models
Low Prices - Same Day Shipping
www.BatteryBob.com
```

Uh-oh, Battery Bob. You just spent $12,000 on clicks in about six hours, with no sales to show for it. (The real Battery Bob would never make such a mistake, of course.)

You can deploy dynamic keyword insertion not only in the headline and description lines, but also in the display URL for marketing purposes and the destination URL for advanced conversion tracking.

Subdomain redirects

The third "black belt" ad technique gives you a chance to test hundreds of display URLs for the price of one. A *subdomain* is the part of your URL that can appear before the main domain name. For example, `books` is the subdomain of this Web site:

```
http://books.fitfam.com
```

With a Web service called `www.zoneedit.com`, you can quickly and easily create new subdomains without needing to know Web design, HTML, server architecture, or how to make vegan oatmeal cookies. (I actually do know how to make delicious vegan oatmeal cookies — send a blank e-mail to `cookies@fitfam.com` for the recipe — but I assure you I could still work ZoneEdit.com without this knowledge.)

My wife had a business selling handmade soap featuring different essential oils and other natural ingredients. Her main Web site address was `www.comfortsoap.com`. Say she wants to test a different domain that works well with various subdomains, `www.soapforyourfamily.com`:

```
lavender.SoapForYourFamily.com
oatmeal.SoapForYourFamily.com
cruelty-free.SoapForYourFamily.com
```

With ZoneEdit.com, which is free for the first five domains (not subdomains, so their free service may be all you'll ever need), she can create subdomains and then redirect them to specific pages on her `www.comfortsoap.com` Web site. She can even mask the pages so the subdomain is what appears in the visitor's browser's address and title bars. With this method, she can test different URLs (which is better, `Natural.SoapForYourFamily.com` or `ChemicalFree.SoapForYourFamily.com`?). She can also use different display URLs in different ad groups: the lavender group, the Shea-butter group, the neroli group, and so on.

Visit `www.askhowie.com/zoneedit` for a video tutorial on using `www.zoneedit.com` for subdomain redirection.

Following Google's Text-Ad Guidelines

I warn you about some commonly broken rules in the following sections, but you should still take ten minutes to read Google's editorial guidelines at

```
https://adwords.google.com/select/guidelines.html
```

Punctuation

Google's rules for punctuation in your AdWords ads are pretty simple:

- ✔ No more than one exclamation point in your text, and not in the headline.
- ✔ No repeated punctuation (Tired??!!).
- ✔ No unnecessary punctuation ($$ instead of *money* or $#!! standing in for an expletive).

Capitalization

The capitalization rules for AdWords ads are that you can't use excess capitalization such as *FREE* or *SIDE EFFECTS*.

However, you can capitalize acronyms (MPH) as well as the first letter of each word in your ad and in your display URL (`LeadsIntoGold.com` is acceptable; `LeadsintoGOLD.com` is not).

Spelling and grammar

Google doesn't like ads that look like they were written by toddlers. Make sure all words are spelled correctly. If you don't have an ear for grammar, get someone who does to take a look at your ad. Spell checkers can't pick up mistakes like using *than* for *then* or *weather* for *whether*.

Copyright and trademark usage

You can't use copyrighted and trademarked terms in your ads without the permission of the rights holder.

This is a thorny and complicated issue for Google. If you sell one brand of mobile phone, can you compare it to a competing brand in your ad? Can you use copyrighted terms in your URL? The law is still being written on this topic — and lawsuits are mounting between companies claiming copyright infringement and "initial interest confusion." (I can throw these terms around thanks to my work as an expert witness at trial; obviously I'm not a lawyer and you should get competent legal advice before doing anything that may get you in trouble.)

Competitive claims

If you say your business is the best, fastest, cheapest, most successful, and such, you need to prove it to Google (and the world) on your landing page.

Offers

If you offer it in your ad, your visitor must be able to get it easily from your landing page. Giving away a free trial download? Put the link in an obvious place on the landing page. If Google's editors visit your site and decide your offer is fraudulent, your ad will be disallowed.

No offensive language

Unlike the late George Carlin, I *can't* tell you the seven words you're not allowed to use on Google. But if they get bleeped out of movies on TV, that's a pretty good clue to omit them from your ads.

Links

The domain of your display URL must be the same as that of your Web site. That is, if someone typed your display URL into his browser instead of clicking your ad (thoughtfully saving you money!), he should still get to the same Web site, if not the exact same landing page.

Your destination URL must work properly and must resolve to a working Web page, as opposed to an e-mail address or document or multimedia file.

Exploring the Other Ad Formats

Google is constantly exploring new places and media for their ads. You can now create graphical ads for Web sites, text ads for mobile phones, local business listings that appear on search results pages and next to Google Maps, and video ads.

Getting the picture with image ads

Image ads are graphical files that display on content sites, but not on Google's or its search partners' results pages. Publishers can choose to display image ads instead of text ads. Perry Marshall has found that image ads typically generate higher CTRs than text ads, but convert to leads and sales at a much lower level. If you're a Web site publisher who gets paid for clicks on the Google ads on your site, image ads can be very profitable because of their high CTRs. For you, the AdWords advertiser, the high CTR can be a double-edged sword. Unless you monitor ROI from each ad, you may be funding Google's expansion at the expense of your own.

If you decide to try display ads, Google provides a Display Ad Builder that allows even those who failed 7th grade art to create decent graphics. You can find it as a link on the ad variations tab at the ad group level of your AdWords campaign management. Go to www.askhowie.com/adwizard for a video tutorial on using the tool.

Joy Milkowski of www.getmoreaccess.com offers the following four suggestions if you decide to try image ads:

1. Focus on a Pain or Problem

The same principles apply to this format as to all your marketing material — does it clearly suggest/address a pain or problem? Often I see ads trying to "feature dump" instead of offering to solve an issue in simple, easy to read language.

2. Keep the Design Clean and Simple

Are you trying to be too busy or use colors that are too bold in order to try to get noticed? If yes, chances are you may be turning prospects OFF. Our eyes are drawn to clean, easily decipherable images and language. Image ads, normally, are not the place to go "Las Vegas."

3. Show People, Not Products

Careful with using pictures of your product on the ad — often the space is so small that you end up either confusing the viewer or making your product seem less than adequate. Instead, I recommend using people. Get the viewer looking at a person — it's hard to NOT notice a person looking right at you!

4. Include an Offer and a Call to Action

Your image ad needs an irresistible offer as well as a compelling call to action. Remember, you're still in a direct response world. Don't let your ego look at the pretty pictures and elevate branding above measurable response.

Compared to text ads, image ads are more expensive and time-consuming to create, more expensive to display, and take longer to generate results. For these reasons, test your message, tone, offer and call to action with text ads before creating image ads.

Making the phone and the doorbell ring with mobile text ads

Google is going mobile, creating content that can be accessed and acted upon seamlessly from your smart mobile phone (and even from your mobile phone of average intelligence but with a nice smile). If your ad includes a link to a Web site, you have to make sure the site is created in a phone-compatible way. If you just want prospects to pick up the phone and call, or drive over and pay you a visit, create your ad and include an offer and call to action.

To create a mobile text ad, click the Mobile Text Ad link from within the Ad Variations tab of an ad group.

You can view your mobile text ad from your SMS-enabled phone by first registering your phone with Google at `http://google.com/mobile`. You can do this from your computer or just point your phone's browser to `http://mobile.google.com`. You can conduct searches and view maps, as well as access several other Google services, such as Gmail and Google News.

Waving to the neighbors with local business ads

If your business caters to a local market, you can still use AdWords to attract clients and customers. For instructions on using regular text ads for geographically limited markets, see Chapter 7. Right now you see how to create a local business ad that will appear as Google Maps business listings as well as other search results.

From within the Ad Variations tab of an ad group, click the Local Business Ads link just above the ad variations. On the next page, enter the business name and address. If you have multiple locations, you have the option to add additional addresses to your ad. If your business is not yet listed in Google's Local Business Center, you'll receive the following error message:

```
No businesses matched the address you entered.
```

In that case, visit `www.google.com/local/add/login` to add your business.

If your business is listed (mine isn't, so I'm going to use the Dogstar Tattoo Co. in Durham, NC as an example in Figure 6-5), you can continue to create your ad.

You can add a business image and even change the icon that appears next to your ad. Figure 6-6 shows what the ad looks like on the Google search page.

When someone searches for your keyword in a local area on Google Maps (`http://maps.google.com`), your ad may appear on the left, below, or above the business listings. Clicking it brings up the ad (including phone number and image) as a callout from the map location, as shown in Figure 6-7.

Figure 6-5:
Creating a local business ad for a business already in Google's Local Business Listings.

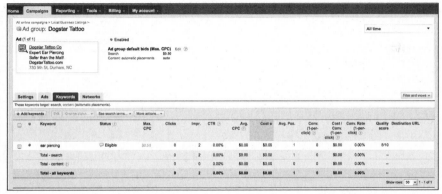

Figure 6-6:
The local business ad on the Google search page looks like a regular listing. The business name is the headline, and the city is the fifth line.

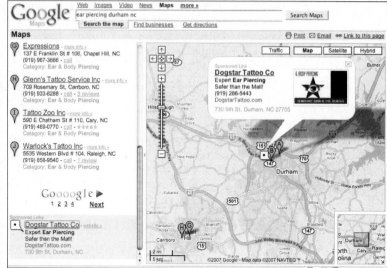

Figure 6-7:
Clicking the
sponsored
link on the
left brings
up the local
business
ad within
the map
on Google
Maps.

Going Hollywood with video ads

To create a video ad that shows on content pages, click In-Line Video Ad from within the Ad Variations tab of an ad group. On the next page, choose an image (Google is very picky about the size of this image, so make sure your graphic designer knows the dimensions Google accepts), enter display and destination URLs, name your ad, and upload your video.

My 9-minute, 30MB QuickTime video took about 7 minutes to load with a fast cable-modem connection, so have a book handy if you plan on uploading lots of large videos.

Adriel Brunson of www.rfyvideo.com, a video advertising expert of many years, studied and experimented with Google video ads in 2006, and sent me this evaluation:

> When Google offered video ads in AdWords, everyone who understood the power of video on the Web cheered. Unfortunately, we may have cheered too soon.

> We wanted video ads in AdWords campaigns on Google search pages. What we got were video ads that only played on AdSense sites that allow graphical ads. Nothing for regular Google search pages. It's not that Google doesn't understand the value of including video in their searches. For a while, they included Video as one of the five links at the top of their search page. Now it's been moved down to the top of the More . . . link.

And videos have been included in the organic search results just like images. This makes it even more important to learn how to include keywords, titles, and other metadata with your online videos.

Google owns YouTube.com and all videos uploaded there are indexed fairly quickly. YouTube.com now accepts HD videos, so quality of online video is more than acceptable. Plus, YouTube.com offers decent capability for metadata including the ability to add your narration as closed captions. That means the text of your video becomes searchable.

But, sad to say, Google's AdWords still treats video like an image ad only. If an AdSense publisher allows image ads, you may be able to get your video ad on their site. It's been my experience that few AdSense publishers allow graphical ads. Most choose the default text-only option. Even the AdSense experts recommend text-only ads to blend in with the site navigation and content. No graphical ads, no video.

On the plus side, Google's AdWords video program does offer powerful options. You can create both keyword and site-targeted campaigns. You can search for AdSense sites matching your keywords. If you find any that allow graphical AdSense ads, you can target those sites.

You may want to explore Google's options for playing ads on cable channels in your area. The technical specs are different than online videos but it may be just the right way to use video to get your message to your market.

My recommendation is to create regular AdWords campaigns and drive traffic to a page with a good headline, embed a good video uploaded to YouTube.com with metadata included, and complete the page with well-written sales copy and offer.

With a regular Google AdWords keyword-targeted campaign, you'll get more control over the traffic, plus you can test everything in the chain — the keywords, the ad, the headline, the video placement, the text and links around the video. You can even test different video edits if you want.

With Google AdWords video ads, you have little or no control over these elements. Go with an AdWords text campaign and a split testing landing page with good video. It's a much better option all the way around.

Because Google runs a *blind* advertising network based on keyword search (meaning you as an advertiser can't tell in advance where your ads will show, and the publishers can't predict accurately which ads will display on their pages), I recommend using Google video — if you must — only in placement-targeted campaigns (more on this approach in Chapter 7).

Part III
Managing Your AdWords Campaigns

The 5th Wave   By Rich Tennant

In this part . . .

The AdWords fantasy is that you find the perfect keyword, write the perfect ad, and retire to Fiji while the money rolls in relentlessly. The reality is that as important as keywords and ads are, the structure of your AdWords campaigns will determine success or failure.

In Chapter 7, you find out how to navigate a dizzying array of settings, including which network(s) will display your ads, how to budget and set bid prices, where in the world and what time of day to show the ads, and others.

Chapter 8 covers the strategy most neglected by AdWords users: creating tight Ad Groups of similar keywords and relevant ads. You discover how to perform ongoing tune-ups of your keyword lists, bids, and ads so your AdWords vehicle runs ever more powerfully and efficiently.

Chapter 9 introduces you to the tools that Google has thoughtfully provided to make your AdWords life easier and more fulfilling. Okay, just easier.by keywords. It covers fundamentals and clever variations to make your ads more compelling and profitable.

Chapter 7

Deciding Where and When to Show Your Ads

*W*hen I install a piece of software on my computer, I often get a screen that asks me whether I want to go ahead with the Typical Installation (always recommended) or the Custom Installation (for advanced users only). To my recollection, I've never chosen Custom. I always worried that I would install a version of Microsoft Word that wouldn't let me type the letter *M*, didn't have a built-in English-to-Esperanto translator, or would omit some other crucial feature.

Google gives you an overwhelming number of choices for configuring AdWords campaigns — but it doesn't really bring them to your attention. Google isn't trying to bamboozle you; instead, the default settings are designed to protect clueless advertisers from themselves. But you, my friend, are no longer a clueless advertiser. By virtue of buying this book (or at least spilling coffee on it at Barnes & Noble), you are hereby officially dubbed *clueful advertiser.*

In this chapter, you see how to tweak the AdWords default settings that aren't appropriate for power users. You discover how to bid intelligently on your own and when to let Google set your bids for you. (I know Google's motto is "Don't Be Evil," but I still wouldn't give it complete control over my advertising spending.) And you figure out how to show your ads to different geographic areas with laser precision and how to separate your search and content traffic for maximum clarity and ROI.

Getting the Most Out of Your Campaigns

If you want to set up one AdWords campaign, put it on autopilot, and never look at it again, feel free to skip this section. The changes I suggest will usually mean more, not less, work for you — more decisions, more overseeing, more risk, even, if you drop the ball. Google gives you a vehicle with an automatic transmission that does your thinking for you. On highways, it works fine, although it will never be as efficient as a well-handled manual transmission. When you take it out for a race, though, you're going to need precision control based on experience — something no computer can do for you. Ready to strap on your AdWords seatbelt and hit the track?

Changing the default campaign settings

From within the Campaigns tab of your AdWords account, click the Settings Rollup tab. You'll see a list of all your campaigns along with a summary of settings for each, as shown in Figure 7-1. Click the campaign name to access a page on which you can change any or all of the settings. Some of the settings are shown to you when the campaign is born, whereas others hide on this page, waiting for you to find them. I explore some options that you haven't yet seen.

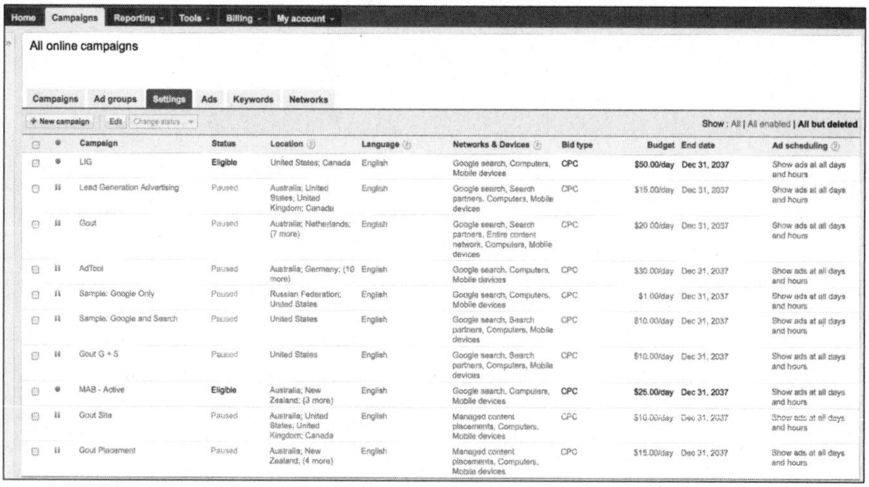

Figure 7-1: You can edit the default campaign settings to gain more control over where and when your ads show.

Audience

You can change three parameters under the Audience settings: locations, languages, and visitor demographics (if you are showing your ads on the content network).

Locations

Google allows you as much geographical precision as you could possibly need. The default setting is by country: Google gives you a list of countries and then you choose the ones whose inhabitants will see your ads. Straightforward and uncomplicated, this setting is common for online businesses that can serve customers pretty much anywhere. If you sell downloadable software or telephone consulting, for example, you don't have any reason to exclude customers from Belgium, Israel, or New Zealand, assuming language compatibility. In my experience, certain African and Asian countries tend to be hotbeds of credit-card fraud, however — and if you don't think a particular country will add a great deal to your bottom line, you may want to leave it off your list.

Click the Edit link next to Locations to take you to a recently updated interface that enables you to target your campaigns as widely or as precisely as you desire. Under the Browse tab, Google lists the most commonly selected 24 countries at the top, beginning with the United States and continuing alphabetically from Australia to United Kingdom. If you click the Show All Countries link at the end of the list, you'll see a complete list of dozens of countries from Afghanistan to Zimbabwe. Select countries by clicking their check boxes. When your list is complete, click the Save button to return to the Edit Settings page.

The Bundles tab, as shown in Figure 7-2, enables you to choose with an even broader brush among 14 country bundles. Notice that these bundles overlap with the United States and Canada bundle contained within the North America bundle, and the last bundle, All Countries and Territories contains, you guessed it, all countries and territories.

If you want to target prospects more precisely, you can drill down into each country listed under the Browse tab. Click a country's expand button (the plus sign next to a country's name) to select or deselect regions/states within that country. Similarly, you can expand regions/states into cities/metro areas and metro areas into smaller cities. To select a single small city, deselect the country, region/state, and metro area that contain it and then select the specific city, as shown in Figure 7-3.

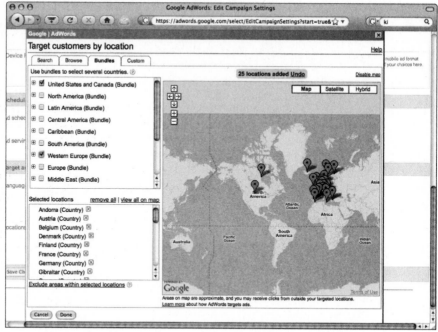

Figure 7-2:
You can
show your
ads to
multiple
countries
and
territories.

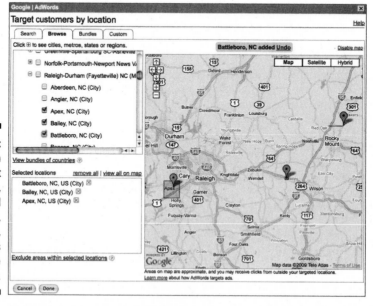

Figure 7-3:
You can
target
regions,
individual
states,
metro areas,
and cities
within one
country.

If you run a local business, the regional and city targeting may not be precise enough for you. After all, no matter how good a dry cleaner you may be, few customers will drive 45 minutes across town to drop off their dress shirts. Enter customized targeting to the rescue. You get to that page by clicking the Custom tab. You're given three options:

✔ **Map point:** This option designates a circular area. After entering a physical address or centering the map at your desired location (zoom way in by clicking the + button at the top left of the map), you can enter a radius around that spot in miles or kilometers. Figure 7-4 shows a radius of 2 miles around Ewing, New Jersey.

✔ **Custom shape:** Occasionally, a circle isn't precise enough. What if, in Figure 7-4, I want to expand the area where my ads show to include the entire triangle between I-95, US 1, and the Delaware River? Google sends a multi-point option to the rescue. Click the Custom Shape link. You can either enter coordinates as if you're a World War I ace, or zoom in to your map location and draw a polygon that defines your target area, as shown in Figure 7-5.

✔ **Bulk:** This option adds a bulk list of locations. Click the Bulk link. You can paste or type up to 100 different locations (cities, states, countries) to create a global patchwork of ad serving.

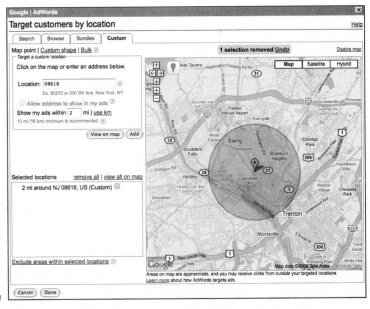

Figure 7-4: Centering the map on zip code 08618 and selecting a 2-mile radius produces a circular area that will see your ads.

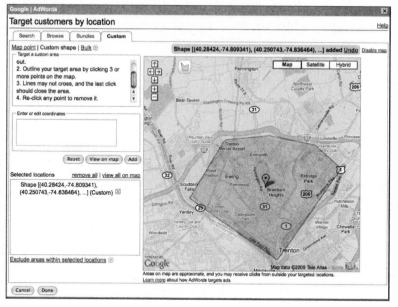

Figure 7-5:
Indulge your
inner artist
by creating
a polygon
within which
to show
your ads.

When you finish specifying the ad serving locations for this campaign, click the Save button to save your changes and return to the Campaign Settings page.

Language

You can specify the language(s) of the users you want to see your ads. Click the Edit link to bring up a list of languages from Arabic to Vietnamese.

Demographic

If your campaign is set up to show ads on the content network, you may be able to see a breakdown of your data by age and sex. (Because I turn 44 this year, I will not be making any middle-age jokes about that last bit.) When you set up conversion tracking (see Chapter 14), you receive data that shows which sex and age groups convert at the highest rates. This data allows you to modulate your bid prices, so you pay less for clicks from some groups than others.

Networks, devices, and extensions

As you may have read in Chapter 1, you can show your text ad in any of three places: Google pages, search partner pages, and the content network. The default setting for each campaign includes all three networks. The trouble with this setting is that the three sources of traffic generally behave very differently, respond to different language and different offers, and don't command the same bid prices. You can set different bids for the content network, but a cleaner way to separate the networks is to put each one in its own campaign. See the section, "Separating your account into three types of campaigns," later in this chapter, for details.

Click the Edit link next to the list of current networks and devices to choose where and on what machines to show your ads. Click the radio button next to Let Me Choose to change any of these options.

Bidding and budget

In this section, you can set the most you're willing to pay for a click across various networks, and even change the way Google sets your bid prices. You can change the daily budget for your campaign so that you don't end up with nasty surprises.

Bidding option

Keep the default here (Focus on clicks, Manual bidding – maximum CPC bids) for now. Don't let Google optimize your budget. See the section, "Bidding Smart," later in this chapter, for a discussion of bidding strategies.

Position preference

Click the plus sign next to the Position Preference, Delivery Method link to show these advanced settings. Click the Edit link next to each item to make any changes.

If you enable Position Preferences by clicking the radio button next to On: Automatically Manage Maximum CPC Bids to Target a Preferred Position Range and saving your changes, you can then designate a position range for each keyword. Now your ad will show for a given keyword when it falls within that position range, and Google will try to keep your ad within that range, given your budget limitations.

Essentially, position preference is like setting your maximum cost per click (CPC), except you focus on the *outcome* (position) instead of the *input* (how much you're willing to pay for that position). If you discover that your ad is most profitable at position 7, for example, you can tell Google to keep it there, instead of allowing it to fluctuate.

To play with position preference, go to the Keywords tab (from within a campaign or from within an individual ad group). In the column named Position Preference, click the word Any to input the highest and lowest position your ad will appear for that keyword (see Figure 7-6).

In Figure 7-7, I've configured the keyword [cold calls] to trigger ads that appear in position 7 only. You can edit position preferences for multiple keywords by checking the box to the left of the keywords you wish to edit, and then clicking the Edit button just above the keyword list.

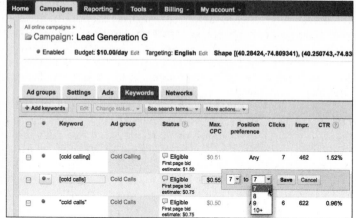

Figure 7-6:
You can change position preferences for an individual keyword.

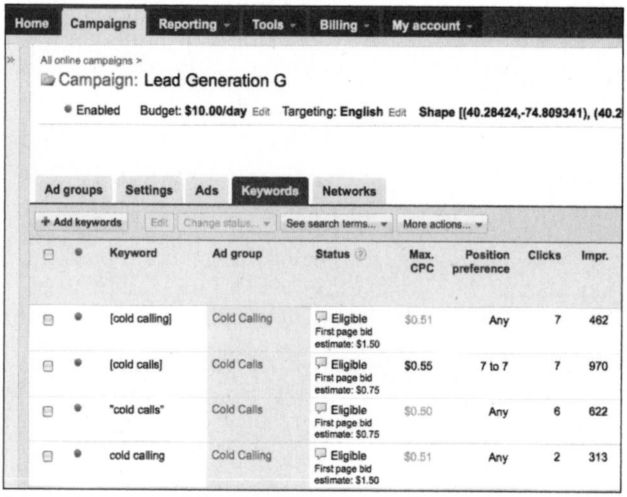

Figure 7-7:
The [cold calls] keyword will now show its ad in position 7 only.

Delivery method

If you exceed your daily budget on a regular basis, you have two choices: tell Google to pace your ads evenly through the day (Standard), or show the ads as often as possible until you run out of money (Accelerated).

Both methods can make sense, depending on the viewing patterns of your market. If your market is global, you probably want to show your ads evenly so you can get your message to your prospect in Singapore as well as the one in Saskatoon. If you run a local campaign for office workers, you may want to accelerate the ad showing if more people buy in the morning than the afternoon.

However, the choice begs an important question: Why are you limiting your advertising spend? The concept of an advertising budget doesn't make sense if each ad is making money. If I offered you a dollar bill in exchange for your half-dollar, how many times would you want to complete that transaction? Does *infinity* sound about right to you? It wouldn't make sense for you to say, "I only trade my 50 cents for your dollar 24 times because my daily budget is 12 dollars."

Limit your daily budget for testing purposes, when you're not yet profitable and you're adjusting your keywords, ads, and Web-site sales process to become profitable. Another case where limiting your budget makes sense is if demand exceeds supply and you can only service so many paying customers. Or if you work for a big company used to advertising that's not directly tied to results, and you're given an ad budget. Or if you haven't read this book and don't yet know what you're doing.

In fact, as you're assessing the competition, if you find that their ads disappear and reappear on the Google search results page as you refresh the page, you can be fairly confident that they aren't profitable yet or they don't understand results-accountable marketing and won't be much of a threat to you.

Advanced settings

Actually, these settings are no more or less advanced than any of the others. But if you want to feel special about messing with them, you have my permission. Click the Schedule: Start Date, End Date, Ad Scheduling link to see the options available for scheduling your ads.

Start and end dates

You can set up campaigns to run for a predetermined time period. This is useful if you have a seasonal campaign (pool toys, Valentine's Day candy, or Happy January 25th cards) or an event-based campaign (tickets to the World Cup or presidential candidate hats and t-shirts in the months leading up to an election). You can specify start and stop dates in advance, thus saving you one more thing to remember to do later. Click the Edit link to set the campaign dates.

Ad scheduling

Click the Edit link next to Ad scheduling and gasp to discover that Google gives you the option to schedule your ads by 15-minute increments, any day of the week, as shown in Figure 7-8. You can run your ads from midnight to 2:45 a.m. Monday, 3:00–3:15 a.m. Tuesday, and so on. Click the Time Period setting for the desired day to specify the time periods for your ads to show on that day. By clicking the Bid Adjustment link near the top of the page, you can even adjust your maximum bids by time period. You may want to be in a higher position on weekends, or just after *The Daily Show,* or during *Monday Night Football,* and so on.

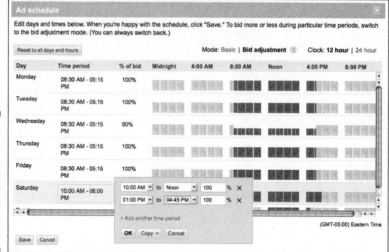

Figure 7-8:
You can
schedule
when your
ads appear
by time and
day of the
week.

Ad delivery

Click the Ad Delivery: Ad Rotation, Frequency Capping link to view the
options here and then click the appropriate Edit link to make any changes.

Ad rotation

Hold on for a short fire and brimstone sermon about the Ad Rotation setting:
Until you start using the Conversion Optimizer, a very advanced tool that I
talk about at the end of this chapter, please do not optimize your ads. I don't
care where you are. Run, don't walk to a Web browser, log in to your account,
choose a campaign, click the Settings tab, click the Ad Delivery: Ad Rotation,
Frequency Capping link, click the Edit link (next to Ad rotation), and move
the radio button from Optimize to Rotate. Then click the Save button.

Done? Okay, now I can get rational and calm again. Let me explain why you
made this change, and why it's so important. When you run two ads in the
same ad group, Google shows them to different people and gives you statistics on how each ad performed (see Chapter 13 for the gory — er, *glorious* —
details of split-testing). If Google optimizes your ad rotation, the ads with
lower click through rate (CTR) are shown less and the ads with higher CTR
are shown more. Eventually, the poor performer stops showing, and Google
declares a winner by default. You set up the test once, and it runs without
you from then on. What could be bad?

First, your tests take much longer when you don't give each ad an equal
chance to be "voted on" by searchers. You need a threshold number of
impressions and clicks for each ad to determine a statistical winner. If one ad
gets fewer and fewer impressions and clicks, it takes longer to declare that
winner.

When you can't declare winners as they happen, you learn slower. Think of how fast bacteria adapt to antibiotics — because they go through so many generations in a short time frame. The more iteration per time frame, the more your ads can evolve and improve. AdWords is a playground where both evolution *and* intelligent design rule.

You also lose money because your campaigns are improving more slowly than they might. Ad groups that could achieve profitability in a few days, based on traffic, will take weeks or even months to start making money.

In the second-to-worst-case scenario, you don't figure out anything about your market because you don't even pay attention to the differences between the winning and losing ads. You don't figure out which headlines work best, so you can't improve your Web site, your e-mails, your expensive offline advertisements, and so on.

If you allow Google to optimize your ads, the absolute worst-case scenario involves Google killing off the more effective ads by mistake. Until you acti-vate Conversion Optimizer (see later in this chapter), Google decides ad effectiveness based on CTR, not whether the visitors who click an ad end up *buying*. Often the highest CTR ads *lose* money because they attract too many nonbuyers.

Frequency capping

If you show ads on the content network, you can control how many times a unique user (the online marketing geek term for "person") sees your ad. Click the Edit link to set a number of views, specify the time frame (day, week, or month), and tell Google whether this limit should be applied to the entire ad group (that is, all the ads you may be rotating), or to each individual ad (called a "creative" here). Because the content network is more of a "brand-ing" medium than search, and since you don't pay for impressions that don't lead to clicks (as long as you don't change the content network–bidding format), I would leave the default No Caps on Impressions. If you discover a very low CTR and you suspect the same uninterested people (oops, I mean "unique users") are viewing your ads over and over again, you can try to limit impressions and see whether your numbers improve.

Separating your account into three types of campaigns

By default, Google wants to show each of your ads to as many people as pos-sible. It's good business for them and possibly for you as well. But until you separate out the traffic streams and evaluate each one individually, you'll never know. For most keywords, Google search converts best; search part-ners second best; and content network worst. So it makes sense to test your ads and keywords where they have the greatest chance of success before rolling them out globally. Google is a little bit like Frank Sinatra's "New York, New York:" If you can make it there, you might be able to make it anywhere.

Separating your traffic by network is a little more complicated than it ought to be, but that turns out to be a good thing. If it were easy, everyone would be doing it and you couldn't gain a competitive advantage.

Google search

Your first campaign should probably be Google search only. Creating a Google only campaign is simple. On the Campaign Settings page, under Networks, Devices, and Extensions, click the Edit link, and then uncheck the Search Partners and Content Network check boxes. Google has a little snit when you uncheck those boxes — and warns you that your ads won't show in those networks. Click the Save button and ignore the entreaty.

This campaign will now show your ads only on Google pages — not AOL search, not EarthLink, not Aunt Tillie's blog. To confirm this setting, visit the Networks tab for this campaign and make sure Search Partners and Content Network are both off.

Search partners

As you've seen, Google happily shares its search results with AOL, EarthLink, and other search partners. Google and AOL users are different from each other in meaningful ways, and those differences can affect how they respond to your ads. You probably can't predict how those differences will affect response, so the safest route is to separate the two streams and market to them separately.

On the Campaign Settings page, uncheck the Google Search box but leave the Search Partners box checked . . . just kidding! You can't do it; Google won't let you. You can't target AOL without also targeting Google. You can separate the streams by following this process:

1. **Create two identical campaigns (see Chapter 9 for some timesaving Campaign Modification tools).**

   The two campaigns should have the same settings, same ad groups, and same keywords. Add the letter **G** (for Google) to the end of one of the campaign names, and add **S** (for Search) to the other.

2. **Change their Networks settings as follows:**

   - *Campaign G:* Check Google Search, uncheck Search Partners, uncheck Content Network.

   - *Campaign S:* Check Google Search, check Search Partners, uncheck Content Network.

3. **For the Campaign S, reduce all your bids to about five cents below the Campaign G bids.**

You've created two campaigns that compete with one another for exposure. When they compete head to head on Google, the Campaign G will win because it has the higher bids. Only Campaign S will show for the search partners because Campaign G isn't configured to show for that network. *Voilà!*

Content network

You can add the content network by creating a third identical campaign, this one with C after the name. For Campaign C, go to the Settings tab, click the Edit link next to Networks and Devices, and then click the radio button next to Let Me Choose. Then remove the check from Google Search and select the radio button next to Relevant Pages across the Entire Network. Click the Save button, and you've just created a keyword-based, content-only campaign.

Next, you're prompted to create an ad group. Name the ad group, write your first ad, and choose some keywords so that Google knows what content to pair with your ad. Set your default bids, and click the Save Ad Group button. You have just told Google to show your ad on sites with content related to the keywords your entered.

Figure 7-9 shows a neat AdWords account with three campaigns each receiving different streams of traffic. The Google search–only campaign has the highest CTR, 0.87 percent, the search partner campaign is second with 0.44 percent, and the content campaign comes in lowest with 0.07 percent. Notice also the difference in average CPC: The search and Google networks cost 10 to 12 cents more per click, respectively, than the content network. These differences suggest that each network requires its own strategy, from ad copy to ad position to keywords. Unless you separate them, you'll never discover what works best for each network.

Although people searching on Google expect organic listings and ads (after all, that's why they're searching), ads on the content network are interruptions. If you're reading an article in the *New York Times* or managing your Gmail, you haven't asked a bunch of advertisers to vie for your attention. Your content ads must be extremely relevant, urgent, or curiosity-provoking to compete against the editorial content of a Web page. Your search ads may only need to highlight a problem and offer a solution.

Your bidding strategy for the content network must achieve the goal of getting your ad at or near the top position. Unlike a search-results page, AdSense pages typically show from one to five text ads. Figure 7-10 shows the online community, at http://psychotactics.ning.com with five AdSense ads on the right, next to the video. Your marketing-related ad needs to be in positions 1–5 to get any play on this social network.

Figure 7-9:
Here the
Google (G),
search part-
ners (S), and
content (C)
traffic are
separated
by cam-
paign so
each source
can be eval-
uated and
optimized
separately.

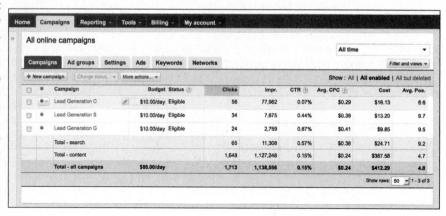

Figure 7-10:
Only the
top five ads
make it onto
the Psycho-
tactics
social
network.

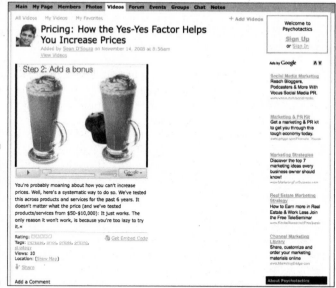

Choosing content placements

If you show your ads on the content network, Google decides by default where to show your ads (automatic placements, based on the keywords you select). But you can regain control here, by telling Google to show your ads on specific sites (managed placements). You can set up a managed placement campaign by following the steps in the previous section and selecting the radio button next to Relevant Pages Only the Placements I Manage. You can later combine the two methods by specifying keyword-optimized pages on specific sites (see the following section, "Combining keyword and placement targeting").

To add managed placements to an automatic placement campaign, click the Ad Groups tab within a campaign, click an ad group name to view the details of that group, and then click the Networks tab. Click the Show details link next to Managed Placements. You'll see a list of all your managed placements (none, to start), along with an Add Placements button. Click that button to bring up another screen with an Add Placements button. Click that button to access a text box where you can type the URLs of Web sites that you want to carry your ads. If you have no idea, click the Try the Placement Tool button next to the magnifying glass.

Placement Tool

When you advertise on the content network, in addition to locations and languages you can also specify user demographics. Basically, you're selecting a group of people in some geographic area, from a small town to the entire world, who visit certain Web sites. You can choose Rap/Hip-Hop fans in the Midwest, Progressives in South Carolina, Evangelicals in Chicago, and so on. Interest groups merged with geography can provide very tight, responsive markets for your ads.

The Placement Tool prompts you to select from categories, such as games or health, enter topic words, name specific Web sites, or describe your audience and let Google suggest Web sites matching that demographic, as shown in Figure 7-11.

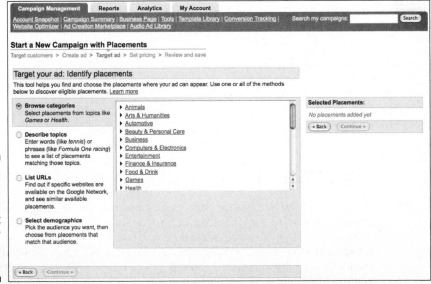

Figure 7-11: Google can help you find the right sites for your ad in four ways.

If you type the topic **Gout** (as shown in Figure 7-12), Google returns a list of Web sites, with locations or categories on those sites, along with information like impressions per day and supported ad formats (text, image, and video). You can filter the results by clicking Choose Ad Format, so if you have a square 300 x 250 pixel image ad, you can choose only those Web sites that have elected to serve ads of that size and shape.

If your desired audience is in the United States and you choose to target the entire country, you can choose Web sites based on demographics. In Figure 7-13, Google will show Web sites visited by 25–44-year-old women making more than $60,000 a year who have children in their household. Figure 7-14 shows the top Web sites returned for those criteria. You can select any or all of them to show your ad. The first one, Aintitcool.com, shares news and reviews of movies, DVDs, and comic books. Ask yourself, "Can I create an ad that will interrupt someone reading an interview with Tom Cruise about the next Mission Impossible movie and make him or her act on my offer? If so, will that person be a good prospect?" If both questions can be answered, "Yes," you may have found a successful content site.

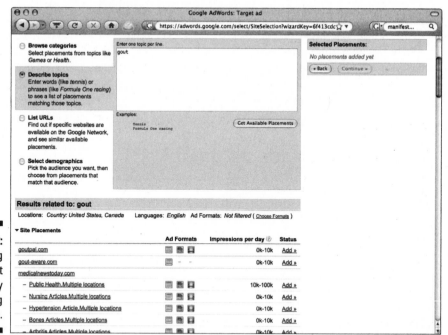

Figure 7-12: Choosing content sites by describing topics.

Figure 7-13:
Demo-
graphic
targeting
allows you
to show
your ad
to men or
women
of differ-
ent ages,
income
brackets,
and ethnic-
ity, whose
households
include
children.

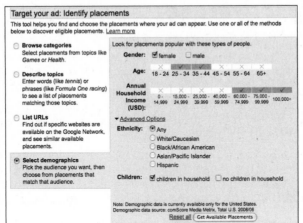

Figure 7-14:
Web sites
whose
visitors are
deemed
to meet
the demo-
graphic
criteria
shown in
Figure 7-13.

Result▼	Site	Details	Ad Formats Choose Formats »	Impressions per day	Add all 68 »
1	vamoose.com	more info		10k-100k	Add »
2	catholicmom.com	more info		10k-100k	Add »
3	reelviews.net	more info		10k-100k	Add »
4	boardingschoolreview.com	more info		10k-100k	Add »
5	phonedog.com	more info		10k-100k	Add »
6	urbanplanet.org	more info		10k-100k	Add »
7	mediaminer.org	more info		100k-500k	Add »
8	videogamesblogger.com	more info		0k-10k	Add »
9	seniormag.com	more info		0k-10k	Add »
10	vacationhomerentals.com	more info		10k-100k	Add »
11	spacepimping.com	more info		10k-100k	Add »
12	vacationrentals411.com	more info		10k-100k	Add »
13	thegrocerygame.com	more info		10k-100k	Add »
14	blackenterprise.com	more info		10k-100k	Add »
15	internetfamilyfun.com	more info		0k-10k	Add »
16	govtech.net	more info		0k-10k	Add »
17	thebestkidsbooksite.com	more info		10k-100k	Add »
18	tripsmarter.com	more info		100k-500k	Add »
19	jamaicans.com	more info		10k-100k	Add »

Combining keyword and placement targeting

You can combine the two targeting methods — keywords and placements — within a single ad group. For example, if you want to show your ads on Webmd.com pages that are about gout, you can choose the URL webmd.com from the placement list, and then refine the targeting by adding gout-related keywords and negative keywords (say, for other kinds of arthritis) in the Keywords tab. This gives you much more control than using either placement or keyword targeting separately.

Bidding Smart

Earlier in this chapter, I urged you not to let Google automatically determine your bids. Eventually, when you have conversion tracking and analytics set up (see Chapters 14 and 15), you can adjust your bids intelligently in response to back-end conversion. When you first bid on a keyword, you want to balance three objectives: getting valid data quickly, generating high CTRs for your best keywords, and not losing the shirt off your back by paying too much for too many unprofitable clicks.

Initial bidding strategies

Richard Stokes, founder and president of AdGooroo, discusses his research-backed bidding strategy in his book *Mastering Search Advertising — How the Top 3% of Search Advertisers Dominate Google AdWords*. He divides keywords into two groups:

- ✔ **Niche keywords:** Keywords with that are at least three words long, that you expect will generate high CTRs.

    Examples: gout foods to avoid, left-handed titanium driver, iPod shuffle blue case

    Bid to get those keywords in positions 2–3. Typically, the costs for positions 2 and 3 are not significantly higher than that for lower positions, while obtaining both a good CTR and conversion rate. Position 1 often has a significant jump in cost and tends to attract unqualified clicks.

- ✔ **Broad keywords:** Category terms that lots of people use at the beginning of their search process; these are usually one- to two-word, short-tail keywords.

    Examples: gout, golf club, iPod

Bid for position 7 for broad keywords. Rarely will you convert enough of these searches to sales to justify the extra expense of positions 1–3, and the traffic for these words can bankrupt you if you generate too many clicks before optimizing your sales process.

If your campaign is showing on the content network, bid to appear in positions 1–3 for text ads, and position 1 for image and video ads. Otherwise, your ads won't appear enough to for you to learn (or profit) from.

When you have data . . .

The initial bidding strategies should give way to data-informed bids as soon as possible. After you set up conversion tracking and analytics (described in Chapters 14 and 15, respectively), run keyword reports and adjust each keyword to be profitable. One position will give you the highest ROI for each keyword, and you can usually find it through trial and error within a few hundred clicks.

Just as this edition was going to press, I received reports from a bunch of AdWords power users that the Conversion Optimizer tool was improving their campaign performance significantly. This tool asks you how much you're willing to pay for a conversion — for example, a lead or a sale. Google then scans the history of all your conversions in a search for the perfect bid price for every occasion to provide you with the most conversions at or below your bid. The amount of data Google considers is awesome (I mean that in the literal sense, not the teenager sense). The Conversion Optimizer fluctuates your bid based on time of day, geographic region, keyword, placement site, and other variables — all in combination with each other.

To enable Conversion Optimizer, make sure your Ad Rotation setting is set to Optimize, not Rotate. You must run your campaign for at least a month with conversion tracking on, so Google can start collecting the data to optimize. If your campaign generates at least 30 conversions during the past 30 days, your campaign is eligible for Conversion Optimizer. Determine the most you're willing to pay for a conversion, and then edit the Bidding Option setting for the campaign. Select Focus on Conversions, enter a maximum CPA (cost per action), and then click the Save button.

When you move a campaign to Conversion Optimizer, you lose all your existing bids. In case things don't work out, make sure you back up your campaign with the desktop AdWords Editor (see Chapter 9 for details). Also, be aware that the tool can take several weeks to discover improvements. The more conversions you generate, the faster it learns. This is one of the most powerful tools in the AdWords arsenal — please read the documentation carefully. You can get to it by clicking the question mark next to Bidding Option on the campaign settings page and then clicking the Learn More link at the bottom of the pop-up.

Chapter 8

Improving Your Campaigns through Keyword Management

In This Chapter

▶ Managing your keyword sales force

▶ Increasing relevance by tightening ad groups

▶ Saving and resuscitating keywords

▶ Avoiding overwhelm with the 80/20 rule

*W*hen you place an ad in the Yellow Pages, you can't change it until the next edition comes out. After the ad is in the Yellow Pages, your job is to answer the phone, take care of customers, and pay the electricity bill.

Your AdWords account, on the other hand, frequently needs changes and requires much more of your attention than a static advertisement. If you like metaphors, you can equate your AdWords account to auto maintenance. If you never change the oil, the engine will eventually die. However, with regular maintenance and tinkering, you can get it to a high-performance state over time — and keep it there. Your AdWords account demands more attention up front and less and less as time goes on.

In this chapter, you discover tactics for improving your AdWords campaign performance over time. I show you how to identify unprofitable keywords, and what you can try before you fire them. I help you improve CTR by grouping similar keywords and targeting your ads more tightly to those keywords. I divulge a strategy for resuscitating keywords rendered inactive because Google doesn't like them. Finally, I show you a triage system that allows you to focus your campaign management where it will bring the highest return.

Nurturing, Relocating, and Firing Keywords

Keywords connect people with ads. If the connection is right, the right people find the right ads. While your AdWords campaigns mature, you'll discover the best relationships between keywords and ads. Think of your keyword list as a commission-only sales force, with each keyword a different sales rep driving up and down the Internet looking for business:

- **Stars:** Some of keywords are stars, bringing in customers and profits on a regular basis.

- **Solid performers:** These are good performers, making their numbers without complaint but not setting the world on fire.

- **Long tails:** Still other keywords are harmless stay-at-homes, making you nothing but costing you nothing either.

- **Underperformers:** A large number of your keywords underperform but might convert into solid producers by relocating to better territories.

- **Negative ROI:** Inevitably, you find keywords that just aren't worth keeping — they may bring you some business, but their expense accounts far exceed the value of their leads.

The following sections look at what to do about each of these keywords.

Star keywords

I'm going to take a wild guess about your AdWords account: I predict that 95 percent of your Web site traffic is coming from fewer than ten keywords. Maybe fewer than five. I know this not because I'm psychic (I knew you were thinking that), but because in five years of helping people with AdWords, most accounts I've seen have been tilted in that direction. In fact, it's not uncommon for an online business to live or die based on a single keyword.

Your most important AdWords job is to identify star keywords and give them everything they need to be happy and healthy. Limos, special diets, bathtubs filled with Perrier — these keywords must receive ongoing attention if they are to perform at a high level.

Of course, keywords aren't really pampered Hollywood stars, so my suggestions in the previous paragraph are meant to be understood metaphorically. What keywords really want are relevant ads in the right positions taking the searcher to an appropriate landing page. All your keywords want this; your job as an advertiser is to give it to them to the extent you can. But if you're building your campaigns correctly, with hundreds or thousands of long-tail keywords, it's easy to lump your star keywords in with the hoi polloi and lose a lot of potential sales.

Give each star keyword its own ad group and landing page. The ads in that ad group include the keyword at least once, possibly twice, and you check your split tests regularly for a winner (see Chapter 13). The landing page tells your visitors within 1.3 seconds that they've come to the right place — to the Web site with the answer to their deepest and most pressing desires.

If you didn't connect with the Hollywood-stars metaphor, here's one inspired by my visit to the North Carolina State Fair last fall: Your hundreds or thousands of keywords are like apples in your orchard, while the star keywords are your prize milk-fed pumpkins. Each pumpkin gets as much attention as an orchard of apples. (If you need more metaphors, you're on your own.)

Finding star keywords

To identify your star keywords, follow these steps:

1. **Log in to your AdWords account at www.google.com/adwords and get to the Campaign Summary page (you may be taken there by default).**

2. **Click the Keywords tab to show all the keywords in your account.**

3. **Click the Impr tab to sort the keywords from most to fewest impressions.**

   You should see all your keywords already sorted by impressions, as shown in Figure 8-1. In many accounts, the top five to ten keywords receive more traffic than all the rest combined. Within individual ad groups, this phenomenon is often even more pronounced.

Figure 8-1: The top two keywords in this ad group have received 94 percent of the search impressions.

		Keyword	Status	Max. CPC	Clicks	Impr. ↓	CTR	Avg. CPC	Cost	Avg. Pos.	Quality score
		gout diet	Ad group paused	$0.20	6,370	433,594	1.47%	$0.18	$1,123.19	7.5	5/10
		[gout diet]	Ad group paused	$0.20	1,194	127,048	0.94%	$0.16	$186.94	8.5	5/10
		"gout diet"	Ad group paused	$0.20	194	13,137	1.48%	$0.13	$26.03	6.6	5/10
		diet gout prevention	Ad group paused	$0.15	107	7,132	1.50%	$0.12	$12.49	7.7	5/10
		diet gout purine	Ad group paused	$0.20	57	3,875	1.47%	$0.18	$10.31	5.1	5/10
		[diet to prevent gout]	Ad group paused	$0.15	7	1,816	0.39%	$0.10	$0.69	9.3	5/10
		diet free gout	Ad group paused	$0.15	19	1,344	1.41%	$0.09	$1.71	8.2	5/10
		anti diet gout	Ad group paused	$0.15	9	1,166	0.77%	$0.10	$0.88	8	5/10
		[gout treatment diet]	Ad group paused	$0.15	3	1,077	0.28%	$0.10	$0.31	11.9	5/10
		arthritis diet gout	Ad group paused	$0.15	8	927	0.86%	$0.10	$0.78	8.5	5/10
		Total - search			8,007	597,064	1.34%	$0.17	$1,367.35	7.7	—

Settings | Ads | **Keywords** | Networks   Filter and views ▾

These keywords target: search, content (automatic placements and managed placements).

+ Add keywords | Edit | Change status... ▾ | See search terms... ▾ | More actions... ▾

Figure 8-1 tells a typical story: The top two keywords, [gout diet] and gout diet, together have received 82 percent of the total search impressions for this ad group (560,642 out of 597,064). A closer examination shows that [gout diet] is significantly underperforming in terms of traffic: Its average position is 8.5, putting it on the second page of search results much of the time. Were I to raise its bid, that keyword would generate even more impressions. (Whether that move would be profitable depends on the cost per conversion for that keyword, which you can explore in Chapter 14.)

Although it's convenient to see all your keywords in one big list, keyword management is best done within individual ad groups. That way you can view each keyword in context, and determine its contribution to its group, and its relative performance. You can easily get to a keyword's ad group by clicking the ad group name to the right of the keyword.

Moving a star to its own trailer

I know, back to the movie star metaphor. It just amuses me to imagine [gout diet] running around in dark sunglasses and a designer shirt. Giving a star keyword its own ad group is a three-phase process:

1. **Create a new ad group in the same campaign as its current ad group, write an ad that connects strongly to the keyword, and add that keyword only to the keyword list. Pause it immediately.**

   If it's an exact match, with brackets, don't worry about negative keywords. If it's a phrase or broad match, include negative keywords.

2. **Create a new landing page specifically for that keyword.**

3. **When you're ready to send traffic to that new page, pause the keyword in the old ad group and unpause it in the new one.**

   If you run into problems, you can always pause the new ad group and unpause the old keyword.

Solid performers

Your *solid performers* are keywords that consistently generate decent numbers of impressions, but nowhere near the stratospheric output of the stars. In Figure 8-2, the first four keywords generate two-thirds of the total impressions. The next 8 keywords are the solid performers, each generating between 1,400 and 6,900 impressions.

		Keyword	Status ⓘ	Max. CPC	Clicks	Impr. ↓	CTR ⓘ	Avg. CPC ⓘ	Cost	Avg. Pos.	Quality score
		Settings Ads Keywords Networks								Filter and views ▾	
		These keywords target: search.									
		+ Add keywords Edit Change status ... ▾ See search terms... ▾ More actions... ▾									
☐	●	"cold calling"	⬚ Eligible	$1.00	615	31,701	1.94%	$0.85	$525.07	3.4	5/10
☐	●	cold calling	⬚ Eligible	$1.00	721	25,134	2.87%	$0.82	$592.31	3.1	5/10
☐	●	cold calling techniques	⬚ Eligible	$1.00	219	15,992	1.37%	$0.86	$189.43	2.3	5/10
☐	●	[cold calling]	⬚ Eligible	$1.00	378	13,422	2.82%	$0.89	$335.59	4.2	5/10
☐	●	"cold calls"	⬚ Eligible	$1.00	156	6,904	2.26%	$0.86	$134.24	2.1	5/10
☐	●	cold calls	⬚ Eligible	$1.00	123	6,115	2.01%	$0.76	$93.54	2.4	5/10
☐	●	cold call techniques	⬚ Eligible	$1.00	50	6,101	0.82%	$0.66	$33.03	2.2	5/10
☐	●	[cold calling techniques]	⬚ Eligible	$1.00	64	5,297	1.21%	$0.91	$58.45	2.6	5/10
☐	●	cold call scripts	⬚ Eligible	$1.00	41	3,577	1.15%	$0.68	$28.06	2.5	5/10
☐	●	"cold calling techniques"	⬚ Eligible	$1.00	17	3,180	0.53%	$0.91	$15.40	2.7	5/10
☐	●	[cold calls]	⬚ Eligible	$1.00	124	2,716	4.57%	$0.69	$85.73	1.5	5/10
☐	●	making cold calls	⬚ Eligible	$1.00	27	1,409	1.92%	$0.55	$14.86	1.9	5/10
☐	●	[cold call scripts]	⬚ Eligible	$1.00	11	871	1.26%	$0.62	$6.80	3.2	5/10
☐	●	"cold call scripts"	⬚ Eligible	$1.00	15	627	2.39%	$0.74	$11.14	1.8	5/10
☐	●	[cold calling for cowards]	⬚ Eligible	$1.00	6	384	1.56%	$0.92	$5.53	2.5	5/10
		Total - all deleted keywords			43	3,781	1.14%	$0.73	$31.57	2.8	--
		Total - search			2,689	129,271	2.08%	$0.83	$2,225.52	2.9	--
		Total - content ⓘ			0	0	0.00%	$0.00	$0.00	0	--
		Total - all keywords			**2,689**	**129,271**	**2.08%**	**$0.83**	**$2,225.52**	**2.9**	--

Figure 8-2:
The keywords from "cold calls" to making cold calls are all solid performers.

Keywords of a feather should flock together

Look at your keywords and see whether you can group them into more tightly focused ad groups, based on word similarity and CTR. For example, the keywords in Figure 8-2 need to be divided into more tightly targeted ad groups, based on word similarity and CTR.

The CTRs for the eight solid performers are as follows:

Keyword	Click-Through Rate
"cold calls"	2.25%
cold calls	2.01%
cold call techniques	0.81%
[cold calling techniques]	1.20%
cold call scripts	1.14%
"cold calling techniques"	0.53%
[cold calls]	4.56%
making cold calls	1.91%

The range of CTRs is huge, with the best performing keyword, [cold calls], generating Web site visitors at almost nine times the rate of the worst performer, "cold calling techniques". And they're all showing for the same ad or ads. What this means is that the ads in this group have the potential to achieve a very nice 4.56% CTR, if they're showing for the right keywords. The keyword "cold calling techniques" is poorly matched to the ads in this ad group. It should be moved to a different ad group with an ad and landing page more specifically targeted to that desire.

The keywords in this ad group that don't generate enough traffic to warrant their own group should be divided as follows:

✔ **Cold Calling Techniques ad group**

- cold calling techniques

- [cold calling techniques]

- "cold calling techniques"

- Any other phrases that include the three words cold calling techniques in any order

- Phrases with the three words with technique misspelled or mis-typed (for example, cold calling tehcniques)

- Phrases with the words cold call techniques (then split those out if the CTRs are different)

✔ **Cold Calls ad group**

- [cold calls]

- "cold calls"

- cold calls

- making cold calls

- [making cold calls]

✔ **Cold Call Scripts ad group**

- cold call scripts

- "cold call scripts"

- [cold call scripts]

- Phrases with the three words with scripts misspelled or mistyped (for example, scirpts)

- Any other phrases that include the three words cold call scripts in any order

Determining your ad's true potential

Sort the keywords in your ad group by the Clicks column. The keyword that's received at least 30 clicks with the highest CTR represents your ad's potential. Keywords that receive significantly lower CTRs don't belong with that ad. Typically, you find that the highest CTR keywords are the ones echoed in the headline of the ad.

Long-tail keywords

The long-tail keywords are the ones receiving low numbers of impressions and the occasional click. They just don't get enough traffic to justify their own ad or landing page, but collectively are worth bidding on because they are cheaper than other keywords and convert better because there's less competition. These two factors lower your global average cost of customer acquisition and can mean the difference between a struggling and a dominant business.

Each long tail isn't anything to write home about, but collectively they may be doing more for your business than any of your top performers are. It's like the hardworking character actors, lighting directors, third associate key grips, and assistant best boys who don't get all the credit but without whom the movies don't get made. The names in the credits at the end of the movie are the long-tail keywords.

Your long-tail keywords can be in big, undifferentiated groups with a generic "problem/promise" ad: Headline describes the problem, Description Line #1 makes a big promise, Description Line #2 includes a feature and call to action. (See Chapter 6 for details of ad writings.)

You will improve performance by grouping the long-tail keywords by concept. For the gout campaign example, I used the following concepts to group long-tail keywords:

- **Diet:** Keywords related to diet indicate, as best as I can tell, potential customers who desire to take control and change aspects of their lifestyle. Ads that reassure that such changes are quick and easy do well with this group.

- **Food:** Food keywords, on the other hand, reflect a narrower mindset related to specific foods to ingest or avoid, rather than a wholesale diet change. Ads that ask ignorance-uncovering questions (What are the 3 worst gout foods? Is cherry juice for real?) will motivate this group.

✔ **Remedy:** People who type **remedy** are looking for home remedies and folk medicine, as opposed to drugs or prevention. They like "secrets" and "what doctors won't tell you."

✔ **Symptom relief:** People searching for `gout pain`, `arthritis gout`, `gout symptoms`, and `gout treatment` view gout as a disease not entirely under their control. An ad that immediately offers information about diet and lifestyle change will alienate this group. Instead, empathize and offer quick results.

Some of your long-tail keywords may be rendered inactive by Google because of low search volume. If that happens, you can leave the keyword in your account in case lots of people start searching for it (new products and trends often take a while to build up search volume), or you can delete the keyword. Google won't penalize your account's quality score for low search volume keywords. The only cost will be an account more cumbersome than necessary.

Underperforming keywords

As we've seen, a keyword will underperform if it points to an ad that doesn't address the right desires, or if that ad is positioned too high or too low (based on that keyword's maximum CPC). If the problem is too few impressions, check your average position for that keyword. Your ad may be showing on page 4, where few searchers are willing to go. Or your ad may be lower than third position in a Content Network campaign.

The quickest way to identify underperforming keywords is to create filters within the Keywords tab. For example, here's how to set a filter for all keywords with at least 200 impressions and a CTR of less than 0.2%:

1. **From the Campaigns tab, select All Online Campaigns, either from the left menu, or if you've hidden it, from the navigation links just below the top tabs.**

2. **Select the date range you want to check.**

   You can use the preset options (Today, Yesterday, Last 7 days, and so on), or select Custom Date Range and specify start and end dates.

3. **Click the Filters and Views button on the right, just below the date range.**

4. **Select Filter Keywords from the drop-down list.**

5. **Change the > to < in the middle field.**

6. **Enter 0.2 in the % field.**

7. **Click the Add Another link just below the filter.**

8. **Select Impressions from the drop-down list. (The > automatically changes to >=.)**

9. **Enter** 200 **in the blank number field.**

10. **(Optional) If you want to use this filter again in the future as a regular part of your AdWords management strategy, check the Save Filter box and give the filter a name you'll recognize later (for example,** Low CTR**).**

11. **Click the Apply button to filter your keywords. (See Figure 8-3.)**

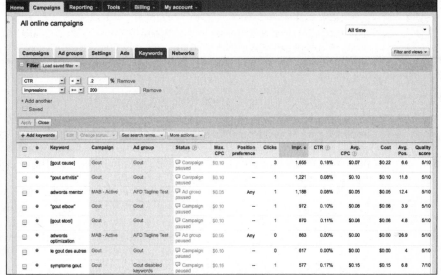

Figure 8-3:
Use filters to quickly identify low CTR keywords in need of attention.

 When your keywords deliver lots of impressions but few clicks, the problem is the connection between the keyword and the ad. Move your keyword to an ad group that addresses the desire represented by that keyword, or increase your bid to move the ad to a more desirable position.

Negative-ROI keywords

After you set up conversion tracking (described in Chapter 14), you discover that some keywords appear to be doing well within the AdWords account — lots of traffic, good CTR — but don't convert to sales well enough to justify the cost of their clicks. This type of underperformance is especially insidious because it's hard to identify. In Chapter 14, I show you how to spot Expense Account Gluttons that cost you more than they make for you.

You deal with negative-ROI keywords by first trying the tactic just described for underperforming keywords: point them to better ads. If the increased CTR doesn't make them profitable, add negative qualifiers such as price and other disincentives to click (see Chapter 6). If nothing works, you have to let them go. Don't worry about them — someone else will blissfully (and cluelessly) continue losing money on those keywords. Just don't let it be you.

Resuscitating Poor-Quality Keywords

Since July 2006, Google has been rolling out occasional changes to its bid price algorithm designed to improve the search experience (and boost its profits). The most important factor in determining your bid price, aside from what your competitors are willing to pay, is your Keyword Quality Score. Quality Score takes into account your CTR (the higher, the more clicks and the more money Google makes) and its determination of the relevance and quality of your landing page to that search.

The Quality Score algorithm continues to evolve, and no one outside the hallowed halls of Google knows exactly what it is, but the trend is clear: Google wants to make money today (high CTR) and tomorrow (your customers can find what they want quickly and easily, with no hassle, so they continue to use Google as their search engine of choice).

Keywords are ranked for quality on a scale of 1 – 10, with 10 being the highest. Google penalizes low quality score keywords by raising the minimum bid needed to appear on the first page. This makes sense from their perspective — if your ad is generating fewer clicks for a keyword than your competitor's ad, Google needs you to pay more per click to make the same amount of money for "renting" you the space on their search results page.

To resuscitate a keyword, follow these steps:

1. **Move it to a new ad group.**

2. **Write a new ad with a message targeted specifically for that keyword.**

3. **Link the ad to a new landing page written with that searcher in mind.**

   (See Chapter 10 for landing page dos and don'ts.)

Managing the 80/20 Way

This chapter is deceptively short, because the work it asks you to do can be time-consuming. It's maintenance, not setup — and it's tempting to do maintenance once and not peek under the hood again until you smell oil. (Yup, back to the car metaphor.) Especially after you've divided your campaigns into many focused ad groups, you can find yourself drowning amid the priorities competing for your attention. This section gives you some guidance in answering the only question that ever matters at this point: "What do I do now?"

The 80/20 Principle states that 80 percent of your efforts lead to only 20 percent of your results, while the remaining 20 percent of your efforts is responsible for 80 percent of your results. The top 20 percent of your keywords will generate 80 percent of your clicks and sales. Don't get hung up on the exact numbers — you'll probably find that the ratio in AdWords is closer to 95/5 or 99/1.

In any case, the moral is the same: Consciously focus your time and attention on the parts of your AdWords account that have the biggest impact on your profitability.

Each AdWords account is different, so I can't give you a formula for how to spend your time. The key skills here are threefold:

- ✔ Know the key priorities for your business.
- ✔ Sort your campaigns, ad groups, and keyword lists by those priorities.
- ✔ Always address the issue that can provide the biggest boost to your bottom line.

The factor limiting the growth of most online businesses is the size of the reachable market. In AdWords, the reachable market consists of people searching for your keywords or visiting Web sites that display your ads. The AdWords metric for this market is *impressions* — instances of exposure to your ad.

After you log in to your account, click the Ad Groups tab and compare the statistics for each ad group. You're looking to answer the question, "Which ad group's improvement will have the biggest impact on my business?" Generally, I focus on the ad group with the highest potential number of impressions. In Figure 8-4, for example, the Causes of Gout PS group's average position is 8.3, meaning it shows on the second page of search results and not at all in the content network. If I increase my bids, the traffic would increase, probably to ten times this amount.

If the average position of an ad group is 7 or better within a search campaign, or 3 or better in a content campaign, then you are theoretically getting as many impressions as possible. If an ad group averages position 8 or worse (4 for content), your ads aren't being seen by as many people as possible.

First, sort by impressions, and note any ad groups whose average positions are too low. They are potential sleepers, if you can afford the bids needed to get your ads in front of people.

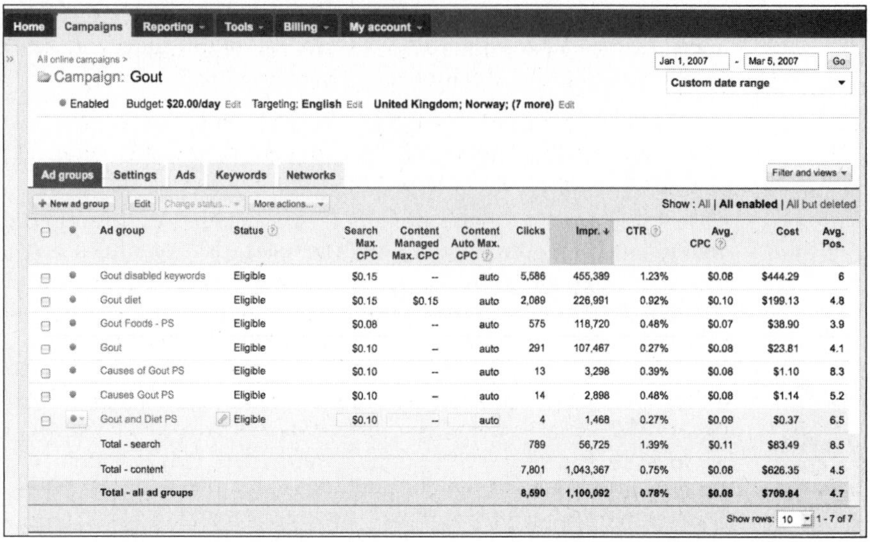

Figure 8-4:
Triage your
ad groups
by looking
at areas of
potentially
big improve-
ment.

Let me plug a microphone into my head so you can hear my thinking about Figure 8-4:

> "Okay, let's see. I have 4 big ad groups, with more than 100,000 impressions so far this year. The most expensive group is the top one. I've spent more than $400 on it since January. Its CTR is OK (1.23%), but I definitely can improve it. If I double the CTR, I would increase my Web traffic by 5,500 people over the next couple of months. If I double the CTR on my next biggest group, Gout Diet, the same amount of effort would get me only 2,000 more visitors. Oh, and look at the fourth group, Gout. The CTR is miserable, just 0.27%. I could probably improve it by a factor of 8, getting it to 2.00% with a little split-testing and rearranging of keywords. That would give me about 2,300 additional visitors (291 × 8). And it's usually easier to improve a bad ad than an OK one, so maybe that's a good place to start."

I click the Gout ad group and view the Networks tab (see Figure 8-5).

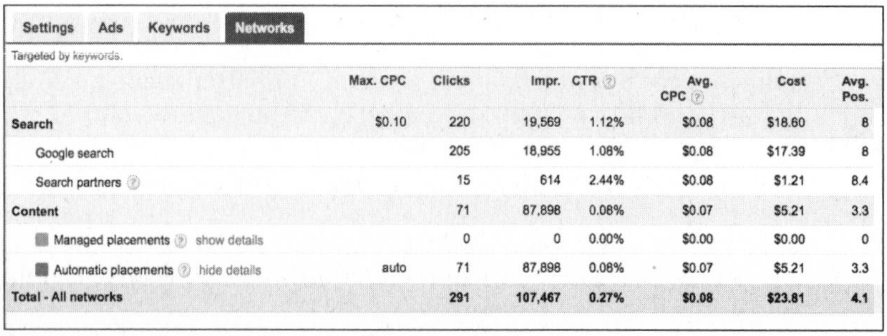

Figure 8-5:
The
Networks
tab tells
that my CTR
problem is
caused by
the content
network.

"Oh, look, the CTR for the Search networks is 1.12%, but for Content only 0.08%. The big problem here is the content network, where my ads are generating lots of impressions but few clicks."

"Obviously my ads are aimed at people who are searching for a solution to their gout problem, rather than people who are reading about gout and need a powerful ad to interrupt them into taking action.

"Good gracious me!" (Yes, sadly, that is how I talk to myself. You have no idea how annoying it can be.) "I need to move the high-potential keywords into their own ad groups, write better ads, and send them to more tightly targeted landing pages. Then my dime bids can get my ads on the first page and skyrocket my traffic without harming my ROI."

When you install conversion tracking, you have another data point upon which to act. When you find an ad group that delivers negative ROI (see Chapter 14), do something at once. Attempt a fix, pause it, or delete it. However, the order in which you act depends on the potential value of the improvement. A miniscule improvement in an ad group that gets lots of impressions is more valuable than a big improvement in an ad group consisting of seldom-seen long-tail keywords.

As you spend time in AdWords, you'll get the hang of where to focus, and you'll develop your own rhythm and intuition for what needs adjustment. The main thing to keep in mind is the 80/20 question: "What can I do now that will make the biggest difference in results?"

Split-testing ads and adjusting your bids are the sexy parts of AdWords management. Putting the right keywords together with the right ads and landing pages is more like nailing up the studs of a house than putting in the fancy trim. (Yes, campers, one final metaphor for today!) Nobody visits a show house and says, "My, those two-by-fours sure are straight." AdWords Consultant Greg Marsden e-mailed me these words of wisdom (so blame him for the metaphor):

> *Simply put, it's the solid scalable architecture of your campaigns that needs to come first before you pick the curtains out and decide what color to paint the door of your store. Virtually everyone I've worked with on AdWords completely misses that point and spends almost all of their time, effort and a ton of wasted money on frantically changing their ad texts just trying to find a "super ad" that'll magically double CTR and save the day.*

Greg went on to relate that three items on his To-Do list increased the amount of traffic to his Web site by 50 percent with no loss of quality:

- ✔ Separating content and search traffic (see Chapter 7).
- ✔ Building separate keyword lists for content and search.
- ✔ Expanding and tightly grouping keywords, particularly on the content side.

Chapter 9

Getting It Done with AdWords Tools

*W*hen my father was 12 years old in 1930, his Uncle Freddie offered to take him to a Newark Bears minor league baseball game. With the Depression raging, he couldn't afford the ticket on his own, so he accepted the offer from his notoriously stingy (and occasionally just notorious) uncle. Upon arriving at the ballpark, Uncle Freddie hustled them away from the turnstiles, around the stadium to the fence abutting the farthest outfield bleachers. Once there, Freddie knelt down and instructed my father to climb on his back and grab the top of the fence.

With a last-gasp boost by Freddie, my father vaulted the fence and toppled into the ballpark, right on top of a pair of cops hired to keep order at the raucous venue. One of the policemen roughly lifted my father up by the collar and inquired of the quivering youth, "Don't you know these games are free for kids?"

A whole industry of third-party tools has grown up around Google AdWords. Some of them, in my opinion, are indispensable (see my recommendations in Bonus Chapter 1, available as a PDF file at www.askhowie.com/bonus chapters). Others are convenient and may be worth it because of the time they save. But many are simply duplicates of free tools included (but buried) within your AdWords account. You may never need most of them. But in memory of my father's early brush with the law, I hereby introduce you to a bunch of tools that come free with AdWords. Don't let Uncle Freddie sucker you into missing out or paying extra.

The purpose of this chapter is to give you an overview of each of the free tools included with your AdWords accounts and its function, so you know to use it when you need it. This chapter is not intended to be an in-depth explanation of each tool's complete functionality. Visit www.askhowie.com/gtools for video tutorials that show you how to use them, one step at a time.

Improving Your Campaigns with the Optimizer Tools

Google offers free tools for your ad campaign on the Tools page. To go to the Tools page, log on to your AdWords account, go to the Campaign Management page, and then click the Tools link under the Campaign Management tab.

Google provides four tools under the heading Optimize Your Ads that, oddly enough, focus entirely on keywords rather than ads. I don't know if Google intended this title as a bit of cryptic wisdom, but wise it is: The quality of the ad is completely dependent on the match between it and the keyword that triggers it.

Keyword tool

You meet the Keyword tool in Chapters 4 and 5, and in this chapter I focus on some different uses. After you enter a keyword and click the Get Keyword Ideas button, select Show All from the Choose Columns to Display drop-down menu. You'll see several additional columns, including Advertiser Competition and Search Volume Trends. See Figure 9-1.

Advertiser Competition

The Advertiser Competition column shows, again in relative terms, how many competitors are bidding on that keyword. If the entire rectangle is shaded, the keyword is highly competitive, at least in terms of number of competitors. Don't let large numbers of competitors scare you away from a keyword or a market without researching further: The competitors may be easy to beat through split testing (see Chapter 13) and intelligent campaign architecture (see Chapters 7 and 8).

Figure 9-1:
Many
"mortgage"
keywords
show high
competition
(the bar is
fully colored
in), and a
number of
keywords
show a
striking
increase
in volume
in October
2008.

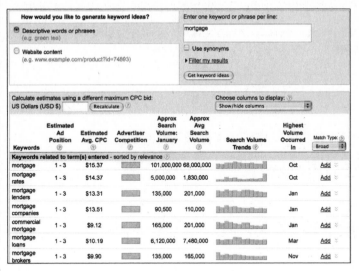

The rightmost column allows you to add any or all of the keywords to the ad group of your choosing. Notice that the column header prompts you for Match Type: Broad, Phrase, or Exact. The Broad match keyword is the default. Try changing it to Exact and see how the search volume and competition data change.

Don't confuse the *broad, phrase,* and *exact* terms at this stage of your keyword research — they are likely to perform very differently. (See Chapter 5 for a detailed explanation of the differences between these three match types.) If you do use this tool for adding keywords to your ad groups, do it carefully. I recommend scrolling to the bottom of the page and downloading the keywords to a text file or spreadsheet first, before dumping them into an ad group. You'll have much more control and will create better organized and better performing campaigns.

Cost and ad position estimates

You can also choose to display cost and ad position estimates for the keyword list, based on a Max CPC of your choosing. Select Cost and Ad Position Estimates from the Choose Data to Display drop-down list, and then enter a value for the maximum CPC in the US Dollars (USD $) text box. If a visitor to your Web site is worth $4.00, for example, you can use this tool to find keywords that will break even at worst. Enter **4** and click the Recalculate button. (See Figure 9-2.)

You can sort by Estimated Ad Position to find the profitable keywords that will position your ad advantageously. If you're building a comprehensive list, remember to repeat the process for all three keyword match types: broad, phrase, and exact.

	Estimated Ad Position ⓘ	Estimated Avg. CPC ⓘ	Advertiser Competition ⓘ	Approx Search Volume: January ⓘ	Approx Avg Search Volume ⓘ	Search Volume Trends (Nov 2007 - Oct 2008) ⓘ	Highest Volume Occurred In	Match Type: Broad ⓘ
Keywords ⓘ								
Keywords related to term(s) entered - sorted by relevance ⓘ								
mortgage	1 - 3	$3.38		101,000,000	68,000,000		Oct	Add ⌄
mortgage rates	4 - 6	$3.50		5,000,000	1,830,000		Oct	Add ⌄
mortgage lenders	4 - 6	$3.12		135,000	201,000		Jan	Add ⌄
mortgage companies	4 - 6	$3.33		90,500	110,000		Jan	Add ⌄
commercial mortgage	1 - 3	$3.29		165,000	201,000		Jan	Add ⌄
mortgage loans	1 - 3	$3.62		6,120,000	7,480,000		Mar	Add ⌄
mortgage brokers	1 - 3	$3.19		135,000	165,000		Nov	Add ⌄
mortgage broker	1 - 3	$3.22		201,000	246,000		Jan	Add ⌄
mortgage leads	1 - 3	$2.37		74,000	110,000		Nov	Add ⌄
mortgage information	4 - 6	$3.34		18,100	27,100		Jan	Add ⌄
mortgage lending	1 - 3	$2.91		74,000	60,500		Oct	Add ⌄

Calculate estimates using a different maximum CPC bid: US Dollars (USD $) 4.00 [Recalculate] ⓘ   Choose columns to display: ⓘ Show/hide columns ▾

Figure 9-2: These broad match keywords are all available for $4.00 or less.

To find out Google's estimate of the CPC for each keyword for position #1, enter **100** (for $100) in the US Dollars (USD $) text box.

Google's bid price estimates are notoriously unreliable. Don't bet the farm or give up in despair based on this data. The best way to find out the actual cost of a click is to take that keyword live in your account. Even one or two clicks will give you more realistic data than all the predictive tools in the world.

Search Volume Trends

The third option in the Choose Data to Display drop-down list is Search Volume Trends. This option gives you the average search volume along with two potentially interesting modifiers: the trend over the past 12 months for which data has been collected (the lag is usually a couple of months), and the month in which the search volume was highest.

The mortgage market is steady, with most keywords' trend lines staying pretty flat. A keyword like gifts shows huge seasonal fluctuation. The keywords birthday gifts and wedding gifts are steady, but Christmas gifts, personalized gifts, and unique gifts skyrocket in December and January and languish for the rest of the year, as shown in Figure 9-3.

I recommend a quick check on the seasonal trends in your marketplace as part of your online due diligence, so you don't start beating up on perfectly good campaigns in February because they've stopped sending you traffic.

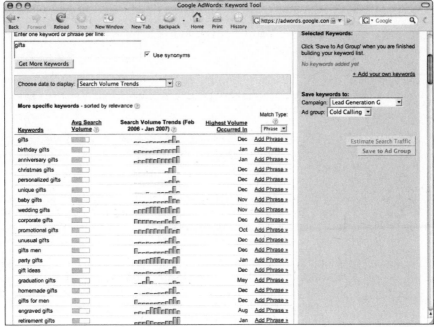

Figure 9-3:
The Gifts
market
fluctuates
wildly by
season.

Possible negative keywords

The Possible Negative Keywords option from the Choose Data to Display drop-down list shows you related searches and gives you an easy way to hide your ads from searches containing irrelevant words. For example, if you sell soccer equipment and clothing in the United States, you would find many negative keywords upon entering **Soccer** in the text box, as shown in Figure 9-4. If you sell Diadora shoes but not Adidas, consider adding **–Adidas** to your keyword list.

Edit your campaign's negative keywords

This tool can save you time and hassle if each campaign represents a broad market. If one campaign includes ad groups for homeschooling math curricula, scuba gear, magic tricks, and seminars on how to take advantage of frequent-flier-miles programs, you have no need for campaign-wide negative keywords. If, on the other hand, your Whiteboards campaign consisted of ad groups for Magnetic Whiteboards, Porcelain Whiteboards, Commercial Whiteboards, Whiteboard Cleaners, Whiteboard Pens, and so on, you can use this tool to consolidate all the negative keywords in one master list. If you create a new ad group, you don't need enter the negative keywords into that group's keyword list. Some negative keywords might include these:

```
netmeeting
Microsoft
java
msn
```

These keywords refer to online *virtual* whiteboards, not the ones that hang on your office walls and are ruined by the schlemiel who uses a permanent marker by accident.

You can generate campaign-wide negative keywords in one of two ways. You can enter the negative keywords manually, or "sweep" them out of individual ad groups into the campaign.

- ✔ **Manual exclusion:** First, select a campaign from the Campaign drop-down list near the top of the page. If your campaign is new, place the negative keywords into the text box and click the Add Keywords button. You'll see them appear in the table at the bottom of the page.

- ✔ **Clean Sweep:** If your ad groups already contain negative keywords, you can consolidate them using Clean Sweep. You can choose to sweep negative keywords found in every single group (choose All Ad Groups from the Campaign drop-down list), at least 75 percent of them, at least 50 percent of them, or keywords found in any ad group. After Clean Sweep runs, you can decide which negative keywords to apply to the entire campaign and which negative keywords to leave in their original groups only.

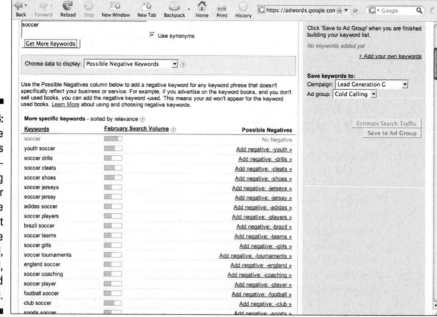

Figure 9-4:
Negative keywords for a business selling soccer gear in the U.S. might include Brazil, England, and Football.

Site Exclusion tool

The Site Exclusion tool allows you to choose particular Web sites (and parts thereof) where you *don't* want your ads to show. This tool is relevant only for campaigns that show in the Content network.

If you want to keep your ads off an entire Web site, enter the top-level domain with and without the www prefix: `www.fitfam.com` and `fitfam.com`. To keep your ads from showing in a specific cheesy subdomain or directory within a Web site, include that information: `cheesysection.fitfam.com` or `www.fitfam.com/cheesysection` and `fitfam.com/cheesysection`. You can also specify a particular page, such as `www.fitfam.com/embarrassing page.html` for exclusion.

You must set site exclusion separately for each campaign.

IP Exclusion tool

Suppose you don't want competitors to see your ads. Maybe you don't want them to know what you're up to. Or perhaps you suspect them of "click fraud" — clicking away on your ads just to cost you money. You can use the IP Exclusion tool to hide your ads for IP addresses that you specify. If you know the IP address of the server used to surf the Internet, you can enter it on a campaign-by-campaign basis.

Traffic Estimator tool

The Traffic Estimator can quickly help you avoid markets and market segments that simply don't generate enough search volume to justify a campaign, as well as help you estimate your sales volume and profitability. This tool calculates search traffic only, from Google and its partners. It does not include clicks you may receive from sites on the Content network.

Begin by entering a keyword or keywords into the text box at the top of the page. Next, enter a very high Maximum CPC. I always start with Google's maximum, $100, to find out what Google thinks I'll have to pay to get position #1. Ignore the daily budget for right now. Because you're talking about $100 clicks, you can enjoy fantasyland a little longer.

Now, choose your customers' languages and locations, just as you would in setting up a new campaign (see Chapter 7). Click Continue to see how much Google thinks you'll pay for the top spot for each keyword, and how many clicks each one will generate. Google assumes your ads' CTRs will be the same as those of current advertisers bidding on these keywords. If your ads are more attractive, your average CPCs will be correspondingly lower.

In Figure 9-5, the top position for Whiteboard keywords can be had for $3–$5 per click. Assuming your ads are as appealing (or unappealing) as everyone else's, Google thinks you'll be parting with $480–$660 per day for the privilege of showing your ads in position #1 to viewers in the U.S. and Canada. Based on its data for ads showing at that position for these keywords, Google estimates 108–117 visitors per day to your Web site (let's call it 112.5 on average). If your Web site can turn exactly 3 percent of your visitors into paying customers, and your average order amount is $500 at a 50 percent profit margin, then your gross daily profit from this campaign will be, on average, $843.75 ($500 × .50 margin × 3.375 sales). Subtracting the daily advertising spend (let's call it $520), your net at the end of each day is $323.75.

Figure 9-5:
Google estimates your daily clicks and cost per day for your keywords, based on how much you're willing to bid and where you intend to show your ads.

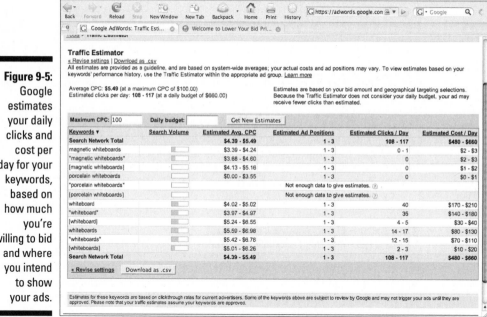

Download this table as a spreadsheet readable by Microsoft Excel by clicking the Download as .csv button at the bottom of the page. After you've saved the table, enter a saner amount in the Maximum CPC text box at the top left, and then click the Get New Estimates button. In Figure 9-6, you can see the results of capping your maximum bid at $2.00.

Now you get around 80 clicks per day for around $120. Assuming the same Web-site conversion process, you average 2.4 sales per day, for a daily profit of $600.00. Subtracting your AdWords costs leaves you with $480 net profit. Bidding lower and generating fewer clicks appears more profitable, based on this simulation.

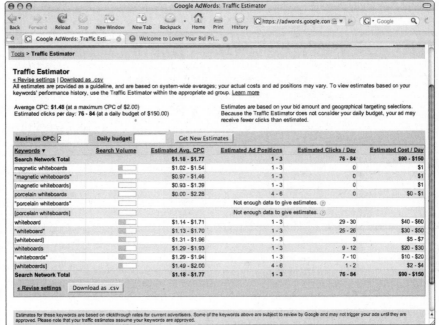

Figure 9-6:
Dropping
your bid
to $2.00
produces
almost as
many clicks
at a much
lower
estimated
daily cost.

The Web-site conversion for clicks *not* from position #1 is likely to be higher, because your ad attracts fewer happy clickers and more serious prospects. The lower bid is likely to be even more profitable than the preceding scenario projects.

Keep playing with the Maximum CPC until you find the scenario that produces the highest net profit. You can become even more granular by adding individual Max CPCs to the keywords, using the `keyword**1.50` format on the first page of the Traffic Estimator. Until you track the actual sales performance of keywords (so you know exactly the optimal bid for profitability), the Traffic Estimator is a good place to start.

Insights for Search tool

This recent addition to the AdWords tool family will help you explore seasonal trends and geographic distribution of keywords. It has far too many features to describe here. If you want to know where in the world the most people search for `ramen noodles` or when `Campus Ladies` was hot, this tool provides hours of fun.

Check out a video demo of the Insights for Search tool at `http://askhowie.com/searchinsights`.

Getting Feedback from Google with the Ad Performance Tools

When you put an ad in your local paper or hire a kid to wear a chicken suit in July and hand out flyers for your Buffalo Wings Shack, it's pretty easy to tell whether the ad appears or the kid shows up and shakes his tail feathers. The world of online advertising is not so apparent, so Google provides some tools to help you monitor where and when your ads are showing.

To use the Ad Performance tools, log on to your AdWords account, go to the Campaign Management page, and click the Tools link under the Campaign Management tab. Click the link for the tool you want to try out under the Analyze Your Ad Performance heading.

The Conversion Tracking tool is important enough to merit its very own chapter, so I don't belabor it in this chapter. Flip to Chapter 14 to find out all about the Conversion Tracking tool.

Ads Diagnostic tool

Want to find out whether searchers are seeing your ads for your favorite keywords? Click the Ads Diagnostic Tool link on the Tools page. With the Ads Diagnostic tool, you can enter a keyword, choose parameters, and ask Google to indicate the ads that appear for a given search term. In Figure 9-7, Google will show the ads that appear in the Chicago, IL area for the phrase-match keyword IT consultant.

Note that you are not limited to the straight www.google.com search; you can also check other Google domains, such as maps.google.com or google.co.za (the South African Google home page), by entering the URL in the Google Domain text box. You can specify a geographic location, just as you do when targeting a campaign, choose the language(s) your customers speak, and even specify individual IP addresses for laser targeting. This is very useful for advertisers who can't see what their far-flung prospects in other regions or countries are viewing during searches.

Google offers a second option to diagnose a missing ad. Option 2: Search Results Page URL, at the bottom of the page, allows you to paste the entire URL of a search page into the Search Results Page URL text box. To use this option, open another Web browser window, perform a Google search, and then select and copy the entire text of the URL in the Address bar.

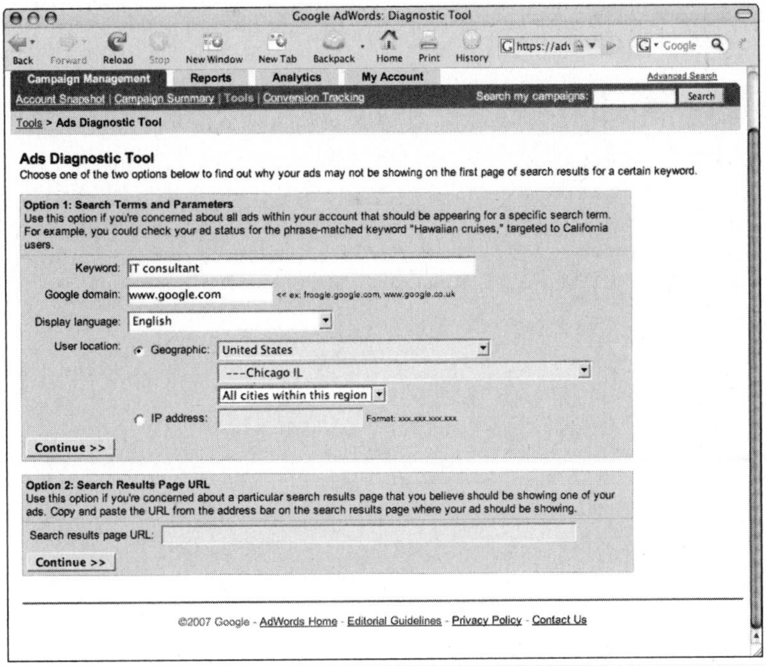

Figure 9-7:
Asking
Google
which ads
display
when some-
one in the
Chicago
area
searches for
the phrase
match "IT
consultant".

To be sure you've selected the entire address, perform the following steps:

1. **Right-click anywhere within the URL in the Address bar and choose Select All.**

2. **Right-click again and choose Copy.**

3. **Return to the Ad Diagnostic tool, right-click your cursor in the Option 2 text box, and then select Paste.**

4. **Click the Continue button.**

For either option, when you click the Continue button, Google shows you not only the ads that will show for that keyword, but also the ads that you would like to show, but aren't. Google also provides tips and strategies for fixing the problem, as shown in Figure 9-8.

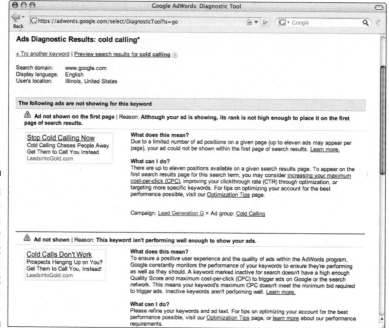

Figure 9-8:
Google
explains
why your
ads aren't
showing
and what
you can do
to fix them.

Your ad might be slacking off for a number of reasons:

✔ **Ad not showing on first page:** Your ad is showing, but not on the first page. Google suggests raising your minimum bid, increasing your CTR, or targeting more specific keywords.

✔ **Ad not shown because of low quality keyword:** Google gives each keyword a quality score (see Chapter 7). If your keyword quality is Poor or OK, Google penalizes you by making that keyword more expensive. Your options here include improving the keyword-to-ad-to-landing-page match (opening your mind) or bidding higher (opening your wallet).

✔ **Ad not shown because one of your other ads is showing for this keyword:** Google lets your campaigns and ad groups compete against each other, but will let only one win at a time. You won't see two of your ads showing for the same keyword, even if you bid on that keyword in multiple ad groups or campaigns. Google chooses the one with the highest ranking, which generally means the one that makes Google the most money (they aren't stupid). If you want the missing ad to show, either decrease the duplicate keyword(s) or raise your bid on this keyword.

✔ **Ad not shown because of paused campaign, ad group, or keyword:** If you pause a part of your account, Google stops showing it. Obvious, yes, but when accounts get large, it's easy to forget that you never turned that ad group back on after pausing it for maintenance.

✔ **Ad not shown because negative keyword or Non-Family Safe classification is preventing your ad from showing:** If you dump a lot of negative keywords into your campaigns or ad groups, you may inadvertently cause a conflict between a positive and negative keyword. The Non-Family Safe classification means that your ad is deemed inappropriate for minors, and will be shown only to searchers who turn off the adult filters (few do). Unless you're selling adult entertainment (I love that euphemism!), make sure your ads would be at home on *Captain Kangaroo*.

✔ **Ad not shown because disapproved ads or keywords:** If your ad is disapproved due to a violation of Google's editorial guidelines (see `https://adwords.google.com/select/guidelines.html` for the actual document you "signed" when you gave Google your first five dollars), use the tool in the next section to discover possible remedies.

Ads Preview tool

I know you want to deduct that 45-country trip as a business expense, but it's not necessary to travel to see the Google search results from around the world. Simply enter a keyword, domain, and language; and then choose a country and region to view (but not interact with) the Google results page that searchers in that area would see.

If you use Firefox for your Web browser, there's a cool third-party tool put out by Redfly Marketing that has more functionality than the Ads Preview tool (and which you can use right on the search results page). Find it at `http://askhowie.com/redflytool`.

Disapproved ads

I'm such a good boy that I can't show you screen shots for disapproved ads. The best I can do is let you see what happens when I try to write one, as shown in Figure 9-9.

Some ads can be fixed by requesting exceptions. If you sell MAS90 accounting software, originally created by Best Software, you may be able to use the Best brand name. If you use a medical term in an ad, you may trigger the "Uh-oh, it's a Canadian Pharmacy" policy. Click the Request an Exception link and explain to a live Google editor why this rule doesn't apply to your ad or keyword in 300 characters or fewer (now's not a good time to go into your childhood).

Figure 9-9:
The word
Best
triggers an
automatic
disapproval,
before
Google even
discovers
the mis-
spellings,
abbre-
viations, and
excessive
capitaliza-
tion.

Create Text Ad

⚠ Your ad doesn't appear to comply with one or more of our editorial guidelines. See problems below. Please review your ad and make any necessary modifications. If you feel this message is in error, you may apply for an exception and continue. Your ad may not run until the request is approved. [?]

STOP COLD CALLING NOW, YO
The best❶ sistem 4
getting salesleads2callu at...
LeadsIntoGold.com
Ad text with errors highlighted.

STOP COLD CALLING NOW, YO
The best sistem 4
getting salesleads2callu at...
LEADSINTOGOLD.COM
Ad text with any revisions you make below.

Headline: | STOP COLD CALLING NOW, YO | Max 25 characters

Description line 1: ✗ | The best sistem 4 | Max 35 characters

❶ **Unacceptable Superlatives** ⓘ
Unless verified by a third party, your ad text cannot contain comparative or subjective phrases such as 'Best,' 'Lowest,' or '#1.' This verification must be clearly displayed on your website. Please remove 'best' from your ad.
▸ Request an exception

Description line 2: | getting salesleads2callu at... | Max 35 characters

Display URL: ⓘ | http:// LEADSINTOGOLD.COM | Max 35 characters

Destination URL: ⓘ | http:// ▾ | SomeOtherWebsite.com | Max 1024 characters

Save Ad | Cancel

Stop Cold Calling Now
Cold Calling Chases People Away
Get Them to Call You Instead
LeadsIntoGold.com
0 Clicks
Served - 100.0%

My Change History tool

The My Change History tool was created for those suffering from CRetTNS (Can't Remember to Take Notes Syndrome). You can find specific changes by filtering out the irrelevant ones. Google allows you to filter changes by date, campaign and ad group, users (in case you set up more than one user for your account), and type of change.

I find this tool useful when I want to examine my campaign or run a report to see the effects of a particular change. You can specify start and end dates in the Campaign Summary control panel and in reports. The My Change History tool helps you remember which dates to select to get a clean experiment.

For example, let's say you lowered a bunch of bids around the beginning of March, but you can't remember exactly when, and you want to see the effect this change has had on your business.

Figure 9-10 shows three Max CPC changes, two on February 13 and one on March 2 at 1:30 p.m. You can now look at the two weeks prior to March 2 and the two weeks following March 2 (for example) to compare your statistics for these two phases of the experiment. You can look at impressions, clicks, average position, total cost, conversions, sales, and such. If the only difference in the two periods is the change you identified, you have learned something by isolating that variable in time using the My Change History tool.

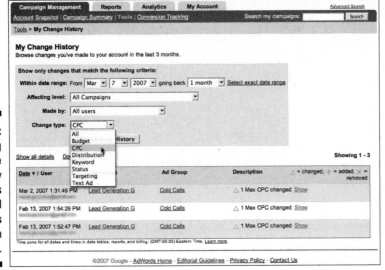

©2007 Google - AdWords Home - Editorial Guidelines - Privacy Policy - Contact Us

Figure 9-10:
Filtering the change history by CPC shows all the bid changes in a given period.

Even though you can fall back on this tool, please spend a buck on a notebook and pretend you're in high school chemistry class again. Taking notes on your questions and changes helps you monitor your account more seriously, and puts you in an observant and curious AdWords mindset.

Website Optimizer

This tool is so cool, it deserves — and gets — its own chapter (Chapter 14).

AdWords Editor

AdWords Editor is a free desktop program that allows you to make changes to your AdWords account while you're offline. After you download it to your computer (they have PC and Mac versions), you can copy and paste ads, keywords, ad groups, and even entire campaigns in seconds.

AdWords Editor includes powerful search features. For example, you can find, all in one list, every ad that includes a particular destination URL. If you need to change that URL, you can do it globally via the editor, instead of piecemeal in the online AdWords interface.

As AdWords consultant David Rothwell of AdWordsAnswers.com points out, you can also use the editor to back up your account, in case your account is hacked or you just make a bunch of changes you later regret.

Part IV
Converting Clicks to Clink

The 5th Wave   By Rich Tennant

"Oh, we're doing just great. Philip and I are selling decorative jelly jars on the Web. I run the Web site and Philip sort of controls the inventory."

In this part . . .

Up to this page, the book has been devoted to AdWords. In other words, you now know how to give money to Google. This part shows you how to make money from paying customers — hopefully, more than you spend on AdWords.

In Chapter 10, I cover the vital importance of dedicated landing pages that quickly begin scratching the itch expressed in the keyword and inflamed in the ad. You uncover how to get your visitors to say "This is for me" within one second of their arrival at your site.

I expound on my favorite topic, e-mail follow-up, in Chapter 11. No matter how wonderful your Web site, if you don't stay in touch with prospects and customers, they forget all about you. This chapter gives you the strategies to stay in touch with your Web site's visitors long after they leave your site and shows you stunningly powerful and inexpensive tools that put follow-up on autopilot.

Chapter 12 covers a wide array of other Web-site strategies, all of them based on the time-tested principles of direct marketing: engagement, calls to action, and ascending levels of value exchange and intimacy.

Chapter 10

Giving Your Customer a Soft Landing on Your Web Site

· ·

· ·

*W*hen (potential) customers click your ad and your Web site appears, they will decide to stay and shop or return to Google within seven seconds. Everything about your landing page will either persuade your visitor to stay and play, or hit the Back button and never darken your door again.

Don't just send customers to your site's home page. You have the ability to send your visitors to the page of their dreams, the one that quickly grants them their fondest wish, that scratches the itch they've never quite been able to reach before, that dreams the impossible dream — sorry, I was channeling Richard Kiley there for a minute. Deep breath. Orchestra fades. Where was I?

The text, the pictures, the design, the loading speed, the contact information, the logos, the multimedia, and the opportunities for interaction all combine to create a gestalt, an instant impression of Perfect Fit, Run Away Screaming, or something in between. Old-school direct marketers have favored text over graphics, based on years of experience with ugly magazine ads and Courier-font, direct-mail sales letters. That works for some markets, but not most. The Web is a different medium from print, one in which design speaks as loudly as words.

Your AdWords landing page must impress two suitors: Google, and your Web site's visitor. This chapter shows you how to make landing pages that are highly relevant to the keywords and ads that point to them. You discover the most important purpose of a landing page, along with several strategies for achieving that purpose. You find out a few sneaky tricks for building multiple landing pages by doing the work just once. I show you the elements of a landing page that you can tweak to improve performance, and discuss briefly the things you need to know about search engine optimization to increase the quality scores of the keywords pointing to your landing pages.

Making Your Visitor Shout "That's for Me!"

Perry Marshall of www.perrymarshall.com shares a wallet-walloping calculation that should convince you to spend a lot of quality time working on your landing pages:

> *Let's say you pay 50 cents for a click and Barbara in Oregon goes to your Web site and spends eight seconds seeing what you're selling . . . then leaves.*
>
> *50 cents divided by 8 seconds is $225.00 per hour.*
>
> *Barbara in Oregon's attention is pretty expensive, wouldn't you say?*

Now, maybe Barbara was never your customer. She clicked because your ad aroused her curiosity, or was cute, or implied or promised something for nothing. Oh, well, can't win them all. But most Web site owners are told to be satisfied with conversion percentages that are pathetically low: half a percent, one percent. The Web is a numbers game, they're told. Get enough traffic and even a mediocre site can pay the rent.

The Web is a numbers game, true. But who says you have to be satisfied with the numbers? The entire premise of AdWords — in fact, the feature that rocketed AdWords past what is now Yahoo! Search Marketing within months of its birth — was the ease with which campaigns could be tested and improved. This improvement doesn't have to stop at the AdWords border with your Web site. You can deploy the market intelligence you gain by testing keywords and ad copy to create compelling landing pages that continue to attract and guide your best prospects.

The goal of each landing page is to build an instant emotional bond with your prospects, show them you understand their needs, and can take away their pains. From that platform, you present your offer and guide them to take action. Your home page, the one that says, "Welcome to Acme Online Sock Emporium," is hardly ever the right place to take AdWords traffic. If someone walked into your retail Sock Emporium and told you, "I'm looking for red-and-white-striped, over-the-calf dress socks," you wouldn't take them back to the front door and say, "Welcome to Acme Sock Emporium, for the finest in men's and ladies' dress and casual socks; sporting socks; and never-washed, vintage baseball stirrup socks worn by members of the 1958 Championship New York Yankees." Instead, you'd lead them directly to the wall displaying the red-and-white-striped, over-the-calf dress socks and ask them, "What size?" That level of specificity is the purpose of your landing page.

Your retail sock store is probably not located next to other sock stores. But your *online* store's landing page is precisely two clicks away from just about every other online sock store in existence. If your landing page doesn't look like the next point on the shortest distance between your prospect's A and B, whoosh! Barbara from Oregon is here one second, Oregon the next. (Hah! Chapter 10 and my first pun. My sister owes me a dollar.)

Achieving relevance based on keywords

As I discuss in Chapter 5, keywords are the keys to your search visitors' desires. You bundle similar desires into ad groups, and send the traffic from each ad group to a landing page focused on that desire. Everything true about ad copy is also true about Web site copy; the message, the tone, the balance of features and benefits, the next call to action all must connect with the conversation already going on in your prospect's mind. The only difference is, on the Web site you are free from the space constraints and most of the editorial shackles imposed by Google. With great power comes great responsibility, as Peter Parker, another famous Webmaster, learned the hard way in the *Spider-Man* comics. Use the power of your Web site to focus not on your business, but on your customer's desires as suggested by their keywords and the ad that triggered their visit.

If your traffic is derived from AdSense, you don't have a specific keyword to build on. Instead, you know which ad interrupted them like a talking white rabbit and caused them to detour into the rabbit hole of your site. In that case, your landing page should continue the conversation begun by the ad.

For example, if you sell computer training videos on DVD, part of your AdWords account and landing pages might look like the example shown in Table 10-1.

Table 10-1		Linking Keywords and Landing Pages	
Ad Group	**Subject**	**Sample Keywords**	**Landing Page Headline**
Ad Group A1	Microsoft Access Tutorial Keywords	`Microsoft access tutorial, access tutorial, ms access tutorial, access database tutorial`	"Master Microsoft Access at Your Own Pace with This Award-Winning DVD-based Course"
Ad Group A2	Microsoft Access Training Keywords	`access training, access data-base training, Microsoft access computer training`	"Microsoft Access Training at Your Own Pace with this Award-Winning DVD-based Course"
Ad Group A3	Microsoft Access Best Performing Keyword	`[ms Access]`	"Become Certified in MS Access in Just 6 Weeks with This Award-Winning DVD-based Course"
Ad Group A4	Microsoft Excel General Keywords	`excel xp training, excel training, excel 2000 training, excel 2003 training`	"Receive Professional Excel Training from the Comfort of Your Home with this Award-Winning DVD-based Course"

Product-focused landing pages

If you sell physical products, like home office telephone systems or paper shredders or runners' watches with GPS, your landing page presents the most specific product you can offer, based on keyword and ad. The keyword `runners watch` takes visitors to your entire display of runners' watches. `Casio runners watch` produces a page dedicated to that brand (or, if you don't carry Casio, make it a turn-the-corner page that explains why your watches are superior to Casio's). And a search for `Casio GPR-100` should take them to a page devoted to that particular watch.

Concept-focused landing pages

Many online stores do not sell a wide variety of merchandise. Instead, they sell one or two items that solve a certain range of problems. For example, maybe you've invented a clever filing system that automatically purges old files, or reminds people when to pay the energy bill, or sends flowers and chocolate to key people on Valentine's Day. You probably will generate most of your traffic not from searches for the solution (because people don't yet know it exists), but from descriptions of the problem:

```
paper clutter
messy filing system
messy office
```

Or they search for the one aspect of a potential solution that resonates with them at that moment:

```
bill pay reminder system
self-purging files
holiday and birthday reminders
```

Each of the six keywords listed previously should go to a specific landing page that addresses that problem or need. The final destination will be the same for all buyers, but the paths they take from problem to solution depends on where they're starting.

Turn-the-corner landing pages

Sometimes the thing you're selling is related only tangentially to what your prospect is looking for at first. The entire field of consultative sales is based on the premise that your prospects don't really know what they need, and your value as a salesperson is to help them discover "the need behind the need" and help them solve their problem at the most fundamental level. For example, many visitors to www.leadsintogold.com searched for ways to improve their cold-calling performance. The Web site doesn't offer any suggestions or tools for cold calling, except to stop doing it. The job of my landing page is to get my visitor to turn the corner from "I've got to learn how to make better cold calls" to "Cold calling is a flawed strategy, and here's a strategy that works much better."

Pleasing Google with the Title tag

At the very top of your Web browser, above the URL even, you can read the "title" of the page you're visiting. For example, the title for www.askhowie.com is "askHowie.com ~ AdWords Help, Advice and Tools." The title tells Google what your page is about. (Most human visitors to your site never even notice the title, so use it to show Google the connection between your keyword and your landing page.)

You or your Web master can edit the title tag in any HTML authoring program. You can find it in the source code for your page, near the top:

```
<title>askHowie.com ~ AdWords Help, Advice and Tools</
            title>
```

If your landing page has a nondescriptive title, like "Page 3" or "Welcome to VintageDirtySocks.com," Google will charge you more for clicks to punish you for sending traffic to a nonrelevant page.

Using PHP to increase relevance

Through the magic of a programming language called PHP, which either stands for Personal Home Page or PHP Hypertext Preprocessor (thrilling fans of recursiveness everywhere), you can increase the relevance of your landing page based on your visitor's keyword, geographic location, type of computer, and several other factors.

Online marketing coach and PHP consultant Rob Goyette has been quoted as saying, in a phrase borrowed from Napoleon Hill, "Anything the mind can conceive, PHP can achieve." Following are some of Rob's favorite uses of PHP on landing pages. You may be able to use dynamic keyword insertion (described in the next section) on your own, but the rest of the applications require considerable PHP expertise combined with marketing savvy. As they say in the car ads, "Professional driver on closed course. Do not try this at home." Meaning, of course, that the following sections describe what's possible with PHP, but you will need to be, or work with, an experienced Web site programmer to achieve those results. I can't go into detail about programming Web sites, because I don't know squat about it — I mean, it's beyond the scope of this book.

Dynamic keyword insertion

Chapter 6 shows how you can include the exact keyword in your ad through a technique called dynamic keyword insertion. You can configure your landing page to perform the same trick. For example, if your visitor surfed to your site on the keyword `messy office`, you can insert that phrase anywhere you like in your headline, your page text, or your call to action. You'll need to configure the destination URL for each keyword individually; then add PHP code where you want the keyword to appear on the landing page.

If your Web site consists of `.html` files (rather than `.php`), you need to enable PHP in your `.htaccess` file. If you don't know what this means, ask your Webmaster or Web site host.

Magically changing the landing page based on keywords

The first *Harry Potter* book featured a cool gizmo called the Mirror of Erised. People who looked into the mirror saw an image of what their heart desired most. An advanced PHP application turns your landing pages into Mirrors of Erised based on keywords. This function allows you to create one landing page that changes itself like a magic mirror. You save a lot of time by not having to create new pages for each keyword. A site selling college sports clothing and gear could create PHP code that would show Duke basketball shirts and sweatshirts to visitors who arrived with `Duke` and `basketball` in their keyword, and similarly create a UNC page for UNC fans.

Likewise, `baseball`, `lacrosse`, `basketball`, `Missouri`, `Gators`, and `Princeton` would all trigger the dynamic creation of other pages, specifically mirroring the desires suggested by the keywords. The program would also serve a default page for keywords not in its database.

Split-testing with cookies

Split-testing, which I cover in Chapter 13, is one of the most powerful tools at your disposal. You can use *cookies* (tiny snippets of code that identify an individual computer as having visited before — like having your hand stamped at a carnival, except each stamp has your name and address on it) along with PHP to discover which of two different landing pages is doing a better job of converting visitors into leads and sales. You can test headlines, bullets, offers, guarantees, frequently asked questions, placement of forms and buttons and links, as well as colors, fonts, inclusion or exclusion of video or audio, or just about anything else. Done correctly, you don't have to worry about your visitors seeing multiple versions of the same page. When a visitor returns to your page, the cookie your site places on her computer tells your Web server to show the first version she saw (provided the visitor is using the same computer).

Survey to customized sales letter or report

Ask your customers what they're looking for before showing them content. Insert their answers into your page, or show them different content based on their answers. If you sell a diet plan, you can show different sales letters to vegetarians and meat eaters, people who travel a lot and people who don't, and people with diabetes or wheat allergies or berry phobias. If your site asks visitors to opt in (see Chapter 11) in exchange for a free e-book or report, PHP can customize those as well.

Based on location

When you surf the Web, the sites you visit know a lot about you, including where your ISP is located. You could program your landing page to show Duke basketball tank tops to visitors from Hawaii and fleece hooded sweatshirts to visitors from Wisconsin. You can display local phone numbers and store locations, and even translate your site into different languages based on the physical location of your visitor.

Based on operating system

You can show different pages to Windows, Mac, and Linux users, a valuable feature if you sell software. Instead of prompting your visitor with too many choices, simply provide the download link appropriate to the visitor's operating system.

Scraping the Internet

You can triangulate your visitor's geographical location with other information you can find and scrape from the Internet, such as the local weather and traffic reports. I could program www.fitfam.com to greet you with, "Hey, it's noon your time, and it's sunny and warm today. Here's a great exercise you can do in your back yard that will only take five minutes."

Scratching your customer's itch

Showing a "That's for Me" page will keep your visitor on your site for 30 seconds rather than 8. Your next task is to scratch their itch by fulfilling the promise of your ad.

Giving them what they want

If your prospects know exactly what they want, then give it to them. Are they ready to buy an Epiphone Les Paul Special II Sunburst electric guitar? Put a photo, a price, a shipping policy, and a Buy Now button right on the landing page. Are they looking for more information to help them decide what to do next? Give them the information. Do they need to talk to a real human being? Put a phone number on your site and hire someone to answer it 24/7, or during business hours, or whenever your customers call.

Agitating the problem

I don't want to get too disgusting here (actually, I don't mind, but my editor does), but I have to point out something important about this itch metaphor. Scratching an itch feels good for a while, but actually makes the itch worse. Sometimes you can scratch so hard that it turns red and swollen and bleeds. Sometimes in the sales process, you have to agitate the problem and make your prospect feel even worse before they will take action.

If you sell a product that prevents rather than cures, you must be willing to paint the awful picture of what happens when the preventable event — hard drive crash, flood, heart disease, death without a will, yellow teeth, whatever — occurs. Scratching the itch in a case like that means taking advantage of your visitors' momentary spasm of responsibility and making them quake with fear at the prospect of not addressing the issue this very minute, and trembling with relief at having found you.

Guiding them with a headline

Each page on your Web site is about something. The headline — a prominent phrase or sentence near the top of the page — helps your visitor decide whether to spend time on a page by summarizing the content, promising a benefit, or tickling curiosity. Imagine a newspaper without headlines, just articles. How would you decide what to read and what to skip? The headline is a relevance shortcut that also primes the reader for the message to follow.

Establishing credibility

In his popular book *Blink: The Power of Thinking without Thinking*, (published by Little, Brown and Company), Malcolm Gladwell shows how we make snap judgments about most things before we've even thought about them. The neural pathways that establish an emotional reaction are pre-thought. Before your prospect has read a word, identified the subject of a photograph, or listened to a word of audio, they've already decided whether they like you and trust you. They'll never be able to tell you why they feel the way they do because those decisions are outside of consciousness. They'll come up with justifications for their gut reactions, but are usually clueless as to the real causes.

Overall look and feel

Visitors will react instinctively to the design of your landing page. They will assume things about you based on logos, colors, shapes, border styles, text fonts and sizes, and movement. Different markets respond to different gestalts. If you're selling a "secret" of some sort, don't put up a standard corporate Web site. If you want to appear like an established company, spend some money on elegant design elements rather than putting up an ugly sales letter. If you offer bereavement counseling, use a subdued color palette. If you sell violent video games, consider light text on a black background. And so on.

The Web site www.probasketballreferee.com tested two landing pages, identical in every respect except for the border and the header. (See Figure 10-1.) The second page, lacking the graphic elements, received twice as many opt-ins as the first.

Photographs can enhance credibility, especially in a medium comprised entirely of electrons. Show visitors your face, your store, your warehouse, your products. Asepco, a firm that manufactures valves for the pharmaceutical industry, put a photo slide show on its site that documented the odyssey of one of its valves from the mountain where the ore was mined to the finished product. It changes location frequently, so check www.askhowie.com/valve for the updated Web address.

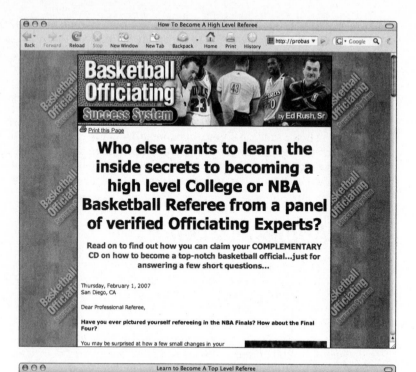

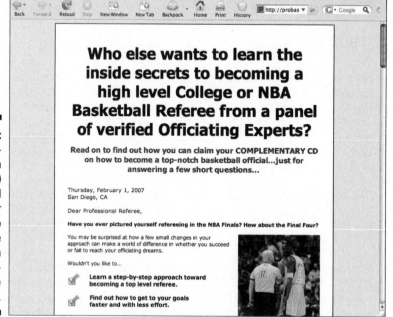

Figure 10-1:
The graphically rich page (top) convinced fewer visitors to request the free CD than did the simpler page (bottom).

Basically, you want to subliminally get across the message that "this trust-worthy business will be around tomorrow." To achieve this, visit successful competitors' sites, talk to graphic designers, and test different designs just as the Pro Basketball Referee site did.

Specific visual cues

In addition to the overall look and feel, you can add specific graphical elements that lend credibility by association, as shown in Figure 10-2. These include credit card logos, PayPal, credit card processors like VeriSign; shippers' logos (such as those of UPS, FedEx, and the U.S. Postal Service); as well as Web site certifications, such as the Better Business Bureau's BBB Online Reliability Program, Hacker Safe, and Trust-e.

Figure 10-2: The My Wedding Favors site devotes a large amount of space to "credibility-by-association" logos.

Another type of visual reassurance is the presence of subliminal "I Am Not a Crook" links, including privacy policy, Web site terms and conditions, shipping and refund policies, disclaimers, and so on. I'm not sure anyone actually *reads* these documents, but their very presence can be reassuring.

Finally, the more contact options you include, the less you look like a fly-by-night with something to hide. Post office boxes don't cut it; instead, get a real mailing address that gives the impression of an office. Give a phone number. Put your e-mail address where people can find it.

When you display your e-mail address on your Web site, put it in an image file rather than a live link. This will prevent spambots from harvesting it and sending you hundreds of unwanted e-mails every day.

Defining the Most Desirable Action for the Landing Page

Before creating your landing pages, as well as every page on your site, ask yourself the big question: What's the one thing I want my visitor to do as a result of visiting this page? The possible actions include reading, watching, and listening; clicking a link; completing a form; making or requesting a phone call; or engaging in live chat.

Most clients I've worked with can identify a "point of no return" for their customers; a place in the sales cycle that, once reached, typically leads to a sale. For example:

- ✔ "Once they request the free DVD, 90 percent of them become customers."
- ✔ "Once I get them to call, I sell 75 percent of them right there on the phone."
- ✔ "After they request a quote, almost all of them sign up for the service."

If you have a step in your sales process that converts lookers to buyers, then everything about your landing page should be engineered to get as many visitors to that step as possible. And in most cases, the first step on the way to the point of no return is getting your visitor's e-mail address.

"Bribing" your visitor to opt in

Sometimes your landing page can go for the sale. In other cases, your prospect needs more information or more time before taking out a credit card. In either case, the big goal of your landing page is to make sure your visitors do not leave your site without giving you a way of contacting them in the future. If that way also includes a financial transaction, so much the better. But it's often more profitable to aim for a second date than to propose marriage on the first date.

Business on the Internet is a multi-step process — a series of small, safe, mutual commitments that allow your prospect to begin to trust you — and allow you to qualify the prospect. This process is the business equivalent of dating. Your job is to get on your prospects' wavelength so quickly and completely that they regard you as their "one and only." Remember, the page after your landing page is three clicks away from your competitor, using the Back button. The deeper they go, the more of a psychological commitment they're making to you.

An *opt-in,* in Internet marketing parlance, refers to a visitor who has given you an e-mail address, at the very least, before leaving your site. Essentially, an opt-in is permission to call them for a date. In the old days of the Internet (pre-2001), all you had to do was offer a free newsletter to get opt-ins. These days, with everyone protecting their e-mail inboxes from mountains of spam, visitors hesitate to sign up for anything. The last thing they need is more e-mail from someone else trying to sell them something, even if you're not peddling fake Rolexes and enlarged body parts.

In order to get their e-mail address and permission to follow up, you need to demonstrate value and promise future value. www.leadsintogold.com contains a long letter about cold calling and its alternatives, which many people have told me is eye-opening in its own right. In several places on the home page, I offer visitors a chance to download two free chapters of Leads into Gold, so they can sample the product before making a buying decision (as shown in Figure 10-3). The request for the opt-in makes sense because I need their e-mail address to send them the free chapters. It is natural, not forced, so it works well. Note that I also ask for their names, which gives me the ability to address my follow-up e-mails to them personally ("Dear Ralph Lauren").

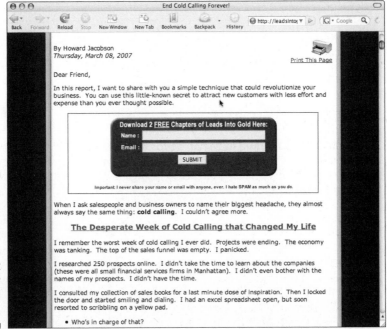

Figure 10-3:
Following up with prospects requires getting at least their e-mail address.

Many marketers make the opt-in the only option on the landing page. The so-called "squeeze page" provides no links, no other navigation, and no context to the visitor. Google now frowns upon these pages, largely because they discovered that their users hated them.

Online marketing strategist Sean D'Souza has crafted a Web site — www.psychotactics.com — that still gets visitors' names and e-mails without forcing anything. Here are his (and my) opinions about opt-in strategy:

Squeeze or No-Squeeze

Imagine you went for a date with a person you hadn't met before. And your date wore a paper bag on his/her head. He/She refused to show you his/her face. That date refused to tell you anything about his/her past. Or let you into any information at all. Yet you had to give them information. Like your first name, last name, blah, blah, blah.

How do you feel?

Well that's exactly how the customers feel. They feel irritated, frustrated, and to choose a mild word: trapped. They know they want the information, but they can't seem to get any information from you without filling in that stupid form.

Squeeze pages are contrary to human nature. They force you into a corner. They force you to part with information based on some random headline and bullet points.

So why do we have so many squeeze pages on the Internet? Why do people catch colds and coughs? Yes, one person has it, and then it spreads. One person put in a squeeze page, then everyone else decided to follow suit. Don't get me wrong. Squeeze pages work. They work wonderfully.

Well, so does Bruno, who's six foot nine inches and weighs 400 pounds. Just because it works doesn't mean you have to follow suit. Because there are other things that work. Like non-threatening, non-Bruno, no-squeeze pages. Pages that get you to sign up not through intimidation and fear. But pages that get you to sign up because you want to do so. Because persuasion is stupid. Persuasion implies that you acted against your nature. And why get customers to act against their nature when they will gladly give you information?

A good opt-in page should entice. It should give you lots of details. It should answer your every question or objection. It should not make you feel icky, like being on a blind date.

At Psychotactics, we've collected names, addresses, home numbers, postal addresses, mobile numbers, city, country on our opt-in pages. All without twisting anyone's arms. We've done it to entice customers to subscribe to the newsletter.

Or to opt-in to a workshop. Or to buy a product or service. Our customers give us bucket loads of information, because they trust us. They believe in us. They know they're not on a yucky blind date.

I'd rather have that kind of customer, wouldn't you? Sure beats being squeezed!

Go to www.psychotactics.com and have a look around. And if you do subscribe (which I highly recommend), you'll experience Sean's noncoercive, warm and fuzzy opt-in process for yourself. (I can attest personally to the effectiveness of this method, as I use it on www.askhowie.com with great results.)

The folks at www.novamind.com sell mind-mapping software. The top goal of their Web site is to entice visitors to download the free 30-day trial version of the product. Because they know that visitors who try the software typically buy the software, they don't even require an e-mail address.

If you can afford to spend real money on leads, you can collect snail mail addresses by offering a physical packet: a CD, a DVD, a book, a report, a 5-day supply of wrinkle cream, and such. E-mail is very cheap, but not very stable. A physical mailing address is not subject to spam filters or the whims of unreliable servers and switches. Also, the avalanche of spam e-mail that floods most people's inboxes daily makes it hard for your legitimate sales messages to get the attention they deserve. The motto for e-mail could be, "When you absolutely, positively don't really care if the message ever gets through."

Getting permission to continue the relationship is such a fundamental goal that I devote all of Chapter 11 to the opt-in and e-mail follow-up.

Engaging visitors in real time

The opt-in allows you to follow up with your visitors by e-mail, in what online geeks refer to as an *asynchronous* fashion. This fancy word (*asynchronous*, not *fashion*) means there is a gap between when the message is created and when it is received. This book is an extreme example of asynchronous communication, as I'm writing it long before you will read it (unless you believe, based on my prescience and wisdom, that I am actually a time traveler from the year 2036 who came back to the first decade of the 21st century and couldn't land a better gig than this book).

This form of communication fits well with the pie-in-the-sky dream of the Internet as a business medium where you never have to deal with customers: You just create a Web site, write a bunch of e-mails that are sent automatically, and check your inbox for incoming orders. That strategy can work, to a degree, but everyone I've worked with has found that adding real-time, live engagement to their Web site boosts sales significantly.

The telephone is a much underused online marketing tool. Get a toll-free phone number, place it prominently on your Web site next to the calling hours ("24 hours a day, 7 days a week" is a good policy), and offer them a reason to call. Figure 10-4 graces the top of the www.unlockthegame.com home page, while Figure 10-5 appears at the top of the www.mywedding favors.com site.

Figure 10-4:
Around the clock customer service.

Figure 10-5:
Set your phone hours to convenient times.

Selling the Most Desirable Action

After you define your sales process, your next big question is, "What stands between customers and the next step?" If you want them to download your free report, what do they need to be feeling and thinking in order to go ahead and do it? If you want them to call, what might cause them to hesitate and then bail? If you're asking for the sale, what action-freezing second thoughts might they be entertaining?

A cliché in the sales world is that you have to work as hard to sell a $10 item as a $10 million item. On the Internet, you have to work just about as hard to give something away free. Your landing pages must answer your prospects' questions, reassure their doubts, assuage their fears, and guide them clearly to what they should do next.

I have an entire library filled with books and manuals dedicated to the creation of effective sales copy. The masters of persuasive copy know a lot of tricks and techniques, but the basis for their effectiveness is a deep knowledge of what their prospects want to have and want to avoid. As you can read in Chapter 4, marketing tricks without having your finger on the pulse of a substantial market is like doing a technically perfect triple gainer into an empty swimming pool. So the following copywriting tasks can be accomplished effectively only against the backdrop of market insight.

Using bullets

Sales bullets are the foundation for all effective sales copy, whether they appear in actual bullet form on the page or not. Ken McCarthy, my copywriting teacher, gave me a very useful phrase to focus on whenever I sit down to write sales copy: Bullets Wound. (*Wound* here rhymes with *swooned*.) In other words, the purpose of the bullet is to highlight and stretch the gap in your visitor's mind between their current and ideal situations. The cure for the bullet is the next action you want them to take: read, click, download, call, chat, buy, whatever. Figure 10-6 shows some benefit bullets that I use to sell my Traffic Surge telecourse at askhowie.com/traffic.

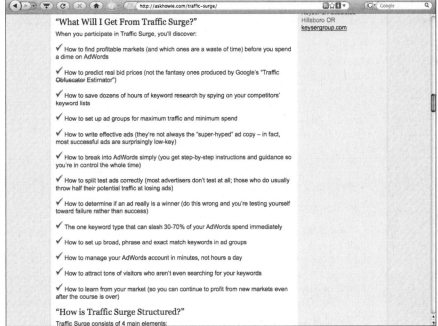

Figure 10-6: Bullets can arouse curiosity, make big promises, and bring features to life.

Translating features into benefits

As sellers, we become intimately acquainted with the facts of our products and services. It glows in the dark; it comes in extra large; it has a self-cleaning button; it's made from shea butter; and so on. After a while, we are in danger of operating under the illusion that our prospects understand why these features are important and beneficial. They don't have a clue, and if we fail to *translate* features into benefits, then we are asking our prospects to do interpretive work they have no interest in doing.

Here's a quick formula for figuring whether a particular statement is a feature or a benefit. Write down the statement. Look at it. Ask yourself whether your most impolite and brash customer could conceivably read it and snarl, "So what?" If so, you've got yourself a *feature*, not a benefit.

To turn a feature into a benefit, write down the feature, add the words ". . . and what this means to you is . . ." and then complete the sentence. Ken McCarthy thinks of this as "bringing the facts to life." For example, one of my clients, poly-D, is a company that manufactures a metered dispensing system (MDS) for household, pharmaceutical, and industrial applications. Isn't that exciting?

Actually, the technology *is* exciting. But calling the feature a "metered dispensing system" asks the prospects — for example, brand managers in charge of cleaning products, toiletries, and food and beverage lines — to do way too much work.

The first pass at turning a feature into a benefit often creates not a true benefit, but a clearer feature set. For example, the MDS uses a button-operated vacuum pump to dispense the liquid, gel, or ointment it contains.

It's the job of the product marketer to bring each of these features to life. The fact that MDS dispenses a product via a button-operated vacuum pump means the product

- Can be dispensed one-handed
- Gives a consistent dose
- Eliminates leaks and spills
- Gets 98 percent of the liquid, gel, or ointment out of the package

Each of those features can become a benefit:

- **One-handed dispensing:** Tired parents can hold a sick, thrashing toddler in one arm and pour the medicine into a cup with the other.
- **Consistent dose:** The tired parents don't have to worry about finding a measuring spoon or misreading the dosing directions.
- **No leaks or spills:** The tired parents don't end up with cough syrup running down their pajama tops or oozing between their toes into the shag carpet.
- **98 percent product evacuation:** The tired parents don't have to hold the cough syrup upside down for five minutes, waiting for the final drips to exit the bottle. No waste — they get to use what they've paid for.

The sales material we created for poly-D brings the features of the MDS to life for the brand managers, as well as for the end user. We didn't assume the brand managers could translate the experience of a tired parent with a sick kid into a benefit relevant to them, so we did it for them. In the white paper available at `www.poly-d.com`, we explain that the MDS instantly gives their existing products a new and dramatically different marketing story. We help them see how effective their advertising campaigns could be, with a real consumer benefit to tout. Make sure your benefits relate directly to what you know or believe your prospects want. Your goal is to help your prospects visualize the movie of their future, a future made rosy by the action they're about to take.

Provoking curiosity

If the next action involves education of your prospects, you have to whet their appetites for the information you have and they don't. Bullets that provoke curiosity include teasers ("The most dangerous seat on an airplane — page 5"), hidden information ("Best-kept secret in the travel industry"), promise of valuable knowledge ("How to spot slot machines that pay off most often"), warnings ("Surprise! Choosing the wrong private school for your child can cost you a bundle in tax breaks"), and questions ("Would you know how to keep your ticket safe if you won the lottery?").

Useful But Incomplete: If I wanted you to go to `askhowie.com/loms` and read the entire sales letter, I would tease you with a partial list in Figure 10-6 and imply that the really good stuff is just behind the curtain, waiting for your visit.

Including third-party testimonials

For several reasons, third-party testimonials can sell more powerfully than you can. They can pull off this bit of magic because they are

- ✔ **Believable:** Your visitors have (unfortunately) been taught many times that salespeople will lie through their teeth to make a sale. Until you prove otherwise, you're presumed to be in that category. Your customers who say nice things about you don't have anything to gain by lying. On the contrary, they're risking their own "credibility capital" by going out on a limb and endorsing you.

- ✔ **Polite:** Grandma said that it's impolite to brag. If you can get your satisfied customers to do it for you, you can look bashfully pleased instead of boastful — while still getting your message across.

- ✔ **Benefit-based:** Testimonials are already formulated to highlight benefits because customers create them rather than you.

You can deploy four testimonial media on your landing page: video, audio, written text, and contact for more information. Video can be extremely effective if done well, but tends to be expensive, time-consuming, and a pain for your customers to give you. Ken McCarthy uses video testimonials effectively at the www.thesystemseminar.org sales page. Because all his customers were in one place — his seminar — it was cost-effective to hire a video crew and collect the testimonials.

Audio testimonials can be almost as powerful, and are much less expensive and time-consuming to produce. You can collect audio testimonials just by asking your customers to pick up a telephone and talk. Try it now: Call (214) 615-6505, extension 6900 and say something nice about this book. I may post your comment at www.askhowie.com/readercomments. You have to pay long-distance charges (because I'm a cheapskate), but you can set up a toll-free audio line for just a few dollars a month. Visit www.askhowie.com/audio for recommended services and advanced testimonial-gathering strategies.

Written testimonials by themselves are the least powerful, simply because you might have written them yourself. But by adding the written text below an audio or video, you can have the best of both worlds: believability and multiple modes of message delivery.

Finally, you can let your visitors know you have "references available upon request." This can work for big purchases later in the sales cycle; on the landing page, focus on delivering needed information immediately.

Giving clear instructions in the call to action

Somebody once said, "A confused mind always says 'no.'" In fact, if you're reading this book out loud, you just said it. Make sure your instructions for the action you want visitors to take are so clear and free of ambiguity that a reasonably intelligent hamster could follow them.

Not only will you explain exactly how to fill out the form, where the form is located, and what to click, but you will also tell them what happens next. What page will be served after they click "Send me the two free chapters!"? What will appear in their inboxes and in what time frame? Do they need to add you to their spam filters' white lists? If they phone you, who will answer? What extension should they ask for?

Tony Robbins likes to say that humans have a simultaneous need for certainty and excitement — a balance between what is known and what is unknown. At the point where someone is considering entering into a relationship with your Web site, your job is to reduce the already considerable uncertainty.

Chapter 11

Following Up with Your Prospects

In This Chapter

▶ Building the relationship with e-mail

▶ "Bribing" your visitors for their e-mail addresses

▶ Putting e-mail marketing on autopilot

▶ Staying on the right side of the spam police

*I*ndulge me for a moment and try this experiment. Think about the Web sites you browsed yesterday (or the most recent day you were online). Roughly, how many sites were there? What were they? Take a minute and write down as many as you can remember. When you're done, open your Web browser and view your browsing history. How many sites did you forget? How many of those sites are you likely ever to visit again?

The point of this experiment: If you're anything like me, you visited a lot of sites, found some of them interesting, but got distracted and left without leaving yourself a convenient and reliable way back. Your Web site visitors are the same. You work like crazy to build a great AdWords campaign, pay real money for visitors, and most of them vanish like dust in the wind (to quote one of my favorite folk-rock songs of the 1970s).

You haven't bored your Web site's visitors, or offended them, or disqualified them. They just weren't ready to transact business with you at that moment. Or a phone call, incoming e-mail sound, fax, co-worker, daydream, flashback, or UFO sighting distracted them. What a shame, too. You spend so much time, money, and energy to get them into a sales funnel that turns out to operate more like a sieve.

In this chapter, I show you some strategies and tools for following up with prospects after they leave your Web site. You discover easy methods for deploying effective follow-up sequences that you create once and put on autopilot. You see how to use e-mail autoresponders and newsletters to become your prospect's one and only. And you integrate telephone and mail strategies to keep your business on the radar screen.

Overcoming Your Prospects' Miniscule Online Attention Span

Your average Web site visitor has the attention span of a guppy — deal with it. Online attention spans are notoriously short, but merchants have known for a long time that a sale delayed is generally a sale lost. The infomercial must get a couch potato to the phone, credit card in hand, before the thumb touches the TV remote. The direct mail subscription pitch must compel action before the reader puts the letter down to grab a cold drink from the kitchen because soon that letter will be in the middle of a pile, instead of at the top. And the salesperson at the car dealership wants the prospect to commit today, before comparison-shopping a better deal in the next county.

Pressure tactics don't work online

The traditional sales approach to any sort of buyer hesitation and reluctance has been to wrestle prospects to the ground, lock them into a half nelson (full nelsons prevent them from signing the credit card slip), and shove a vacuum cleaner hose into their pocket or purse and suck out the money. In the offline world, this translates into pressure tactics, fake scarcity, fake urgency, aggressively overcoming objections, and various sleazy tricks. Salespeople are taught that, "I'll think about it" means "No, and you can kiss your commission goodbye."

That attitude is crazy. Sure, prospects lie to avoid conflict and to keep from hurting our feelings. But sometimes prospects are telling the truth when they say they need to think it over. If they are forced into a decision before they're ready, the decision will almost certainly be *no*. If the high-pressure tactics work, the buyer's remorse refund rate will be astronomical. Moreover, those customers will not be sources of referral business because they want to protect their friends from unpleasant experiences.

I could debate the relative effectiveness of these tactics in the face-to-face world, but it's clear that they don't work so well on the Internet. Don't like a Web site? It's gone at the click of a button, no hard feelings. Give yourself a reality check about online manners and inhibitions by visiting a Yahoo! chat group some time. Perfectly mild-mannered folks who wouldn't dream of so much as coughing if someone cut in front of them in the supermarket line turn into raving lunatics online, slinging mud and brimstone safe in the shelter of their anonymity. Trust me: The second your visitor is annoyed by your site, he or she disappears faster than Roadrunner in a cloud of smoke. (Insert your own sound effects.)

Build a relationship so you can make the sale when your prospect is ready to buy

Your mission, should you choose to run a successful online venture, is fourfold:

- ✔ **Get your prospects' contact information.** You want their e-mail at the very least, more if you can get it. The more you ask for, the fewer prospects will convert to leads (I define a *lead* as someone you can follow up with), and the more serious they will be.

- ✔ **Receive their explicit permission to stay in touch.** People don't always realize that you will be using their contact information to contact them, probably because it occurs so rarely in the offline world. Prospects are used to dropping their business cards into a fishbowl for a chance to win dinner for four, or giving the supermarket all their contact information in exchange for a loyalty card, and never hearing a peep after that. If you assume that an e-mail address represents an open invitation to visit their inbox, you'll be rudely awakened faster than they can hit the Report Spam button in their e-mail program. Enough spam complaints and your Web site is basically out of business.

- ✔ **Provide such helpful and credible advice, guidance, and support that your visitors never ever go searching on that topic again.** Perry Marshall refers to this as "taking your prospect off the market." When prospects are actively searching for information, they go wide, looking at a lot of sites and getting the lay of the land. They don't want to become the world expert; they're just looking for someone to trust, to hold their hand and lead them. Your follow-up will determine if you become that trusted resource or not.

- ✔ **Build a relationship that leads naturally to a win-win outcome.** Database marketing consultant Lori Feldman (www.thedatabasediva. com) reminds us, "The purpose of a business is to grow a customer." Not just to get the sale. A sale is a one-time transaction. A customer is a living, breathing asset. The relationship you build with leads may lead to sales, referrals of their friends, testimonials, and more. But the goal of the relationship is not to close the deal, but to determine if a sale is a win-win outcome or not. The most expensive customers in your database are the ones you shouldn't be selling to. They take up too much time, demand too much special help, and don't buy anything else from you.

Spinning a Web with an Opt-In

In Chapter 10, I identify the opt-in as one of the top goals of any landing page. An opt-in refers to a prospect who has opted into your database with the expectation of receiving follow-up communications from you. Depending on the market, the quality of traffic to your landing page, your offer, and how you describe that offer, you can aim for an opt-in rate from 20–50 percent, sometimes higher. If your opt-in rate is lower than 20 percent, you're doing something wrong. This chapter helps you fix your opt-in process.

Unlike a spider that spins a web to ensnare — and subsequently eat — its prey, you spin a customer-catching Web site to ensure a second date with your prospects. The opt-in takes all the pressure off the first visit. They can buy if they like, but, hey, no big deal if they don't. If your Web site has to make the sale on the first visit, your prose is likely to come across as desperate. And desperate is not attractive, not at junior high school dances, and not in sales. The more desperate you seem, the more it looks like there's something wrong with you.

The most common method of acquiring an opt-in is through a form on your Web site. Figure 11-1 shows a form that I use on www.askhowie.com to get visitors to download my AdWords ER Report, "Why Most AdWords Campaigns Fail, and How to Make Yours Succeed." Opt-in forms can also be embedded into sales copy, as I do in the body of the www.askhowie.com home page. (Notice that the entire function of this page is to get the visitor to subscribe — even the testimonials refer specifically to the ER Report and the BOPzine (Breakthrough Online Profits e-zine) that they get in exchange for their e-mail address.)

Figure 11-1:
A short
opt-in form
offering
an Action
Guide.

Whatever e-mail service you use to send e-mails and manage your list will help you generate the HTML code or JavaScript that puts the form on your Web site. Later in this chapter, I show you the vendor I use and recommend a few others for comparison.

If you thought you could do e-mail marketing using Outlook Express or Yahoo Mail, you were mistaken. If you have more than 20 leads in your database, you will need a specialized application to get the e-mails out, manage your list in accordance with anti-spam rules, and keep your sanity.

Generating an opt-in form using AWeber

For the purposes of this chapter, I'm going to use my preferred vendor, AWeber Communications, to show you how to set up and manage e-mail fol- low-up. If you already have a shopping cart with e-mail capabilities, you will have to adapt the instructions accordingly. If you don't yet have an e-mail- marketing provider, sign up for an account at www.aweber.com. (For a video tutorial and overview of the e-mail marketing process, visit www.askhowie. com/email first.) Currently, AWeber costs $19 per month for the first 500 subscribers. Just to put this cost in perspective, you can now send unlimited e-mails to up to 500 people at a time, as many times as you want. If you give $19 to the U.S. Postal Service, you can buy 43 first-class stamps and still have eight cents left over for envelopes and paper. (That's as of summer 2009, so you'll have to do the math yourself when rates rise again.)

Before you build the opt-in form, you need a place to send your visitors after they complete the form. This page should confirm the success of their opt-in ("Thank you for signing up for the Nose Hair Removal Secrets 42-Day E-mail Course"), describe what they'll be receiving next and where and when to look for it ("Check your e-mail inbox in about 5 minutes for Installment 1: Don't Use a Butane Lighter While Waiting at a Gas Station"), and suggest a next action ("While you're waiting, let me tell you about an amazing new way to remove nasal hair without tweezers, dry ice, or gas flames . . . "). Don't worry about getting it perfect — for our purposes right now, all you need is a working URL to send your lead. Name the page something like www.*yoursite.com/* signupthanks.html and remember the name.

When the thank-you page is done, you're ready to sign up for an AWeber account as follows:

1. **Go to www.aweber.com and click the Order button at the top.**

   Choose any plan you like, from one month to a full year — you get 30 days during which you can get a full refund. If you like it, the annual plan is the best value; e-mail marketing is a long-term tool.

2. **After placing your order, you're taken to a page with a link to log in to the Control Panel. Click that link.**

AWeber immediately sends you an e-mail with your login and password.

3. **Enter your new login and password, click Account at the top right, and change your password to something you'll remember.**

4. **Return to the Home page and click the Getting Started — Setup Guide link.**

5. **Choose Web Form Wizard to create your first opt-in form.**

6. **On the next page, click the green Create Web Form button in the center of the page and fill out the form details (see Figure 11-2).**

7. **In the Form Name text box, enter a name for your form that you'll remember later.**

   Only you see the form name, so don't worry about being clever. Just describe it so you can find it later among the many forms you'll create.

8. **Select the type of form you're using.**

   The form type can be in-line (that is, within the Web page itself), or a pop-up, pop-under, or pop-over/hover. Google won't let you use pop-ups, exit pops, or pop-unders on a landing page, and they really annoy people, so forget about those options. The pop-over/hover isn't actually a pop-up; instead, it's a graphic that's technically part of your Web page even though it appears to float above it. Google has mixed feelings about this; sometimes it disables your ads if they point to pages with pop-overs, and sometimes it doesn't. Stick with an in-line form for now.

9. **Enter a URL that you created for your "Thank you for opting in" page in the Thank You Page text box.**

   The page must exist already, or else AWeber gets persnickety. If you don't have a thank you page ready, either enter your home page for now, or leave the AWeber default page. Just don't forget to come back and change it later. I talk about strategies for this page later in this chapter.

10. **As the instructions say, leave the Forward Variables check box blank if you don't know what it means.**

    Later on, you can use this feature to customize the thank-you page, just as you can do with PHP on the landing page (see Chapter 10).

11. **(Optional) Enable ad tracking by entering some unique description for this form in the Ad Tracking text box.**

    You can use ad tracking to segment your list based on the particular form your lead used to opt in. This ability to segment comes in handy, say, if each ad group leads to a different landing page. You can name the traffic source or the page in the Ad Tracking field so you can find all the leads who were interested in red wagons as opposed to green tricycles. If you place a form more than once on the same page (at the top of the right sidebar and below the landing page text, for example), you can even track which form collected the opt-in.

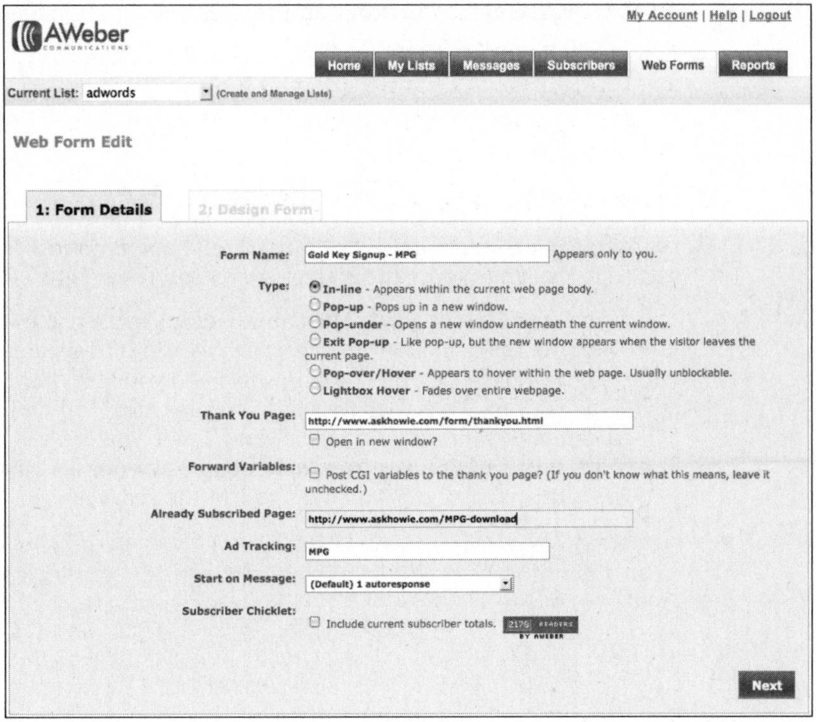

Figure 11-2:
Creating
an opt-in
form using
AWeber.

12. **Leave the Start on Message drop-down list at the default for now: (Default) 1 Autoresponse.**

An *autoresponse* is an automatic e-mail that your leads get from you. The default setting means they'll receive all the autoresponse e-mails in the sequence, starting with the first one.

13. **Click Next to design the form:**

The instructions for this part are pretty straightforward on the AWeber site:

a. If you hover your mouse pointer over the Name field on the left, you see a plus sign. Click it to add that field to your form.

b. Just below the Name field, you can click the Add New Field link to add more fields if you want to collect a visitor's address, phone number, pet's name, favorite flavor of Vice Cream, annual income, innie or outie belly button, and so on.

c. When you add a new field, you see a check box labeled Subscriber Update. Check this box if you want your lead to be able to change this information later.

d. You can change the order of the fields by clicking and dragging them up or down. Edit a field by holding your mouse over it and clicking the pencil icon. Four options appear to the left:

Required: Does your prospect have to fill out this field to opt in, or is it optional?

Type of Field: In addition to plain text, you can include drop-down lists and radio buttons for multiple choice questions, check boxes for yes/no, and a larger text area to give the prospect the visual cue that they can write a short novel here.

Label and Default Value: The Label text box is used in conjunction with the Default Value field (see the following) to segment your list later. For example, if you put this form on your Juggling Scarves for Kids page, you can include a hidden field called Product and make the default value Jr. Juggling Scarves. Later, you can search for this value and send a scarf coupon to people on your list who opted in from this page and haven't yet bought the scarves (see Figure 11-3).

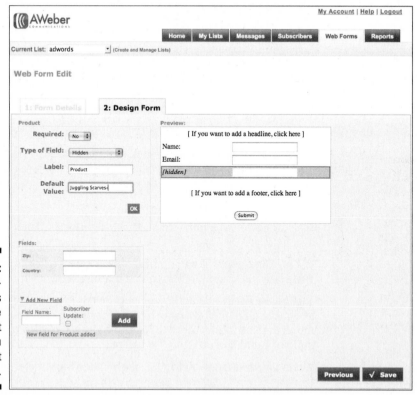

Figure 11-3: Use hidden fields to include data that will help you segment your list.

14. **(Optional) Click the Submit button at the bottom of the form to rename it.**

    I generally give the button a title that sounds like my prospect making a request: "Send Me the Action Guide!"

15. **When you finish editing the form, click the Save button (bottom right), and you're ready to get the code for your opt-in page.**

Placing the form on your Web site

After you create your Web form on the AWeber site, you need to get the code that you'll place in your opt-in Web page. In the AWeber List Settings tab, select Web Form from the submenu. If you've created your first form, you'll see it in the list. Click Preview to see what the form looks like by itself. If everything is in the right order and you're ready to stick it on a page in your site, close the pop-up window and select Get HTML.

AWeber gives you a new window with two code options. The top one, shown in Figure 11-4, is in JavaScript, and consists of a single line of code that you place on your page's HTML where you want the form to appear. The script goes to AWeber's Web site and pulls the form onto your page. As long as you don't need to change the look and feel of the form, this is a good option. It allows you to collect statistics on how many times the form was displayed, which you need to determine your opt-in rate.

Figure 11-4: To use the form without making design changes, add this snippet of code to your Web page.

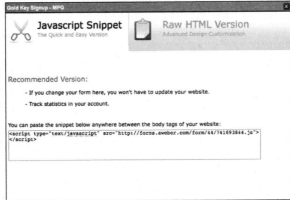

If you want more control over the design of the form, select and copy the raw HTML code from the lower box. Your Web designer can use this code to make the opt-in form blend in with the rest of your page. You can see an example of a designed AWeber opt-in form; visit www.poly-d.com and click through to the white paper offer.

Visit www.askhowie.com/forms to see examples of both codes.

Generating opt-ins via e-mail

You can also generate opt-ins via e-mail. For example, if you send a blank e-mail to askhowie@aweber.com, within about a minute you'll get an e-mail with the subject line, "RESPONSE REQUIRED: Confirm your request for information from askhowie" or something like that. When you click the first link within that e-mail, you're added to my list and will start receiving my e-mail messages. (See the following section for a discussion of this double opt-in process.)

Importing and adding leads yourself

AWeber and most other e-mail marketing services allow you to import existing lists and add new leads manually as well. The better services — the ones you want to use — send all these prospects a RESPONSE REQUIRED type of e-mail to make sure they want to receive your messages. It's a pain, but if your service doesn't require this, I predict that a lot of your e-mail messages will not make it through the spam filters. It's counterintuitive, but I won't use a service that *doesn't* verify my imported lists.

You and I are honest and ethical, of course, and would never send out thousands of spam messages to people who don't want them. But if the e-mail service I use allows *other* people to do just that, the spam filters will catch my e-mails as well as those of the spammers, because they are all being sent from the same server. Using a lax e-mail service is like putting the return address *Seedytown* on your envelopes. Don't risk it.

How to "Bribe" Your Prospects to Opt In

The mechanics of the opt-in are straightforward: Place a form on your site, tell people to fill it out, send them to a thank-you page, and start e-mailing. The only thing missing is the answer to your prospect's question, "Why on earth should I give you my name and contact information?" People protect their inboxes like geese protecting their nests. The last thing they want is a bunch of annoying e-mails trying to sell them something. The keys to achieving a high opt-in rate are to

- ✔ Give away something of value.
- ✔ Make the opt-in in a logical next step in the relationship rather than a form of online extortion.
- ✔ Offer your visitors something they really want.
- ✔ Reassure them.

Give away something of value

When I was little, my dad used to take me to Sonny Amster's bakery on Vauxhall Road in Millburn on Sunday mornings to get rolls and bagels for brunch. My most vivid memories of those trips were the hundreds of free cookies I consumed. Mr. Amster understood the power of giving away a free sample before asking for the sale. He knew that if he could give away something of value before asking for the sale, he was likely to ring up a bigger order than if he insisted on payment before the munching began.

Not only did my dad sometimes add a dozen cookies to our order, he felt compelled to buy as an act of reciprocity. As Robert Cialdini explains in his book, *Influence: The Psychology of Persuasion* (published by Collins), when someone does something nice for us, we feel a powerful urge to balance the scales by doing something nice in return. This principle is often used to manipulate us, but works even better when it's genuine.

 You can give away something of value as a prequel to the opt-in. If you sell unicycles and generate traffic with a Unicycle Beginners ad group, give away a free guide on the seven steps to learning to ride. Put Steps 1 and 2 right on the landing page, and offer the remaining five steps in an e-mail. Make the first half of an article about choosing your first unicycle available on your site, and ask for an e-mail address to send them the second half. Put a video on your site showing the first step, and offer a series of how-to-ride videos in exchange for the opt-in.

Make the opt-in a logical next step

To grasp the concept of a logical next step, return with me to the metaphor of the museum where people go to find the love of their life. You're standing next to an attractive person whom you'd like to know better, looking at the postmodern painting of a 12-foot-high piece of lined notebook paper. The person glances in your direction, smiles, and says something like, "I wonder what music the artist was listening to while she was painting this." You say, "I'll tell you what I think if you give me your e-mail address." End of conversation, no?

The request for their e-mail address had nothing to do with the prior conversation. On your Web site, your opt-in will not work if it's just a thinly veiled attempt to build your list.

If you need inspiration, consider the tech-support hotline model. Have you ever waited on hold for 20 minutes for tech support, listening to cheesy music or endless repetitions of "Your call is important to us, and we will answer your call in the order it was received"? And then you get a live person, start explaining the problem, and 30 seconds later you hear a click and a busy signal? After years of this treatment, I finally got a technician who began the call by asking for my phone number and e-mail address "in case we get disconnected." Boy, was I ever so happy to give away my information. I received a logical reason to share that information, so I did.

Why do you need your visitors' e-mail addresses? What are you going to send them via e-mail? Why do they want it? If you ask for a phone number, how will they benefit from your call? Spell it out: "Leave your phone number if you'd like to talk about which perennials will thrive in your garden."

I asked Seth Godin (www.sethgodin.com), author of the very important book, *Permission Marketing: Turning Strangers into Friends and Friends into Customers* (Simon & Schuster), his thoughts about trying to compel your visitors to opt in because you're trying to build your list. Seth didn't beat around the bush:

> *What you want is irrelevant. Of course, it matters what you want if you have power, if you can force people to do what you want. The reality is that the new paradigm demands humility. You will either engage people on their terms or you will fail to engage them. Your choice.*

Offer your visitors something they really want

Every marketing campaign consists of three factors:

- ✔ **The market:** In the case of your AdWords landing page, the market is initially determined by the keyword and then funneled through your ad.

- ✔ **The creative:** This is everything you show your market to get them to accept your offer — text, graphics, audio, video, and so on.

- ✔ **The offer:** This is the bait, the thing they really want.

Marketers like to spend a lot of time massaging the creative part because it's fun and they have the most control over it. But the success (95 percent of it, anyway) of your campaigns depends on one thing: how well the offer matches the market. In other words, is this bait something your visitors want?

In dating, someone gives you their phone number for one reason only: they're hoping you give them a call some time. Your job is to become so appealing that your prospects actually want to hear from you again. They look forward to your e-mails. They get value (and perhaps entertainment) from every point of contact.

You already know what your AdWords traffic wants because they told you by clicking your ad. You can use the ad to split-test features of your offer (free report, e-mail course, PDF delivered by e-mail, fax, small lead-lined box flown to your door by 72 carrier pigeons, whatever). See Chapter 13 for the details of split-testing, and read the later section, "Creating a lead-generating magnet," for a discussion of types of things you can offer in exchange for your visitors' contact information.

Reassure your visitors

Basically, three things motivate human beings: seeking pleasure, avoiding pain, and conserving energy. Of the three, pain avoidance is usually the strongest. Most of the time we're just acting out of damage control, asking ourselves, "What's the worst that can happen here and how can I prevent it?" At the threshold of opting in, prospects want to be reassured that you won't spam them; that they can stop the flow of e-mails easily at any time; and that you'll respect their privacy and not sell, rent, barter, or give away their contact information to anyone else.

Legendary copywriter Gary Bencivenga puts the following sentence below his www.bencivengabullets.com opt-in form: "No obligation . . . Nothing to buy . . . Your e-mail address will never be shared or rented."

To sell or to get the opt-in?

When I present the opt-in strategy to clients, they sometimes object on the grounds that the opt-in strategy will get in the way of the main objective of the site: the sale. They understand the sales funnel, and worry that a side-ways step will upset the process and destroy sales.

A sale is a fragile thing, and you can certainly sabotage your sales by creating a clumsy opt-in process. And you'll get fewer initial sales if you go for the opt-in first, rather than the sale. But if your sales conversion of a new visitor is 0.5 percent (meaning 1 out of every 200 visitors buys from you) and your opt-in percentage is 20 percent (meaning 1 out of five visitors opts-in to your list), you will almost certainly make more sales from ongoing follow-up than from the one-shot approach.

If your prospect wants to buy right now, don't put an opt-in in their way. Online sales include all the information you could ask for, including the lovely credit card number and expiration date. Consider the sale a super opt-in.

Make sure your thank-you page offers a path back to the sales funnel, rather than a dead end.

The thank-you page

Perry Marshall uses two clever techniques on his thank-you pages to keep the sales process going while the prospect is still hot. You can see his thank-you page by opting in to his five-day AdWords e-mail course at www.perrys marshall.com. Even though the first autoresponse e-mail actually hits your inbox within 30 seconds of clicking Start Your Mini-Course Now, Perry tells you to check your inbox "in about 10 minutes."

The second technique in use on this page is the dynamic redirect. The page tells the visitor, "In a few seconds, I'm going to tell you about the latest tools for making the most of Google. . . ." And the page is coded to send you straight to a sales letter about 15 seconds after it first appears.

Here's the code, which you place between the <HEAD> and </HEAD> tags in the page's HTML code:

```
<meta HTTP-EQUIV="REFRESH" content="0; url=http://
www.yourdomain.com/nextpage.html">
```

Replace the two elements in bold. Instead of 0, put in the number of seconds you want this page to show before redirecting. Replace the example URL with the next page.

The thank-you page is also a great place to explain to your leads what to expect from you next, and what they have to do to get it. When you download the two free chapters from Leads into Gold at www.leadsintogold.com, you're taken to a download page that includes the download link and instructions on downloading the chapters in PDF format.

It also includes a mini-sales pitch for the autoresponder sequence you just signed up for (and may not have known about):

Important Note: I'll be sending you a series of e-mail tips to help you get the most out of the two free chapters. They have incredibly valuable insights, and a lot of subscribers think I'm crazy for giving it away for nothing.

I've always been a show-off — just ask my sister.

Here's the thing: Your ISP's spam filter may consider these e-mails to be spam, and will prevent you from reading them.

To ensure you receive the e-mails (you can unsubscribe at any time), please add me to your trusted list of senders. Here's how . . .

Notice that I put the download link right on the thank-you page. That strategy raises an interesting question: Do I care if someone can get to that page by giving me a fake e-mail address? If I put the link in an e-mail, I know that the e-mail must be real for them to get the two free chapters. In this case, I want to get the two free chapters into as many hands as possible, because those chapters do such a good job of selling the rest of the product. If you follow up with leads manually, or don't want your lead-generating magnet available except to your subscriber list, then don't put the link on the thank-you page.

To see an example of this without having to opt in to a list, visit `www.ask howie.com/redirect` and wait 12 seconds.

Creating a lead-generating magnet

You have many choices about what sort of lead-generating magnet (LGM) to create. You can offer information, a free sample, a demo version, a limited time free trial, or a coupon. If your Web site is a catalog store with many items available for purchase, the LGM can be as simple as an invitation to receive a 5 percent discount off the first purchase. Software vendors can offer demo versions, either time-limited or with features disabled.

If you sell high-margin consumables — such as skin care products, health supplements, and perfumes — you may find a free trial to be a cost-effective way to build your customer list. Free or low-cost trials also work with high-margin intangibles, such as membership Web sites and newsletter subscriptions. I offer a low-cost one-month trial of my Ring of Fire AdWords support club, because one month gives my prospects a chance to experience the benefits without commitment or fear of making a mistake. Many of them sign up for a full year after their trial month.

Informational LGMs

The economics of the Internet favor giving away information. After you create the LGM, digital copies are all free, so you incur no marginal expense by giving away a million as opposed to a hundred. When your business includes a healthy back end, you can afford to pay more up front to mail letters and packages.

Formats

Informational LGMs can take many formats:

- Free Report/White Paper (PDF)
- Newsletter (PDF, Web page, e-mail)
- Book (self-published)
- Magazine/Journal
- Resource Guide
- Analysis/Planning Template
- Electronic Book
- Recorded Message
- CD/DVD
- Preloaded iPod/mp3 player
- Restricted Access Website
- Audio/Video download
- E-mail Course
- Live Seminar/Workshop
- "Cheat Sheet"

Content types

Three basic types of information LGMs lend themselves very well to the purposes of attracting, building trust, and selling. These are special reports, consumer guides, and how-to guides.

- **Special Report (often called *White Paper* in the corporate world):** The free report is the tool of choice when your prospect is not yet educated or motivated enough to take action of any kind. The free report essentially names a problem faced by your prospects, gets them emotionally involved in the horrible consequences of the problem, unveils a generic solution, and then introduces and sells your version of the solution.

By contrast, the Consumer Guide (see the following bullet) works better when the prospects know they have a problem, know they need to solve it, and are looking at you and your competitors side by side.

Visit www.askhowie.com/reports for examples of a special report for consumers (by an indoor air specialist writing to parents of children with asthma) and a business-to-business white paper (about maximizing profits from your customer list).

✔ **Consumer Guide:** The consumer guide is most effective when your prospect is actively shopping for a solution and trying to figure out which solution to buy. A variation is the Consumer Alert, which warns prospects about all the ways they can be scammed or make a wrong decision. A popular format for this is the "Seven questions to ask before choosing a. . . ." You name your profession, and teach your prospect how to find a qualified and honest practitioner.

✔ **How-to Guide:** The How-To Guide doesn't have to refer to your product at all. What it does is teach your prospects how to solve a problem somewhat related to the problem that your product solves.

For example, if you sell bookkeeping services for small businesses, your prospects typically have grown to the point where they are overwhelmed by the amount of start-up stuff they haven't outsourced or hired for. Think about what other problems owners of growing small businesses have: inefficient purchasing systems, not enough time to market and sell, nagging questions about incorporation options, and so on. If you can offer information that solves those problems, you can be pretty sure that the people who raise their hands in interest are good prospects for you as well.

If you need to bid on turn-the-corner keywords, create a How-To Guide that qualifies your prospects and gets them into your funnel, even if it doesn't directly sell your products or services. You now have the ability to build the relationship through the most revolutionary communications medium of the last 50 years: e-mail.

Staying on Your Prospects' Minds with E-mail

Imagine for a moment that Google changes its policies and bans all your ads. Imagine further that it changes its search algorithm, thereby excluding your Web pages from its listings. What would happen to your online business?

Aside from pointing out the foolishness of putting all your business eggs into one Google basket, the scenario I just described points out the importance of having a customer list. As Fred Astaire sang to Ginger Rogers on a ferry deck in *Shall We Dance,* "They can't take that away from me."

As Ken McCarthy says, one goal of your list is to support your business if all your traffic disappears. The glue that binds your list to you is e-mail. In spite of all the spam, a person's e-mail inbox is an intimate space. Think of how much more upset people get about spam than junk mail to appreciate just how intimate we want it to be. Writing e-mails that grow the relationship is one of the most important skills you need to succeed online.

You can send two kinds of e-mail: autoresponses and broadcasts. They serve different purposes, and can complement each other to create a powerful e-mail customer-building strategy. Before I cover these methods, I want to discuss a much-debated topic in e-mail marketing: verified opt-in.

Verifying your lead

Suppose you come to my Web site and sign up for my newsletter. You enter the name U. Big Dope along with the e-mail address of some person you don't much like. What happens next is that your "friend" gets an e-mail from me addressed to U. Big Dope. You're anonymous, your acquaintance is mad at me, and I'm innocently confused by the whole thing. I may end up being blacklisted by spam filters for too many of these lapses. (This actually happened to me a couple of years ago, but the actual name was much more offensive than U. Big Dope. The perpetrator targeted a couple of guys in his office as recipients of this prank, for which I was blamed. Needless to say, I've tended toward verified opt-in ever since.)

AWeber and other e-mail-marketing services have "solved" this problem, sort of, by creating a higher category of opt-in: *verified* or *double opt-in.* In this system, people who opt in receive one e-mail with a link they can click to really join the list. Essentially, this step says, "I'm going to make sure you are who you say you are by sending you this e-mail. If you didn't request this information, you don't have to do anything. Sorry about that."

Verified opt-in protects you from accusations of spamming. No matter how often you send out e-mails, some of your leads will wake up one morning with no recollection of your existence, find your e-mail in their inbox, and report it as spam with a single click. If they opted in using verified opt-in, you can prove to the spam police that you weren't e-mailing without permission.

Also, verified opt-in gives you a higher quality list. The more hoops people have to jump through to receive your e-mails, the hungrier they are for your information.

The one big problem with verified opt-in is that it depresses sign-ups. Especially if your market acts impulsively, your prospects may have cooled down in the 10 minutes it took your e-mail to meet their eyes. Instructions on your landing page and customization of the confirmation e-mail can improve your conversion rate, but you won't build as big a list with verified opt-in.

Following up automatically with an e-mail autoresponder

The e-mail autoresponder is one of the coolest tools ever invented, right up there with Pez dispensers and bicycle brakes. You can preload a series of e-mail messages, and when someone opts in to your list, they receive the series in order, according to the schedule you set. You can merge fields to make the e-mail look exactly like a personal correspondence. Done right, your autoresponder sequence will mimic what you would write to each prospect if you had all the time in the world. You can schedule e-mails days, weeks, months and even years in advance. Figure 11-5 shows an autoresponder sequence of eight e-mails, the first four of which are scheduled as follows (the Interval column is in number of days):

> Message 1: immediately
>
> Message 2: 1 day later
>
> Message 3: 3 days after message 2
>
> Message 4: 3 days after message 3

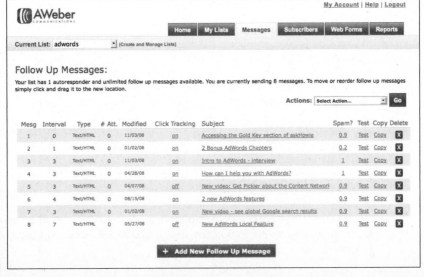

Figure 11-5:
A short auto-responder sequence consisting of an instant response and seven subsequent follow-up messages.

But wait, there's more! You can create multiple lists, and set rules about subscribing and unsubscribing based on certain conditions. For Leads into Gold, my sequence consists of 18 messages sent over about two months. But what if someone buys on Day 17? Do I want to keep asking them to buy? Obviously not. I created a rule that says, "When someone on the list buys Leads into Gold, remove them from the prospect list and add them to the customer list." My customer sequence consists of 12 messages, also spread over about two months, that give advice, offer support, and tell them about other things they may want to buy.

I'll show you how to perform this magic again using AWeber, the service I use and recommend. You discover how to use the AWeber Control Panel to build an opt-in form earlier in this chapter. If you haven't yet signed up for an AWeber account, go to `www.aweber.com` and order now. You have 30 days in which to change your mind and get a full refund.

Changing your list name

From the AWeber home page, click List Settings to change the name of your list to something relevant to your business. If you use verified opt-in, the list name will be the main clue your prospects will see as they decide whether to opt-in. Would you agree to receive e-mails from someone named `default389178`? If your ideal name is taken, think of variations — you have 15 characters to play with. My list names for my Gout e-book include `gout-recipes`, `gout`, and `goutbook`. For my marketing business, I use list names like `adwords`, `adwordscoaching`, `askhowie`, `coachmarketing`, `email-club`, `emailstrategy`, `guide`, and `question`. I improved my verified opt-in percentage when I changed the name of my Leads into Gold prospect list from `2freechapters` to `leadsgold-2free`.

Changing to verified opt-in

To change to verified opt-in, follow these steps:

1. **From the List Settings tab, click the Verified Opt-in tab in the submenu.**

2. **Click the OFF link to turn on Verified Opt-in for your Web forms, as shown in Figure 11-6.**

3. **Say yes to the pop-up warning and you're in complete compliance with e-mail-marketing best practices.**

   Give yourself a pat on the back.

Next, you need to customize the verification message your prospects will receive. Your job is to get them to open the e-mail by choosing or creating the right subject line, and then getting them to click the link that puts them on your list. Click the Subject box to bring up the Pre-Approved Subject drop-down list and scan the subjects first. Which one most closely connects with what you promise? Is it a subscription? A request for information? Do you want to include a capitalized pre-head like RESPONSE REQUIRED? Do you want to include or omit the @aweber e-mail suffix? (Hint: Omit it.)

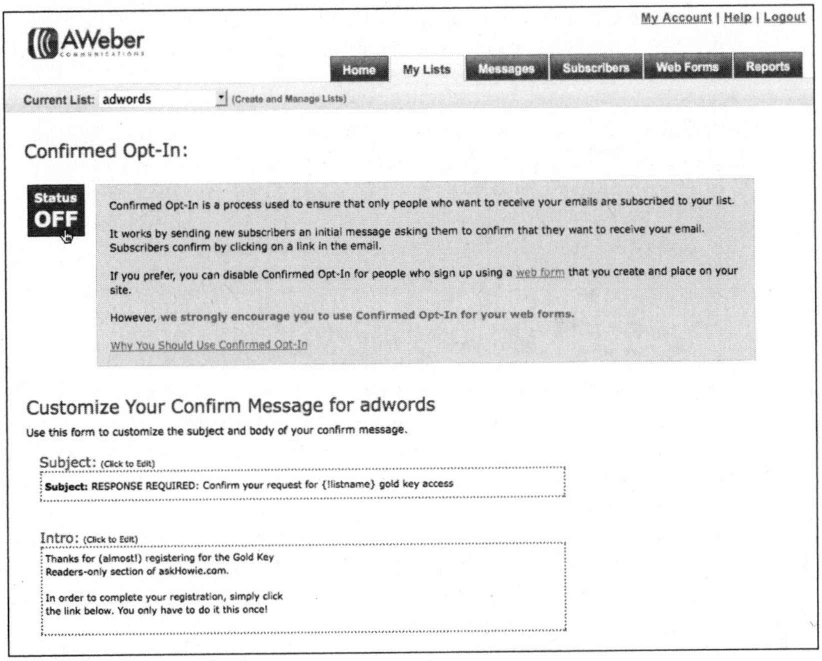

Figure 11-6:
Change to
verified
opt-in to
prevent
spam
complaints
and worse.

The advantage of using a pre-approved subject line is, well, they're pre-approved. I prefer to write my own custom subject lines, enter the text in the Custom Subject text box, and wait for the AWeber folks to approve them. One of my favorites is, "Making sure you signed up on purpose for {!listname}." That helps them connect to me while saying exactly why I'm sending this e-mail.

In the Custom First Paragraph text box, simply repeat the offer and tell them what to do. For example:

```
Hi {!firstname_fix},

Congratulations on your purchase of Leads into Gold!
To receive the promised bonuses, simply click the
link below.
```

Save your changes by clicking the Save button at the bottom right; then review the verification message you've edited. When you're satisfied, click the Messages tab to start creating your autoresponder sequence.

Planning your e-mail sequence

When Abraham Lincoln was asked how long a man's legs should be, he famously retorted, "Long enough to reach the ground." When I am asked how long an e-mail sequence should be, I give the same answer and watch my clients' heads spin in confusion. Actually, I paraphrase Honest Abe and say, "Long enough to turn your best prospects into buyers." It really depends on the circumstances: the market, the keyword, the offer, the first sale.

Ask yourself: What is your prospects' interest cycle? How long will they focus on this itch before losing interest? Some itches go away by themselves after a few minutes or hours. In those cases, your best strategy is to go for the sale right away. Other itches can linger for years — soundproofing a noisy restaurant, losing 15 pounds, learning to play the ukulele. Your e-mail scheduling strategy depends on their interest cycle and the urgency of their need.

Your choices for e-mail content are so vast that I could write a book just on e-mail–autoresponder marketing. (Hey, maybe that will be my next *For Dummies* book!) Here are several strategies to choose from as you create your sequence:

- **Consumption of your LGM:** Just because people download your special report or software demo, doesn't mean they're going to read it or start using it. In fact, thanks to ferret-on-caffeine attention spans, they probably don't remember where they saved the file, or that they have the software. Your first e-mails should help them consume your LGM in manageable chunks. Reassure them: "If you haven't gotten to the white paper yet, I understand. You'll get to it when you get to it. When you do, I'd love to hear your thoughts."

  Remind them why they wanted your LGM in the first place. Tell them about the great strategy on page 9. Show them a cool way to create a color-coded mind map using your software.

- **Soliciting engagement:** My most successful autoresponder message of all time goes out one day after my prospect has opted in. I've used this for my products and for various clients, and it always gets a great response:

  ```
  Hi Betsy,

      Yesterday you visited FitFam.com and downloaded the Action Guide.

      (If you haven't gotten your copy yet, it's at www.FitFam.com/home/
  Actionguide.)
  ```

> I just wanted to ask you, was it helpful? What were you looking for
> when you came to the site? (If you haven't read it yet, I
> totally understand. You'll get to it when you get to it.)
>
> If you'll hit reply, I'd love to hear from you. I want to make sure
> the information on the site is as helpful as possible.
>
> All the best,
>
> Howie Jacobson, Ph.D.
> www.FitFam.com

This chatty e-mail starts a dialogue with prospects. They reply out of courtesy, because it looks to them like I sat down and wrote this just to them, and it would be rude not to reply. I always reply to their reply, thanking them for their feedback, and asking more questions about their situation. Before you know it, I'm doing consultative selling with zero sales resistance. I'll offer to help them over the phone, and very often can take the prospect to the next step in the sales funnel just by virtue of this e-mail.

✔ **Teaching and guiding:** My Leads into Gold e-mail sequence contains some very long e-mails. Each one is a short chapter on direct marketing. For people hungry for information on how to grow their business, these e-mails make me a valuable resource. Some of them reason, "If this is his free stuff, imagine how good his paid stuff must be."

✔ **Offering more good stuff:** If you have a second white paper, an audio interview, or a free teleseminar, you can build goodwill and establish yourself as the expert by offering them to your prospects. Remember, most people start their search wide, looking in lots of places for information, but quickly narrow their informational intake filter to let in one primary source. Your goal is to be that one source.

✔ **Selling:** Yes, you can make offers and convince your prospects to take you up on those offers in e-mail. You'll be more successful in converting those offers if they are the minority of your e-mails, and if the e-mails that do sell educate or entertain (preferably both).

The best way to learn about what works is to get on a bunch of lists and experience various autoresponder sequences. Create folders in your e-mail program for each sequence, print the e-mails and study them. What's the ratio of valuable content to sales pitch? Is the tone professional, folksy, in-your-face, or humorous? Are their motives transparent or veiled? Are the messages short, medium, or long? What's the purpose of each e-mail? Was it effective for you? Would it work in your market? And so on.

Go to www.askhowie.com/autoresponders for a list of autoresponders to study and model.

Pay special attention to the two most important elements on an e-mail: the Subject line and the From line.

✔ **The From line:** Before we read an e-mail, we look to see who sent it. If your leads know you only as Pat the Welder, they probably won't open an e-mail from Patricia McLaughlin. You can change the From address at the bottom of the AWeber List Settings page. The name next to the checked From/Reply box is the one your prospects see in the From line.

✔ **The Subject line:** The subject line serves one function: to get the user to open the e-mail and read it. You can use curiosity triggers, benefit triggers, and any of the strategies discussed in Chapter 6. Your subject line is the headline of your e-mail, the thing your prospect spends a millisecond scanning before deciding whether to read the message or delete it.

Creating an autoresponder sequence using AWeber

After you rename your list and set your verified opt-in preferences (described earlier in this chapter), you're ready to create e-mail messages. Click the Messages tab to see a list of your current messages (none, if you haven't created any yet). Click the Add Message button to create your first autoresponse.

If you are already collecting leads, they will receive your autoresponse e-mails. If you're just playing around, create a second list that only you will see, as shown in Figure 11-7. You can create new lists by clicking the small Create and Manage Lists link next to the current list name at the top left, and then clicking the bright green Create a New List link on the next page.

Creating a message

For now, my advice is to stick with plain text e-mails, not HTML. Plain text e-mails are delivered at higher rates, are simpler to create, and mirror the normal e-mails your prospects send and receive every day. They won't neces- sarily stand out and scream, "You can ignore me because I'm not from a real person."

If you select the Click Tracking check box, you can see how many leads click links within your e-mails, which is very useful information. However, the downside of using plain text messages is that your pretty links (www. fitfam.com/actionguide, for example) will turn into hideous AWeber links with lots of funny characters and may scare people into not clicking.

Type your subject (the default, "Insert Your Subject Here" is not recom- mended) in the Subject text box, and then type your plain text message or import it from a text file or Word document into the Plain Text Message box. AWeber shows you its recommended width of 68 characters per line. If you click Wrap Long Lines after inputting your message, AWeber will automati- cally reformat it to that width.

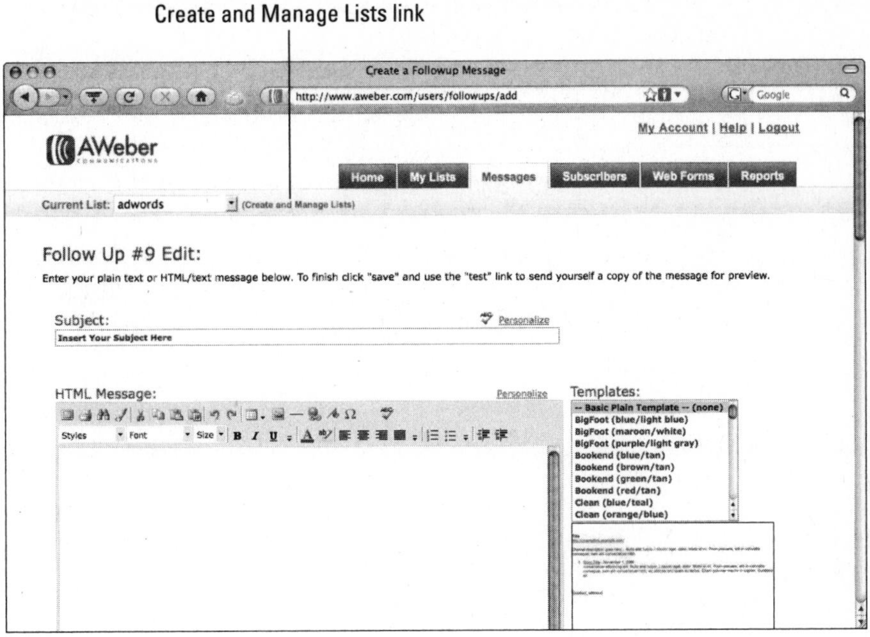

Create and Manage Lists link

Figure 11-7:
Create auto-
response
messages
on this
AWeber
page.

I often make my e-mail messages half that width, or about 35 characters per line, to make them very easy on the eye and encourage my readers to scroll all the way to the end. After creating the message, save it (by clicking the Save button at the bottom right) to return to the message list.

Using personalization fields

You can personalize the e-mail message to each lead, using dozens of different fields, some of which are shown in Figure 11-8. I generally include the first name in the salutation, as follows:

```
Hi {!firstname_fix}
```

The _fix at the end capitalizes the first letter of the name and makes the rest lowercase, in case someone typed in his name as HOwie and you don't want to show him those two capital letters in every e-mail.

To view the actual e-mail generated by the message in Figure 11-8, visit www. askhowie.com/personal and complete the form. It's verified opt-in, so you have to confirm the first e-mail to receive the second. How close to your actual city did AWeber get? In my case, within about 270 miles — not very impressive. Oh well.

Figure 11-8:
Using
personaliz-
ation fields,
you can
customize
e-mails to
each lead.

Click Test to send yourself a copy of the message. Do this with every e-mail you ever put into AWeber. Click every link within those e-mails. You'll save yourself a lot of "oops" e-mails, the ones where you say, "Gee, I'm sorry that the links didn't work in the last e-mail I sent out." Take the time to get it right, so you don't raise unnecessary doubts about your competence.

Scheduling your next message

For all autoresponder messages after the first one, you have to decide when you want the e-mail to be sent. AWeber allows you to choose any number of days, from 0 through 999, following the previous message. If you have a sequence that sends an e-mail a day for 5 days, then once a week for 3 weeks, and then once every 28 days forever, you configure it as follows:

Message 1: Instantaneous

Message 2: 1 Day Delay

Message 3: 1 Day Delay

Message 4: 1 Day Delay

Message 5: 1 Day Delay

Message 6: 7 Day Delay

Message 7: 7 Day Delay

Message 8: 7 Day Delay

Message 9: 28 Day Delay

Message 10: 28 Day Delay

And so on . . .

Generally, you want to send more frequent e-mails at the beginning of the sequence, and drop down to a stay-in-touch-once-a-month frequency after a month or so. The last thing your prospect wants is to go on vacation for a couple of weeks and return to an inbox full of you. (Actually, an inbox full of "Send this e-mail to 20 people within 10 minutes or your nose will fall off" might be worse, but you get the point.)

Scheduling an e-mail is simple: Click the Add Message button at the bottom of your list of e-mails to create a new one. At the top of the next page, the first field you can edit has the default number 4 in it. If you leave it as is, this message will be sent four days after the previous message. To send this message the very next day, change it to 1 (see Figure 11-9). If you're using a different autoresponder service, make sure you understand their format. Some of them ask you to schedule based on the signup date, rather than the previous e-mail.

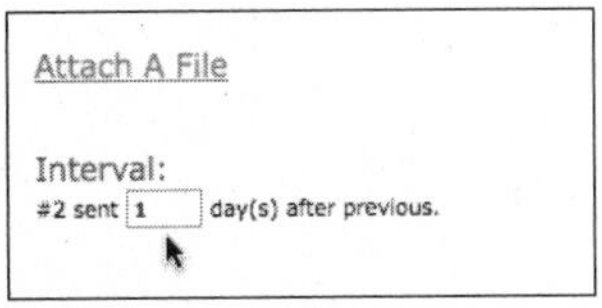

Figure 11-9:
Change the
scheduling
of an e-mail
by entering
the number
of days after
the previous
message.

Attach A File

Interval:
#2 sent 1 day(s) after previous.

Your autoresponse e-mails fall into one of two categories: obvious parts of a sequence, or simulated real time e-mails. If you offer an e-mail course, the messages that deliver the course don't have to "pretend" to be a note you just dashed off. Something as simple as

```
Hi Howie,
Here's Part 1 of the 17-Part E-mail Course, "How to Clean Your Fingernails"
+ + + + + + + + + + + + +
Part 1: Finding Your Fingernails

Many of my clients have such dirty fingernails, they can't even find them
anymore. Here's where to look: at the ends of your fingers, just opposite the
part with the fingerprint . . .

And so on . . .
```

will get the job done. After the course is over, you can start communicating in a chattier and natural way:

```
Hi Howie,
I was recently talking to a client who complained, "Fran, my fingernails are now
spotless, but my toenails are a mess. What do you suggest?"

Goodness, but I guffawed when I heard that one. Did he think I had another
17-part course about toenails?

The answer, obviously, is "Wear shoes and nobody will notice."

But then we started talking about the spring wedding season approaching, and it
occurred to me that you might find occasion to don footwear with open toes in
the coming months.

And so on . . .
```

Try to keep these messages "evergreen" by avoiding references that will date them. Don't say, "I was watching the Oscars last night," because someone on your list will receive your message in September and dismiss you as a liar or TiVo addict. Do read over your messages once or twice a year to nip stale-ness in the bud. If you talk about a celebrity who has died since you wrote the e-mail, it may come across as offensive, if not just outdated.

The goal of the autoresponder is to automate what you would do anyway if you had a million hours a day and nothing better to do. When you plan each message and each sequence, ask yourself, "Knowing what I know about this lead, what would I write to them today?"

The purpose of your first autoresponder sequence is to turn your lead into a buyer (or at least to help your lead to decide whether they should become a buyer). Your e-mails continue to hammer at pain points, educate, offer solutions, build credibility, invite feedback — everything you would do if you were the account manager and this lead was a hot prospect.

Using autoresponders to move leads and customers through your sales funnel

Say you sell three products, and you want your customers to buy them in this order: Product 1, Product 2, Product 3. You can set up three autoresponders as follows:

- ✔ **Prospect List:** A sequence of e-mails to get your opt-ins to buy Product 1.

- ✔ **New Customer List:** A sequence of e-mails to get your customers to buy Product 2.

  Here's the coolest feature of all: when someone buys Product 1, AWeber automatically adds them to the New Customer list and unsubscribes them from the Prospect List. You don't have to subject your customers to a sales pitch for a product they already bought. You can also avoid the worst-case scenario of offering a better deal for something they already bought.

- ✔ **Returning Customer List:** A sequence of e-mails to get your customers who already own Products 1 and 2 to buy Product 3.

Setting up automatic unsubscribe

To set up automatic unsubscribe, follow these steps:

1. **Create a second AWeber list by clicking Add New next to the list name at the top left.**

2. **On the next page, click the green Create List button and complete and save the forms on the Success page.**

   This new list will be for new customers who just bought your first product.

3. **Change the list to your first list by selecting it from the drop-down list next to Current List, as shown in Figure 11-10.**

4. **Once you're managing the list that leads will unsubscribe from when they subscribe to the new list, go to the List Settings tab and click Automation from the submenu.**

5. **From the drop-down list in the center of the page, select Unsubscribe from List {*name of first list*} When Lead Subscribes To {*name of second list*} (see Figure 11-11).**

6. **Next, select the new list name from the drop-down list under the List column.**

7. **Click the Save button to save the changes and read the Action you've saved, to make sure it's what you want AWeber to do.**

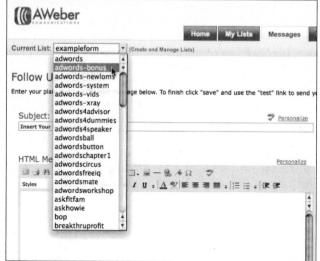

Figure 11-10:
Select a list
to manage
using the
drop-down
list near the
top left of
the page.

Figure 11-11:
You can set
up AWeber
to remove
people auto-
matically
from one list
when they
are added to
a different
list.

If you have an online shopping cart, you can set it up to forward the customer information to AWeber after a sale is made. AWeber will then perform the auto-mated rule, removing the customer from the prospect list and adding the name to the customer list. If you don't yet have an online shopping cart, go to www.askhowie.com/cart for some recommendations.

Don't be an accidental spammer

No discussion of e-mail would be complete without a foray into the wacky world of *spam* (junk e-mail). I know you get hundreds of them a week, if not each day, and you're saying to yourself, "But I would never send out an e-mail offering a fake Rolex. I don't even know where to find fake Rolexes." Or you're saying, "I've had enough of this chapter. I'm going to put this book down and try that new Indian restaurant, the one next to the beauty shop and the pizza place." (Sorry, I can't reveal how I do that trick.)

Spam has become such a huge annoyance to e-mail users that many Internet Service Providers (ISPs) have become hyper-aggressive in their spam filtering. Your e-mails may be going to leads who opted in and are hungering for them; the e-mails may be completely appropriate, but the big dumb filters are programmed to stop everything that doesn't come from Aunt Sadie and Uncle Lou.

If AOL or EarthLink incorrectly tags your e-mails as spam, you may find yourself sending 2,000 e-mails but having only 400 delivered. Spam is a big topic, but the following tips will help you avoid the worst mistakes made by innocent marketers.

Use plain text instead of HTML

Spammers use HTML to do all sorts of nefarious things in e-mails. A brand of spamming known as *phishing* creates e-mails that look exactly like big companies, such as financial institutions, eBay, or PayPal, sent them. Their goal is to get unsuspecting customers to click to fake sites that look like the real ones and enter sensitive data. If your e-mails are in plain text, it shows you're not hiding anything. Spam filters like that transparency, and bother plain text e-mails less.

Keep links to a minimum

Avoid putting lots of links in your e-mails. Remember, each e-mail should compel a single action. Too much choice is bad marketing, regardless of spam considerations. You can repeat a link at the top and bottom of a long e-mail, but don't give your reader half a dozen choices.

Avoid common spam trigger words

Words like `free`, mortgage, `pornography`, spam, `make money`, enlargement, and others alert filters that a message may be spam. In the past, you could fool a filter with punctuation tricks, such as `fr.ee` and `m@ke m0ney`, but the filters now look at tricks like these as spam markers.

So what do you do if you're in the mortgage business, or a similar legitimate enterprise that uses spammy words? One solution is to put your e-mails on your Web site, and write short e-mails with links:

```
Hi Bartleby,
Today's installment of "Affording a New Home" is available at
www.yoursite.com/newhome23

It talks about the three mistakes that can cost you big time, as well as a time-
saving resource you'll wish you had discovered years ago.

Enjoy,
Maury Gage Lender
```

TIP

Random e-mail tip

Leave a space after a URL before adding punctuation. Web browsers often include periods
and commas that appear at the end of the URL,
so someone might click your working link and
end up with that nasty "Page Not Found" error.

Wrong: `www.askhowie.com.`

Right: `www.askhowie.com .`

Putting your e-mails online will reduce readership, so you have to work hard
to entice your reader to click the link and view your message.

Don't send attachments

If you have a legitimate attachment, such as a PDF document or software
demo download, put a link in your e-mail to a Web page where that file can be
downloaded. Files attached to your e-mails can contain viruses. Also, large
attachments can crash your readers' e-mail servers or just get your messages
hung up in cyber-limbo.

ON THE WEB

For more tips on beating an undeserved spam rap, visit `http://www.ask`
`howie.com/spam` . (See that extra space before the period? Just a subtle
reminder, courtesy of the "Random e-mail tip" sidebar, elsewhere in this
chapter.)

Broadcast e-mails

The other e-mail workhorse for your online business is the broadcast. This
works just like a combination of regular e-mail (you pick a recipient, type
something, and send it) and the AWeber system (you can merge fields just
like the autoresponses; you can schedule it to go out at a particular date and
time; you can send it to hundreds or thousands of people at once).

To send a broadcast, go to the AWeber site, click the Messages tab, and
choose Broadcast from the submenu. Click the green Create Broadcast
Message button in the center of the page to get started. The first thing you
notice is that this form is the same as the form for creating an autoresponder,
with only tiny yet crucially important differences:

✔ Instead of choosing a sending interval, you are prompted to enter a date and time. The default is right now.

✔ You can segment this list by creating a view and sending only to leads who meet certain criteria (see the "Managing your e-mail list" section, later in this chapter, for instructions on creating and using views.)

The default views in the drop-down list use time and deliverability as the criteria. You can send a broadcast e-mail to all leads who subscribe within a certain period. You can also resend a broadcast to leads who, for some reason, haven't been able to receive your regular e-mails because of spam filters or other problems.

✔ Instead of sending the message to just one list, you now can send it to multiple lists. You can also exclude lists. Just click the Send To Multiple Lists Or Exclude Lists link to open a table where you can choose the lists to include or exclude.

I use broadcasts to send my weekly BOPzine (Breakthrough Online Profits e-zine), let my customers know about special events, send time-sensitive information, and to send out newsletters. I also use broadcasts to fill my autoresponders while making sure that my newest leads don't miss anything good.

Special events

Often I run webinars (live on-screen demos along with conference calls) to which I invite my customers and subscribers. Recently I sent an e-mail to several of my marketing-related lists, letting them know about a webinar demonstrating the features of the just-released new AdWords interface (recording available for viewing at www.askhowie.com/interface-webinar, if you're interested). Obviously, I can't put a message like that in an autoresponder.

You can use broadcasts for sales, announcements, coupons, news, opportunities; anything that is time-sensitive and of interest to a significant segment of your list.

E-newsletters

E-newsletters, also called ezines (which nobody knows how to pronounce), are regular communications from you to your customer base. You can create a publishing schedule or just send one out when the mood strikes. The most successful e-newsletter publishers I know stick to a schedule and never deviate. Because you can schedule a broadcast for a future date, you can create six newsletters and have AWeber send them out weekly while you drink yak milk and climb K2.

Writing great newsletters

E-newsletter wizard Michael Katz, of www. bluepenguindevelopment.com, is one of the few people whose newsletters I read as soon as they arrive. Michael teaches professional service providers — coaches, consultants, trainers, accountants and other people who sell their expertise — to build relationships with prospects through regular e-mail newsletters. Here's Michael on the four commandments of e-newsletters:

What I'm about to tell you is so valuable, that I frankly wouldn't blame you if after reading it, you felt compelled to take $5.00 out of your wallet, stuff it in an envelope and send it directly to me. Here's why: What I'm going to share with you now are the four guidelines we use to make sure that all the newsletters we're involved in stay on track. Here they are:

✔ *Make It Useful:*

With a business-to-business newsletter in particular, it's difficult to get any traction with readers if you don't give them some kind of actionable "aha" with every issue you send. They are barraged with e-mails, and eager to click the delete button as often as possible.

Your goal therefore, is to give them pause. To make them live in fear that if they delete your newsletter, they will miss some insight that would have made a significant impact on their success. Useful information rises to the top of the pile, and when your newsletter is on top, you need not worry about how big the pile is.

✔ *Make It Interesting:*

I don't know who started the rumor that significant and profitable businesses must also be serious and boring, but it seems to have caught on nonetheless. That's good news for you and me. Because with all the dry as dust E-Newsletters out there, all trying to sound like the front page of the Wall Street Journal, we can make our newsletters shine with little effort.

Personal anecdotes, conversational language and the occasional joke here and there will keep your readers involved long enough for them to hear the "real" information you're trying to give them. They probably won't read it just because it's interesting, but they certainly won't read it if it's not.

✔ *Make It Simple:*

An effective newsletter isn't a doctoral thesis; it's not even a case study. It's what I like to call, "a nugget." One insight or tip or concept that your readers can take in, understand, and hopefully remember long enough to put into practice. If you give me too much information (even if it's good), I'm likely to stockpile your newsletters until I delete them in one, "I'll never get around to reading these old ones anyway" frenzy. Give your readers something small enough to understand and remember.

✔ *Make It Authentic:*

Done right, your E-Newsletter is the voice of your company. It reflects your unique personality and culture, whatever that happens to be.

I've walked into enough companies to know that each of them — even the ones in seemingly straight laced, hard to differentiate industries — has its own language, pace, sense of humor and approach. Don't hide all that in an effort to sound "professional." Marketing is the opposite of fitting in — do yourself a favor and fit out!

For more of Michael's wit and wisdom, go to www.bluepenguindevelopment.com to read his latest newsletter and join his list. He might even reveal how to pronounce *ezine.*

Repurposing broadcast e-mails to build your autoresponder sequence

Say you've created an autoresponder sequence that lasts five months and then stops. One day you're driving on the highway and this idea hits you for a great next e-mail for that sequence. You rush home and type the e-mail into your autoresponder sequence, 30 days after the last message. Let's call it the 180th day of the whole series.

Now everyone on that list who hasn't been on your list for more than 179 days will receive that message. But it's sad that the people who have been on your list for more than six months will never see your message. You could put it in your autoresponder and send it as a broadcast, but then all the new people will get the same e-mail twice.

 The solution, as revealed to me by Perry Marshall during the intermission of a Blue Man Group performance in Las Vegas, is simple and elegant: Calculate how many days after subscribing someone will receive the autoresponse e-mail. Send the e-mail today as a broadcast, and make a note on your calendar to enter it into your autoresponder sequence that many days in the future.

Continuing with our example, let's say today is March 16. You will add the message to your autoresponder sequence on day 180. Send the broadcast to your list today, and on September 16, add the message to day 180 of your sequence. That way, everyone on your list will receive the message once, and no one will receive it twice.

Managing your e-mail lists

You can manage your e-mail lists by clicking the Leads tab on the AWeber site. You can search and sort by any of the data you collect. Click Select Field in any of the drop-down lists to view your choices. You can select filters and a sort order and save that view, in case you need to come back to it again. Once you generate the view (or just click Display View with All Leads showing to see your entire list), you can manage individual leads.

You can stop the autoresponder sequence for a lead by checking that person's box in the Stop column. You can reset the last message they received to put them backward or forward in the sequence. You can erase them entirely — when someone complains to me about spam but doesn't unsubscribe via the link that appears at the bottom of every single e-mail I send them (what, me frustrated and bitter?), I erase them from the list to prevent future problems.

If you click the e-mail address, you can edit more information about your lead in the pop-over window: name, e-mail, ad tracking, last message delivered, and a miscellaneous notes field.

As your list grows, you will benefit from tutorials on advanced list management techniques. You can find these and other AWeber tutorials at www.ask howie.com/aweber along with other articles about e-mail marketing.

Going Offline to Build the Relationship

When you start conducting business online, it's easy to be seduced by the automation and anonymity of e-mail and Web site. Imagine a business that never requires you to talk with customers, lick a stamp, buy an envelope, or write a check. You could die and keep making money for years!

What many online-only businesspeople don't realize is they're sacrificing growth for convenience, or perhaps laziness. If you collect phone numbers, you can follow up via the telephone. Ditto for the fax machine, which is making a comeback as a permission-based follow-up medium that's considerably less cluttered than the e-mail inbox. (And faxes are less likely to be blocked than mass e-mail messages.) The mail, including the postal service as well as private carriers like FedEx and UPS, is a great way to stay in touch with prospects.

I can't begin to cover offline follow-up strategies in this book about AdWords. (Remember AdWords? This is a book about AdWords.) But they are so near and dear to my heart, I want to share one quick and clever way to use e-mail, your Web site, and the telephone together to grow your business:

1. Choose a time and date for a teleconference call.

2. Go to www.freeconferencecall.com and sign up for a free 96-person conference call line.

3. E-mail your list to let them know about a teleconference you will be holding to answer their biggest questions. Include a link to a page on your Web site where they can take a short survey to register for the call.

4. Look over the survey results and pick the questions you will answer on the call.

5. Ask a friend or colleague with a nice voice to interview you by asking you the questions you've chosen. If you're brave, they can also moderate and help you field live questions from teleconference participants.

6. Record the call, using the www.freeconferencecall.com recording feature (free, but not such great quality), or an audio-recording service, such as www.audioacrobat.com.

7. Download the recording, and either edit it with the free Audacity program (available at http://audacity.sourceforge.net) or the audio editing software of your choice, or post it as an .mp3 file to your Web site.

8. E-mail your list, letting readers know that the teleconference is available for them to listen to online or to download to their PC or iPod.

9. If you've said some good stuff, pay a transcription service to turn the recording into a Word document. (You can find freelance transcriptionists by posting a project at www.guru.com or any similar freelance brokerage site.) Edit it, make it graphically pretty, turn it into a PDF document, and put it on your Web site.

10. If you've shared some great material that your prospects and customers want, you can do any or all of the following:

    a. Give it away free on your site.

    b. Give it away free as an LGM in exchange for an opt-in.

    c. Turn it into a CD and/or printed manual and sell it as a product.

    d. Use it as a bonus to compel some other desired action.

    e. Let other people reproduce the CD and manual and include them as bonuses with their products.

    f. Come up with a brand new use that no one has ever thought of before.

Go to www.askhowie.com/phone for the detailed instructions and vendor list for the teleconference process.

Chapter 12

Building a "Climb the Ladder" Web Site

*Y*our business is just a system for turning complete strangers into great customers. AdWords finds you the strangers, your ad invites them in, and your landing page opt-in and e-mail give you the ability to keep the conversation going. Your Web site contains the content that will turn leads into buyers, buyers into repeat customers, and customers into referral sources and advocates.

One way to look at your Web site is purely numerically: traffic in, money out. In a nutshell, the game of online marketing can be reduced to that equation. Your Web site, in this view, is a tool for extracting cash from visitors. You set up conversion tracking and analytics and reports to find out how good your Web site is at extracting a purchase from which visitors (see Chapters 14 and 15). You run split tests to increase the amount of money you get per visitor (see Chapter 13). But when you actually design and build your Web site, sales and money should be the farthest thing from your mind. Instead, you focus on growing customers.

The big goal of your Web site is to develop the relationship between you and your customers. Sales are part of that relationship, and an important part — after all, you can't take *satisfaction* or *good will* to the bank or the grocery store or the music store on Broad Street with the gorgeous Weber mandolins — er, excuse me, where was I?

Oh, yes, the relationship. The typical online business can identify several stages of customer: first-time buyer, second-time buyer, third-time buyer (now the customer is a habit, not a fluke), referral source, and advocate. You may be protesting that your business is different because you only have one thing to sell to a customer. That may be true, for now, but the real competitive advantage online is not the best AdWords campaign, or the best Web graphics, but the best relationship with customers. If your customers are worth more to you than your AdWords competitors' customers are worth to them, you eventually win — and win big.

Your Web site can be a potent partner in farming the seeds of leads into fruit-bearing customers. (Hey, that last sentence was poetically metaphorical. Excuse me while I high-five myself.) This chapter shows you how to use various tools on your Web site to grow customers, clients, and an enthusiastic volunteer sales force.

Identifying the Rungs of Your Business Ladder

Take a few moments now to sketch the perfect trajectory of a new visitor to your Web site. What's the first measurable outcome you desire? An opt-in? A sale? To engage you in a chat? To ask a question via a form? To call your business phone?

After they take that step, what's the next one? If they opted in, it may be a sale, a second opt-in to a new list, attending a teleseminar, or scheduling a phone call. If they already bought, maybe you have an upsell they should get. Maybe you want them to send you a testimonial, to refer five friends, or to use the product they bought, instead of putting it on a shelf unopened.

What's the top rung of your customer ladder? Think of the top 20 percent of your current customers — what puts them in that category? If you have customers who've maxed out your business, can you build a new rung at the top so they can ascend even higher? A private coaching club? A membership site? A chocolate-themed cruise?

Every business is different; take a few minutes now to identify the rungs of your business before continuing. When you know where you want to go, it's much easier to help visitors get there. Let's look at a few rungs that are common to most businesses:

✔ **The Lead:** The bread and butter of the online business is the *lead* — the visitor with whom you can communicate even after he or she leaves your site. In Chapter 11, I cover strategies and tactics for getting visitors to opt in to your list. I also share how you can use e-mail to bring them back to your Web site. E-mail is great, but limited. The e-mail inbox is too competitive and distracting a space to hold an intimate conversation. It's like trying to have a date in a restaurant booth surrounded by comedians, competitors, fake-Rolex peddlers, and all their friends and family. Also, spam filters make it hard to say much of anything related to selling. The wise online marketer uses e-mail to bring leads back to the Web site.

The lead has uttered a soft, tentative "Maybe" in response to your overtures. Your job is to make the leads glad for the chance they've taken, and provide value far beyond their expectations. You are aiming for the three magic verbs: *know, like,* and *trust.* When your leads think they know you, feel warmly toward you, and believe you to be trustworthy, they'll take a chance with a first purchase.

✔ **The First-Time Buyer:** The one-time customer has taken a leap of faith. The "Yes" is followed by "Okay, show me what you've got." Don't think of the first sale as *closing* anything. Your customer just opened the door and invited you into the front hall. The customer hasn't taken your coat, or invited you to sit down. Now is the time to prove yourself.

✔ **The Second-Time Buyer:** The second sale shows that you've passed the first customer test. Your product or service did what you said it would, or more, and you haven't alienated the person with poor customer service. Your job now is to take your prospects off the market entirely, so they will never consider patronizing a competitor's business. They must feel that you are their protector, watching out for their best interests and more concerned for their needs than your own.

✔ **The Third-Time Buyer:** The third-time buyer has established a trend and a habit. These buyers have committed part of their self-esteem to proving themselves right, and will continue to buy from you as long as you don't ignore or mistreat them. Your goal is to get them to the point where they feel comfortable telling their friends about you.

✔ **The Referrer:** Visitors to your Web site who have been referred by someone they trust is completely different from search engine or pay-per-click traffic. They come with positive expectations and an optimistic filter, and will doubt and argue less than a complete stranger. When your customers take the time and effort to send others to you, you have a business that can survive just about any change in Google's algorithm. There's just one more rung to take them to. . . .

✔ **The Loyal Advocate:** Is there a business in your town that you feel so good about, you would be angry if a competitor opened up? Those feelings are what you want to inspire in your customers. You want them to act as your advocates, your advisors, your eyes and ears around the marketplace. You want them to post comments and questions to your blog, to agree to be recorded and filmed for testimonials, and to shout to the world that you run a great business.

Using Web Tools to Help Your Visitors up the Ladder

Let's simplify human behavior for a moment. Peter Bregman (www.bregman partners.com), author of *Point B: A Short Guide to Leading a Big Change*, points out that people take action when three things are true:

1. They know what to do (knowledge)
2. They can do it (capability)
3. They want to do it (motivation)

This chapter focuses mostly on the third element, motivation. How to get people to know, like, and trust you; to show them that the action you want them to take will help them avoid pain and gain pleasure; and that it's the easiest, quickest, and cheapest way for them to get there. However, the first two points are just as important. If your Web site design is poor, it doesn't matter how magnetic or persuasive you are. You can't convince visitors to click a Buy button they can't find.

Design

The design of your Web site will either guide your visitors toward rungs of your ladder or make those rungs invisible or inaccessible. I've seen too many Web pages that look like they were designed to *prevent* sales: tiny fonts, distracting graphics, gratuitous Flash animation (as Lemony Snickett would say, "'Gratuitous' here means 'your Web designer spent a lot of time and money learning how to use that animation software and by golly, they're going to use it every chance they get'"), navigation systems determined by a template rather than what will get the visitor's attention, and shopping carts that require more clicks than a Wheel of Fortune booth in Point Pleasant Beach.

Is your navigation self-evident? If visitors wanted to buy *kettlebells* (big hunks of iron with handles used by hardcore fitness fiends), could they figure out how to find them from your home page? Do you use graphics and borders to shine a light on the most-looked-for links on your pages? Or do they have to drill through pages like Shop and Weights and Free Weights and Miscellaneous to find your Kettlebell selection?

I often coach online entrepreneurs who show me Web sites where the most important links are buried in long navigation bars or hidden below the scroll bar. When I tell them that I can't find how to get to the page for restaurant owners, they say things like, "It's in the submenu on the left. Just click Most Popular Pages and you'll see it."

As Mike Psenka of Ethority (www.ethority.com) points out, if you have to train your visitors to use your site, the navigation isn't, to use a software-design buzzword, *self-evident*. For Mike, *self-evident* isn't nearly strong enough a term. He strives to create software and reporting that is, in his words, "User Ridiculously Obvious." Take a look at your Web site with new eyes: Is it User Ridiculously Obvious?

The next time you're surfing and searching, pay attention to sites that seem easy and obvious to use. Notice where they place their buttons and links, and what they call them. Avoid the mystery buttons with icons and no names. Keep your design clean and functional — use everything you need, but no more. Look at the difference between the home pages of American Airlines (Figure 12-1) and JetBlue (Figure 12-2). The American page is busy, with lots of links, multiple offers, and several competing graphics. The big graphic at the top is animated, and keeps changing as you try to figure out where to go to conduct your business.

JetBlue's home page is simple and sparse, with few colors and a big obvious form for the number-one action on this page: booking a flight. The headline, "Free TV with purchase," next to a graphic of the video monitor in the back of an airplane seat, emphasizes the JetBlue difference: 36 TV channels on every flight.

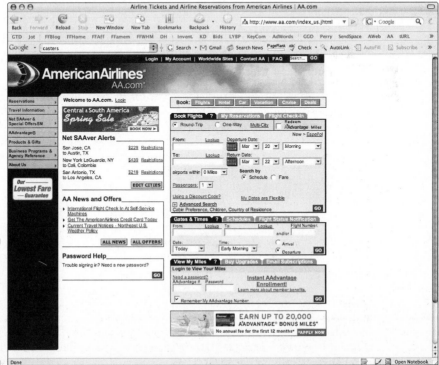

Figure 12-1:
American Airlines' home page is cluttered and confusing.

Figure 12-2:
JetBlue's
home page
is simple
and clear,
focusing
the visitor
on the flight
booking
form.

When you start clicking into the site, the differences become even more
apparent. Clicking American's Reservations navigation button brings down a
long sub-menu with a huge array of options (Figure 12-3). By contrast, when
you click Where From to start booking your flight on the JetBlue site, a
beautifully designed list of departure cities appears above the page, as shown
in Figure 12-4. User-friendly? User Ridiculously Obvious.

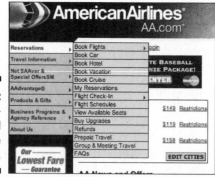

Figure 12-3:
Avoid hard-
to-read
menus like
this one.

Figure 12-4:
JetBlue's
menus are
slick and
easy to
read.

And if you're not convinced of the power of simplicity, perhaps you haven't seen this page: www.google.com. Google became the 900-pound gorilla of search partly by making it so easy to conduct a search. No competing graphics or links — just a plain box in the center of a nearly empty page. Other search engines competing with Google in the late 1990s were trying to cram every pixel on their home page with juicy content. Google won by not intimidating or confusing its users, as well as by delivering quick and relevant content.

Sales copy

Sales copy refers to the words you use to convince your visitor to take some action. You sell opt-ins, you sell free downloads, you sell phone calls, and of course you sell products and services.

Even in the dawning multimedia era of the Web, words matter. Your sales copy is what ultimately persuades visitors to take actions. We're creatures of inertia and hesitation when it comes to doing business. We don't want to get burned (again). We don't want to make big mistakes that will be cumbersome and costly to undo (again). As you write, focus on two elements: proof of performance and risk reduction. Assuming I want the big benefit you're promising, I will buy from you if I believe it will work for me and if I'm not taking a risk.

Proof can come in many forms. If you can demonstrate effectiveness, that's the best. Think of the vacuum-cleaner salesperson who shows that the vacuum can suck up a bowling ball — hard to argue with that! Online, many products defy demonstration, although video is expanding the horizon. The next best thing is to get testimonials and endorsements from real customers, describing in their own words what your product or service has done for them.

How long your sales copy should be has been the subject of a decades-long (and utterly pointless) debate in marketing circles. Sales copy should be exactly long enough to get the job done, and not one word longer. The comprehensiveness of your sales pitch depends on the price of the product (more expensive items generally require more substantiation), the severity of the need (the ER doctor doesn't need to give a long speech about why it would be good to staunch the flow of blood from the patient's aorta), and your visitor's familiarity with the product or the producer (I could probably sell J.K. Rowling's next book in five words — "Buy J.K. Rowling's New Book" — but it would take me considerably longer to convince you to buy my new Yiddish-style magic/fantasy novel, *Chaim Mendel and the Enchanted Phylacteries of Thomashevsky*).

Think about the length of your sales copy this way: How long would you talk on a live sales call if your prospect was interested? Would you say 25 words and then shut up? Don't underestimate your prospect's capacity for interest in solving a problem or attaining a goal.

Articles

Not every word on your Web site needs to convince. You build credibility, trust, and reciprocity by sharing your expertise. Remember, your sales copy is only as good as your reputation. Well-written and helpful articles establish your reputation as someone who knows what's good, and who seeks to be helpful.

In addition to building your credibility, articles support the sales process by building the need for what you're selling. For example, if I sell meditation CDs for parents and kids, I could include articles about meditation: health effects, methods, instructions, stories about transformation brought about by meditation, and so on. If I sell special dichromatic green light bulbs for use during meditation, I can include articles about the healing properties of green light.

Articles can also dispel confusion and help your visitors take action. If you sell four brands of flat-screen TV, your visitor may become overwhelmed at all those choices — and do nothing. You can write reviews that compare the brands and models, and help visitors decide which one is right for them.

Blog

A Weblog, or *blog*, is a way of publishing Web content without requiring any design or coding skills. If you can write an e-mail, you can publish a blog. The way blogs have evolved, with bloggers linking to each other and carrying on hyperlinked discussions and arguments back and forth, lend themselves to platforms for expertise.

From its origins as a communications outpost for the hopelessly techie and its phase as a self-absorbed tell-all medium for high school kids, blogging has evolved into a powerful business tool. To be a credible blogger, you not only have to know your stuff, but have your pulse on the rest of your market. You'll discuss industry trends, amplify or argue points made by other blogs and Web sites in your industry, and act like a key opinion leader in your space.

Another feature of blogs is reader interactivity. Your visitors can add comments and questions, engaging in a conversation with you and each other. It's *your* blog; you benefit from being the host of the party.

Dave Taylor of www.intuitive.com teaches clients to blog for business purposes. Go to www.askhowie.com/blogrules to find his article on the 7 Don'ts of Business Blogging.

Your keywords' Quality Scores can benefit from an active blog on your site. Google has spent much of the past three years raising the relevance requirements of AdWords listings. You can improve the relevance of your landing page if it links to dozens or hundreds of other relevant pages. Google schedules its inspections of your site according to how often it thinks you update the site. An active blog, including comments by visitors, induces Google to visit more frequently. The more your site changes, the more up-to-date and relevant Google assumes it to be.

Audio

The biggest drawback to the Internet as a business medium is its impersonal nature. Since people can't look each other in the eye and shake hands, trust will always be a big hurdle in developing business relationships online. Psychologists tell us that most human communication is nonverbal — body language and tone of voice. The sound of your voice on your Web site can go a long way toward making you more real and trustworthy.

You can easily spend thousands of dollars on Web-audio equipment, and in some cases, the investment can be well worth it. But if you just want to see whether the addition of a human voice can improve your conversion, start with a tool you already own and know how to use: the telephone.

Audio Acrobat offers a service for $20 per month that allows you to create audio files for your Web site by talking into a telephone or recording them on your computer. You can easily embed the files in your Web site or send them via e-mail. Visit www.askhowie.com/audio for a demonstration of the service, as well as a video tutorial that shows how to get audio onto your Web site within minutes.

Four ways to spice up your Web site with audio include these:

- **Welcome messages and guidance:** Robert Middleton puts his message and personality right in the center of his home page with an audio introduction. He qualifies the prospect, introduces himself and his Web site, acknowledges common objections, and ends with a clear call to action. The message lasts about a minute, and gives the visitor time to browse the home page and see Robert's smiling face to the left of the audio button. By the time the message is over, Robert's visitors have been welcomed, agitated, reassured, guided, and gently pushed toward the next step. Experience it for yourself at www.actionplan.com — and make sure your computer speakers are turned on.

- **Mini audio sales letters:** Mike Stewart takes the introductory audio message approach one step further with a mini sales letter. He includes two snippets of audio testimonial, and explains why information publishers need to add audio to their product mix. You can listen at www.internetaudioguy.com by clicking the Play button at the right.

- **Testimonials:** Audio is a perfect medium for testimonials, which I cover near the end of Chapter 10. The more testimonials you can collect, the more credible your sales message. Ken McCarthy of www.thesystem seminar.org once remarked at a seminar that business owners should think of their business as a machine to create testimonials. I've collected many testimonials for Leads into Gold by requesting them at the end of a surprise bonus consultation that I offer. I e-mail some of my customers and offer them a 15-minute action consultation, and I set aside half an hour. After the consultation, I ask if they would do me a favor and phone in what they would say to someone who was on the fence about buying Leads into Gold. You can hear some of the best ones at www.leads intogold.com near the bottom of the page.

Audio Acrobat (www.audioacrobat.com) allows you to create multiple testimonial lines, each with its own phone number, so you can provide recorded instructions specific to the product or service your caller is praising.

✔ **High perceived value in your content:** You can answer questions, interview experts or have other people interview you, read articles you've written, comment on current issues, solve common problems, and do it all over the phone without having to suffer writer's block. I discuss a teleseminar strategy at the end of Chapter 11; you can extend this method to collecting and deploying many kinds of valuable audio content.

One way to increase the perceived value of your online audio is to offer the same audio for sale as a CD. Your visitors have the choice to buy the CD for $24.95, or they can simply download the audio in MP3 format free.

If you find you need to edit your audios, you'll find that a well-constructed sound-editing program is easier to use than a word processor. For PCs, I love Sony's Sound Forge Audio Studio program because it's cheap, powerful, and simple. The URL for Sound Forge is ridiculously long, so I'll post it at `www.askhowie.com/sonyaudio` as a live link. A more complicated but free program is the open-source sound editor Audacity, available at `http://audacity.sourceforge.net`. Audacity is also available in a Mac version.

Stick with two forms of online audio:

✔ **Streaming audio:** One format, used by Robert Middleton at `www.actionplan.com`, is streaming audio that can be heard online but not saved or downloaded. It's great for short clips, but a pain for long messages.

You can use the inconvenience factor to your advantage, by offering a downloadable version of the streaming audio in exchange for contact information. You can also sell the same audio on your Web site as a shippable CD, but allow people to download it free. Knowing something has a price automatically increases the perceived value of a free item.

✔ **MP3 files:** The second format is the MP3 file, a format that can be played online through a player or downloaded and saved on a computer, where it can be synced with an iPod or other MP3 player. Think of your customers listening to your wisdom while driving in their cars or working out at the gym — what a rush!

Stay away from Real Media and Microsoft's Windows Media as formats — their players annoy users with constant pop-ups and reminders to buy or upgrade. MP3 is a universal format that sounds great and plays on virtually all players.

Video

As more and more Web users upgrade from dialup to broadband connections, the Internet is ready to serve as an interactive multimedia channel. YouTube has already trained us to watch video online. If you sell products, you can combine the visual and auditory richness of a QVC or infomercial with the click-to-buy immediacy of a Web page with AdWords' ability to show the right message to the right person.

You can use video to demonstrate products, to show even more of your personality to your visitors, to display powerful testimonials, to chat with your market, and much more. With a decent video camera and good lighting, certain types of video content are almost as easy to create as text and audio.

How to use Web video to increase sales

by Joe Chapuis (www.webvideozone.com)

Adding video to your Web site can help attract visitors, add value, and increase site visibility. But you've got to do it right. If you're not careful, putting video on your Web site can actually backfire, chasing people away and causing a lot of headaches for you in the process.

It's never been easier to create and add video to your Web site. But just like with anything else, there is a learning curve, and there are pitfalls. Just because it can be done, doesn't mean it should be done. You need to know when and where to use Web video — and when not to.

In addition, not everyone has the same programs and players on their computers. For example, if you produce all of your videos in QuickTime .mov format, people who don't have (or want to use) QuickTime will never see your video.

Your goal should then be to create videos that are accessible to the greatest common denominator. You'll want to make sure any video you offer is viewable to as many visitors as possible, while minimizing hassles and tech problems for your viewers.

And while it's true that placing video on the Web is now quite easy, that doesn't necessarily mean it's always a good idea. Sometimes, your message can be better told using text with a few images. In other instances, an audio message will suffice. Video isn't the end-all solution for everything you have to say.

So before you rush into posting video on your Web site, consider these important points:

1. Web video done poorly is worse than no video at all.

   This is especially true if your video clips don't play properly, or if the quality of the video reflects poorly on you or your site. In these cases, it would be better not to use Internet video on your site.

2. Internet video may not work for all visitors.

   Some Web surfers are still using Windows 98 or older operating systems. Many of these older systems do not support the playing of video very well. One solution is to offer your video clips in as many different video formats as possible. Unfortunately, this can be a frustrating and time-consuming process for you.

3. Know your target market.

   Not everyone experiences the Internet the same way. People access the Web at very different connection speeds. While more than half of the U.S. Web-connected population now enjoys a high-speed broadband experience (and for these people, video is no problem), there are still many people connecting via painfully slow telephone modems.

   By knowing who you are targeting, you can better determine if video makes sense for your site, as well as the best way to deploy it.

4. Video requires a lot of storage space.

   On average, a one-minute video clip of average quality and resolution often requires at least 2MB of Web hosting space. If you offer that same clip in the six most popular formats, it is possible that you would need 20MB of space — just for that one minute of video! And if you offer a total of 20 minutes of video, and provide it in all different formats, you could easily consume 400MB of Web space.

5. Video is a bandwidth hog.

   If 100 people click to view your 5-minute video at the same time, they could jointly require and consume 2GB of bandwidth, all at the same time! Depending upon your hosting package, that alone could exceed your allocated monthly bandwidth.

   Imagine what would happen if 1,000 people clicked to view your 5-minute video . . . your Web host would likely crash, due to the inability to fulfill the huge bandwidth request. And your Web host won't be very happy. And neither will you, when they send you their bill.

6. Clicking away from your site and your Internet video is effortless.

   Even with the fastest Web connection, viewing high quality video on a computer monitor can be tedious — especially compared to watching that same video on TV. For best results, Web video clips should be short (under three minutes) and to the point.

   Once the novelty wears off (and it will, once video becomes commonplace — very soon), people are going to be less willing to sit there and watch some idiot skateboarding off his roof.

   In order to grab and hold attention, and get some kind of result, Internet video needs to be compelling, useful, and/or entertaining.

7. Be careful when choosing an Internet video format.

   Whether the video you plan to offer is a computer screen tutorial, or live video footage shot with a camcorder, you may want to offer your video in multiple formats, making it viewable by as many people as possible.

   But at the same time, too many choices may confuse and overwhelm your audience. In addition, there are time and cost considerations for creating and deploying your videos. If you offer five different choices, you need to create and upload five different videos. (And what happens if you need to make a change to the video?).

Joe Chapuis is the founder of www.web videozone.com, *which offers tools, tips, and tutorials to help businesses profit from Web video. Go to* www.askhowie.com/video *for Joe's reviews of various video formats and methods of hosting video files, as well as his take on the right and wrong way to use YouTube/Google Video.*

Saying "make yourself at home" with video

Online video can serve as a warm welcome to your Web site; a way to say hello, orient your visitor, and create an immediate emotional bond. If you think of your Web site as your home, and your visitors as, well, your visitors, you can open the door; smile; invite them in; take their coats; and offer them a chair, a cup of tea, and directions to the bathroom. Michael Katz accomplishes this with a short and charming video welcome at `bluepenguindevelopment.com`. (It begins, "Hi, I'm Michael Katz, and if you've never seen what I look like before, let me just say, I share your disappointment.")

Giving a shop tour with video

Josephine Canovas is a professional horse breeder and trainer in Spain. She sells Andalusian horses internationally. Obviously, most of her customers will not travel to her horse farm to view the horses and their living conditions. She uses video to show, rather than tell, about her horses and the care they receive. At `www.andalusians-for-you.com/break-page-1.html` you can view raw video of the stable and its daily happenings.

Running a Home Shopping Channel on your site

The Web boasts several significant advantages over TV shopping shows:

- ✔ The production costs are much lower.

- ✔ You are showing products to people who are searching for those products, rather than just channel surfing during commercials.

- ✔ Your visitors can program your channel to show the exact product they're interested in right now, rather than wading through hours of knives and dehydrators to get to the levitating steamer basket.

- ✔ You can make money with small market items because you're attracting high-quality traffic and you don't have to keep paying to air your show.

- ✔ You can complete the transaction in the same medium as you're selling. When you watch TV, you can't buy the product using the TV — you need to pick up the phone.

At `www.myweddingfavors.tv` (shown in Figure 12-5), you can watch a home shopping–style show and choose among Beach Favors, Seasonal Favorites, Bridal Shower Favorites, and others. When the hosts show and describe an item, the Web page changes to display that item to the right of the video, along with buttons for More Info, E-mail a Friend, and Buy This Item.

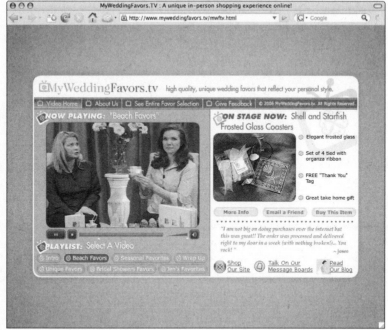

Figure 12-5:
The videos on My Wedding Favors.tv bring products to life in ways that static text and photo Web pages cannot.

Displaying customer testimonials

As marketing consultant Dan Hollings of www.danhollings.com says, "The most important thing a marketer can possess is a good review or testimonial, and there are only two reasons why you might not have a bounty of these on hand: 1) your product or service stinks or 2) you're not asking." A slew of video testimonials reassures your prospect that they aren't going to be your guinea pig, that you have a history of success and happy customers.

To reassure meeting planners that I can deliver a great talk, I've compiled dozens of video testimonials at askhowie.com/videopraise. (See Figure 12-6.) I collected them using a $100 Flip Video camera. After my talks, when people come up and say thanks, I whip out the camera and ask, "Could I record your comments to use as a testimonial on my site?" If they say yes, I coach them briefly ("Say your name, where you're from, and one specific thing you found helpful.") If they say no, I look extremely sad and start to sniffle — works like a charm.

Figure 12-6:
The author
collects
video
testimonials
from
audience
members at
live events.

Teaching with video

Whatever your business, you have expertise that other people lack. When you make that expertise available online, you gain credibility as an expert helper, not just a self-interested peddler. Video offers the highest emotional bandwidth for your visitors to assess your knowledge and your character. Oliver Sachs wrote in *The Man Who Mistook His Wife for a Hat* about a group of patients in the aphasia ward who were laughing hysterically at a speech given by then-president Reagan. Although the patients had lost the ability to understand language, they ascertained he was lying by observing his facial expressions, gestures, and vocal tones and cadences. Just as video can destroy trust, it can also build trust when your goal is to be helpful and straight with your market.

The Kabbalah education site www.arionline.info features instructional videos that introduce the subject of Kabbalah and the instructors. Through music, spoken word, and moving images, the videos not only instruct but also elicit emotional reactions. Just as many of us have developed crushes on total strangers because we see them in Hollywood movies (I still have a thing for Amy Irving in *Crossing Delancey*, heaven help me), skillful video can create relationships with customers you haven't met yet, and may never meet in person.

The *For Dummies* people wouldn't let me include actual videos on these pages, even though I know it can be done from watching *Harry Potter* movies. While I can't show you any video examples in these pages, you can go to `www.ask howie.com/video` for links and discussions of good and bad uses of Internet video.

Recognizing and welcoming returning visitors with PHP

In Chapter 10, I show you how the PHP programming language can serve your visitors customized Web pages straight from the AdWords click. You can also use PHP to recognize returning visitors, so you can present them with relevant information and offers.

You've seen this in action if you're an Amazon.com customer. You're greeted by name, which is nice, but the really powerful application is the personalized recommendations based on your previous shopping history. In Figure 12-7, Amazon.com asks me whether I'm aware that it sells organic food. Actually, I wasn't aware of it because I've never bought groceries from Amazon.com before. So how did it know/figure out/guess that I'm into healthy eating? Hmmm, do you think my prior purchases of *Disease-Proof Your Child: Feeding Kids Right,* by Joel Fuhrman (St. Martin's Griffin), and *The China Study: The Most Comprehensive Study of Nutrition Ever Conducted and the Startling Implications for Diet, Weight Loss, and Long-Term Health,* by T. Colin Campbell and Thomas M. Campbell II (Benbella Books), had anything to do with it?

Amazon.com uses its enormous database of customer behavior to make targeted offers. You can accomplish the same thing, on a much simpler scale, by engaging a PHP programmer to create a script that recognizes people who've visited your site before, and make the next offer. Rob Goyette of `www. howtomarketbetter.com` gives the following example of a simple returning customer page headline for an online sporting goods store: "Welcome back, Howie, I hope you're enjoying your new ping-pong table. Do you want to see our line of tournament-quality paddles and balls?"

Figure 12-7:
Amazon.
com offers
me organic
food,
probably
based on my
history of
buying and
browsing
healthy
cookbooks
and other
books on
natural
health.

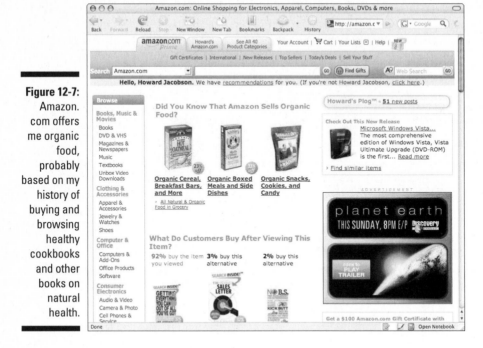

Part V
Testing Your Strategies and Tracking Your Results

The 5th Wave   By Rich Tennant

"Hey-here's a company that develops short memorable domain names for new businesses. It's listed at www.CompanyThatDevelopsShort-MemorableDomainNamesForNewBusinesses.com."

In this part . . .

*O*ne of my favorite things about the Internet is how cheaply and quickly I can fail — and how much I can learn from each failure. This part reveals simple strategies that virtually guarantee success if you implement them diligently, no matter how many failures you encounter.

Chapter 13 explains how to continually improve your ads by running multiple ads simultaneously and showing the different versions randomly to Google searchers. (Hint: Write two ads — Google does this automatically if you know how to change the default campaign settings.) Here's where you also get a handle on split-testing pages on your Web site.

Chapter 14 continues the split-testing theme by introducing you to Google's free Web Site Optimizer tool, which allows you to perform simple split tests and robust multivariate tests (in English: "really cool and powerful stuff") to improve the performance of your Web site.

The immensely powerful AdWords conversion-tracking feature is covered in Chapter 15. I show you how to add code to your Web site so Google can tell you how much money you're making or losing from every single ad and keyword. Armed with this intelligence, you can dramatically improve profitability and reduce your AdWords spend.

In Chapter 16, I introduce Google Analytics, a comprehensive Web-site statistics program that ties in with AdWords to give you even more information about how to design an effective Web site.

Chapter 13

How You Can't Help Becoming an Advertising Genius

In This Chapter

▶ Exploring split testing with AdWords

▶ Setting up simple and powerful split tests

▶ Declaring winning and losing ads

▶ Generating ideas to test

Most people find that writing an effective AdWords ad is challenging. In the old days (2004, actually), advertisers found their ads swatted down constantly by the 0.5% CTR (click-through rate) threshold. That is, not even 5 in 1,000 searchers would click their ad, and Google felt that an ad so unattractive did not deserve to remain active.

The difficulty of successful ad creation is understandable — you have 130 characters to convince someone to choose your offer over 19 other close-to-identical listings on the same page. Plus, writing good ads is tough in the best of circumstances.

Perry Marshall gave a talk in which he demonstrated the need for split testing by challenging audience members — professional marketers all — to choose the more effective ad or headline from a series of 10 split tests. The best of us got no more than 4 or 5 out of 10 correct. As we held our hands up high and proud for having achieved 50 percent on the test, Perry shot us down: "If I had flipped a coin, I would have done as well as you. Congratulations. You guys are as smart as a penny."

If you want to be smarter than a penny, you must apply the most powerful tool in the marketer's arsenal: split testing.

In this chapter, I show you how to set up split testing with AdWords and analyze the results. I tell you about split-testing landing pages, as well as your entire sales process. Also, you discover only what you need to know about *statistical significance* (which, in this case, relates to your confidence level that the split-testing results are repeatable) to make the best choices about your ads.

Capturing the Magic of Split Testing

Nothing leads to improvement faster than timely and clear feedback. While a million monkeys typing would eventually produce the entire works of Shakespeare, they would get there much faster if they got a banana every time they typed an actual word and an entire banana split when they managed a rhymed couplet in iambic pentameter. (Can you tell I've been reading *Shakespeare For Dummies,* by John Doyle and Ray Lischner?) And for every nonword, someone would chuck a copy of *Typing Shakespeare For Monkeys* at them.

Now suppose the monkeys could keep and understand a written record of the characters that produced bananas, banana splits, and no reward. After a while, you would see more and more real words and Shakespearean phrasing, and fewer xlkjdfsdfsr. Ouch!

AdWords contains the world's simplest mechanism for getting timely and clear feedback on your ads. You can create multiple ads, which AdWords shows to your prospects in equal rotation, and you can receive automatic and ongoing feedback.

Split testing is not an AdWords innovation — direct marketers have been testing customers' response rates since Moses got two tablets of commandments. *Readers' Digest* used to choose headlines for its articles by sending postcards to readers, asking which articles they would be interested in reading in an upcoming issue. The list of articles was actually a list of headlines for the same article.

Here's how split testing works in AdWords:

1. **Run multiple ads simultaneously within a single ad group.**

2. **Monitor the effectiveness of all ads at eliciting the customer response you want.**

   Continue monitoring until one of those ads has proven itself better at its calling.

3. **Declare the proven ad the winner (or, in marketing geek-speak, the *control*).**

4. **Retire the less successful ad, replace it with a new challenger, and repeat the contest.**

   If the challenger does better, it becomes the new control. If the control maintains supremacy, you send a different challenger up against it.

The beauty of this split-testing system is that you can't help but improve your results over time. If a new ad proves worse than your control, simply delete it. And the added beauty is that you don't even have to know what you're doing to improve your ad's effectiveness. While market intelligence, creativity, and writing skill help, mere trial and error — when funneled through split testing — can boost your results significantly.

One of my early AdWords projects was an ad for a direct-marketing home-study course for small businesses (see the series of ads in Figure 13-1). An early ad, headlined "Cold calling — now illegal," achieved a 0.7% CTR. The final ad I used — "Cold calling not working?" — nearly quadrupled that with a 2.7% CTR. The big lesson from this long series of ads is this: I had no idea what I was doing at the time, yet I still succeeded. Take a few minutes and examine each of the ads carefully. Be honest — could you predict which of these ads would do better than the rest? I couldn't. I still can't. But the numbers don't lie, and I was able to turn a marginal product into a success thanks to split testing.

Cold calling not working? Discover a powerful alternative. Free report and 2 chapter download. www.LeadsIntoGold.com — 2.60%	**End cold calling forever** Small business marketing system. Download 2 chapters for free. www.leadsintogold.com — 1.35%
Cold calling not working? Discover an effective alternative. Free report and 2 chapter download. www.LeadsIntoGold.com — 2.35%	**Stop cold prospecting.** Small business marketing system. Free report and 2 chapter download. www.leadsintogold.com — 1.04%
End cold calling forever Lead generation system explained. Free report and 2 chapter download. www.LeadsIntoGold.com — 2.28%	**End cold calling forever** and make more money. Free report and 2 chapter download. www.leadsintogold.com — 1.00%
End cold calling forever Lead generation system explained. Free report and 2 chapter download. www.leadsintogold.com — 2.26%	**End cold calling forever** Small business marketing system. Free report and 2 chapter download. www.leadsintogold.com — 0.83%
Cold calling ineffective? Discover a powerful alternative. Free report and 2 chapter download. www.LeadsIntoGold.com — 2.22%	**Stop cold calling forever** Small business marketing system. Free report and 2 chapter download. www.leadsintogold.com — 0.82%
End cold calling forever Attract customers automatically. Free report and 2 chapter download. www.leadsintogold.com — 2.18%	**Cold calling -now illegal** Effective alternative explained. Free report and 2 chapter download. www.LeadsIntoGold.com — 0.76%
End cold calling forever Attract customers automatically. Free report and 2 chapter download. www.LeadsIntoGold.com — 2.04%	**End cold calling forever** Free report and 2 chapter download. Attract customers automatically. www.leadsintogold.com — 0.00%
End cold calling forever Free report and 2 chapter download. Lead generation system explained. www.leadsintogold.com — 1.95%	**Stop wasteful advertising** Small business marketing system. Free report and 2 chapter download. www.leadsintogold.com — 0.00%
End cold calling forever Small business marketing system. Free report and 2 chapter download. www.leadsintogold.com — 1.76%	

Figure 13-1:
The author ignorantly split tests his way to profitability.

Conducting Split Testing with AdWords

Split-testing with AdWords follows the four-step process outlined in the preceding section. You can prepare yourself to launch a series of split-testing ads by getting curious about what messages will be most compelling to your prospects. Turn each message into an ad and get ready to have fun.

Creating a challenger ad

Creating your second ad is even easier than creating your first (see Chapter 3 for step-by-step instructions):

1. **From the Campaigns tab, click the Ads rollup tab group name to see a list of all the ads in your account.**

2. **Click the Ad Group name to the right of the ad you wish to challenge.**

3. **Click the New Ad button just above and to the left of the list of ads.**

4. **Choose Text Ad from the drop-down list.**

   An ad template with sample copy appears on-screen, as shown in Figure 13-2.

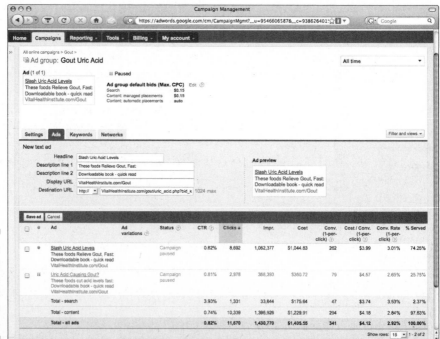

Figure 13-2: Creating a new ad on the Ad Variations tab.

5. **Type over the existing copy and URL with your challenger ad's copy and URL.**

6. **Click the Save Ad button.**

After your challenger ad is in place, you want to make sure that your two ads will compete fairly. Google assumes you're too busy (or lazy) to monitor your split tests, so the default setting is for AdWords to show the ad with the higher CTR more, and gradually let the poorer-performing ad slip into oblivion.

You want to override this setting for two reasons:

✔ An ad with a lower CTR may still be the more profitable ad (see Chapter 15 for details of this apparent paradox).

✔ When you let AdWords evaluate the ads without your supervision, you don't learn anything that makes you a smarter advertiser. The faster you declare winning and losing ads, the faster your marketing improves.

Here's how you override the AdWords default setting that may kill an ad without your approval. (***Note:*** You establish this setting on the campaign level, so you may need to do this with each campaign.)

1. **From the Campaigns tab, click the Campaigns rollup tab to generate a list of all campaigns in your account.**

2. **Check the name of the campaign you wish to edit.**

3. **Click the Settings rollup tab.**

   A page with various campaign-level settings appears.

4. **Scroll down to Advanced Settings at the very bottom of the page, and click the Edit link next to Ad Rotation.**

   If you can't find the Ad Rotation setting, you may have to open the Ad delivery section by clicking the Ad Delivery: Ad Rotation, Ad Frequency Link at the bottom of the page.

5. **Click the radio button next to Rotate: Show ads more evenly.**

6. **Click the Save button at the bottom of the Campaign Settings page.**

Now you're split-testing properly. Once you install conversion tracking (see Chapter 15), you have the ability to compare the profitability of your ads. Until then, the only thing you can compare is the CTR.

If you ever deploy Google's Conversion Optimizer tool on a campaign, you must revert to the default option, where Google shows your better performing ads more often.

Monitoring the split test

Just as you wouldn't put a cake in a 350° F oven and not pay attention to when it was done, you wouldn't set up a split test and then ignore the results. You have three ways to check up on your cake to make sure it doesn't burn and the fork comes out clean:

- **Haphazardly:** Check up on your cake when you think of it. As long as you catch it before the smoke alarm does, the cake might turn out okay.

- **Annoyingly:** Set your watch to beep every few minutes to remind you to check the cake.

- **Geekily:** Install a sensor in the oven that alerts you when the cake is done.

These three methods are available for monitoring your AdWords split tests as well:

- **With the haphazard method,** you can look at each ad group once a day, once every three days, once a week, whenever Dartmouth wins a football game, and so on. The interval you choose should relate to the amount of traffic your ads are getting. For example, if you get 50 clicks per day, you might want to check your ads every day. A huge stream of traffic will give you a winner much quicker than a trickle, all other things being equal. But even if your traffic is massive, wait at least a couple of days before declaring a winner. Visitors checking out your ad at three o'clock in the morning on Sunday are likely to be very different from Monday afternoon visitors. You want to collect a representative sample to be sure your results are accurate.

- **With the annoying, repetitive method,** you can create reports within AdWords and schedule those reports (see Chapter 15).

- **With the geeky, pass-the-buck method,** you can subscribe to a third-party service that monitors all your split tests and e-mails you when you have a winner (see the section, "Automating your testing with Winner Alert" later in this chapter).

Declaring a winner

Okay, so you're watching your split tests with eagle eyes and keen concentration. How do you know when one ad has outperformed another? After all, as the investment ads say, "Past performance doesn't guarantee future results." Fortunately, the testing process is simple and straightforward when you're running a single test of two different ads. You just want to answer the question, "Is this result real, or just a random coincidence?" That's where your friend and mine — statistical significance — makes a welcome appearance.

Understanding statistical significance

If I flip a coin twice and it lands heads both times, should I assume that coin would always come up heads? Of course not — two flips do not give me enough data to reach that conclusion. What about four flips, all heads? Less likely, but still plausible? What about ten flips, all heads? Are we getting a tad suspicious now? It could still be due to random chance — after all, every single flip of a fair coin has an equal chance of landing heads or tails — or, possibly, this is no fair coin. If I get to 20, 30, or 100 flips with no tails in sight, I can be pretty sure something's up.

In your AdWords split testing, you're looking for information that will tell you that something's up. You want to know that one ad is truly better than another, and that the difference in CTR is not because of randomness. Just as with the coin, you can never know for absolute certain. Statistical significance tells you the probability that you're making the right choice.

Testing for significance

If you're doing it yourself, here are the steps to assessing the significance of your results and deciding whether to declare a winner:

1. **From your AdWords account, click through to the Ad Group you want to test.**

2. **Click the Ad Variations tab, and write down the following numbers:**
    - Number of clicks for Ad #1
    - Impressions for Ad #1
    - Number of clicks for Ad #2
    - Impressions for Ad #2

3. **Go to www.askhowie.com/split and enter the four numbers in the appropriate fields.**

4. **Look at your confidence interval and see whether you have a winner.**

I'm willing to accept a 95% threshold for my split testing. I can live with the knowledge that 1 out of every 20 split tests is giving me a bogus sense of confidence. Below that, I want to keep running the test until I achieve significance or until I'm satisfied that there really is no difference between the two ads.

What if you have no winner?

Say you're testing two ads, and they're running neck and neck for days. Weeks. Months. In this case, you're losing money by continuing the test. Sure, at some point, the data might tip one way or the other, but the simple fact is the difference isn't going to be important in real life. Drop the challenger (keeping the control makes sense because it has more history behind it) and get a new challenger. Pull the plug on a test when each ad has at least 100 clicks.

Mechanics of Split Testing in AdWords

Because of the way Google assigns quality scores to keyword/ad combinations, you need to make sure you're giving your challenger ads a fair chance. Google, like most people, prefers old friends to new acquaintances. This means that an ad that's been running for a while and doing well (meaning, good CTR and clearly relevant) will have a higher quality score than a new ad. Therefore, the control ad will display in a higher position, which gives it an artificial boost in CTR. So, you may incorrectly keep a control ad because of its unfair advantage.

The solution is to create a copy of the control ad and test it against the challenger. Both ads start out with zero impressions and an assumption of equal quality. Even though the copy is an exact clone of the control ad, Google doesn't recognize it as an old friend. Therefore, your split test will compare the ads fairly, allowing you to choose the real winner.

While you're at it, I recommend creating three copies of your control ad, not just one. That way, you get to show your control ad (that is, the one you know is working the best) to 80 percent of searchers, rather than 50 percent. Think about it — would you trust half your business to a new, totally untested salesperson? By creating multiple copies of the control ad, you're reducing your risk in case the new ad is a total failure. (See Figure 13-3.)

Figure 13-3:
The control ad (top) achieved a much higher CTR than its three identical clones because of a better Quality Score.

Variations	Actions	Status ▼	% Served	Clicks	Impr.	CTR	Cost
Hire a Nanny in LA FT, PT, Live-in & Live Out Nannies Prescreened, CPR Certified, Legal www.NeverlandNannies.com/LA	Edit	Active	20.6%	8	104	7.69%	$17.71
Hire a Nanny in LA FT, PT, Live-in & Live Out Nannies Prescreened, CPR Certified, Legal www.NeverlandNannies.com/LA	Edit	Active	18.4%	3	93	3.22%	$6.81
Hire a Nanny in LA FT, PT, Live-in & Live Out Nannies Prescreened, CPR Certified, Legal www.NeverlandNannies.com/LA	Edit	Active	19.2%	3	97	3.09%	$7.10
Hire a Nanny in LA FT, PT, Live-in & Live Out Nannies Prescreened, CPR Certified, Legal www.NeverlandNannies.com/LA	Edit	Active	17.8%	2	90	2.22%	$4.08
Find a Nanny in LA FT, PT, Live-in & Live Out Nannies Prescreened, CPR Certified, Legal www.NeverlandNannies.com/LA	Edit	Active	9.9%	1	50	2.00%	$2.34

Also, as Richard Mouser of www.scientificwebsitetesting.com points out, the different CTRs of the three identical copies of the control ad will converge at the point of statistical significance. So if you have three identical copies at CTRs of 3.1%, 1.6%, and 0.8%, then you know instantly you haven't run the test long enough to be confident in the results.

Strategies for Effective Split Testing

Many AdWords beginners understand the concept of split testing, but do it haphazardly and without strategy. They learn that split testing is too confusing and complicated, and give up on the most powerful weapon in their marketing arsenal. The following sections discuss three strategies to assure a streamlined and effective split-testing process.

1. Start wide, get narrow

When you begin to split-test in an ad group, choose two very different ads. You may want to focus on different markets (stay-at-home dads versus divorced/widowed dads with full custody), different emotional responses (greed versus fear), or different benefits (lose weight versus prevent heart disease). Get the big picture right before drilling down to the details. It does you no good to test *easy* versus *simple* in a headline if your prospects don't care about ease or simplicity, but just whether it can run on batteries.

After you discover the right market, key benefits, and the emotional hot buttons of that market, you can start testing more specific elements (see the upcoming section, "Generating Ideas for Ad Testing").

2. Keep track of your tests

Remember high school chemistry class? You had to buy a marble notebook and keep track of all your experiments, including date, hypothesis, experiment design, and results.

Chances are that your bright ideas about ad testing are not new. If you don't keep track somehow, you'll find yourself repeating experiments to which you already know the answer. Keeping track of your results in a marble notebook, or its digital equivalent (a Word document, private blog, or Excel spreadsheet), is therefore crucial to moving forward efficiently.

3. Split-testing is just asking questions

Split-testing can become so mechanical, it's easy to forget the purpose is to make you smarter by learning what makes your customers tick — er, *click*.

Perry Marshall distinguishes between true market research and what he calls "opinion research." Opinion research is what people *say* they'll do. Market research is what they *actually* do. Split testing is a powerful form of market research that will provide answers to whatever questions you ask. As computer programmers are fond of saying, "Garbage In, Garbage Out." If you ask intelligent questions, you'll get useful answers.

So before you run a split test, take a moment to write down (in your lab notebook, of course) the question you want your prospects to answer for you. Then design a split test that asks that question.

The following figures show some examples of good questions and the split tests that were set up to answer them:

How much traffic do I give up if I put the price of the product in the ad? (See Figure 13-4.)

Figure 13-4:
Including the price in an ad cuts my traffic in half.

Variations	Clicks	Impr.	CTR ▼
Beat Gout with Food. End the pain - take control. Downloadable book - quick read. VitalHealthInstitute.com	66	31,931	0.20%
Beat Gout with Food. End the pain - take control. Downloadable book - $17.77 VitalHealthInstitute.com	34	32,024	0.10%

Will positioning my product as a "professional shares his secrets" increase clicks, compared to flagging the benefit of family fun? (See Figure 13-5.)

Figure 13-5:
The "pro-tells-all" approach is a clear winner.

Variations	Clicks	Impr.	CTR ▼
Get started Beekeeping. Set up hives, harvest honey - stay safe and have fun! A pro tells all. www.Beekeeping-Secrets.com	287	6,071	4.72%
Get started Beekeeping. Set up hives, harvest honey - be safe and have fun! Family activity. www.Beekeeping-Secrets.com	203	4,781	4.24%

Generating Ideas for Ad Testing

You want to test broadly different ideas before getting into details. Don't worry about whether description line 2 should have a comma in it before you've figured out the answers to your big questions. Imagine that you're searching for the most delicious plum in the world. First, you test the orchard to make sure it has plum trees and not orange trees. When you find the plum orchard, start testing trees to find the tree with the best plums. When you find the best tree, see whether you prefer the plums near the top or closer to the ground. On the north or the south side. Then taste the fruit on different limbs, and after you find the most promising limb, see which branch yields the best fruit.

David Bullock's (`www.davidbullock.com`) list of big questions from Chapter 6 comes in handy here:

- Who is looking?
- What are they looking for?
- Why are they looking for it?
- What will be the result of their search?
- What does the searcher want the ultimate outcome to be?
- What is the emotional good feeling they seek?
- What emotional outcome are they trying to avoid?
- Who does the searcher care about?
- What does the searcher care about?

In other words, split-test the ads to discover the demographics and psychographics of your market. Who are they — working mothers or single professionals taking care of aging parents? What big benefit are they looking for in your product — saving time or assuaging guilt? Are they angry with their company or do they feel grateful? Who do they want to help them with this problem — Walter Cronkite or Jon Stewart?

Use your split tests to answer these questions as best you can. Write down a hypothesis and brainstorm two ads that will prove or disprove it. After you test the big ideas, turn your attention to the little things that can make a big difference:

- **Order of lines:** If you're highlighting the benefit on line 1 and explaining a feature on line 2, try switching the order of the two lines.

- **Display URLs:** If you buy a bunch of domain names related to your main domain, you can point them all to the same Web site and test which domain name attracts the right customers. If you have the `.com` and `.org` for the same domain, will one outperform the other?

- **Capitalization:** Finding the right capitalization of your URL to make its meaning stand out is an art form. For example, I found that `LeadsintoGold.com` did better than `leadsintogold.com` in almost every test.

✔ **Synonyms:** Try variations of your benefits: simple/easy/quick/no sweat.

✔ **Punctuation:** Perry Marshall talks about the cadence of an ad — the way the searchers hear it in the mind's ear can subtly influence whether they resonate with it. Use punctuation to make the phrase more melodic and persuasive. Figure 13-6 shows what happened when I used a comma to put the emphasis on *You* rather than *Instead*:

Figure 13-6:
In this split test, a comma quadruples the CTR.

Variations	CTR ▼
Cold Calls Don't Work Prospects Hanging Up on You? Get Them to Call You, Instead! LeadsintoGold.com	2.02%
Cold Calls Don't Work Prospects Hanging Up on You? Get Them to Call You Instead! LeadsintoGold.com	0.49%

The ad with the comma is four times as effective as the other one. Without testing, there's no way I would have predicted the effect would be so profound.

Tools for Split Testing

With the proper tools, split testing can be the most powerful tactic in your entire marketing strategy. The following tools allow you to split test faster to improve faster.

Automating your testing with Winner Alert

My AdWords account is quite large at this point. I have 27 separate campaigns. Many of the campaigns include dozens of ad groups. Each of these groups is running a split test pretty much all the time. I probably have to monitor well over 100 split tests simultaneously. If I were to go into each ad group, pull out the data, and enter it into a statistical significance calculator, it would take me the better part of a day just to assess the tests. And that doesn't even include the time it takes me to think up new ad variations to challenge the winners.

If you're just starting out and you're running fewer than 10 ad groups at a time, you won't feel my pain. But after your campaigns grow, you'll either stop tracking the results of your tests or you'll wait too long to find winners. Wait too long and you're ignoring profit-growing market data and showing prospects suboptimal ads.

To help alleviate this problem, I created a Winner Alert tool that automates the process of tracking statistical significance, and e-mails you whenever one of your split tests produces a winner. It's a great tool, and when you're ready for it, you can try it free for a month. Go to www.askhowie.com/winner for video demos and your coupon code.

Turbocharging your testing with Taguchi

The Taguchi Method lets you test hundreds of variations in a fraction of the time it would take if you used a standard A-B split. It's not for beginners; the methodology is so complicated, it's easy to fall into the Garbage-In-Garbage-Out trap and believe you have the answer to Life, the Universe, and Everything because the printout looks so impressive.

You should consider Taguchi testing if and only if your keywords get at least several thousand daily impressions each, and if the person setting up your test has experience using Taguchi for marketing. Taguchi testing was originally developed to reduce manufacturing errors, and many practitioners misapply a manufacturing mindset to the marketing process. David Bullock is the premiere Taguchi marketer who applies the method to AdWords. You can find an article he wrote to protect you from incorrect and unnecessary use of Taguchi at www.askhowie.com/taguchi.

Split-Testing Web Pages

Although you can split-test other elements of your Web site using ad split testing (for example, running two visually identical ads with different destination URLs), you get better results by using Google's free Web Site Optimizer tool (see Chapter 14 for details).

Chapter 14

Making More Sales with Website Optimizer

In This Chapter

▶ Deciding what to test

▶ Setting up landing page tests

▶ Interpreting test results

▶ Testing continually for massive improvement

In the movie *Groundhog Day,* Bill Murray plays a surly, cynical weatherman fated to relive the same day — February 2 in Punxsutawney, Pennsylvania — over and over again. Along the way, he learns to sculpt ice, play piano, and dance. Eventually, he falls in love with his producer, played by Andie McDowell. In his quest to win her heart, Murray's character fails repeatedly to impress and attract her. But he learns from every failure and adapts his behavior, until he has transformed himself into a suave, considerate, and heroic companion.

When you split-test pages on your Web site, you can accomplish the same sort of trial-and-error adaptation with your visitors and prospects, without having to spend quasi-eternity in Pennsylvania. Your tool of choice, compliments of Google, is the free, powerful, and elegant Website Optimizer.

Website Optimizer allows you to test different variations of your Web pages to see which ones give you more of the results you want. Will your visitors respond better to a product photo, video, or testimonial in a given region of the page? Will more people buy if you offer a 50 percent discount or a two-for-one sale? Should your headline read, "Natural Soaps for All Occasions" or "You Probably Stink"?

Testing, part of the DNA of direct marketing, has been practiced for well over 100 years. In the old days, advertisers would test direct mail campaigns at a cost of thousands or tens of thousands of dollars, and would get results months after initiating the test. On the Web, you can generate the same quality of data with a few minutes of setup and a few days or weeks of data gathering. Most site owners never test, so they never discover that they're missing 50 percent to 100 percent increases in sales — and that range is conservative, because you won't believe the real possibilities until you experience them for yourself.

In this chapter, I borrow heavily from the expertise of Richard Mouser, testing genius and proprietor of www.scientificwebsitetesting.com. Richard launched an e-commerce site, www.mrwaterfilter.com, in 2004, and tested his way from losing money to becoming highly profitable in a very competitive market, home water filters. Richard and I guide you to create a testing strategy, set up tests, analyze the results, and take action to produce more effective and profitable Web sites. Richard should get credit for all the good information in this chapter. But all the bad jokes are mine.

Deciding What to Test

Website Optimizer makes it so easy to set up and run tests, you may be tempted to jump right in before doing the necessary planning and preparation. So before I show you how to crank your testing engine, I talk about how to develop a strategy that gets you going in the right direction. The first step is to figure out what to test.

Here's the problem: Your landing page consists of dozens of different elements — headlines, subheads, body copy, navigation bars, images, fonts, color schemes, and on and on — and each can be changed in practically infinite ways. If you were to test each element randomly, you'd feel like a monkey at a keyboard aiming to produce *King Lear*. It would take forever, you'd have no guarantee of ever getting there, and you'd develop a nasty case of simian carpal tunnel syndrome.

And, you've already created the best site you could build. So where can you go for new ideas?

Testing Principle #1: Start big, get smaller

In Chapter 13, you see some examples of very tiny changes in ad copy that lead to very different results. The addition of a comma increased my CTR four times! So you might think that similar small changes would work for site testing as well. Generally, they don't. Instead, go for giant differences. That way, you'll get clearer results faster.

For example, you may want to find out if your visitors will respond better to a video or a still image at the top of the page. That's a big difference. Do they prefer a short page or a long page? A professional-looking site or one that could have been put together by your nephew in about 15 minutes?

After you answer the big questions, you can look at the nuances and details. But if your first tests are showing no difference in results, the difference between options A and B aren't big enough to matter.

Testing Principle #2: Tests are just questions in action

Maybe you still have flashbacks to 11th grade chemistry class, where you had to write down hypotheses and experimental methods in your marble notebook, and then try to avoid setting your hair on fire with a Bunsen burner? If so, please relax when it comes to scientific Web site testing. Running a test is just asking a question and inviting your visitors to answer with their actions.

One of my tests started with the question, "How much do the visitors to this page know about me already?" Do I need to spend time introducing myself and establishing credibility by telling them I'm my mother's favorite AdWords author or cut right to the chase and entice them to purchase the *Look Over My Shoulder* AdWords Video Series?

My test had to put that question into action, by creating an option that assumed familiarity and an option that didn't. I created two pages, cleverly named Long and Short. The long page introduced me in depth before getting down to business, and the short page started talking about their situation and why watching short online videos was the answer to their prayers.

Testing Principle #3: Test to overcome objections

While you brainstorm questions to turn into tests, familiarize yourself to all the reasons your visitors aren't doing what you want. Is it too hard? That is, do you have a usability issue of complicated menus, cumbersome forms, and hidden buttons? Or are visitors unpersuaded? If so, you need to work on the elements that create comfort, build credibility, and describe relevant and desirable benefits.

Karl Blanks and Ben Jesson of `www.conversion-rate-experts.com` make this simple with their objection/counter-objection approach. First, you determine the likely objection. Then, make changes that address that objection.

For example, if the objection is, "I don't trust you or your company enough to buy something or give you my contact information," then you add trust elements such as endorsements; photos of your staff, office or warehouse; years in business; Hacker Safe seals, and so on.

If they can't differentiate your product from your competitors', then test elements that show the advantages of your product. If they're afraid of making a mistake, introduce and test risk-reduction strategies, such as a free trial or money-back guarantee.

In other words, don't focus your testing on the elements of your site ("Red or blue headline here?"). Focus on what the users need in order to feel good about doing what you want them to do.

Testing Principle #4: Look for things that don't work

Testing isn't always about finding things that work better. Sometimes you learn more when your great idea falls flat. Instead of shaking your head and saying, "Well, that bombed," get an inquisitive look in your eyes and ask, "Now why didn't my visitors go for that?"

That question gets you out of your head and into the heads of your visitors — the people who are interacting with your site in an attempt to achieve a personal goal. When you understand what your visitors don't like, and what gets in their way, you can apply that knowledge to the rest of your marketing — online and off.

When you test, you're developing your instincts for what works and what doesn't work. Over time, this is where testing really pays off. By experiencing success and failure, you gain insight into your market and become better at creating effective promotions for them.

Creating a Testing Plan

After you generate your testing ideas, your "I wonder . . ." questions, and the likely objections, you can build your testing plan. Richard recommends three simple steps to get you started (and hooked on) testing.

1. Make a list of things you want to test.

2. Prioritize that list.

3. Start testing and keep adding to the list based on test results.

The next few sections discuss these steps in detail.

Making your list of things to test

You might not feel like you have any ideas that are worth testing at this point, but don't worry. You just need to start getting ideas down on paper regardless of whether the ideas are good.

If you follow this process, you'll end up with more ideas than you have time to test and you'll never stop adding to your list. The most promising ideas will bubble to the top of your list, your Web site will get a little better with each test, and your marketing skills will get sharper in the process.

One important thing, carry around a piece of paper or an index card to capture ideas. Inspiration comes at the strangest times; you don't want to forget a good idea.

Richard's story

When I launched my first Web site, www.mrwaterfilter.com, I was just seeing whether I could successfully drive traffic to an e-commerce site by using AdWords. I didn't want to spend a lot of money on the site. One thing I skimped on was security, or credibility seals. The seals were expensive at the time, so I didn't want to spend the money without being sure that I could generate sales without them.

I started making sales as soon as I turned on the AdWords traffic, but I was losing money with an initial conversion rate of 1.2 percent. Because the site was making *some* sales, I decided to take the plunge and test credibility seals on the site, and my sales conversion rate improved to 1.5 percent almost immediately. That may not sound like much, but it made the difference from losing money to making money. It was the first time I tasted blood and saw that testing could actually work.

My graphic artist misunderstood some instructions of mine and created a header that wasn't what I wanted. I was disappointed, but I let the design stand because I was in a hurry to take the site live. But when I got around to testing my original concept, sales increased. So good-bye artist's rendition.

Sometimes testing went the other way. I *knew* that making the first part of each bullet point bold was tasteful and effective. It drew the eye to the key points that would help visitors decide to buy. Except that when I tested it, I was dead wrong. Bold text suppressed sales. So despite my love of a well-placed bit o' bold text, I use almost no bold on the site today.

My sales conversion rate from AdWords traffic is 5.5 percent. Actually, it's higher than that, because I'm not yet tracking phone sales. But the big lesson is that it's rare to be profitable with AdWords right from the start. If the only modifications you make are to ads and keywords, you're missing the lion's share of profits.

Think back to when you launched your Web site

In the frenzy of getting a Web site built, there are always compromises. No one has the time to create the perfect Web site on the first try. And even if you had all the time and money in the world, how could you possibly know for sure what "perfect" would look like?

Take a deep breath, follow my pocket watch swinging back and forth, and feel your mind free-floating back, back, back to when you were creating your site and thought:

> "OK, that's good enough for now."
>
> "Not exactly what I had in mind, but I guess it works."
>
> "We don't have time to do it over again."

Browse your site to jog your memory. Look for areas of compromise, of "Good enough for now," or "Gee, I hope that works." Make a list of every element that just maybe could improve.

Getting inspired by your competition

Next, take a good look at your competitors' sites. Compare their landing pages to yours. Ask yourself:

- ✔ What are they doing better than I am? Do they have better copy, headlines, pictures, design, or something else? Can I use their site as a template on which to improve?

- ✔ What's on their site, but missing from mine? Can I test adding that?

- ✔ What's on my site, but missing from theirs? Can I test removing that?

- ✔ Is their site more focused on the customer, the customer problem, or the solution?

- ✔ Does their site seem more credible or professional than mine?

- ✔ Do they have more elements or different elements above the fold (visible without scrolling) than my site? Could I test these changes?

- ✔ Does their site deliver on the promise made in their AdWords ad?

- ✔ Is their checkout or sign-up process more intuitive and easier to follow than mine?

Your competition can give you lots of ideas on what to improve, what to add, and what to remove from your Web site. Sometimes you can find good ideas by studying and modeling your competitors. But don't assume something is good just because someone else is doing it — most online markets consist of the clueless copying the clueless. Until you test, be skeptically curious.

For example, Richard noticed that his competitors showed only the manufacturer's stock photos. In many cases, the pictures weren't even sized correctly, so they appeared stretched and grainy in visitors' Web browsers.

Richard replaced his stock photos with high-quality photos that he took, using an inexpensive light box and a digital camera. Even though the water filters he sells are in many cases identical to those sold by competitors, he achieves a competitive advantage by making it easier for his customers to visualize and evaluate the products. When Richard surveys his customers, they consistently tell him that good, clear pictures are an important factor in their decision to buy from him.

Asking your visitors and customers

Your visitors and customers can provide a wealth of information on how to improve your Web site.

Here are a few things you should put in place to gather information from your visitors:

- ✔ Google Analytics to track visitors and sales, compare bounce rates on various pages, learn how users progress through your sales process, and more. See Chapter 13 for more information about Google Analytics.

- ✔ A high profile, easy way for visitors to ask questions (see Figure 14-1). This lets you know the questions you need to answer with your Web site. This also provides you with words that customers use when talking about your product or service.

- ✔ Surveys to determine visitor needs or satisfaction with your Web site. Surveys can give you an overview of what people are trying to accomplish on your Web site and how satisfied they are with your site.

Figure 14-1:
MrWater
Filter.com
encourages
visitors
to ask
questions
by soliciting
them at the
top left of
every page.

Visit 4Q at `http://4q.iperceptions.com` for a free survey tool that's easy to install and configure. You'll be amazed at the valuable information you can get from a simple four-question survey. Your visitors will tell you — if you let them — what they like and dislike about your site and how you can change it to make them happier.

With the information from the above tools, you can start to ask interesting questions, create some theories, and then test those theories. For example:

- ✔ If you find a high percentage of survey respondents are attempting one task and they have a lower satisfaction than visitors attempting other tasks, you should focus some testing in that area.

- ✔ If you find that visitors consistently ask a particular set of questions, you might test answering those questions on the product page or in a Frequently Asked Questions section (hence the name) or article with prominent links to your product page.

- ✔ If you find that there are fewer sales from one of your high traffic pages than from other lower traffic pages, you should test some changes to the high traffic page. Analytics allow you to focus your effort where the biggest payoff is possible.

All this combines to create a steady stream of information from and about your visitors. Evaluate that information to design tests that look for ways to serve your visitors better.

Here's an example. By running a 4Q survey, Richard found that 47 percent of his visitors to the *shower water filter* page wanted to compare products, and that they were considerably less satisfied with their experience on the site than were people attempting other tasks, such as checking prices or making a purchase. The survey revealed an opportunity to improve those visitors' ability to compare products. So Richard is now testing ways to allow comparison shopping for that category. He uses visitor and customer data to drive continuous improvement of his site.

Prioritizing your list

After you set up tools to capture information about visitors and use that information to generate ideas to test, it's time to grade each idea so you can prioritize the tests based on expected ROI. You move the ideas with the highest grades to the top of the list and test them first.

Apply the following 11 criteria to each item you're thinking of testing. The items that receive the most checks rise to the top of your testing list. These represent your first tests. (In case of a tie, I recommend flipping a coin — I like the 2005 Oregon quarter with a picture of Crater Lake, but that's totally up to you.)

- ✔ The item is on a high traffic page.
- ✔ The test result, if positive, can be applied to other pages on the site.
- ✔ The item is above the fold (that is, most visitors can see it without having to scroll down or sideways).
- ✔ The item is the most prominent feature on the page.
- ✔ The item relates to a high leverage conversion, such as an opt-in or first sale. (High leverage items in most businesses are gateways to multiple purchases and customer loyalty.)
- ✔ The item addresses a frequent customer question or problem.
- ✔ This item affects all customer sales (as part of the checkout process, for example).
- ✔ The item fills a competitive gap.
- ✔ The item enhances the credibility of your site.
- ✔ The item contributes to your site's uniqueness.
- ✔ The new version of the item is very different from what is shown on your site.

This exercise provides you with a prioritized list of what to test on your site. When you come up with new ideas, add them to the list, but be sure to re-prioritize before you select the next item to test.

Start testing (and never stop)

Are you ready to pull the top idea off the list and start testing? First, you need to create the resource to test. You already have your original, that's your A version. Now put together your B version. You might have to write some copy, create an image or video, and get some HTML code to tie it all into a working page. Upload that page to your site, and commence testing!

When you're testing elements of your marketing, you're acting like a scientist. Don't just ask questions; ask clear questions in an elegant way so the answers mean what you think they mean. Exclude other variables so that the only reason for the difference in outcome is the different inputs you controlled.

Also, run the test enough times to reduce the effects of random chance. Finally, don't stick the end of a Bunsen burner hose onto a sink faucet instead of the methane gas supply. Although hilarious, it also got me suspended.

Here are four rules to help you achieve useful and valid test results:

1. **Test one thing at a time.**

   If you test the headline font and header graphic simultaneously in an A/B split test, you won't know which element mattered and which element didn't. (You can test multiple synergistic effects using the more complicated (and therefore left out of this *For Dummies* book to keep your blood pressure down) Multivariate Testing. Visit `http://askhowie.com/multivariate` when you're ready for some advanced testing methods.

2. **Repeat each test to be sure.**

   If you have enough traffic, engage in the luxurious practice of validating your tests by running them a second time. Website Optimizer makes this one-click simple (keep reading this chapter to find out how).

3. **Keep traffic streams separate.**

   Each ad group should send visitors to a unique landing page, so when you're testing elements on that page, you're looking at how a specific market segment interacts with it. If you send all your traffic to a single page, you will almost certainly miss chances to optimize the page for different groups of people. If all of Richard's AdWords traffic went to his home page, for example, he would not be able to optimize the page for people searching for *shower water filters* in order to compare products.

4. **Identify a measurable outcome.**

   Sure, you want your Web site to be better, but what exactly does *better* mean? To conduct tests, you have to operationalize *better* into some visitor behavior that you can see and count. If you collect leads on your site, one measure of a landing page is how well it turns visitors into leads. Another measure is sales. You might also count downloads of software or marketing documents, or views of a key page.

To use Website Optimizer, you must identify a page on your site that visitors arrive at *after* they convert — that is, after they take the action you want them to take. Just to make things really clear, I'll call this the thank-you page. Two things must be true for the test to be valid:

   ✔ Every visitor who converts must make it to your thank-you page.

   ✔ No visitor who *doesn't* convert can make it to your thank-you page.

Testing with Google Website Optimizer

Here's the step-by-step method for setting up your first experiment in Google Website Optimizer (GWO, which sounds like Elmer Fudd encouraging his plants).

1. **Start GWO.**

   You don't need AdWords to use GWO, but Google provides a handy link right in the AdWords menu bar. (See Figure 14-2.)

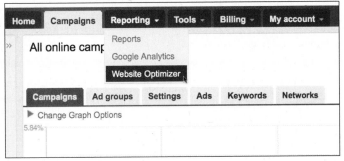

Figure 14-2:
Get to GWO from within your AdWords account.

   If you haven't set up your AdWords account but you want to begin testing anyway, visit `www.google.com/websiteoptimizer` and log in with your Google account.

   After you log in, Google requires that you specify your location and time zone and then agree to GWO's terms of service.

   The first GWO page you see is the Experiment List page. Naturally, no experiments are listed, so let's fix that right away.

2. **Click the Create Experiment link at the bottom of the Experiment List box to get started. (See Figure 14-3.)**

3. **Choose the type of experiment you'll be running.**

   The choices are an A/B Experiment (a simple two-option split test) or a Multivariate Experiment (where multiple elements of the page are tested at one time).

   Select an A/B Experiment, in which you create one or more variations of your page and compare results of each to the original. (See Figure 14-4.) This is the simplest experiment to create and understand, so it's a good place to start. Even when you become a testing ninja, you'll want to start improving a page with A/B tests because they give you big answers quickly. After you feel comfortable with A/B experiments, you can visit `http://askhowie.com/multivariate` to see how to create a multivariate experiment.

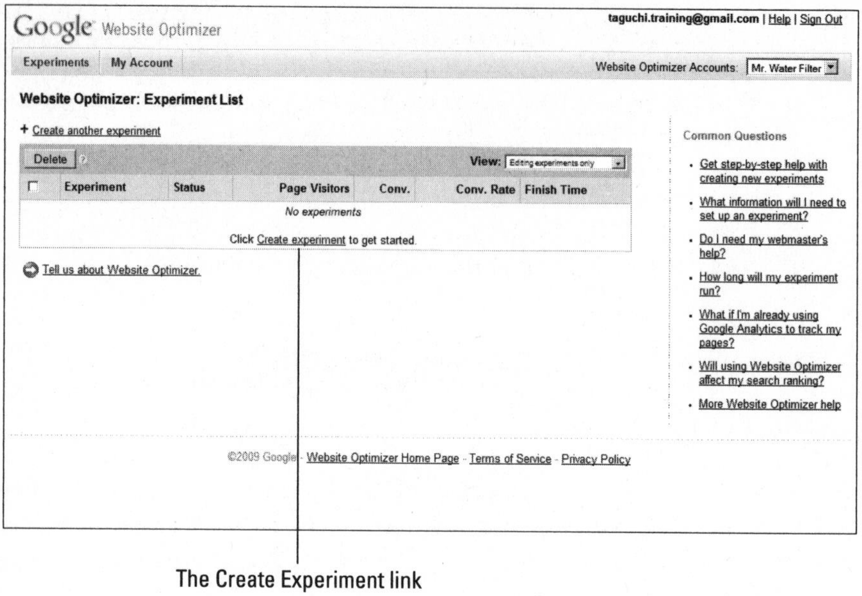

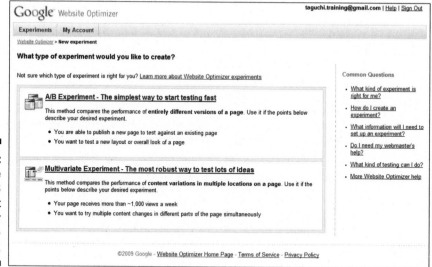

Figure 14-3:
The Create
Experiment
link gets you
started.

The Create Experiment link

Figure 14-4:
Choose the
simple A/B
Experiment
for your
first experi-
ments.

The next page is a checklist of what you need to complete before the test can go live. (See Figure 14-5.) Identify the original page and at least one variation you've created. At first, stick to one variation — you'll get results much quicker and they'll be much clearer than if you compare several pages.

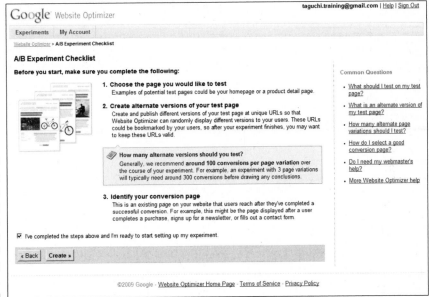

Figure 14-5:
Google
reminds you
of the three
elements
necessary
to begin
a test.

4. **When you have this information readily available, check the I've Completed the Steps Above box and click the Create button to continue.**

   At the beginning of the chapter, I give you a process to help you decide what to test. Now you tell Google the URL of the B version of your original page, as well as the URL of your thank-you page.

   In Figure 14-6, you see how Richard completed the setup form for an experiment that he was just beginning when we started working on this chapter. If you're curious, visit `http://askhowie.com/testresults` to find out the winner and get some commentary from Richard and me on what it means for his site.

Figure 14-6:
Setting up a test of two new pages against the original.

The Add Another Page Variation link

Specifying Experiment Details

The following list helps you get the details right. Use it to specify the details on your first experiment in Google Website Optimizer:

1. **Name the experiment.**

   Enter a meaningful name for your experiment; this is how you will find it in the experiment list. (After you start testing and improving your profitability, you *will* create many more tests.)

2. **Enter the URL for the original page.**

3. **Enter a name and URL for the variation page you are testing.**

4. **Click the Add Another Page Variation link (refer to Figure 14-6) and repeat Step 3 if you want to add more variations.**

5. **Enter the URL of the conversion page (your thank-you page).**

The conversion page is the page that visitors land on *after* they complete the action you wish to optimize. For example, after a sale, visitors generally land on a thank-you page, which is an ideal conversion page for GWO testing.

Google checks the URLs as soon as you type them, to make sure the pages exist. If every page receives a happy green check mark, you're ready to generate the tracking script that's installed on each page involved in the test.

Website Optimizer uses JavaScript tags on the pages to track visits and show different versions of the page to different visitors. Your job is to copy and paste these JavaScript tags into your pages. If you aren't terrified of HTML, you can easily do it yourself, in which case you choose the option, You Will Install and Validate the JavaScript Tags. (See Figure 14-7.)

If you don't want to do this yourself, you can have your Webmaster do it for you by choosing the option, Your Web Team Will Install and Validate JavaScript Tags. Just remember that the whole process should take about five minutes, so make sure you're billed accordingly.

Figure 14-7:
You can install the tags yourself or have the code and instructions sent to your favorite Webmaster.

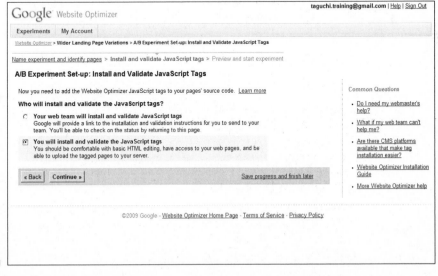

For the sake of your comprehensive AdWords education, I'm going to assume you selected the Do It Yourself option. The next page gives you the JavaScript tags and allows you to validate proper installation on your pages. (See Figure 14-8.)

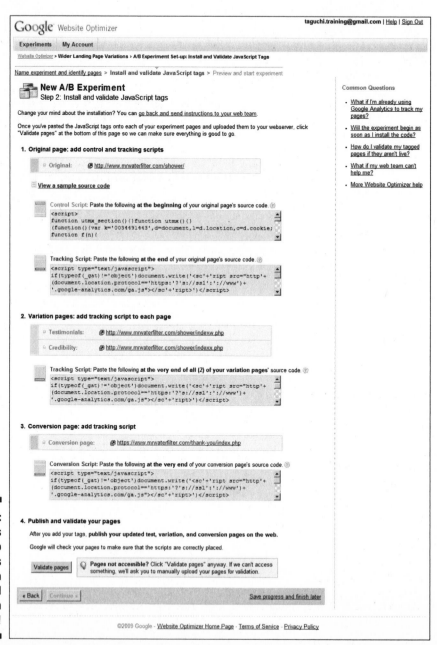

Figure 14-8: Stick this code onto the pages involved in the test and let the fun begin!

This feature of GWO rocks big time (that's online marketing slang for "is a very useful feature"). It ensures that your tests actually provide you with valid results or the tests don't even start. Take it from someone who once sent $250 of AdWords traffic to the wrong page, and almost stopped selling the product because he thought it wasn't selling — you can't be too careful here.

Adding and validating your own JavaScript tags

GWO uses an elegant configuration of JavaScript tags to send traffic to multiple pages without slowing down your Web pages or relying on external servers.

Follow these steps to place the JavaScript tags:

1. **Original page: Add the control script and tracking script.**

   On the original page, you will install two JavaScript tags, the control script and the tracking script. The control script goes at the top of the page, just after the `<head>` tag. (See Figure 14-9.)

   The tracking script goes at the bottom of the page, just before the `</body>` tag. (See Figure 14-10.)

   To copy the JavaScript tag, click anywhere in the shaded blue area to select the entire code snippet. Then copy it as you normally would.

   Open your original page in your HTML editor, select the option to view the HTML source, and then paste the JavaScript tag at the top of the page.

Figure 14-9: The control script goes near the top of the page, just below the `<head>` tag.

```
<!DOCTYPE html PUBLIC "-//W3C//DTD XHTML 1.0 Strict//EN"
  "http://www.w3.org/TR/xhtml/DTD/xhtml1-strict.dtd">
<html>
<head>

<script>
function utmx_section(){}function utmx(){}
(function(){var k='0034491443',d=document,l=d.location,c=d.cookie;function f(n){
if(c){var i=c.indexOf(n+'=');if(i>-1){var j=c.indexOf(';',i);return c.substring(i+n.
length+1,j<0?c.length:j)}}}var x=f('__utmx'),xx=f('__utmxx'),h=l.hash;
d.write('<sc'+'ript src="'+
'http'+(l.protocol=='https:'?'s://ssl':'://www')+'.google-analytics.com'
+'/siteopt.js?v=1&utmxkey='+k+'&utmx='+(x?x:'')+'&utmxx='+(xx?xx:'')+'&utmxtime='
+new Date().valueOf()+(h?'&utmxhash='+escape(h.substr(1)):'')+'"'+
'" type="text/javascript" charset="utf-8"></sc'+'ript>')})();
</script><script>utmx("url",'A/B');</script>

<meta http-equiv="content-type" content="text/html;charset=utf-8" />

<title>Chlorine Shower Filters - Shower Water Filters - Shower Filters - Mr. Water Filter</title>

<meta name="Description" content="Shower water filters protect your health by removing chlorine from
and the steam you breath while showering.  Removal of chlorine also gives you softer skin and
hair."/>

<meta name="Keywords" content="chlorine shower filter, remove chlorine, shower water, kdf-55, chlor
```

Figure 14-10:
The tracking
script for
the origi-
nal page
belongs
just above
the </body>
tag on that
page.

```
</div>

<script type="text/javascript">
if(typeof(_gat)!='object')document.write('<sc'+'ript src="http'+
(document.location.protocol=='https:'?'s://ssl':'://www')+
'.google-analytics.com/ga.js"></sc'+'ript>')</script>
<script type="text/javascript">
try {
var pageTracker=_gat._getTracker("UA-244866-5");
pageTracker._trackPageview("/0034491443/test");
}catch(err){}</script>


</body>
</html>
```

2. Variation page: Add the tracking script.

Place the variation tracking script at the bottom of each variation page.
Figure 14-11 shows the variation tracking script in its proper location,
just above the </body> tag.

Figure 14-11:
The tracking
script for
the variation
page
goes just
above the
</body> tag.

```
</div>

<script type="text/javascript">
if(typeof(_gat)!='object')document.write('<sc'+'ript src="http'+
(document.location.protocol=='https:'?'s://ssl':'://www')+
'.google-analytics.com/ga.js"></sc'+'ript>')</script>
<script type="text/javascript">
try {
var pageTracker=_gat._getTracker("UA-244866-5");
pageTracker._trackPageview("/0034491443/test");
}catch(err){}</script>


</body>
</html>
```

3. Conversion page: Add the conversion script.

Add the conversion script to the bottom of the conversion page, just
above the </body> tag. (See Figure 14-12.)

Figure 14-12:
The conver-
sion script
goes just
above the
</body>
tag on the
conversion
page.

```
<?php
/*  website optimizer code for wide landing page test...
 */
?>

<script type="text/javascript">
if(typeof(_gat)!='object')document.write('<sc'+'ript src="http'+
(document.location.protocol=='https:'?'s://ssl':'://www')+
'.google-analytics.com/ga.js"></sc'+'ript>')</script>
<script type="text/javascript">
try {
var pageTracker=_gat._getTracker("UA-244866-5");
pageTracker._trackPageview("/0034491443/goal");
}catch(err){}</script>
```

At the top of Figure 14-12, the `website optimizer code for wide landing page test` comment helps you identify which test is connected to the script, so you can remove it after the test is over. Placing `/*` before the comment and `*/` after the comment lets the browser know to ignore it, so it doesn't affect anything on the visible page.

After you're hooked on Website Optimizer, you can end up with quite a few of these conversion scripts on your conversion page. Manually adding a comment helps you figure out which ones can be deleted because you'll recognize the completed experiments.

4. **Upload the changed files to your Web server.**

   When all the JavaScript tags are in place, upload the files to your Web server using an FTP program. When the updated pages are in place, you're ready to validate the JavaScript tags.

   Click the Validate Pages button at the bottom of the page (refer to Figure 14-8) to make sure everything is in the right place. Website Optimizer checks the pages and the JavaScript tags to be sure your experiment is ready to run. When validation completes, you see the Congratulations message, as shown in Figure 14-13.

   Click the OK button, and then click Continue to go the experiment console.

5. **Preview the experiment pages.**

   Before starting your experiment, take a minute to preview your pages. In the experiment console, click the Preview link to verify your pages are showing what you want to show. (See Figure 14-14.)

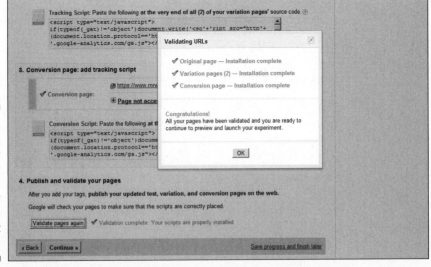

Figure 14-13: Google lets you know that your tags are properly placed on the right pages.

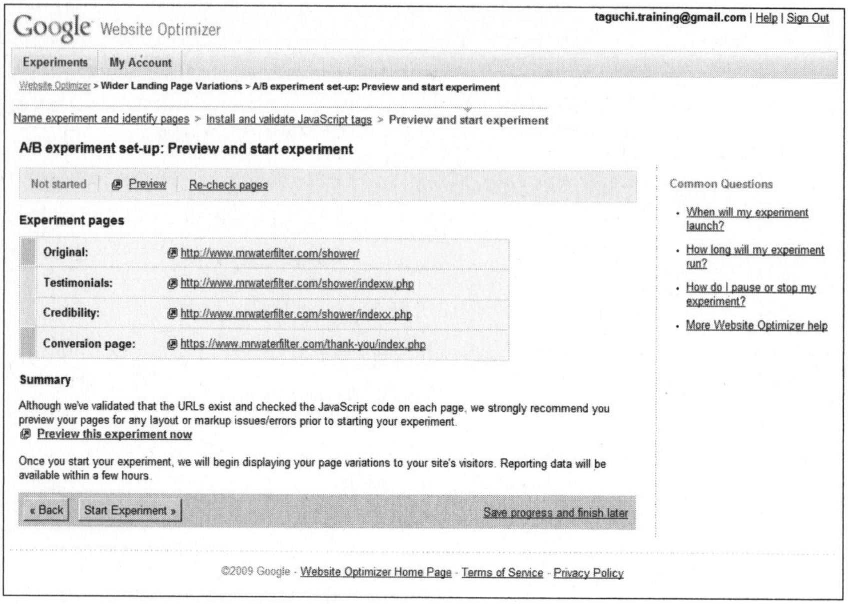

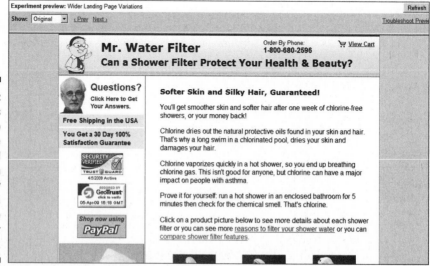

Figure 14-14: Click the Preview link before starting the experiment to view the control and test pages.

The experiment shown here includes the original and two variations. Figure 14-15 shows the original page within the GWO frame at the top.

Choose Variation 1 from the drop-down menu at the top left to view the first variation page. (See Figure 14-16.)

Figure 14-15: GWO allows you to preview the original and variation pages easily within a single browser window.

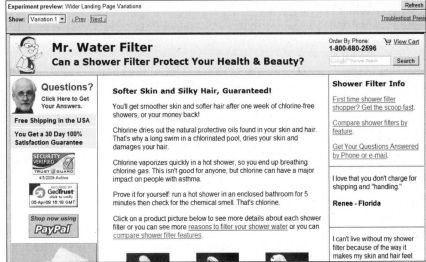

Figure 14-16:
The varia-
tion page
in this
experiment
is wider,
with three
columns.

In this experiment, I created a second variation, a wider page with the credibility elements (Trust Guard, GeoTrust, PayPal) moved to the right column. (See Figure 14-17.)

If you're curious which of these three pages contributed to the most sales, visit `http://askhowie.com/testresults` to make a prediction and see the results.

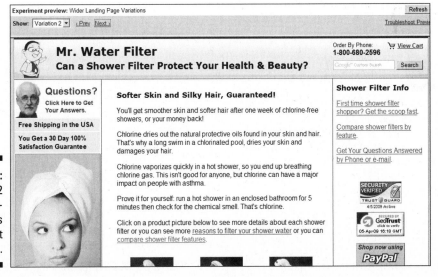

Figure 14-17:
Variation 2
adds cred-
ibility seals
to the right
column.

6. Start the experiment.

If the pages all look good, close the preview window and click the Start Experiment button. (Refer to Figure 14-14.)

An experiment status page appears, as shown in Figure 14-18.

Your experiment is now running and may begin to show you preliminary results within a few hours, depending on traffic. One of the most awesomely cool things (marketing jargon for "nice features") of GWO is that it tells you when the test is complete. Unlike ad split testing (see Chapter 12), GWO bakes your test and sounds a timer when the results are statistically significant.

7. Decide how much traffic to send to the variation pages.

At the bottom of the experiment status page, you can select a percentage of the traffic to send to the entire test. The default, 100%, means that if you are testing one variation, 50 percent of the visitors will see the original and 50 percent will see the variation.

If your original page is already working well, I recommend dialing down the amount of traffic you're sending to an untested page. Choosing 50% from the drop-down menu will exempt half of your traffic from the test, so those visitors will go directly to the original page. The other half will be split evenly between the original page and the variation page. Therefore, only 25 percent of your traffic will be subjected to the untested version of the page. If you are testing two variation pages, the original page will receive 66.67 percent of the traffic (50 percent plus one-third of the remaining 50 percent), while each variation will get 16.67 percent. The more traffic you send to the test, the faster you get a statistically valid result, but the greater the risk of losing leads and sales to a poorly performing challenger.

Don't worry too much about a visitor returning and seeing a different page. GWO places a cookie on all visitors' browsers, so if they return, GWO "remembers" them and shows them the same page they saw the first time. That's why the preview tool is necessary — you wouldn't be able to see the other pages in your test otherwise. The only ways visitors could see another version of the page are if they use a different browser, use a completely different computer, or clear the cookies from their browser.

8. Interpret and act on the results.

When your test is live, GWO counts the number of visitors who see each variation, and how many of them convert. These numbers tell you at a glance how your original and variations are doing. Figure 14-19 shows a test in progress in which both variations are performing worse than the original. The second variation has already lost (it's color-coded red for "loser"), while the first variation is losing, but hasn't amassed enough data for a conclusive call.

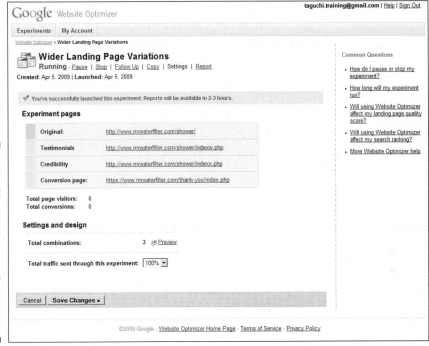

Figure 14-18:
Once your
experiment
launches,
you can
specify
what per-
centage
of your
visitors will
participate
in it.

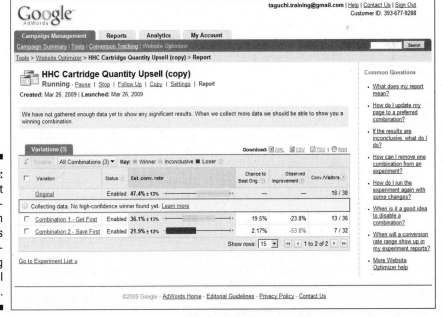

Figure 14-19:
In this test
in prog-
ress, both
variations
are under-
performing
the original
page.

Here's what each of the columns means:

- *Est. Conv. Rate:* The estimated conversion rate is the rate at which visitors to that page end up on the conversion page. The original in Figure 14-19 is converting at 47.4%, with a margin of error of plus or minus 13%. The margin of error is large because the test hasn't run long enough to be statistically significant.

- *Chance to Beat Original:* What are the chances that this particular variation will outperform the original in a head-to-head test? 50% is a dead heat, so anything less than 50% means the original is probably going to be the winner.

- *Observed Improvement:* How much better is this variation than the original? In both cases in Figure 14-19, this number is negative, indicating that the original is in the lead.

- *Conv./Visitors:* The raw data for each page. The original has converted 18 out of 38 visitors (which is where Google got the estimated conversion rate of 47.7%). The first variation converted a respectable 13/36, which is 23.8 percent worse than the original (hence the observed improvement of –23.8%). The second variation only converted 7 out of 32 visitors, which makes it a clear loser — even at this early stage. Google will continue to send traffic to losers, but you can manually "prune" them from your test by clicking the box to the left of the variation name and then clicking the Disable button at the top of the table.

9. **Run a follow-up test to validate the results.**

   Figure 14-20 shows a test in which one variation (Combination 1) has outperformed both the original and the other variation, but not quite to the point of statistical significance. Despite Google singing along with Maurice Williams and the Zodiacs, "Won't you stay, just a little bit longer?", the account owner has decided that a 92.7% chance to beat the original (with a conversion rate of more than 40% compared with the original's 34%) is good enough. Even if you heed Google's advice and keep the test running until you reach the magic 95% confidence interval (and see the bar turn from yellow to green), you still want to be on the safe side and run a follow-up test.

   Click the Follow Up link at the top of the test to launch the follow up. Google handles the thinking for you here by selecting the best variation and pitting it, head to head, against the original. As an added service, Google sends most of the traffic to the better performing page. The worse page gets just enough traffic to confirm that it should retire and produce a line of kitchen product infomercials (or whatever defeated landing pages do for a second career these days), and not enough traffic to significantly hurt sales. When the follow-up test proves conclusive, you can crown (or re-crown) your champion and get ready to run your next test. (See Figure 14-21.)

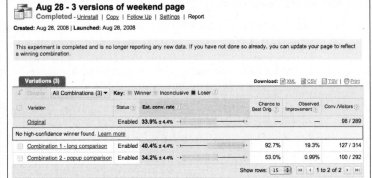

Figure 14-20: Combination 1 is almost certainly the best of the three pages in this test.

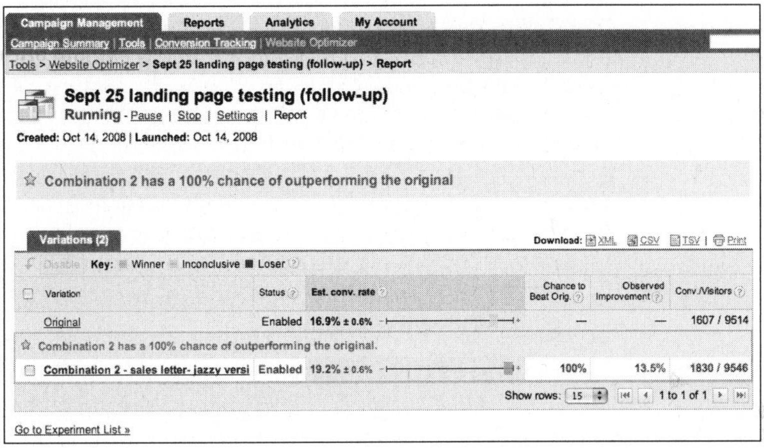

Figure 14-21: This follow-up test confirms that the variation Combination 2 out-performs the original, and should now become the new control.

10. Declare a winner and start a new test.

At this writing, no automatic notification system exists to alert you by e-mail, SMS, or gentle electric shock that you have a winner. So you must keep checking GWO until Google declares a winner.

Now you can return to your list of ideas for testing, and choose the next-most significant one. Create the landing page variation that embodies your question, and then begin a new test. Thoughtful and consistent testing is the single-most powerful strategy for turning a lackluster AdWords campaign into a big winner. So go forth and test!

Chapter 15

Slashing Your Costs with Conversion Tracking

Say you're split-testing two ads, and one gets a click through rate (CTR) of 1.00%, while the other attracts only 0.77%. The first ad is definitely a keeper, right? Without conversion tracking, you might think so. But what if the first ad attracts lots of nonbuyers, while the second ad gets clicks from buyers? Remember that a click on your ad means one thing: You just paid Google. When you think about it this way, your AdWords strategy shifts from trying to get the highest CTR to enticing only the most qualified prospects to your site. In order to tell which ad leads to sales and not just clicks, you need to install conversion tracking.

By *conversion,* Google simply means an action that you want a visitor to take on your Web site. When you can track a visitor's actions on your site, you know what clicks lead to sales. Conversion tracking also allows you to bid more intelligently on keywords. You may find that a high-traffic keyword that's costing you a lot of money isn't actually generating leads and sales. You can then lower your bid, change your offer, or fire the keyword. Without conversion tracking, all your campaign-management efforts are shots in the dark, tinkering with inputs without really knowing what's happening at the other end. It's like learning to shoot free throws in basketball with no feedback about whether your shot went in or missed left, right, too far, or too short.

Conversion tracking is simply a snippet of code added to your Web site that places a cookie on your visitors' computers. This cookie tells Google where the visitors came from, down to the keyword and the ad, and what they did on your site. You can see which ads and keywords are making you money, and which aren't. In this chapter, I show you how to set up conversion track-ing correctly (do it wrong and you'll suffer from the GIGO — Garbage In, Garbage Out — Syndrome and make lots of bad decisions). You see how to read and interpret the data generated by conversion tracking, and how to improve your account based on this new intelligence. You also discover how to design quick-scan reports that can be generated automatically and e-mailed to you on a regular basis.

Setting Up Conversion Tracking

From the Tools tab, choose Conversion Tracking from the drop-down list. Google allows you to track the performance of online ads and traditional media ads. I focus on online ads in this book. Click the Create an Action button to continue.

On the next page, name your conversion. In Figure 15-1, I'm tracking Ring of Fire subscriptions, specifically 1-month trials of the Lava Lounge member-ship level (turns out volcanoes and earthquakes provide an endless source of metaphorical amusement for me).

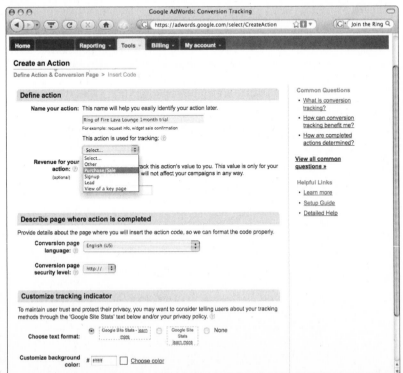

Figure 15-1:
Naming
your
conversion.

Choosing a conversion type

Google identifies five different types of conversions that you may want to track: sales, leads, signups, views of a page, and other, as shown in Figure 15-2. You can track as many different conversions as you want. The following list gives you a look at the five types of conversions so you can determine when it makes sense to use each one:

- **Purchase/Sale:** If you sell products online, you can determine exactly how much money you make from each ad and keyword.

- **Lead:** If you collect contact information so you can follow up with Web site visitors, you can track leads. If you don't sell products online, and use the Web mostly for lead generation, you can get very powerful information on cost-per-lead for your ads and keywords.

- **Signup:** Google distinguishes between signups and leads; I don't. If someone subscribes to my online newsletter, then by golly, I think of him as a lead. If you maintain two lists, you can distinguish them by treating one as a list of leads and the other as a list of signups.

- **Views of a Key Page:** Say you have a certain page that you want visitors to see because you've noticed a connection between traffic to that page and the success of your business. Maybe it's the About Us page, maybe a powerful testimonial, or maybe your daily menu. You can determine which ads and keywords reliably generate visitors who get to that page.

- **Other:** I can't think of any others. If you can, this is the one to use.

Choose one of these types for your first conversion to track.

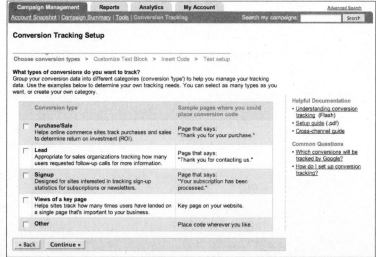

Figure 15-2:
You can track several types of conversions simultaneously.

Revenue for your action (Optional)

Enter a number in this box if you wish to assign a monetary value to the conversion. The easiest example is a sale: If you sell a product for $37, that conversion is worth $37 to your top line. You can enter the sale price or your net profit as the conversion value, whatever makes more sense. I prefer to use net profit, so I can see that a keyword with a CPC of $0.35 is worth $0.75 in my bank account, after expenses.

You can create conversions of many different values. If you sell three versions of the same product, you can put different-valued conversion code on the thank-you page for each version, as shown in Table 15-1.

Table 15-1		Sample Conversion Values by Product	
Product	**Price**	**"Thank You for Buying" Page**	**Conversion Code Value**
Product A: Basic	$17	`/productAthanks.html`	17
Product B: Value	$97	`/productBthanks.html`	97
Product C: Deluxe	$497	`/productCthanks.html`	497

If you can track the value of each conversion, the knowledge you gain can dramatically improve your AdWords results. One client installed conversion tracking with specific values on February 7, and by March 31 had slashed monthly AdWords spending by almost $14,000 — without sacrificing any profit. We simply eliminated all the keywords and ads that weren't leading to sales.

Describe page where action is completed

Before generating the tracking code, you need to tell Google three more things: the language of your Web page (English, Spanish, Russian, and so on), the security level of the page on which you will place the code, and the type of page.

- ✔ **Language:** From the drop-down menu, select the language of your text block. Google will translate the `"Google Site Stats — send feedback"` text block into that language.

- ✔ **Security Level:** The tracking code goes on the page following the conversion. You are concerned only with the security level of that confirmation page, the one where you put the code. You have two choices, based on the URL prefix:

```
http:// - normal security
https:// - heightened security
```

In other words, if the URL of the page your visitor goes to *following* the conversion starts with `https://`, then choose the https:// option from the Select a Security Level drop-down list. Not doing so will cause your visitor to see a nasty little security-alert pop-up.

✔ **Markup Language:** If your visitor is browsing your Web page on a regular desktop or laptop computer, keep the default setting, **html**. The other settings are for Web pages designed for various mobile devices.

Customize tracking indicator

In this section, you can design the block of text that lets your Web site visitors know that Google is monitoring their online activity. The default is one line of white text on a gray background. Google automatically adjusts the text color — either white or black — to be visible against the background you choose. Customize this text block to keep it from standing out on your Web page. Generally, I leave the default alone. Click the Save Action & Get Code button at the bottom of the page to continue.

Generating and copying the code

You now can generate the code that goes on your Web page (for example, if you're tracking sales, you'd insert the code into your "Thanks for your purchase" page). Click anywhere in the text box to select the entire code snippet, as shown in Figure 15-3.

I recommend copying the conversion code and pasting it into a plain text document (a `.txt` file, not a `.doc` or `.rtf`) for safekeeping, rather than immediately dropping the code into your Web page. That way, you have a saved version of the code if you ever need it again. Make sure you give the text document an obvious-but-descriptive name, such as `Google Conv Tracking.txt`. Do not save the code in a Microsoft Word format such as `.doc` or `.docx` because those formats add filler code that can render the code ineffective.

That's it! You've generated the tracking code. You don't need to click the Return to Conversion Tracking button; simply go back to the Campaigns tab in the Campaign Management submenu. You should see six new columns — Conv. Rate, Cost/Conv., and Conversions, each in two flavors, many-per-click and 1-per-click — filled completely with zeroes. (If you can't see these columns, click the Filter and Views button just above the right-most column, select Edit Columns from the drop-down list, and check the Conv. box to show all six columns. Click the Save button to return to the Campaign view, now with the conversion columns.) When you place the code on your Web site, Google replaces the zeroes with actual data.

Figure 15-3:
Clicking
inside the
text box
containing
the code
selects the
entire
snippet.

Putting code on your Web site

The code snippet goes on the Web page that your visitor reaches *after* successfully taking the action you're measuring. In other words, if you want them to opt in, the code goes on the "Thank you for opting in" page. For conversion tracking to be accurate, three things must be true about this page:

1. *Every* visitor who performs the desired action goes to the confirmation page (into which you insert the conversion code) following that action.

2. A visitor who *doesn't* perform the desired action will not get to the confirmation page.

3. Vistors can't refresh the confirmation page to create false multiple conversions. (See www.askhowie.com/norefresh for a demo, as well as details on how to do that with PHP. Pay special attention to the last sentence before refreshing the page.)

If the conversion is a page view, then the code goes on the viewed page itself. In other cases, the confirmation page is the next page. If you are using an e-mail–management service, such as AWeber (see Chapter 10), put your code on the page you designate as the Thank You page in the autoresponder setup.

Where to place the snippet

The conversion-tracking code should go just above the `</body>` tag on your confirmation page, as in Figure 15-4.

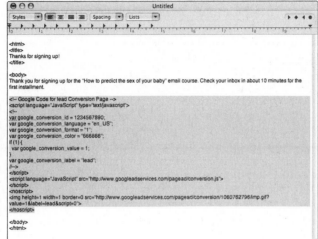

Figure 15-4:
Place the conversion tracking code in your HTML editor, just above `</body>`.

Visit `www.askhowie.com/conversioncode` for a video tutorial on putting code on your Web site.

Common tracking-code mistakes

The following list gives you a rundown of the common mistakes people make when inserting the conversion code (by reading this list and taking it to heart, you can avoid these mishaps!):

✔ **Putting the code in the header or footer:** If you place the tracking code in the header or footer of a page, it may show up on every single page in your Web site. Every page view will then be counted as a conversion.

✔ **Putting code on the wrong page:** Don't put the tracking code on the conversion page itself, but on the page that is served following successful conversion. (An exception is a page view conversion, where the confirmation page and the page itself are one and the same.)

✔ **Putting the code on the same page multiple times:** With complicated Web pages, it's easy to forget that you already placed the tracking code on the page.

If you're not sure whether your tracking code is on your Web page, view the source code of the page. Here's the drill:

1. Choose View➪Source in your browser.

   The source code appears in a text editor window.

2. Choose Edit➪Find, and enter **Google Code** in the Find What text box.

3. Click the Find Next button to search the code.

Tracking sales from a shopping cart

You can configure conversion tracking to record the total amount your visitors spend by using dynamic fields generated by your e-commerce system. For example, if you use Yahoo! Stores or eBay/PayPal shops, you can modify the code snippet to tell Google how much a visitor spent on your site. You can also get this information from a shopping cart written in ASP (Active Server Pages), JSP (Sun Java Server Pages), or PHP.

See Chapter 17 for more on the power of this level of tracking.

If you aren't a proficient coder and don't know what CGI means, please don't try this yourself. Send your Webmaster to `https://adwords.google.com/select/setup.pdf` for full documentation on configuring dynamic shopping carts for conversion tracking.

Testing conversion tracking

To see whether Google is tracking the conversion you set up, you have two choices: the quick and (possibly) expensive way or the natural way. The quickest way to confirm correct setup is to search Google for your keyword, click your ad, and perform the desired action. You should see that conversion in your campaign summary screen as a non-zero number somewhere in the six new columns (see the following section). If you don't want to waste a click, your other choice is to wait for a real visitor to convert. I recommend spending the money yourself and making sure that you're getting useful data.

Introducing Six New Columns

Once you trigger conversion tracking by generating the code snippet, Google shows you six new columns in the campaign management pages: Conv. Rate (conversion rate), Cost/Conv. (cost per conversion), and Conv. (conversions), as shown in Figure 15-5 (I've removed the other columns to keep the image uncluttered). These columns also appear at the ad group, keyword, placement, and ad levels, so you can see the effectiveness of every unit of your AdWords account. Until you place the conversion code on your site and visitors start converting, you will see zeroes in those columns. Also, expect a 24-hour delay in reporting a conversion.

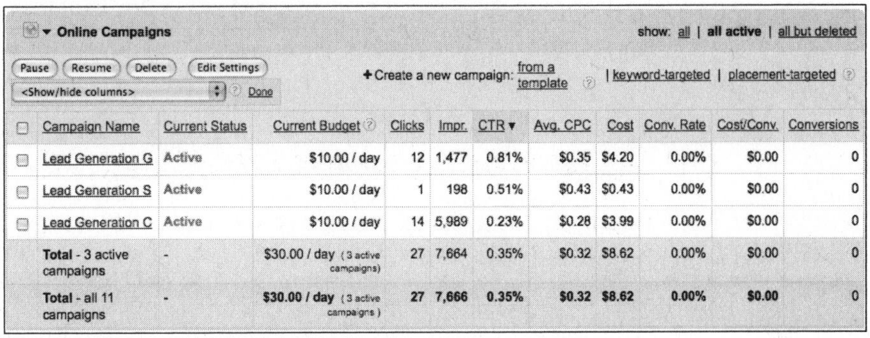

Figure 15-5:
Six new columns appear after you initiate conversion tracking.

Campaign Name	Current Status	Current Budget	Clicks	Impr.	CTR ▼	Avg. CPC	Cost	Conv. Rate	Cost/Conv.	Conversions
Lead Generation G	Active	$10.00 / day	12	1,477	0.81%	$0.35	$4.20	0.00%	$0.00	0
Lead Generation S	Active	$10.00 / day	1	198	0.51%	$0.43	$0.43	0.00%	$0.00	0
Lead Generation C	Active	$10.00 / day	14	5,989	0.23%	$0.28	$3.99	0.00%	$0.00	0
Total - 3 active campaigns	-	**$30.00 / day** (3 active campaigns)	27	7,664	0.35%	$0.32	$8.62	0.00%	$0.00	0
Total - all 11 campaigns	-	**$30.00 / day** (3 active campaigns)	**27**	**7,666**	**0.35%**	**$0.32**	**$8.62**	**0.00%**	**$0.00**	0

Conversions (many-per-click and 1-per-click)

These columns tell you how many conversions were generated by the element in that row; campaign, ad group, keyword, placement, or ad. Many-per-click counts each conversion by the same visitor. 1-per-click counts all conversions by the same visitor as one single conversion. In Figure 15-6, you can see six ad groups in the Gout campaign, two of which have led to conversions. The Gout Disabled Keywords ad group generated 41 many-per-click conversions, but only eighteen 1-per-click conversions. If Alberto came to my site and downloaded a free chapter, bought my e-book, and then downloaded a bonus report, that would count as 3 many-per-click conversions, but only a single 1-per-click conversion.

Conversion rate (many-per-click and 1-per-click)

The conversion rate is the percent of visitors from that campaign, ad group, ad, or keyword who complete a conversion. Let's drill down to the ad group level to make this clear. In Figure 15-6, the first group, Gout Disabled Keywords, received 2,211 clicks and converted 0.81% of them to at least one other action. When you add multiple conversions by the same person, the conversion rate rises to 1.85%. If all your conversions are product sales, then it makes sense to pay close attention to the many-per-click conversion rate. If most of the conversions are intermediate steps — a newsletter subscription or the completion of a quote request — and the sale happens only once, then the 1-per-click numbers are more important.

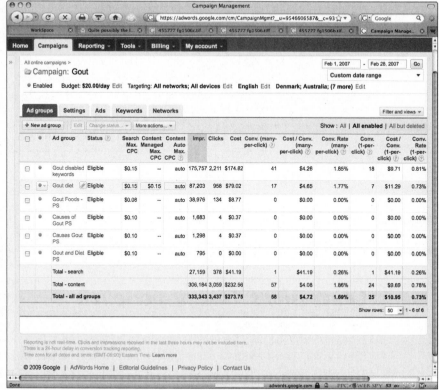

Figure 15-6:
Conversion
statistics
help me
calculate
the ROI
of my ad
groups.

Cost/Conv. (many-per-conversion and 1-per-conversion)

The third new metric, Cost/Conv., refers to how much you spent on AdWords, on average, for each conversion. In the Gout Disabled Keywords group, for example, I spent $9.71 for each person who completed at least one conversion. Whether that's good or bad depends on how much the conversion is worth to me. In this case, a conversion is worth at least $17.77, so I'll take that gross profit of $8.06 per conversion. Again, because multiple conversions don't make me any more money than a single sale, I don't pay much attention to the average cost of all the conversions. Instead, I separate the conversions and measure the cost and return of each one. I can do this with AdWords Reports (discussed later in this chapter), or in the Conversion Tracking module (discussed in the next section).

Actually, I'm making less than $8.06 per conversion because I have to pay for credit card processing. When your margins are tight, make sure you're accounting for *all* costs when you determine your ROI.

The second ad group is bringing in customers for $11.29 each, or a profit of $6.48 per conversion. Still okay, but not as good as the first group. In general, the lower this number, the better you're doing. The exception is when the cost-per-conversion is zero.

Look at the next four groups to see this clearly: no sales, so a $0.00 cost per conversion. Zero is the worst number to see in this column, because it means you've achieved nothing. Luckily, my AdWords expenditures for these groups are low (see the numbers in the Cost column). Also, they haven't generated enough clicks during this period to yield statistically significant results (see Chapter 13 for a discussion of split testing and statistical significance).

Measuring Actions in the Conversion Tracking Module

From the Tools menu, select Conversion Tracking from the drop-down list. After you create your first action, you see a list of all the actions you're tracking, the nature of the action (lead, sale, and so on), and the number of 1-per-click and many-per-click conversions (see Figure 15-7). Click the action name to view detailed statistics about the action, including the number of conversions and conversion rate by ad group.

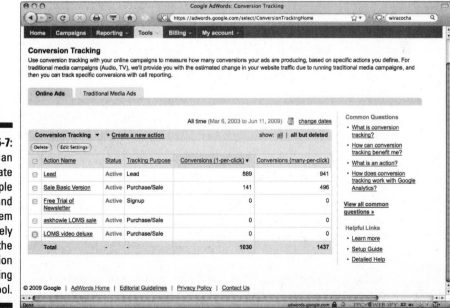

Figure 15-7:
You can create multiple actions and track them separately with the Conversion Tracking tool.

The figure shows the Google AdWords: Conversion Tracking screen.

Conversion Tracking

Use conversion tracking with your online campaigns to measure how many conversions your ads are producing, based on specific actions you define. For traditional media campaigns (Audio, TV), we'll provide you with the estimated change in your website traffic due to running traditional media campaigns, and then you can track specific conversions with call reporting.

Online Ads | Traditional Media Ads

All time (Mar 6, 2003 to Jun 11, 2009) change dates

Conversion Tracking ▼ + Create a new action   show: all | all but deleted

Action Name	Status	Tracking Purpose	Conversions (1-per-click) ▼	Conversions (many-per-click)
Lead	Active	Lead	889	941
Sale Basic Version	Active	Purchase/Sale	141	496
Free Trial of Newsletter	Active	Signup	0	0
askhowie LOMS sale	Active	Purchase/Sale	0	0
LOMS video deluxe	Active	Purchase/Sale	0	0
Total	-	-	1030	1437

Common Questions
- What is conversion tracking?
- How can conversion tracking benefit me?
- What is an action?
- How does conversion tracking work with Google Analytics?

View all common questions »

Helpful Links
- Learn more
- Setup Guide
- Detailed Help

© 2009 Google | AdWords Home | Editorial Guidelines | Privacy Policy | Contact Us

In Figure 15-8, you can see all the sales of the basic version of my gout e-book from the Gout campaign. The Gout Diet ad group, for example, generated 64 sales from 27,085 clicks, for a conversion rate of 0.24 percent. That's useful information, but still doesn't let me compare the most important numbers: cost and return. To achieve the holy grail of results-accountable marketing, you need to track return on investment (ROI) of every element of your account.

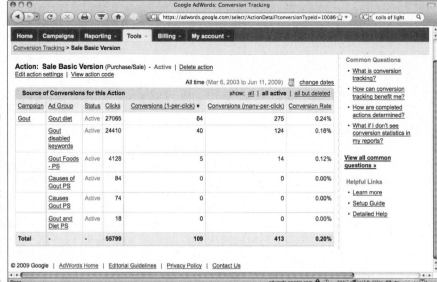

Figure 15-8: You can attribute specific product sales (in this case, an e-book) to individual ad groups.

Tracking ROI of Ads and Keywords

The information at the level of campaigns and ad groups is nice, but not particularly useful. Where conversion tracking becomes a powerful driver of action is at the levels of specific ads and keywords.

Identifying the profitable ads

After you have conversion tracking in place, you can compare two ads competing in the same ad group, not just to see which one attracts more clicks, but which one attracts more qualified clicks. The method I outline works both with text ads purchased on a CPC basis and image ads bought on a cost-per-thousand-impressions basis because you reduce all the data to a single number: *profit per thousand impressions.*

I began this chapter with a hypothetical example of two ads with CTRs of 1.00% and 0.77%. Without conversion tracking, you would declare the 1.00% ad the winner and start testing a new ad. As you can see in Figure 15-9, you could be making a big mistake.

Figure 15-9:
The lower-CTR ad is almost four times more profitable than the higher-CTR ad.

Variations ▼	CTR	Conv. Rate	Cost/Conv.
Never cold call again. Get prospects to call you instead. The System Revealed - download now www.LeadsintoGold.com	1.00%	9.1%	$9.19
Never Cold Call Again. Get prospects to call you instead. Free Report and 2 chapter download www.LeadsintoGold.com	0.77%	33.3%	$2.37

The conversion in this case was an opt-in, to receive two free chapters of the Leads into Gold home-study course. The first ad, the one with the "better" CTR, converted fewer than 1 in 10 visitors to leads. The second ad, while attracting fewer clicks, converted 1 out of 3 visitors to leads. You can see the difference in dollars and cents when you compare the two ads' cost per conversion metrics. Each lead cost me $9.19 when the first ad was shown, compared to only $2.38 when the lead saw the second ad.

Why is the second ad so much more effective at delivering qualified prospects? Look at the call to action in the second description line: "Free report and 2 chapter download." Visitors are enticed by the promise of a two-chapter download; the real question isn't why so many of them converted, but why so many more *didn't* opt in to download the two chapters.

Higher CTR often means lower site conversions

Lest you think the previous example was a fluke, I'm going to draw back the curtain a little more on my AdWords campaign. Figure 15-10 shows a second set of ads, almost identical in language, in which the same inverse relationship exists between CTR and site conversion.

Figure 15-10:
One word makes a world of difference in this split test.

Variations ▼	CTR	Conv. Rate	Cost/Conv.
Cold calling not working? Discover a powerful alternative. Free report and 2 chapter download. www.LeadsIntoGold.com	2.53%	10.5%	$7.45
Cold calling not working? Discover an effective alternative. Free report and 2 chapter download. www.LeadsIntoGold.com	2.28%	14.0%	$5.58

Why should the word *effective* improve my site conversion from 10.5% to 14% compared to the word *powerful?* I can't know for sure, but my guess is that *powerful* is a more attractive word and therefore casts a wider net than *effective,* while *effective* attracts more serious business owners who are predisposed to take the time to study my Web site and accept my offer.

Please take the moral of this story to heart: CTR is usually far less important than the cost per conversion. But until you set up conversion tracking, you're like the guy in the joke (for some reason, it's always a *guy* in the joke) who's looking for his keys under the street lamp, even though he lost them in the dark on the other side of the street. When asked why he's looking in the wrong place, he answers, "Because the light's better here." As business strategist Peter Senge reminds us, "We can't expect what we don't inspect." If you want higher CTRs, you can get them without paying attention to conversion. But if you want higher profits, you must inspect your site conversion data.

Balancing CTR and cost per conversion

CTR still matters. It's related to profitability because of Google's bid price formula: The higher the CTR, the lower the CPC. Also, you might run an ad with a miserable CTR that nevertheless converts at a high level. But because it sends so little traffic to your site, the high conversion rate contributes little to your bottom line.

You can balance an ad's CTR and cost per conversion by calculating a metric based on initial input and ultimate output: How much are 1,000 impressions worth to you? Table 15-2 presents an example in which three ads receive 5,000 impressions each.

Table 15-2		Balancing CTR and Cost per Conversion				
Ad	Impressions	Clicks	CTR	Total Cost	Conv. Rate	Cost/Conv.
Ad #1	5000	300	6.0%	$150	12%	$4.17
Ad #2	5000	150	3.0%	$100	18%	$3.70
Ad #3	5000	25	0.5%	$25	60%	$1.67

Which ad do you keep? If you look solely at CTR, it's easy: Ad #1 is the clear winner. But now that you've added conversion tracking, you can compare the ads' respective cost per conversion. By that measure, Ad #3 is the winner, generating a conversion for $1.67, compared to Ad #2's cost per conversion of $3.70 and Ad #1's bloated $4.17.

The trouble with Ad #3 is the tiny amount of traffic it generates. What you really want to know is which ad makes the most money? To calculate profit per ad, you need two more numbers: total number of conversions and value of a conversion.

Calculating the total number of conversions is easy: just multiply number of clicks by the conversion rate and divide by 100. Ad #1's total conversion is $300 \times 12 \div 100 = 36$.

The value of a conversion answers how much one of that action is worth to your business. If you're tracking hard sales data, Google can give you this information in the Reports section (see the "Creating Easy-to-Understand Reports" section, later in this chapter). If you're tracking throughput data, such as leads or page views, you may need to estimate the value of a conversion to your business. In this example, let's assume that a conversion is a $45 sale, of which you get to keep $40 after cost of goods and processing fees. Now you can redo Table 15-2 as shown in Table 15-3.

Table 15-3			Conversion Values			
Ad	Impr.	Tot. Cost	# Conv	Conv. Value	Total $ (Profits — Cost)	Profits/ 1000 Impr.
Ad #1	5000	$150	36	$40	$1290	$258.00
Ad #2	5000	$100	27	$40	$980	$196.00
Ad #3	5000	$25	15	$40	$575	$115.00

When you deposit your check in the bank, it doesn't give you extra money for having a high CTR or a low cost per conversion. When split-testing ads within a single ad group, the most important number is the amount of money you make per thousand impressions, after paying for your clicks.

The preceding example reflects a situation where your first sale is your only sale. If you make the lion's share of your profits from *back end* sales (sales after the first one), and if those sales occur online, you can still use the average cost per impression metric to choose a winner. If you can't track the lucrative back end sales through Google, you may just want to treat your AdWords campaigns as pure lead generation: whichever ad produces the most leads (in the case just cited, Ad #1) is the winner.

Keywords

You can also track ROI for each keyword in your Google search, and search partners' campaigns. Armed with this information, you can tighten your ad groups, lower or raise your bids on individual keywords to improve ROI or increase traffic for profitable keywords, and pause or delete keywords that cost more than they make.

Figure 15-11 shows an ad group for Leads into Gold. The overall cost per conversion for this ad group is $23.86, far too high to be profitable. Say that my break-even is $18.00 per conversion. All the keywords with a cost per conversion greater than $18.00, or at $0.00, are current money losers. They include `cold calls` at a whopping $76.66 per conversion, all the way down to `cold calling techniques` at an almost-acceptable $19.94. The keywords with cost per conversion between $17.15 and $4.73 are all fine, but the one below those are generating no conversions at all, just costing me Google clicks.

The keyword conversion data can be fed back into campaign management (see Chapters 7 and 8) to continually lower your costs and increase your profits.

Figure 15-11: Only 6 keywords out of 33 in this ad group are generating a positive ROI, with a positive cost/conv. under $18.00.

Keyword	Status	Max. CPC	Position preference	Cost	Conv. (1-per-click)	Cost / Conv. (1-per-click)	Conv. Rate (1-per-click)
Total - all keywords				$2,231.01	84	$23.86	3.47%
cold calls	Campaign paused	$1.00	Any	$94.50	1	$76.66	0.97%
"cold calls"	Campaign paused	$1.00	Any	$134.24	2	$67.12	1.28%
[cold calling techniques]	Campaign paused	$1.00	Any	$58.45	1	$58.45	1.56%
cold calling	Campaign paused	$1.00	Any	$593.04	9	$51.65	1.58%
cold call techniques	Campaign paused	$1.00	Any	$33.03	1	$30.44	2.17%
cold calling techniques	Campaign paused	$1.00	Any	$189.43	7	$19.94	4.32%
[cold calls]	Campaign paused	$1.00	Any	$85.73	5	$17.15	4.03%
"cold calling"	Campaign paused	$1.00	Any	$526.99	31	$17.00	5.02%
"cold calling techniques"	Campaign paused	$1.00	Any	$15.40	1	$15.40	5.88%
[cold calling]	Campaign paused	$1.00	Any	$336.53	24	$14.02	6.33%
[no more cold calling]	Campaign paused	$1.00	Any	$5.99	1	$5.99	14.29%
"making cold calls"	Campaign paused	$1.00	Any	$4.73	1	$4.73	16.67%
cold calling for cowards	Campaign paused	$1.00	Any	$11.92	0	$0.00	0.00%
no more cold calling	Campaign paused	$1.00	Any	$1.75	0	$0.00	0.00%
cold call scripts	Campaign paused	$1.00	Any	$29.00	0	$0.00	0.00%
"cold calling for cowards"	Campaign paused	$1.00	Any	$0.00	0	$0.00	0.00%
[cold calling for cowards]	Campaign paused	$1.00	Any	$5.53	0	$0.00	0.00%
stop cold calling	Campaign paused	$1.00	Any	$1.69	0	$0.00	0.00%
end cold calling	Campaign paused	$1.00	Any	$0.00	0	$0.00	0.00%
making cold calls	Campaign paused	$1.00	Any	$14.86	0	$0.00	0.00%
[stop cold calling]	Campaign paused	$1.00	Any	$10.80	0	$0.00	0.00%
[no cold calling]	Campaign paused	$1.00	Any	$10.27	0	$0.00	0.00%
[end cold calling]	Campaign paused	$1.00	Any	$0.00	0	$0.00	0.00%
[cold call scripts]	Campaign paused	$1.00	Any	$6.80	0	$0.00	0.00%

Creating Easy-to-Understand Reports

Google allows you to create reports that distinguish between leads, signups, page views, and sales. You can see which ads and keywords are making you money, and exactly how much. You can identify the keywords that are doing their job — that is, generating more money than they cost. And, you can automate the reporting to receive exactly the numbers you need in your inbox on a daily, weekly, or monthly basis.

To create a report, follow these steps:

1. **From within your AdWords account, click the Reporting tab and select Reports from the drop-down list.**

2. **Click the Create a New Report link in the center of the page to create your first report, as shown in Figure 15-12.**

   If you've already run reports, you'll see a list of the last five reports that have run, as well as any saved report templates at the bottom of the page.

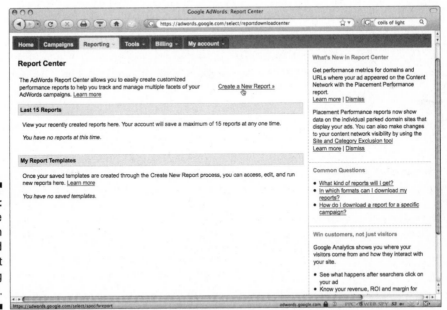

Figure 15-12:
Click the link shown by the hand to start generating reports.

Types of reports

Google enables you to choose from several different types of reports, including:

- ✔ **Placement/Keyword Performance:** This report tells you how each keyword is doing. Earlier in this chapter, the two conversion columns in the campaign management console mushed all the conversions together into one undifferentiated pile. In a report, you can separate out multiple conversions and assign a monetary value to each one.

- ✔ **Ad Performance:** This type of report lets you know which ad in a split test is the most profitable based on ROI and total profit. Depending on your Web site's sales process, you may place more value on generating leads or on sales numbers; you can configure reports that give you exactly the numbers you need in order to make profitable decisions.

- ✔ **URL Performance:** This report evaluates your destination URLs. You can split-test landing pages this way, but it's messy. You're better off using a third-party tool (see Chapter 13 for the details of split-testing) to test landing pages; you can swap pages in and out in one place, rather than in the destination URLs of perhaps dozens of different ads.

- ✔ **Ad Group, Campaign, and Account Performance:** These three report types (Ad Group, Campaign, and Account Performance) are useful for two reasons: their ability to show you hourly results and a metric called Impression Share (IS). You can find out what time of day you receive the most impressions, the highest CTR, the most clicks, and the highest and lowest CPC. This information can help you schedule ads so they don't show at certain unfavorable times of day.

    Impression Share compares the number of impressions your ads receive to the total number they could have received if you were bidding as high as possible with as large a budget as possible. An impression share of 24 percent, for example, means that your ads did not show 76 percent of the time that they could have if you just loosened the purse strings.

- ✔ **Demographic Performance:** If you are advertising on the content network, you can see how your campaigns perform differently with men and women, and with different age groups.

- ✔ **Geographic Performance:** This report parses your traffic by geographical region. You can see, for example, that visitors to your Web site who live in Costa Rica are more valuable, on average, than visitors from Quebec.

- ✔ **Search Query:** This report shows you exactly what people searched for prior to clicking your ads. If you bid on a broad match keyword like `unicycle parts`, you might see keywords like `24" unicycle parts`, `giraffe unicycle parts`, and `unicycle movie parts`.

You can then add the "good" keywords to your account, and add negative keywords (like `movie`) to prevent those searches from triggering
your ads in the future. A modified version of this report (without the ROI
metrics, sadly) is available as an inline report within the Keyword tab at
the campaign or ad group level of your account (`www.askhowie.com/
interface-webinar` has a video demo of this and other cool hard-to-
show-in-book-form features of the new AdWords interface that started
popping up in Spring 2009).

✔ **Placement Performance:** If your ads are showing on the content network,
this report tells you which Web site and pages are displaying them and
how they're doing on each. See `http://askhowie.com/placementvid`
for a short video tutorial on how to get the most from this report.

Settings

Your settings choices change depending on the report type. Basically, you
have to make three choices:

✔ **View (unit of time):** How do you want the data chunked by time? You
can view a summary of all the data; or look at individual years, quarters,
months, weeks, or days. Some of the reports allow you to look at the
data on an hourly basis. Hourly (by date) shows each individual hour.
Hourly (regardless of date) combines the data to show the average
hourly activity — that is, over the entire date range you're looking at,
how does your traffic at 3:00 a.m. differ from traffic at 10:00 a.m. or
3:00 p.m.?

✔ **Date range:** Over what time frame do you want to examine the data?
You can choose a default period from the drop-down menu, or specify
an exact range. Depending on your traffic, you want to choose a period
that can give you statistically significant results. In other words, if you
receive only 100 impressions a day, it doesn't make sense to view one
day at a time. Instead, choose a period that allows trends to emerge —
say, a week or a month.

✔ **Campaigns and ad groups:** You can choose to show every ad group in
every campaign, or look at select ad groups. I like to choose a single ad
group per report, so I can focus on just the relevant data that can help
me make decisions. As you'll see, the amount of data you can generate
with reports is staggering. The art of running reports is not to generate
as much data as possible, but as *little* as allows you to take intelligent
action. When you choose to manually select campaigns and ad groups
from a list, a drop-down list of campaigns will appear. You can add the
campaign directly, or click a campaign name to view its ad groups, which
you then can add individually.

Advanced settings

Configure the advanced settings to create truly useful reports:

✔ **Add or Remove Columns:** You can select the data to appear in your report. Depending on report type, you may have half a dozen options, or as many as 50. See the upcoming section, "Customizing Your Reports to Show the Most Important Numbers," for suggestions on which columns to display and which to ignore.

✔ **Filter Your Results:** You can limit the scope of the report by showing keywords, or ads, or ad groups, or campaigns that match any of a number of search criteria, as shown in Figure 15-13. Here are just two examples:

  • You can choose to display only active ads in active ad groups in active campaigns.

  • You can look at content-targeted campaigns only or keywords whose average CPC is (say) greater than $3.25.

If you find yourself overwhelmed by gigantic report spreadsheets, spend some time looking at filters to see whether any of them will reduce complexity while retaining the key information.

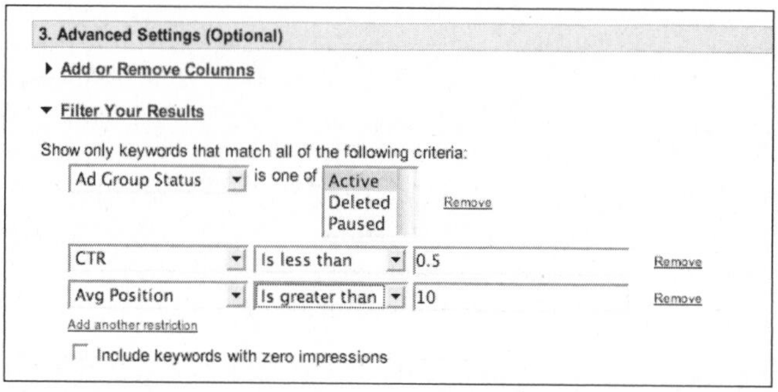

Figure 15-13:
Use filters
to create
smaller
reports that
are easier to
understand.

> **3. Advanced Settings (Optional)**
>
> ▶ Add or Remove Columns
>
> ▼ Filter Your Results
>
> Show only keywords that match all of the following criteria:
>
> | Ad Group Status ▼ | is one of | Active | Remove |
> | | | Deleted | |
> | | | Paused | |
>
> | CTR ▼ | Is less than ▼ | 0.5 | Remove |
>
> | Avg Position ▼ | Is greater than ▼ | 10 | Remove |
>
> Add another restriction
>
> ☐ Include keywords with zero impressions

Templates, scheduling, and e-mail

You don't have to go through the whole report-creation process every time. You can save reports as templates and schedule them to run automatically on a daily, weekly, or monthly basis. I like to schedule reports to run weekly that show me activity for the previous 30 days. I can print them, study them, and archive them in a binder to understand trends and compare results from one month to the next.

I create new reports to answer questions, test hypotheses, and explore my campaigns from different angles. When I find a new report to be valuable, I schedule it to run on a weekly or monthly basis. My accounts don't justify daily reports, but if you get a lot of traffic on a daily basis, you may want to devote 10 minutes a day to glancing at the day's reports. In general, you want to spend more time monitoring new campaigns than mature ones.

Create a report as a template to save yourself the time and effort of making the same choices over and over again for different reports. You can create a template with specific columns and filters, and just change the ad group, instead of creating each new ad group report from scratch.

You can view reports in HTML format from the Report Center, and/or download them in several formats. I like the HTML view for sorting by different columns, just like the campaign-management interface; I like the .csv Excel format for printing and performing additional calculations.

Customizing Your Reports to Show the Most Important Numbers

Some numbers matter more to your business than others. Let's explore customizing the columns for the keyword performance and ad performance reports.

Customizing keyword performance reports

Your column choices for keyword reports are shown in Figure 15-14. Basically, your goal is to remove as many columns as you possibly can and still get the information you need. So before you choose columns, get clear on what are the important questions you want a report to answer:

- ✔ If you have an e-commerce Web site, your most important keyword question will likely be, "Which keywords are making money and which are losing money?"
- ✔ If the primary purpose of your site is lead generation, you want to know how much each lead costs you.
- ✔ If you are generating traffic for clients, you are probably most interested in page views.

Sometimes you want to see a bunch of statistics next to each other. I often am interested in leads versus sales for particular keywords, so I'll select leads count, sales count, and sales value. I may discover that a certain keyword attracts a disproportionate number of buyers, even though it doesn't compel more opt-in conversions.

Your report will display these columns:

Campaign	Ad Group	Placement / Keyword	Match Type	Keyword Status	Est. First Page Bid	Quality Score	Current Maximum CPC	Keyword Destination URL	Impressions	Clicks	CTR	Avg CPC	Cost	Avg Position

Level of Detail : These columns reflect this report's coverage and level of detail

☑ Campaign   ☑ Ad Group   ☑ Placement / Keyword

Attributes : These columns report on your current ad settings and status

☑ Match Type   ☑ Keyword Status   ☑ Est. First Page Bid

☑ Quality Score   ☐ Ad Distribution   ☐ Ad Distribution: with search partners

☐ Daily Budget   ☑ Current Maximum CPC   ☐ Content Bid

☐ Highest Position Preference   ☐ Lowest Position Preference   ☑ Keyword Destination URL

☐ Ad Group Status   ☐ Campaign Status

Performance Statistics : These columns feature data about how your ads are performing

☑ Impressions   ☑ Clicks   ☑ CTR

☑ Avg CPC   ☑ Cost   ☑ Avg Position

Conversion Type Columns : These columns enable you to view conversion statistics broken down by type

☐ Action Name   ☐ Action Description   ☐ Action Category

Conversion Columns : These columns provide statistics on ad conversions and conversion rates

☐ Conversions (1-per-click)   ☐ Conv. Rate (1-per-click)   ☐ Cost/Conv. (1-per-click)

☐ Conversions (many-per-click)   ☐ Cost/Conv. (many-per-click)   ☐ Total Conv. Value

☐ Value/Conv. (1-per-click)   ☐ Conv. Value/Cost   ☐ Conv. Value/Click

☐ Sales Conv. (many-per-click)   ☐ Sales Conv. Value (many-per-click)   ☐ Leads Conv. (many-per-click)

☐ Leads Conv. Value (many-per-click)   ☐ Sign-up Conv. (many-per-click)   ☐ Sign-up Conv. Value (many-per-click)

☐ Page View Conv. (many-per-click)   ☐ Page View Conv. Value (many-per-click)   ☐ Other Conv. (many-per-click)

☐ Other Conv. Value (many-per-click)

Local Business Ad Interaction Columns : Information about user interactions with your local business ads on Google Maps ⓘ

☐ Info window open from left hand side   ☐ Info window open from map marker   ☐ "Get directions" clicks

☐ "Street view" clicks   ☐ Clicks to website from info window

Figure 15-14: You can choose from dozens of columns to create keyword performance reports.

For example, in Figure 15-11 earlier in this chapter, most of the keywords in the ad group aren't generating positive ROI, based on the average value of a conversion. The keyword cold calls is the top offender at over $75 per conversion. The problem with this data is that I can't distinguish between an opt-in and a sale. When I run a keyword-performance report — choosing the conversion metrics of cost per conversion, value per click, sales count, and sales value (shown in Figure 15-15), I discover a much more nuanced and useful picture.

The keyword cold calls turns out to be my best, not worst, keyword. I pay an average of $0.86 per click and make an average of $2.18 from each click. None of the other keywords led to sales at all.

The bottom-line number for keywords is value per click, also known as *visitor value*. This number answers the question, "How much money is a visitor to my Web site worth to me, on average?" You should know this number for each of your sales channels. When you know your visitor value, you know exactly how much you can spend on advertising. The higher your visitor value, the more you can afford to pay for traffic. And when you discover that a promotion produces less or more revenue than you would expect given your averages, you can decide whether it's worth repeating.

Google AdWords: LIG cc techniques all time: Mar 28, 2007 11:12:11 AM PDT

Keyword	Keyword Matching	Keyword Status	Impressions	Clicks	CTR	Avg CPC	Cost	Avg Position	Cost / Conversion	Value / Click ▲	Sales Count	Sales Value
cold calls	Phrase	Active	6,904	156	2.26%	$0.86	$134.24	2.1	$67.12	2.18	1	337.00
cold calling	Phrase	Active	31,701	615	1.94%	$0.85	$525.07	3.4	$16.94	1.61	2	958.00
making cold calls	Phrase	Active	237	6	2.53%	$0.79	$4.73	1.5	$4.73	0.17	0	0.00
no more cold calling	Exact	Active	116	7	6.03%	$0.86	$5.99	5.3	$5.99	0.14	0	0.00
cold calling	Exact	Active	13,422	378	2.82%	$0.89	$335.59	4.2	$13.98	0.11	0	0.00
cold calling techniques	Phrase	Active	3,180	17	0.53%	$0.91	$15.40	2.7	$15.40	0.06	0	0.00
cold calling techniques	Broad	Active	15,992	219	1.37%	$0.86	$189.43	2.3	$19.94	0.05	0	0.00
cold calls	Exact	Active	2,716	124	4.57%	$0.69	$85.73	1.5	$17.15	0.04	0	0.00
cold call techniques	Broad	Active	6,101	50	0.82%	$0.66	$33.03	2.2	$30.44	0.02	0	0.00
cold calling	Broad	Active	25,134	721	2.87%	$0.82	$592.31	3.1	$51.57	0.02	0	0.00
cold calling techniques	Exact	Active	5,297	64	1.21%	$0.91	$58.45	2.6	$58.45	0.02	0	0.00
cold calls	Broad	Active	6,115	123	2.01%	$0.76	$93.54	2.4	$75.70	0.01	0	0.00
[no cold calling]	Phrase	Active	54	2	3.70%	$0.74	$1.47	7.8	$0.00	0.00	0	0.00
cold call	Broad	Deleted	83	0	0.00%	$0.00	$0.00	1.5	$0.00	0.00	0	0.00
cold call script	Broad	Deleted	437	5	1.14%	$0.68	$3.41	2.0	$0.00	0.00	0	0.00
cold call scripts	Broad	Active	3,577	41	1.15%	$0.68	$28.06	2.5	$0.00	0.00	0	0.00
cold call scripts	Exact	Active	871	11	1.26%	$0.62	$6.80	3.2	$0.00	0.00	0	0.00
cold call scripts	Phrase	Active	627	15	2.39%	$0.74	$11.14	1.8	$0.00	0.00	0	0.00
cold call selling	Broad	Deleted	1,473	8	0.54%	$0.76	$6.07	1.9	$0.00	0.00	0	0.00
cold call techniques	Exact	Active	362	9	2.49%	$0.92	$8.28	2.5	$0.00	0.00	0	0.00

Figure 15-15: The keyword `cold calls` cost $134.24 to show and earned $337, for an average value per click of $2.18.

Perry Marshall often talks about the Unlimited Traffic Technique: Start with AdWords, but don't end there. Use AdWords to improve your sales process — meaning, to increase your visitor value. When your visitor value is high enough, you can buy all the traffic you want. You can hire search engine optimization consultants to boost your organic rankings. You can advertise your site on other Web sites, on the radio, in magazines, wherever — because you know exactly how much a visitor is worth to you.

Customizing ad performance reports

Your ad performance reports should answer the primary question, "Within each ad group, which is the best ad?" In an e-commerce situation, this means the ad that puts the most money into your bank account per impression. As of this writing, Google does not include a Value/Impression column in its reports, so you need to figure this out manually or add a column in a spreadsheet. Figure 15-16 shows my recommended selections for an e-commerce ad performance report. I eliminate as many details as possible so I can see all the numbers on one page.

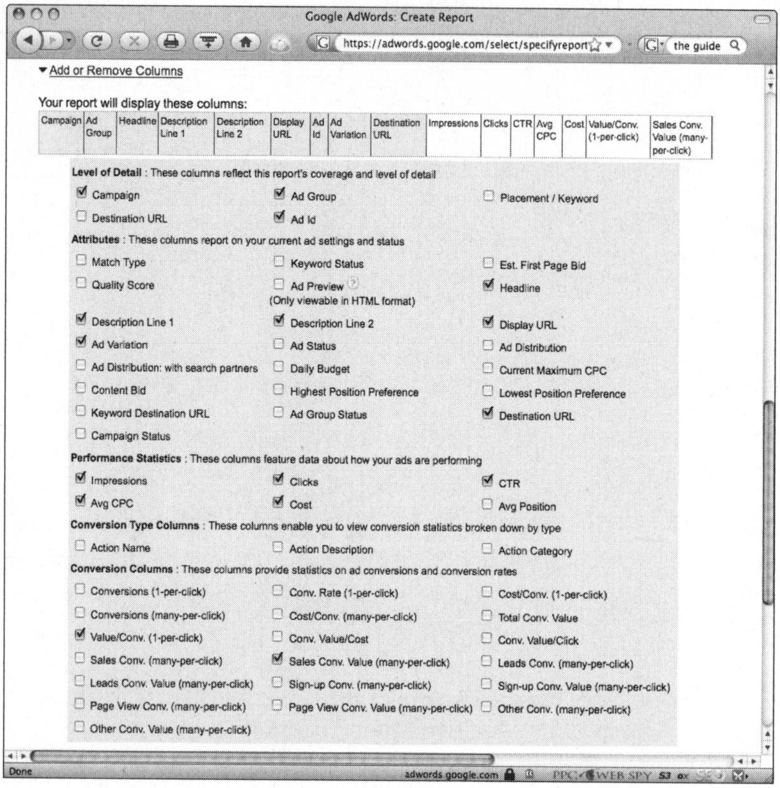

Figure 15-16:
Customize reports by choosing what you want to see and deselecting what isn't necessary.

In Figure 15-17, you can see the results of the choices I made in Figure 15-16. Some columns are mandatory in the report, such as Ad ID and Destination URL, but I can easily remove them in Excel because they don't help me. I can also move columns around in Excel, putting related numbers next to each other. Most important, I can create additional columns that give me the numbers I really need.

In this case, I created a new column (in bold) called **Value/Impression*100**, which is how much every impression is worth to me, multiplied by 100 so I can make better sense of the data. The absolute number is less important than the comparison of the ads that I'm testing. In rows 13 and 14, the two ads in question are identical, except for the end of the Display URL: the one with VitalHealthInstitute.com/BeatGout is almost twice as profitable as the one with the URL VitalHealthInstitute.com: $0.63 versus $0.32.

Rows 15 and 16 feature two ads, identical except for quotes around "Gout Cure" in one. The ad without quotes is almost three times more profitable than its competitor, $0.35 versus $0.12. Rows 17 and 18 show again that adding a subdomain to the main Display URL has increased profits, $0.24 versus $0.14.

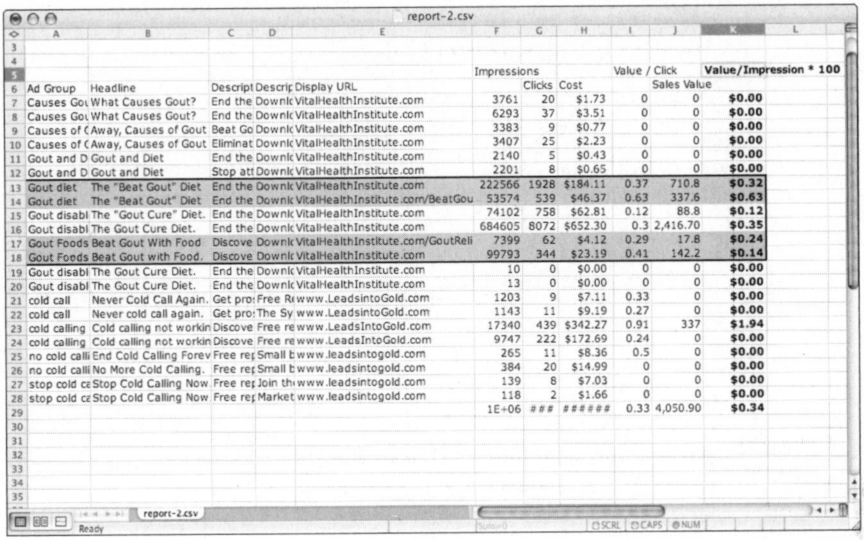

Figure 15-17:
The shaded
rows show
that some
ads are
much more
profitable
than their
competitors.

	A	B	C	D	E		F	G	H	I	J	K	L
							Impressions			Value / Click		Value/Impression * 100	
								Clicks	Cost		Sales Value		
6	Ad Group	Headline	Descrip	Descrip	Display URL								
7	Causes Gou	What Causes Gout?	End the	Downl	VitalHealthInstitute.com		3761	20	$1.73	0	0	$0.00	
8	Causes Gou	What Causes Gout?	End the	Downl	VitalHealthInstitute.com		6293	37	$3.51	0	0	$0.00	
9	Causes of C	Away, Causes of Gout	Beat Go	Downl	VitalHealthInstitute.com		3383	9	$0.77	0	0	$0.00	
10	Causes of C	Away, Causes of Gout	Eliminat	Downl	VitalHealthInstitute.com		3407	25	$2.23	0	0	$0.00	
11	Gout and D	Gout and Diet		End the	Downl	VitalHealthInstitute.com		2140	5	$0.43	0	0	$0.00
12	Gout and D	Gout and Diet		Stop att	Downl	VitalHealthInstitute.com		2201	8	$0.65	0	0	$0.00
13	Gout diet	The "Beat Gout" Diet	End the	Downl	VitalHealthInstitute.com		222566	1928	$184.11	0.37	710.8	$0.32	
14	Gout diet	The "Beat Gout" Diet	End the	Downl	VitalHealthInstitute.com/BeatGou		53574	539	$46.37	0.63	337.6	$0.63	
15	Gout disabl	The "Gout Cure" Diet.	End the	Downl	VitalHealthInstitute.com		74102	758	$62.81	0.12	88.8	$0.12	
16	Gout disabl	The Gout Cure Diet.	End the	Downl	VitalHealthInstitute.com		684605	8072	$652.30	0.3	2,416.70	$0.35	
17	Gout Foods	Beat Gout With Food	Discove	Downl	VitalHealthInstitute.com/GoutReli		7399	62	$4.12	0.29	17.8	$0.24	
18	Gout Foods	Beat Gout with Food.	Discove	Downl	VitalHealthInstitute.com		99793	344	$23.19	0.41	142.2	$0.14	
19	Gout disabl	The Gout Cure Diet.		End the	Downl	VitalHealthInstitute.com		10	0	$0.00	0	0	$0.00
20	Gout disabl	The Gout Cure Diet.		End the	Downl	VitalHealthInstitute.com		13	0	$0.00	0	0	$0.00
21	cold call	Never Cold Call Again.	Get pro	Free R	www.LeadsintoGold.com		1203	3	$7.11	0.33	0	$0.00	
22	cold call	Never cold call again.	Get pro	The Sy	www.LeadsintoGold.com		1143	11	$9.19	0.27	0	$0.00	
23	cold calling	Cold calling not workin	Discove	Free re	www.LeadsIntoGold.com		17340	439	$342.27	0.91	337	$1.94	
24	cold calling	Cold calling not workin	Discove	Free re	www.LeadsintoGold.com		9747	222	$172.69	0.24	0	$0.00	
25	no cold calli	End Cold Calling Forev	Free rep	Small b	www.leadsintogold.com		265	11	$8.36	0.5	0	$0.00	
26	no cold calli	No More Cold Calling.	Free rep	Small b	www.leadsintogold.com		384	20	$14.99	0	0	$0.00	
27	stop cold ca	Stop Cold Calling Now	Free rep	Join th	www.leadsintogold.com		139	8	$7.03	0	0	$0.00	
28	stop cold ca	Stop Cold Calling Now	Free rep	Market	www.leadsintogold.com		118	2	$1.66	0	0	$0.00	
29							1E+06	###	######	0.33	4,050.90	$0.34	

report-2.csv

You can create a Value/Impression*1000 Column in Excel by dividing the
sales value by the number of impressions, and multiplying by 1000. Go to
www.askhowie.com/valueimp for a video tutorial on creating the Value/
Impression*1000 column in Excel.

Or, if you're as lazy as I am, you can get a tool to do all this for you. After
years of doing manually what I describe previously, when I started training
my business partner, Elizabeth, to do it, she rebelled and created a software solution that does it all in about 6.3 seconds. For more info, check out
http://magicadwordsbutton.com.

Discovering What to Do with the Data

Before taking action based on the data, make sure the data is accurate.
Google is usually not the culprit when data is faulty; instead, you most likely
made an error in placing the code on your Web pages. If you're measuring
opt-ins and sales, it won't take long to verify the data. Count the number of
leads Google says you've acquired over a given period, and compare it to the
number of opt-ins to your autoresponder or newsletter list for the same date
range. If the two numbers are fairly close, you can be confident that you're
reading useful data. (Expect the numbers to be slightly off to account for time
delays between initial click and conversion.) Similarly, compare the sales
count and sales value for an e-commerce site with the actual sales data from
your shopping cart or merchant account. Again, they should be close, not
necessarily identical.

Use the report data to split-test your ads — not on CTR, but on profitability (refer to Figure 15-17). As a rule of thumb, wait until each ad has generated at least 30 clicks before declaring a winner to make sure your results are statistically significant and not just a fluke occurrence.

You're looking for keywords that aren't paying for themselves, or aren't as profitable as they could be. When you find these keywords, you can adjust your bid price (and average position) to reflect their value, you can move them into a different ad group and match them to a different landing page (see Chapter 8), or you can pause or delete them to stop the bleeding.

If you find a keyword that costs $0.35 per click and has a value per click of $0.27, you're losing 8 cents every time someone clicks your ad. Before deleting the keyword, lower your Maximum CPC to $0.26. You may find your visitor value increasing because lower positions tend to generate higher-quality clicks. Worst case, you're slightly better than break-even for the keyword. If you're advertising on the Content network, then think of placements like keywords — specific media channels that are either paying for themselves, or not.

If your break-even bid doesn't generate enough traffic because it puts you on page 9 of search results, or is below Google's minimum bid, then you can try moving the keyword to a different ad group and matching it more closely to the ad and the landing page. Sometimes getting the keyword quality score to Great is all you need to do.

The goal of keyword bid management is to maximize profits per keyword. Test your high traffic keywords in different positions. Pay for position 1 for a week, and then drop it to position 7 for another week. Tally your sales and costs: Which position is more profitable? Over time, you'll find the sweet spot for each keyword. Obviously, if your campaigns contain thousands of keywords, you'll want to focus on the top traffic keywords.

Chapter 16

Making More Sales with Google Analytics

In *Why We Buy: The Science of Shopping* (Texere Publishing), Paco Underhill shares the insights gleaned from 20 years of his study of the science of shopping. Some of these include

✔ Putting shopping baskets all over bookstores.

✔ Making the women's clothing aisles wide to avoid the irritation of "butt-brush."

✔ Putting fitting rooms next to the men's clothing section because men buy mostly based on fit, while women consider many other factors.

These findings may seem like common sense to you, but I wouldn't have come up with them in a hundred years. And neither did the giants of retail until they hired Underhill to study shopper behavior and redesign their stores. Underhill's company Web site, www.envirosell.com, describes the methodology for a typical engagement:

✔ *Twelve Staples stores were studied in different markets across the country for two days each.*

  • *Shoppers were observed throughout their visit by in-store observers.*

  • *Video, focused in different areas of the store, recorded shopping patterns for eight hours each research day.*

> • *Shoppers were intercepted and interviewed after they completed their shopping visit.*
>
> • *A manager and an associate from each store were interviewed by researchers to gather their insights on the store.*

I bring this up to explain how incredibly lucky you are as a Web site proprietor to *not* to have to go through this to improve the effectiveness of your site. You can observe your customers without hiring armies of consultants, without intercepting them for interviews, and without watching hours of video. All you have to do, in fact, is install Google Analytics tracking code on your site and you'll be able to evaluate and redesign your online store with greater accuracy, less risk, and greater speed than you could ever manage offline.

You can view — in minute detail — the parts of your site that frustrate or detour your visitors. You can compare this month to last month. You can define goals and funnels and watch your visitors convert or bail at every point on the navigation path. You can identify pages that don't work, and replace them in minutes. And you can automatically connect all this data to your AdWords cost-and-conversion data to segment your traffic by keyword (and other characteristics).

In this chapter, I draw heavily on the expertise generously provided by Timothy Seward of ROI Revolution, online at www.roirevolution.com. (Especially since Google completely overhauled Analytics three weeks before my book deadline — thanks, Sergey and Larry!) Including even one-tenth of what Timothy has taught me would have turned this book into a medicine ball, so I'm limiting the information on Analytics in two ways:

- ✔ **I just show you how to track AdWords traffic.** You can configure Analytics to tell you cool stuff about all your visitors; in fact, it will tell you all about organic search engine traffic by default. I'm going to ignore all that and let you explore it on your own. (Once you understand how Analytics deals with AdWords traffic, the rest isn't hard.)

- ✔ **I don't get into complicated installations**, including integration with e-commerce shopping carts or the tracking of downloads or outbound links. If you are (or know) someone who's a code jockey or has years of IT experience, feel free to play with these settings. Otherwise, start simply — and hire an Analytics expert when you're ready for advanced tracking.

Instead, I show you how to install and configure Analytics to get clean and actionable data. I introduce you to some very powerful data screens, and show you how to set up experiments and answer interesting questions with these data. After you have the data, you discover what to do with it to get more leads and sales.

Installing Analytics on Your Web Site

The Google Analytics installation process consists of three steps:

1. Creating and configuring an Analytics account
2. Adding tracking code to your Web pages
3. Creating filters to keep your data clean and useful

Creating an Analytics account

Within your AdWords account, click the Analytics tab. Click the Continue button to enter Web site information for your first profile (each Web site requires its own profile), as shown in Figure 16-1. You can create multiple profiles, but for right now let's keep it simple.

Figure 16-1:
Make sure
the two
check boxes
are checked
so your
AdWords
data is
included.

Analytics: New Account Signup

General Information > Accept User Agreement > Add Tracking

Please enter the URL of the site you wish to track, and assign a name as it should appear in your Google Analytics reports. If you'd like to track more than one website, you can add more sites once your account has been set up. Learn more.

I don't need to complete this form. I already have a Google Analytics account.

Website's URL:	http:// ▾ www.cheesemongr.com
	(e.g. www.mywebsite.com)
Account Name:	www.cheesemongr.com
Destination URL Auto-tagging:	☑ Automatically tag my ad destination URLs with additional information useful in analytics reports. Learn more.
Apply Cost Data:	☑ Automatically apply your AdWords cost data to all profiles in this Analytics account for reporting calculations.

(Cancel) (Continue »)

Enter the Web site URL, and give this account a name. Very important: Make sure the check boxes are checked next to Destination URL Auto-tagging and Apply Cost Data. Auto-tagging adds information about which keywords your visitors typed and which ads they clicked to arrive at your site.

Google warns that a small percentage of Web sites can't handle Auto-tagging. If you start getting errors when you click your ads, turn off Auto-tagging and tell the following to your Webmaster: "Please configure my site to allow arbitrary URL parameters." When your Webmaster has done this, turn Auto-tagging back on.

Checking the Apply Cost Data check box connects AdWords bid costs to your Analytics data, so you can calculate the costs and values of various Web site conversions.

On the next page, read the epic novel titled *Google Analytics Terms of Service* — and if you agree with each and every provision, check the agreement box at the bottom and click the Create New Account button to get started.

Adding tracking code to your Web pages

On the next page, you see a text block containing the Analytics tracking code. Click inside that box to select the whole thing, then copy it and paste it into every page on your Web site that you are planning to track. The code goes just above the </body> tag, near or at the bottom of the source code for each page. Your source code may end something like this:

```
<script type="text/javascript">
var gaJsHost = (("https:" == document.location.protocol) ?
   "https://ssl." : "http://www.");
document.write(unescape("%3Cscript src='" + gaJsHost +
   "google-analytics.com/ga.js'
   type='text/javascript'%3E%3C/script%3E"));
</script>
<script type="text/javascript">
try {
var pageTracker = _gat._getTracker("UA-1234567-1");
pageTracker._trackPageview();
} catch(err) {}</script>

</body>
</html>
```

Don't copy my code! No ethical objections, just practicality: Each account comes with a unique number, which follows the UA- prefix in the code.

If your Web site is built on a template, you can add this code just once and it will automatically be added to every page. If you don't know what I'm talking about, just e-mail the code to your Webmaster and tell him or her, "Place this code just above the </body> (close-body) tag on every page of my site."

When you click Continue, you're taken to the Analytics Overview. Unless you've added your tracking code already, you'll see an exclamation icon in the status column indicating that the tracking code has not been detected on your home page (as shown in Figure 16-2). The exclamation icon will change to a green check mark when it's satisfied that you've added the code correctly.

Be cautious about installing the Analytics tracking code yourself if any of the following conditions exist:

Figure 16-2:
Check the
status of
your
tracking
once you've
had the
code added
to your Web
site.

✔ You want to track visitors across more than one domain (for example, `http://unicyclesforkids.com` and `http://whoneedstwowheels.com`).

✔ Your site includes subdomains (such as `http://stunt.unicyclesforkids.com` and `http://distance.unicyclesforkids.com`).

✔ You want to track file downloads (PDFs or MP3s, for example).

✔ You have a third-party shopping cart or an e-commerce site.

✔ Your visitors can pay you with PayPal or Google Checkout.

✔ Your site uses frames (if you're not sure, ask your Webmaster).

✔ Your site generates pages dynamically but the URL remains static (if you're not sure, gently let go of your mouse and move away from the computer).

Check out Michael Harrison's cautionary blog post at `www.roirevolution.com/config` for a case study of a mismanaged Analytics installation that generated junk data long after the error was corrected.

If you want to add more Web sites to your Analytics account, click the Add Website Profile link and repeat the process.

Configuring Analytics

While you're waiting for tracking validation, you can configure your Analytics account to allow other users full or restricted access, and to eliminate junk data. From the Analytics home page, choose the profile you want to configure and click Edit. From this page, you can edit your profile information, create conversion goals and funnels, apply filters, and manage additional users.

Adding users

You may want to give other people full or restricted access to your Analytics account and data. You can add more users and specify their rights to change and view the account. For example, you can give your Webmaster access to Webmaster reports only, and you can allow an assistant to view data but not change the account configuration.

Add users by clicking the User Manager>> link near the bottom of the Analytics control panel (refer to Figure 16-2). Click + Add User at the top right, enter their e-mail, and choose an access type: View Reports Only, or Account Administrator. See Figure 16-3. If you've selected View Reports Only, select the profile(s) you want the user to see, and then click Save Changes.

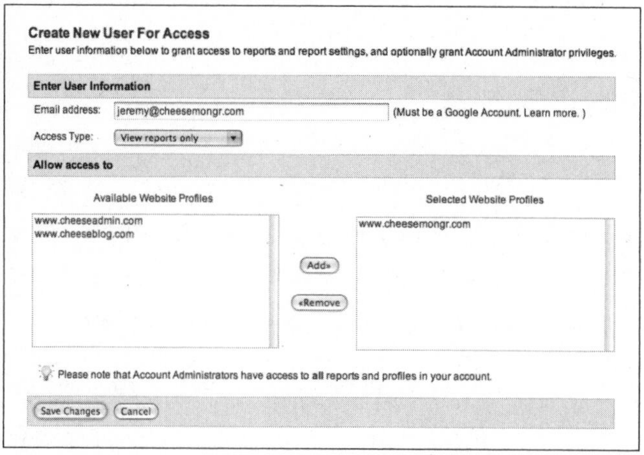

Figure 16-3: Give additional Analytics users limited access to reports by creating profiles just for them.

Choosing a default page

Every Web site has a default page, defined as the page your Web server shows to visitors who enter your Web site name only. For example, someone typing www.askhowie.com is automatically redirected to the page http://askhowie.com/index.php. In this case, index.php is the default page. If you aren't sure of the name of your default page, ask your Webmaster.

If you don't tell Analytics your default page, then views of your root domain (www.askhowie.com) will be counted separately from default page views (www.askhowie.com/index.php), even though these two pages are actually the same.

From the Profile Settings page, click Edit to configure the Main Website Profile Information. Enter your Web site's default page, not including the root domain. You will enter something like this:

```
index.html
index.htm
index.php
```

Click the Save Changes button at the bottom of the page when you're done.

Filtering out internal traffic

A Jewish folk tale from the mythical town of Chelm tells of when Schlemiel and his wife opened a lemonade stand on the outskirts of the town market. Early in the day, one customer bought a glass for 25 cents. After that, nobody bought. Finally, Schlemiel picked up the 25-cent coin and gave it to his wife, requested a glass of lemonade. Shortly thereafter, Mrs. Schlemiel returned the coin to her husband in exchange for a glass. So they went back and forth the rest of the day, until the entire supply of lemonade was gone. They celebrated their good fortune at having sold out their stock, but couldn't figure out where all the money had gone, and why they had only 25 cents to show for their efforts.

You may laugh, but if you don't create a filter to exclude internal traffic to your site, you're making the same mistake. Internal traffic refers to visits to the site by insiders — you, your Webmaster, your colleagues. You don't want these visits to contaminate the important data: the visits by prospects and customers.

A filter to exclude internal traffic is pretty simple to set up:

1. **From the Analytics Settings page, click the FilterManager link and click + Add Filter.**

2. **Select Add New Filter for Profile.**

3. **In the Filter Name text box, enter** Internal traffic.

4. **From the Filter Type drop-down menu, choose Exclude All Traffic from an IP Address.**

   Google fills in the next field with something like 63\.212\.171\. (shown in Figure 16-4).

5. **Enter your own IP address and the addresses of anyone else you consider internal traffic.**

   Each computer has its own IP address, so if you work at multiple computers, you'll want to filter them all. You can find your IP address at www.whatismyip.com. It consists of four blocks of numbers, separated by periods.

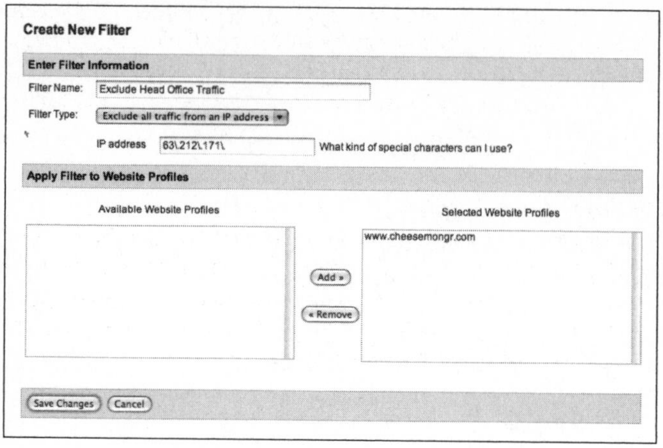

Create New Filter

Enter Filter Information

Filter Name: | Exclude Head Office Traffic

Filter Type: | Exclude all traffic from an IP address ▼

IP address | 63\.212\.171\. | What kind of special characters can I use?

Apply Filter to Website Profiles

Available Website Profiles | Selected Website Profiles

www.cheesemongr.com

[Add »]

[« Remove]

[Save Changes] [Cancel]

Figure 16-4:
Ignore
internal
traffic by
filtering
out the IP
addresses
of internal
users.

If your IP address is 12.34.56.78, for example, you enter the following into Analytics:

```
12\.34\.56\.78
```

The \ character is a backslash, located just above the Return or Enter key on most keyboards.

When you've created filters for all internal users, you can apply those filters to all Analytics profiles (see the next step).

 6. **Select Apply Existing Filter to Profile and you can choose from a list of filters to apply to that profile.**

Analytics allows you to create many different kinds of filters. You can find a list if you choose Custom Filter from the Filter Type drown-down menu. For now, don't worry about adding more filters. When you start receiving data, you'll quickly see pages that are unnecessarily segmented by Analytics, and you can create filters to correct the problems.

For more information about how to configure filters and determine that you need them, check out www.roirevolution.com/filters on the ROI Revolution blog.

Configuring goals and funnels

A *goal* refers to something you want your Web site visitors to do — such as fill out a form, buy something, visit a particular page, download a file, and so on. Except for file downloads and clicks on links to other Web sites, you configure a goal by identifying the page your visitor goes to after completing the conversion.

If the goal is an opt-in to your newsletter, the Goal page is the thank-you page visitors arrive at after completing the opt-in form. For a goal page to work, two things must be true: The only way someone ends up on that page is by doing what you want them to do, and everyone who takes that action ends up on that page.

Creating a goal

Click the Edit link next to the first goal, labeled G1. On the next page (shown in Figure 16-5), enter the Goal URL, the name, and make sure the Active Goal is set to On. Scroll to the bottom of the page and click the Save Changes button. If you'd like to define a navigation funnel for that goal (an optional step), see the following section for details.

Defining a funnel

Google defines a *funnel* as "a series of pages leading up to the Goal URL." Sometimes you won't be able to define a funnel. Your visitors may choose their own path to a particular goal, or there may be many equally plausible paths to the same goal.

If the goal is a purchase, you can usually identify several required steps that must occur in order. Shawn Purtell of www.roirevolution.com offers the hypothetical example for an online cheese shop in Figure 16-5.

If you're not sure of the path, set up your best guess as a funnel. Even if you're completely wrong, you'll see graphically how visitor behavior on your site deviates from the ideal.

Determining a goal value

If your goal is an e-commerce goal, a configuration beyond the scope of this book, leave the value blank or at $0.00. If the goal is a lead, a page view, or a download, you can estimate the value of that goal and input it in the Additional Settings section. For example, say you generated $24,000 in income last month from 750 leads. Each lead is worth, on average, $32 ($24,000 ÷ 750 = $32). You can set the value of that goal at 32.00 (making sure to omit any currency sign), and then save your changes by clicking the Save Changes button.

E-commerce setup

If your Web site includes an e-commerce shopping cart, you definitely want to get it hooked up to Analytics. You'll discover which keywords are making you money and which are not. You'll find the optimal path for your AdWords visitors, from keyword through ad through landing page all the way through your site.

Goal Settings: G1

Enter Goal Information

Active Goal: ◉ On ○ Off

Match Type ⦾ : [Head Match ▾]

Goal URL ⦾ : [/catalog_request_success.htm]
(e.g. For the goal page "http://www.mysite.com/thankyou.html" enter "/thankyou.html")
To help you verify that your goal URL is set up correctly, please see the tips here.

Goal name: [Catalog Success!]
Goal name will appear in Conversion reports.

Case sensitive ☐
URLs entered above must exactly match the capitalization of visited URLs.

Goal value · [10]

Define Funnel (optional)

A funnel is a series of pages leading up to to the Goal URL. For example, the funnel may include steps in your checkout process that lead to the thank you page (goal).

Please note that the funnels and 'Required step' that you've defined here only apply to the Funnel Visualization Report.

Note: URL should not contain the domain (e.g. For a step page "http://www.mysite.com/step1.html" enter "/step1.html").

	URL (e.g. "/step1.html")	Name	
Step 1	/index.htm	Home	☐ Required step ⦾
Step 2	/catalog_request.htm	Catalog Request	
Step 3			
Step 4			
Step 5			
Step 6			
Step 7			
Step 8			
Step 9			
Step 10			
Goal (see above)	/catalog_request_success.htm	Catalog Success!	

(Save Changes) (Cancel)

Figure 16-5:
Configuring
the funnel
for a catalog
request.

Unfortunately, there are simply too many variables for me to explain how to do it: brand of shopping cart, Web server, and so on. If you think you can configure it yourself, you can learn a lot from Google's tutorials at www.google.com/support/analytics. If you're looking for a consulting company to set up your Analytics correctly, you can choose with confidence from Google's own list of accredited Analytics partners, located at www.google.com/analytics/support_partner_provided.html. Google vouches for all 25 (the current number of North American partners); I can't speak highly enough about the talents of my Analytics advisor, Timothy Seward of ROI Revolution. Visit www.roirevolution.com to sign up for their free Webinar, get their newsletter, or pick up tips on their blog.

Actually, the fact that e-commerce Analytics is so complicated is a good thing — the harder something is, the bigger your competitive advantage when you implement. Analytics can provide you with black-belt skills in a white-belt world.

Making Sense of the Data

Analytics allows you to track much more than AdWords traffic, but if I got into the entire range of Analytics' capabilities, this book could double as *Weightlifting For Dummies*. I'm going to limit this section to AdWords only, and ignore organic search traffic, banner ads, newsletters, offline promotions, and direct entries. But once you've mastered the AdWords part of Analytics, you will definitely want to explore the whole range of possibilities.

Checking for data integrity

Before studying your Analytics data, compare the number of clicks between AdWords and Analytics to see whether your Analytics profile is working properly. I once placed Analytics code on a redirect page and the actual landing page by mistake — and got reports of twice as many visitors as I actually received. Comparing the clicks in your AdWords control panel and your Analytics tables can tell you if there's a problem but not what the problem is.

Shawn Purtell of ROI Revolution cautions that the numbers should be close, but probably won't be identical. Analytics and conversion tracking handle repeat visitors differently, and if a visitor clicks today and converts in a week or a month, the data in the two systems will log those events in different time frames. As long as the data are basically telling the same story, you're okay.

Viewing your data in the Dashboard

When your tracking is correctly set up and verified, it's time to start amassing insights on your visitors' behavior. From the Analytics tab in your AdWords account, click the View report link for the profile you want to examine. You'll begin with the Dashboard, which you can customize by adding views that you'll want to see a lot.

The Dashboard consists of, as you might expect, the just-the-facts graphs and charts that give you a quick picture of how your Web site is doing, as shown in Figure 16-6. It includes a graph of visits by day, as well as more in-depth information about those visits.

Figure 16-6:
The
Dashboard
screen
includes
overview
information
about your
visitors.

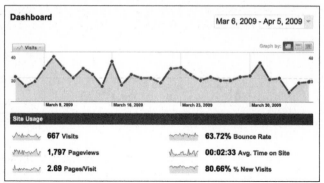

Visits-by-day graph

You can play with the visits-by-day graph, which by default shows you the last 30 days of data, by clicking the arrow to the right of the second date. You can change the date range by length and start date by clicking a date (or several) in the Calendar view or by selecting (much easier and more elegantly) the Timeline tab above the calendar. Click your cursor inside the box and hold your mouse down to drag it backward or forward, or click and select either edge to expand or contract the date range.

Below the Date Range boxes is a check box labeled Compare to Past. Check that box to superimpose a previous date range over the current one. For example, you can quickly compare your Web traffic in May and March. Analytics will automatically generate a range of the same number of days as the current one.

Many other screens also feature a top graph similar to the visits-by-day graph, and you manipulate them all the same way — by changing starting and ending points and comparing two time periods.

Playing with Analytics is really simple after you've seen it done. Head over to http://askhowie.com/dates for a series of short video tutorials that will have you playing with your data in no time.

Site Usage statistics

The Dashboard shows you important data about how often your site is visited in the Site Usage section. The Site Usage section provides the following data:

✔ **Visits, Pageviews, and Pages/Visit:** Shows for a given period how many visitors came to your Web site and how many pages they looked at. In Figure 16-6, 667 visitors were served 1,797 pages over the 30 day period, for an average of 2.69 pages per visit.

✔ **Avg. Time on Site:** Shows how long the average visitor hung around your Web site before leaving. Figure 16-6 shows a time of 2 minutes, 33 seconds.

✔ **Bounce Rate:** Google defines a *bounce* as a single-page visit. If people leave your landing page without going deeper into your site or opting in to a list, your landing page isn't doing its job. Figure 16-6 shows a bounce rate of 63.72%, which means that the majority of visitors to this site are indifferent to the landing page, and I'll probably never get the chance to do business with them.

✔ **% New Visits:** What percentage of your visitors have never been to your site before? (Remember, Analytics tracks computers, not people.) Figure 16-6 shows 80.66% of the visitors are new to your site.

Visitors Overview graph

The Visitors Overview graph shows you the number of unique visitors, rather than the number of visitors. If Sean from Toronto comes to your site on Sunday, Tuesday, and the following Saturday, that counts as three visits, but only one visitor (assuming, of course, that he used the same computer all three times).

The Visitors Overview and following sections can all be removed from the Dashboard by clicking the small X in the right-hand corner of the header.

Map Overlay

A world map shows you at a glance where in the world your visitors live. The darker the shading, the more visits from that location. Click on a land mass to zoom in to a continent. Keep clicking to go deeper, into countries, states/provinces/regions, and cities.

Traffic Sources Overview

This graph shows you the comparative traffic production of direct visitors (those who type your URL directly into their browser), search engine traffic by engine, and other referring Web sites. Click the small View Report link for a detailed breakdown of which search engines and referring sites. Note that Analytics distinguishes between paid search (CPC) and organic search for Google, Yahoo!, and MSN.

Content Overview

You can see the five most viewed pages on your site, based on the number of *pageviews* (how many times visitors saw that page). The % Pageviews column shows what percent of all the pageviews on your site were generated by that particular page.

Goals Overview

The Goals Overview gives you a quick look at the number of visitors completing your defined goals.

The AdWords Campaign screen

In the Dashboard, you can see the number and percentage of visits generated by each AdWords campaign. Click the View Report link to go deeper into the AdWords reporting, the part of Analytics I describe in the rest of this chapter.

In addition to a link on the Dashboard, you can access this screen directly from the left navigation by clicking Traffic Sources, then AdWords, and finally AdWords Campaigns.

The top chart, as usual, shows visits over time. Below, a table segments your traffic by campaign and shows the number of visits, pages/visit, average time on your site, percentage of new visits, and bounce rate for each campaign. Click a campaign name to get the same information on the ad group level, and click an ad group to see the same data for each individual keyword. Figure 16-7 shows how Analytics drills down into the French campaign (which cost a total of $74,544.64) to the Brie ad group (accounting for $40,164.41, or 53.88% of the total) and even deeper to the individual keyword `brie` (which cost $1718.42, or 2.31% of the advertising spending for the entire campaign).

Figure 16-7:
You can discover how each AdWords campaign, ad group, and keyword produces different business results.

If the traffic comes from the content network, it's labeled (content targeting). You can search for specific keywords using the search box below the keyword list.

Clicking on an individual keyword brings up actionable data in three tabs:

✔ **Site Usage tab:** How visitors from that keyword behaved on your site: average time on site, bounce rate, pages/visit, and percentage of new visits. Interesting, to be sure, but the next two tabs will really blow your mind (if you're into that sort of thing).

✔ **Goal Conversion tab:** How visitors from that keyword converted to each of your defined goals, and the goal value per visit (that is, how much the average customer who types that keyword is worth to you). Armed with this information, you can set your AdWords bids so that no keyword is costing you more than you're making back on your site.

✔ **Clicks tab:** The monetary value of a click generated by that keyword: including total number of clicks, value of each click (RPC — Revenue-Per-Click, the average revenue you received for each click based on e-commerce sales and the value you assigned to your goals), your profit (or loss) margin, and the overall ROI of that keyword.

Ad content segmenting

Choose Ad Content from the Segment drop-down list to see the same data, this time by individual ad. (You can find the Segment drop-down list above the Site Usage, Goal Conversion, and Clicks tabs.) Only the headlines are shown, so if you're running different ads with identical headlines, you're not going to find this particular view very useful.

Views

To the right of the Site Usage, Goal Conversion, and Clicks tabs, you find five views to choose from. From left to right, they are Table, Pie Chart, Horizontal Bar Graph, Comparison Against Site Average, and Mini-histogram (that's a line chart, not a medical test).

Showing you all the views here would fill up another book. Check out www.roirevolution.com/graphs for a more in-depth discussion of the Analytics graphs. Play around with different segmenting options and views, and feel free to explore. You can't break anything in the Analytics report section — it's all read-only.

The Keyword Positions view

From the left navigation, choose AdWords and then Keyword Positions. Below the obligatory line graph of visits over time, you see a list of your keywords, and the number of visits generated by each one. Click any keyword, and a magical view appears to the right of the keyword list. This view shows you how many clicks were generated by that keyword in each position on the search results page. The view itself is a mockup of the search results page, on which ads can appear on top of the organic results to the left (labeled Top 1, Top 2, and Top 3) or down the right side (labeled Side 1 through Side 10), as shown in Figure 16-8. You can use this information to find and bid on your keyword's "sweet spot" on the search results page.

Figure 16-8:
The Keyword Positions view shows which ad positions generate clicks for a given keyword.

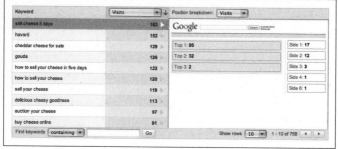

You can also determine position for ads showing on the content network. If an advertiser runs an AdSense tower of five ads, your ad could be in positions one through five in that ad block.

Automating Analytics reporting

At the top of almost every screen, Analytics gives you the option to export or e-mail the results in one of four formats: PDF (for Adobe Acrobat Reader), XML (a Web language), CSV (for Microsoft Excel) and TSV (Tab Separated Values, for other spreadsheet applications). You can also add the view to the main Dashboard.

When you create an e-mail report, you can customize it and schedule it to be sent to whomever you want at regular intervals. You can even include a date comparison, so you can see changes in the key numbers each week or month. Under the Schedule tab, just check the box labeled Include Date Comparison.

Acting on Your Data to Make More Money

Throughout this chapter, I show you examples of data that you can act on to improve Web site conversion. In this section, I recap some of the low-hanging fruit that you can pluck with even a simple, non–e-commerce Analytics setup.

Optimizing your site for your visitors

The more you know about your visitors, the more successfully you can create a Web site that serves their needs and invites their business. Begin with the Web Design Parameters screen in the Webmaster view. View and print your visitors' browser versions, screen resolutions, and connection speeds for the past week, month, and three months. Note the most popular types of each characteristic.

The next step will take a little work, but is well worth the effort. Go and navigate your Web site using the browsers, resolutions, and connection speeds used by your visitors. How long does your site take to load via dialup? What part of your landing page is visible on an 800 x 600 screen? What does your order form look like in Safari or Firefox?

If you interact with your site using only your computer, you have no idea what your visitors experience. Take the time to put yourself in their shoes, or on their mouse, and you may discover simple design tweaks that will double conversion literally overnight.

Improving site "stickiness"

If visitors leave your site after viewing only one or two pages, you may have a "stickiness" problem. A *sticky site* is one that keeps visitors engaged for a long period of time, so they have a chance to get to know you, find answers to their questions, and feel more comfortable with the idea of doing business with you.

The Average Pageviews per Visit metric, available on many screens, is a good indicator of how sticky your site is. If you spend all your energy on your AdWords campaigns yet lose visitors within a page or two on your site, you know where you need to improve.

From Timothy Seward of ROI Revolution: "To calculate your target for pageviews per visit, count how many pages it would take to complete the core goal of your site. For example, if your site is an e-commerce site, then count how many pages it takes from the home page to make it all the way to the receipt page. That resulting number is a good target to shoot for."

Loyalty and recency

Loyalty refers to the number of times visitors return to your site. *Recency,* like it sounds, refers to how recently they've been back. Most successful businesses display high loyalty and recency metrics: Their customers come back again and again, and a large percentage of their customers have purchased recently.

Click Visitors on the left, then Visitor Loyalty, then Loyalty. You see a bar chart showing the number and percentage of visitors who have visited your site once, twice, three times, all the way up to 25–50 visits (as shown in Figure 16-9). If your online business depends on repeat customers to be profitable, you should improve the effectiveness of your e-mail follow up sequences and other means of generating repeat traffic.

Figure 16-9:
The vast majority of visitors to this site are first time visitors, a problem if the site depends on repeat business to be successful.

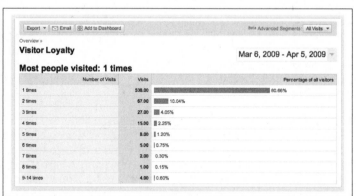

The report just below Loyalty is Recency. A healthy site attracts its visitors back at a regular interval, whether it is daily, weekly, or monthly. Figure 16-10 shows a site that encourages visitors to return on roughly a bi-weekly or monthly basis. The site, www.peaceweavers.com, does so by means of a regular newsletter and an updated photo blog.

Figure 16-10:
More than
10% of the
site visitors
over the
past month
had been
on the site
between 1
week and 2
months
previously.

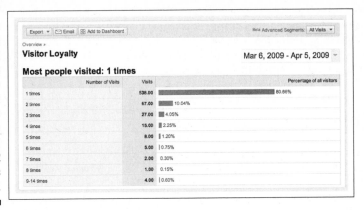

As AdWords matures and competition heats up, the value of the first transaction will trend toward break-even. If you want to be successful, you must cultivate recency and frequency in your customers. E-mail autoresponders and broadcasts (see Chapter 11), special events, teleseminars, referral contests, quizzes, new articles, and sales can all make your Web site a recurring destination rather than a one-shot deal.

Evaluating Web site changes

You can apply the date range comparison function to goal tracking and goal conversion. For example, say that you made a change to your opt-in landing page on July 1, and you want to determine the effect of that change. You can compare the goal conversion for your opt-in for July 1–30, compared to June 1–30 of the same year.

In your AdWords Campaign report (or most other reports), first click the date range at the top right of the screen. Set the date range by clicking and selecting the start and end date, and then check the Compare to Past check box. By default, you see the previous week or month, depending on your current date range. To change the comparison range (for example, to the same month last year), choose the Timeline tab and drag the slider to the left until you reach the beginning of the comparison date range.

The graph now contains bars of two different colors, representing the different time periods. In Figure 16-11, the total number of visits and unique visitors were up from March to April, but the time on site, average pageviews, and bounce rate all got slightly worse. The owner of this site needs to spend more time improving the site, rather than generating new traffic.

Figure 16-11:
Compare
two date
ranges of
data to track
changes
over time.

Page and funnel navigation

The visually coolest part of Analytics is the navigation. You can see how visitors abandon the funnel you've defined, and where they go. You can also analyze any page on your site in terms of where visitors come from before landing on that page — and where they go afterward (shown in Figure 16-12).

Figure 16-12:
For any
page,
discover
where your
visitors
come from
before
viewing and
where they
go after
viewing.

72.17% Entrances		53.91% Exits	
27.83% Previous Pages		**46.09%** Next Pages	
Content	% Clicks	Content	% Clicks
/index.htm	10.61%	/index.htm	10.61%
/products/brie/index.htm	2.43%	/products/brie/index.htm	9.04%
/products/index.htm	2.26%	/products/index.htm	7.83%
/products/cheddar/index.htm	2.26%	/learn/about.htm	3.30%
/catalog_request.htm	2.09%	/products/cheddar/index....	2.96%

Page navigation

Click Content from the left navigation. Identify your most viewed pages on the left, under the Top Content header, and click each URL to see how that page fits in your visitors' navigation. You can learn how visitors found that page by clicking the Navigation Summary link. You'll discover that some of your pages are sending visitors in the wrong direction, and you can take steps to correct the problem. You can make links bigger and more noticeable. You can move buttons and forms left or right, above the fold, or repeat them several times on a page. You can highlight text, use arrows or animation to draw eyeballs, or deploy audio or video.

Funnel Visualization

From the Goals section in the left navigation, choose Funnel Visualization. You can select any of your (up to four) goals. You will see how well your funnel moves visitors from entry to goal achievement, and where and why they are abandoning your funnel, as shown in Figure 16-13.

Timothy Seward offers the example of a detour from the shopping cart checkout page to the guarantee page instead of the completed sale. Upon discovering that, a clever merchant would add the guarantee to the checkout page and keep their visitors on track to a sale.

Figure 16-13: 2,443 visitors entered the funnel, and 113 exited successfully by requesting a catalog. Funnel Visualization shows where the other visitors went.

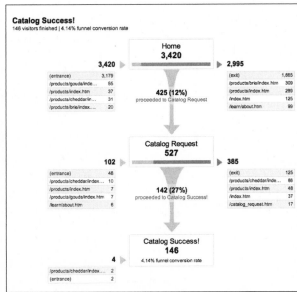

Reverse Goal Path

Also under Goals, check out Reverse Goal Path. This view shows you how visitors actually get to your goals; not what you think your funnel is, but what your visitors think it is. You may uncover your visitors' unanswered questions and objections by studying the reverse path to each goal. If a lot of visitors are coming through your privacy policy page, a page usually ignored by viewers, perhaps your site doesn't seem trustworthy enough. You may want to add credibility elements such as logos, anti-spam assurances, and more professional design.

Part VI
The Part of Tens

The 5th Wave — By Rich Tennant

"Look-what if we just increase the size of the charts?"

In this part . . .

This part covers important stuff that didn't quite fit in the rest of the book. I gathered these tidbits and assembled them into top-ten lists.

I gathered the worst beginner's mistakes I've encountered in my years as an AdWords consultant and coach for Chapter 17. Avoid these and you shave two years off your learning curve.

Chapter 18 contains case studies that highlight the principles revealed in this book. You find a broad range of businesses, challenges, and solutions that are meant to bring the concepts to life and inspire you to make your own AdWords success stories.

Because I had so much fun writing Chapters 17 and 18, I wrote two more top-ten lists and made them into Bonus Chapters 1 and 2. You can view and download these chapters as PDF files at http://askhowie.com/bonuschapters.

In Bonus Chapter 1, I share a bunch of the online tools I use and recommend highly. Some are free and some aren't; start with the free ones and then pay for other tools out of your AdWords profits.

Bonus Chapter 2 was my excuse to contact some of the best copywriters in the world and get them to return my e-mails. You get a first-class education from these tips on writing great Google ads.

Chapter 17

The Ten (Or So) Most Serious AdWords Beginner's Mistakes

In This Chapter

▶ Split-testing snafus

▶ Campaign calamities

▶ Ad agonies

▶ Keyword, er . . . problems

AdWords can have a steep learning curve, as well as an expensive one. In this chapter, I quickly run through the most common and expensive mistakes I've seen as an AdWords consultant and fixer.

Neglecting to Split-Test Your Ads

Even the world's best marketers are wrong more often than they're right. If you run a single ad, the chances of that ad being the best of all the possible ads in the universe are laughably small. When you compare two very different ads head to head, one of them will almost always be better than the other — more compelling, more attractive, or more in tune with the innermost desires of your market.

When you've run the test long enough to have statistically significant data, you gracefully retire (or unceremoniously fire, whichever you prefer) the losing ad and put up another challenger. You continue the process, directing the survival of the fittest ad until you find the one unbeatable control that maximizes your business goals.

In the old pre-Internet days, split-testing was complicated and expensive, a high-level business process reserved for huge companies with giant mainframe computers and millions of dollars on the line. Now, Google AdWords makes split-testing as easy as sending e-mail; when I see advertisers neglecting this fundamental improvement strategy, I feel like the mom telling her kid to eat his peas because there are children starving somewhere else in the world. I want to shake them and shout, "Don't you realize how lucky you are to be able to split-test so easily and cheaply and achieve such quick and conclusive results?"

If you aren't split-testing at this point, contact my office. I'll pack my WrestleMania Split Test Avenger outfit, fly (business class only, please) to your place of business, and shake some sense into you.

Practical advice:

✔ When you set up a new ad group, always have two different ads ready.

✔ Think of split tests as experiments you're conducting to satisfy your curiosity. Keep a journal of questions, prioritize them, and always have another split test waiting in the wings.

✔ Split-test wide variations first, and then narrow down to smaller details.

✔ Check for statistical significance before declaring a winner. Don't mistake randomness for rock-solid trends.

✔ Split-test landing pages and e-mail sequences as well as AdWords ads. With the right tools, these split tests are almost as easy as the AdWords split-testing interface.

See Chapter 13 for best practices in split-testing.

Letting Google Retire Your Ads without Testing

Another campaign setting that you need to override is the Ad Serving option in the Advanced Options section. From your campaign management console, click into a campaign and then click the Edit Campaign Settings link near the top. On the next page, Campaign Settings, find Ad Serving under Advanced Options (on the left). Do not optimize ad serving. Do not let Google show better performing ads more often. Instead, select the radio button next to Rotate: Show Ads More Evenly.

If you're split-testing, you have two goals: You want to identify the winner as quickly as possible, and you want to learn something from the test that will help you connect better with your market.

When you let Google take control behind the scenes and quietly retire your low-CTR ads, you allow tests to drag on unnecessarily. It's like holding a race, not specifying its length, and running it until the winner is miles away and the losers are gasping for breath at the side of the road. A much more efficient method is to establish a finish line and identify the winner as soon as the tape is broken. When Google retires your ads behind your back, you lose the market intelligence that your split tests often provide.

Finally, as I show in Chapter 15, the ad with the best CTR is often the least profitable. Yet Google chooses winners based on CTR, not conversion.

The only exception is when you turn on the Conversion Optimizer tool — in that case, you must keep the Optimize setting in your campaign.

Split-Testing for Improved CTR Only

Ads that generate high CTR can be wonderful. They attract more visitors to your site at lower cost, and rank higher than other ads bidding the same amount. They also teach you about your market's desires and fears.

But when you split-test two ads and choose the winner based solely on CTR, you are in danger of worshipping a false god. Understand that the AdWords game is based on one rule: Get more outputs for your inputs than anyone else. Okay, CTR is a key throughput — but leads, customers, and dollars are what you're after.

A mention of Paris Hilton in your ad text may generate a high CTR, but just like the old magazine ads with the four-inch red headline of the word "sex," she may be attracting eyeballs belonging to nonbuyers. Remember that lots of clicks translate into lots of money for Google, not for you. Getting the right clicks is more important than getting lots of clicks.

When you split-test your ads, make sure you run conversion reports, and don't rely on CTR alone.

Creating Ad Groups with Unrelated Keywords

The easiest way to set up an ad group is to write an ad, dump every keyword you can think of into that group, and send it to your home page. Heck, that should take you about 10 minutes of work if you're using some of the powerful keyword tools I talk about in Chapter 5. It's much more complicated and time-consuming to create tight ad groups, based on a narrow set of related keywords matched closely to the ads and the landing page. But your results will be well worth the extra time and effort.

Keywords unrelated to ads and landing pages produce poor CTR and conversion results — and cost a lot of money because of the poor Quality Score penalty. Remember that each keyword represents a mindset; take the time to group your keywords by similar mindsets, and write your ads and landing pages to address the desires and fears attached to those mindsets.

You can tell when your ad groups are too broad if the CTRs of different keywords in the same group vary wildly. You may discover that the successful keywords are found in the ad headline and repeated in the description or URL. Peel the underperforming keywords out of that ad group and stick them into their own group, with an ad written just for them.

Muddying Search and Content Results

Many beginners rely on Google's default settings when creating campaigns. Remember that Google's defaults usually serve to simplify your account and to increase Google's revenue. Sometimes those two goals are compatible with your goals, and sometimes they aren't. One of the campaign settings you need to change right away, because you prefer profitability to simplicity, is Networks. (See Figure 17-1.)

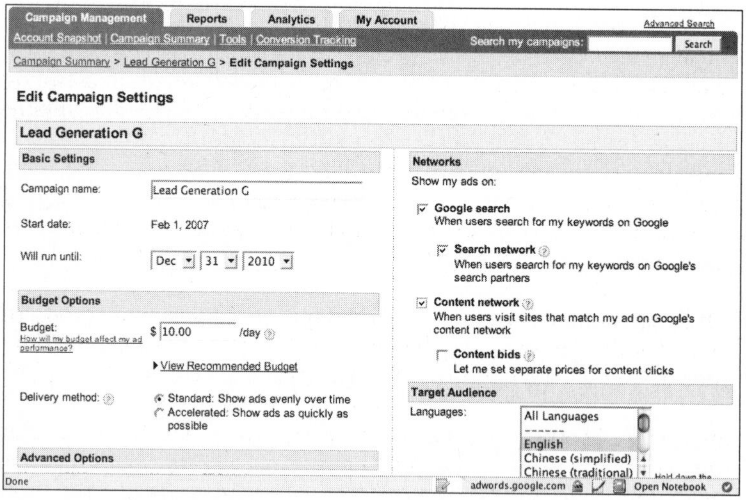

Figure 17-1: Separate content from search network from Google traffic on the Edit Campaign Settings page.

If you run all three streams of traffic (Google, search partners, and content network) through the same ad group, you lose the ability to distinguish among the very different kinds of traffic. *Content network traffic* consists of people who were interrupted while they were reading or surfing or watching something else. *Search network traffic* consists of people who are actively looking for your keywords. Not only do they arrive at your site driven by different motivations and desires; they respond differently to your ads and offers.

In many cases, content traffic overwhelms search traffic. When that's true, you lose the ability to split-test ads properly; your accurate CTR and conversion data from the search traffic is drowned by the flood of content traffic. Figuring out what your market is telling you is like trying to hear a cricket at a heavy metal concert.

When you choose winning ads and identify profitable keywords based on poorly converting search traffic — and try to apply those lessons to your search marketing — in essence, you're surveying penguins to try to sell to chimpanzees. The two market channels are very different, and should be studied and treated differently.

See Chapter 7 for detailed instructions on how to split Google, search partner, and content network traffic into three different campaigns.

Ignoring the 80/20 Principle

The 80/20 principle, applied to AdWords, states that the vast majority of outputs (impressions, clicks, leads, sales, and such) are caused by a very small minority of inputs (ad groups, ads, and keywords). Instead of diffusing your efforts, focus on the vital few rather than the insignificant many.

When you follow my advice and create Best Practice AdWords campaigns, you inevitably create a fair amount of complexity. With so many variables to monitor, juggle, and adjust, it's common to become overwhelmed and wonder, "What do I do now?"

I often see consulting clients spend days massaging an ad group that has no potential to make a significant contribution to their bottom line, while ignoring the big keywords in the important ad groups.

Keep reminding yourself that the AdWords game is about maximizing outputs from fixed inputs. In this case, inputs are impressions and advertising cost. Spend your time fixing the things that will make the biggest difference:

1. Sort your campaigns by impressions.

2. Sort that campaign's ad groups by impressions.

   Assess the ads in that group — do you have a clear winner?

3. Sort keywords by impressions, and look at the top five keywords.

   Are they making you money? Do you need to adjust their bids? Peel and stick them into a new ad group? Pause or delete them?

Here the number of impressions is your limiting factor. If you have two ad groups, one with 50 impressions a day and the other with 20,000, a 50 percent improvement in conversion might translate into one additional sale per month for the smaller group and one to two more sales per day for the larger group. Where do you want to spend your time?

One exception: you may be artificially limiting impressions in two ways:

- By ignoring potential high-traffic keywords
- By bidding for a position on page two or worse

Make sure you check your average position for each keyword, ad, ad group, and campaign before assuming you've maxed out its traffic.

Declaring Split-Test Winners Too Slowly

Once you set up split-testing, you want to identify winners as quickly as possible, so you can learn and improve faster than your competition. If you can double your CTR and maintain the same quality of traffic, you get twice as many visitors for the same amount of money. When you double your Web site's traffic, you can run your landing-page and sales-page split tests twice as fast as well. The faster you split-test, the faster you improve.

I commonly look at new clients' accounts and point out that they have been running a split test for weeks longer than they need to. Not only are they showing an inferior ad half the time, they're also wasting the most precious resource of all: *meaningful insights about their market.*

Set up reports to run on a regular basis that just look at ad performance. Make it a habit to run the numbers through the statistical significance tester at www.askhowie.com/split and identify split tests that have yielded conclusive, action-producing results.

You can automate this process and receive e-mail notification of split-test winners by subscribing to www.winneralert.com.

Declaring Split-Test Winners Too Quickly

If your ad group receives a lot of traffic, your split tests may achieve statistical significance after only an hour or two. The problem with this speedy outcome is that the people searching during that particular window of time may be different from people searching at other times. If you choose a winner based on traffic from 2 a.m. to 4 a.m. on Sunday, you may be picking an ad that has less appeal to people searching at noon on Wednesday.

To be safe, run each split test for at least a week, so you don't put too much weight into a cyclical blip. You can run reports by date and time to identify differences in impressions, CTR, and conversion by day of the week and time of day.

If your weeklong split test threatens to become too expensive because of the volume of traffic, you can limit your traffic geographically by creating a campaign that targets a few low-population metropolitan areas but shows your ad 24/7.

Forgetting Keywords in Quotes (Phrase Matching) or Brackets (Exact Matching)

When you put a keyword in quotation marks, you tell Google that the quoted words or phrase must appear exactly as written somewhere in the keyword. Brackets are even more specific: They signify that the searcher must enter the keyword exactly as it appears within the brackets, with nothing added or removed.

When you use broad match keywords only (putting no quotes or brackets on the keyword), you don't really know what your visitors actually entered as search terms. You lump many different searches into a big vague basket and miss some valuable market intelligence.

Phrase and exact match keywords often achieve higher CTRs than broad matches achieve because you can create ads that speak directly to the exact words and phrases that your visitors type.

Because of the hierarchy among broad, phrase, and exact match keywords, be aware that phrase match keywords cannibalize their broad match counterparts, and exact match keywords steal impressions from both. If the CTRs differ among the three match types for high-traffic keywords, peel the underperformers and stick them into their own ad groups. (See more about keyword matching in Chapter 5.)

Ignoring Negative Keywords

Negative keywords keep certain searchers from seeing your ads. If you get significant traffic from broad or phrase match keywords, you may find that Google is matching your ad to some irrelevant searches. If you want to deter tire-kickers from costing you clicks, you may want to add negative keywords like `free` and `complimentary`.

If you target upscale buyers, you can improve your ROI by eliminating `discount` and `cheap`, as well as certain brand names that have low-end connotations. If some of your search terms are ambiguous (for example, `anthrax` refers to both a disease and a heavy metal band) or could refer to two different niches of the same market (`auto glass` and `plate glass` windows), save your click money by adding negative keywords to your keyword list.

Monitor your keyword-conversion performance over time to find new negative keywords. If you sell golf clubs and none of your `golf instruction` keywords convert, you can add `instruction` as a negative keyword.

Keeping the Keyword Quality Score Hidden

Google introduced the keyword Quality Score in 2006, without much fanfare or documentation. It's often not even shown in the default ad group Keyword tab screen. You must add the Quality Score column to the Keyword tab to manage this crucial metric.

Quality Score tells you how much you must bid in order to show your ad for a given keyword. A low Quality Score puts you at a huge competitive disadvantage in your market; for this reason, I advise my clients to improve their Quality Scores before dealing with anything else on their sites or AdWords campaigns.

AdWords was the first advertising medium in the world to penalize advertisers for showing irrelevant content to their users. Their algorithms are based on years of comprehensive data collection — the keyword Quality Score contains information based on far more than your measly account. Ignoring it means you are missing the opportunity to make your sales process more customer-friendly and effective.

Activate the Quality Score column by clicking the Keywords rollup tab, clicking the Filter and Views button, and then selecting the Customize Columns link from the drop-down list. Check the box next to Quality Score in the Performance column on the left. If your browser isn't wide enough to view the Quality Score column, you can click and drag the green Quality Score column up to the top of the green columns, so it appears next to Position Preference. Click the Save button to return to the keyword list.

Spending Too Much or Too Little in the Beginning

Marketing Consultant Joy Milkowski of `www.getmoreaccess.com` reminded me of another big beginner's mistake: Over- or under-spending during the first weeks and months of your AdWords campaigns.

If you open your wallet too much by specifying too high a monthly budget or daily spend, you'll lose all your money before you have time to learn the ropes. When you figure out that something isn't working, turn it off right away while you make changes. Chances are — even with this book under your belt — you'll take some time to get the feel of AdWords and develop proficiency. If you rush, you'll blow through your budget several times and walk away going, "This stuff doesn't work."

If you ever took a driving lesson, you may remember that your instructor made you drive slowly for a long time, showing you how to steer and brake and stop fiddling with the radio dial, before ever letting you open up on a highway. Your AdWords budget is your MPH — take it easy until you learn how to drive safely.

Other clients are so hesitant that they set daily and monthly budgets far too low to generate enough traffic. They don't get enough impressions to split-test and improve their ads and keywords, and they give up in frustration. Without enough statistically significant data, they don't know how to improve their campaigns and quit in frustration. That's like learning to drive by never going faster than five miles per hour. The experience of going 55 MPH (or 85, which I wouldn't know about, especially not on I-95 in Maryland just south of DC, I swear) is qualitatively and quantitatively different from inching along in an empty parking lot. The super-slow experience just doesn't transfer to the real thing.

The happy medium involves setting a "learning budget" and sticking with it. Do your homework (see Chapter 4) to estimate the amount of traffic you can expect. Your advertising spend (as well as the daily or weekly attention you'll need to give your account) depends on the velocity of that traffic. At first, don't expect to make money, or even come close to breaking even. You're not advertising to earn it back; instead, you're running market tests so you can come out swinging when you open up your wallet and your traffic. Your goal is to get your ROI into the black within a few months.

Chapter 18

Ten (Or So) AdWords Case Studies

The best way to see the strategies and concepts from this book in action is by viewing actual examples. I can't show you all the details because successful advertisers guard their keywords, strategies, and metrics like the recipe for Coca-Cola. I've compiled case studies from consultants who hope you'll think they're clever enough to hire them, from clients who hope you'll go to their Web sites and buy their products, and from friends egotistical enough to want to see their names in a book. Among these three groups, you'll see enough gems to keep you busy for a while.

Using Sales Conversion Data to Save $14k per Month

A client who sells a consumer product online and doesn't want to reveal its identity was spending about $35,000/month on AdWords. The client was tracking conversions but not the actual dollar amount of each sale. When we connected the shopping cart data to AdWords conversion tracking, we could now see the exact ROI of every keyword, site placement, and ad in the client's account.

We began collecting data on February 7, 2008. I started split-testing ads at that point. After 3 weeks, I ran a keyword performance report and paused negative ROI keywords. I ran a placement performance ad and excluded the negative ROI placements. I ran an ad performance report and deleted the inferior ads.

As you can see from Figure 18-1, the client's AdWords spend dropped significantly, but their total sales remained the same. Before, they spent $35 to make $100. After, they spent only $20. In their case, that amounted to a monthly savings of almost $14,000.

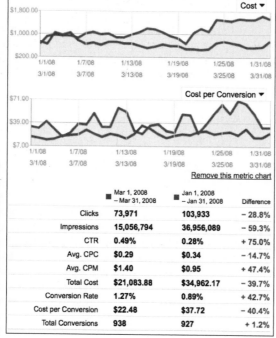

Figure 18-1:
By deleting
ROI-negative
items,
spending
dropped
dramatically
without
affecting
sales.

	Mar 1, 2008 – Mar 31, 2008	Jan 1, 2008 – Jan 31, 2008	Difference
Clicks	73,971	103,933	– 28.8%
Impressions	15,056,794	36,956,089	– 59.3%
CTR	0.49%	0.28%	+ 75.0%
Avg. CPC	$0.29	$0.34	– 14.7%
Avg. CPM	$1.40	$0.95	+ 47.4%
Total Cost	$21,083.88	$34,962.17	– 39.7%
Conversion Rate	1.27%	0.89%	+ 42.7%
Cost per Conversion	$22.48	$37.72	– 40.4%
Total Conversions	938	927	+ 1.2%

Here's the really cool thing about this case study. Go back to the first paragraph and read carefully what I did. Notice: There was no creativity involved. No new ads. No clever keyword variations. No insightful market analysis. Just looking at each element and asking, "Is this paying for itself?" And when the answer was no, out came the axe.

Going Global and Tracking Conversions with Analytics

Shane Keller of www.gcflearnfree.org, a non-profit organization that offers free online computer, technology, and life skills training to help people improve their lives, visited my office on May 8, 2008. We talked for a while, I looked at his AdWords campaigns, made a few suggestions, and he left.

Shane shared his actions and results on August 15, 2008. Here are the relevant excerpts:

After I met with you, I came back and we adjusted our campaign setting to target a worldwide market instead of just the US. The AdWord campaigns exploded into action. We started maxing out our budget by noon every day. Now, finally I could start to see how each test and adjustment affected the results.

I worked the system — outlined in your book — each and every day and saw immediate improvements week after week. This led to a run of seven consecutive record-breaking weeks of stats for our website, the adoption of Google Analytics to track our conversion rate.

Week of April 28–May 4	Week of June 16–June 22
Clicks = 3,935	Clicks = 7,177
Imp = 101,625	Imp = 80,639
CTR = 3.42%	CTR = 8.93%

We added Analytics the week of July 7th – July 13th. Now it was all about the conversions. We now have a conversion rate of 15.42% on our AdWords campaign. We are averaging around 6,600 new unique signups each week and we're now heading into what's typically the busiest period for us. Here is a screen shot of our website signup growth. (See Figure 18-2.)

Figure 18-2: Account optimiza-tion led to a surge of new traffic for this client.

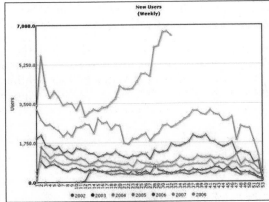

And here's what it did for our Spanish side of things! (See Figure 18-3.)

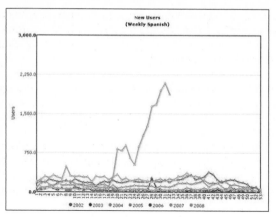

Figure 18-3:
The increase in traffic was even more pronounced for the Spanish language campaign.

We now are trying to take everything we are learning from AdWords and utilize it in order for us to increase our organic search positions.

Throwing a Bigger Party with Broad Match and Negative Keywords

David Rothwell of www.adwordsanswers.com took over the AdWords account of a client, www.perforce.com, which provides versioning and collaboration tools and systems for software development companies. When David took over the account, the main challenge was the lack of traffic. Originally, the account had been set up with thousands of long-tail (three- to five-word) keywords to take advantage of the low bid prices. The trouble was, keywords like "embedded software development tool" and "software development management tool" were getting almost no searches.

David relaxed the keyword specificity; began using more common, shorter-tail keywords, such as version control, software configuration management, and software configuration tools; and put them into lots of tightly focused ad groups.

Because they were now bidding on common keywords in broad match format, they had to pay attention to the searches they no longer wanted. David did so by running the search query report on a regular basis, and adding negative keywords to the appropriate ad groups. For example, "kitchen design software" and "website design software" both showed up, so -kitchen and -website were both added to the software design group.

David reports that long-tail keywords, once a best practice, appear to be losing their effectiveness because Google prefers to show ads for keywords with significant search volume. After all, if nobody's searching, then nobody's clicking, and Google isn't making money.

Results: Perforce had been frustrated by their inability to spend more money on AdWords. As they offer a fully functional two-user free trial software download, the targeted search traffic they get converts quite well.

Once David added conversion tracking and removed the negative-ROI keywords and ads, not only did the impressions and CTR increase, but also cost per lead went down. As an added bonus, the extra traffic now allows for more robust split-testing of landing pages, including new ones with video demos.

Originally, the AdWords account had targeted only the United Kingdom. Perforce is building on the success of the UK-based campaign to roll out campaigns in Germany and Sweden.

Getting Cheap and Hungry Traffic by Bidding on Your Own Brand Name

Christian Bedard of www.calimacil.com sells high-end and high-quality form swords for live action role-playing aficionados. Christian thought he had tapped out all the potential keywords in the swords, shields, and live action weapons department, but recently, he had a brainstorm and bid on the keyword Calimacil and headlined the ad "Calimacil Official Site." (See Figure 18-4.)

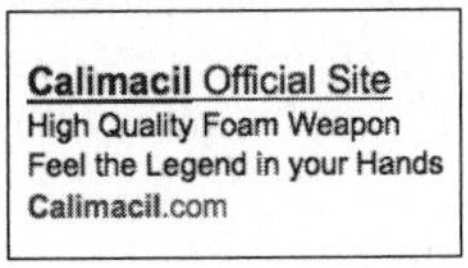

Figure 18-4: An effective ad that capitalizes on searches for their own brand name.

Calimacil Official Site
High Quality Foam Weapon
Feel the Legend in your Hands
Calimacil.com

He got this idea not from a competitor in his industry, but from copying the AdWords strategy of Dell Computers. (See Figure 18-5.) One of the smartest things you can do as an AdWords advertiser is to pay attention to what other advertisers are doing that catches your eye when you're searching. Most innovation is just borrowing a good idea from somewhere else and applying it where it has never been applied before.

Figure 18-5:
Calimacil
borrowed
the idea for
its ad from
this Dell ad.

Dell.com - Official Site
www.dell.com   Shop Home, Office & Small Business. Find Great PCs w/ Intel Technology.

Even though the Calimacil listing comes up at the top of the organic listings for the keyword `Calimacil`, the ad and organic listing combined generate more traffic and sales than just the top organic listing by itself. Rather than cannibalize the free clicks, the sponsored link reinforces Calimacil's domination of the page. The ad's CTR is 26%, with a very high sales conversion rate, and very low bid price because there are no competitors.

Adding a Welcome Video to the Landing Page

Ken Evoy, president of `www.sitesell.com` (a turnkey Web hosting and e-commerce business-building system), thought that he had fully optimized his Web site conversion process through years of comprehensive testing. Nothing he tried could beat his control site. But he found that adding a short, friendly Welcome to My Website video to his home page dramatically increased sales for his Site Build It! service. The video helped increase sales by 30 percent by explaining the product and building an emotional connection with visitors.

With the help of Web video consultant Joe Chapuis of `www.webvideozone.com`, Ken created a 3-minute video shortcut for the SiteSell homepage that walks prospects through a quick tour of his site and service. Ken explained, "Site Build It! is a big product that takes a lot of words to explain. Video enables us to get so much more information across so much more efficiently."

Ken added the video to the top of his home page, using the Flash video player available at `www.webvideozone.com`. Joe Chapuis explained the importance of video placement: "If you want someone to watch your video, you need to have it at the top of the page where it will get noticed, as well as on a Web page that prospects are likely to visit."

Ken reported that sales increased by 30 percent since he added video to the home page: "Video is incredibly powerful, especially for a product like SBI. . . . We have never been able to communicate so precisely, effectively, nor with such emotion."

Getting the Basics Right

Kelly Conway kindly saved me several hours of work by providing the following case study. Notice the simple steps that cumulatively produced stellar results.

I met David O'Hara, a product-development expert, when he was looking for help in selling one of his products, the Breatheasy blood-pressure reduction system, via PPC advertising. David's goal for this ad campaign is to drive visitors to a landing page where he makes a one-time sale of either a CD or downloadable product. Two landing-page examples include www.highbloodpressurehq. com *and* www.highbloodpressurehq.com/about_me.html

The campaign includes 30–40 ads, which we continuously split-test. Examples include:

```
15 Minutes to Lower Blood
Pressure - 6 Weeks to a Better Life
Free from High Blood Pressure
HighBloodPressureHQ.com
2,070 Clicks | 3.49% CTR | $0.12 CPC


These Breathing Exercises
Lower High Blood Pressure
Naturally - Just 15 Minutes a Day
HighBloodPressureHQ.com
220 Clicks | 4.90% CTR | $0.24 CPC


How To Lower Blood
Pressure - 15 Minutes/Day - 6 Weeks
to Freedom from High Blood Pressure
HighBloodPressureHQ.com
137 Clicks | 6.82% CTR | $0.23 CPC


Lower Blood Pressure
Start Immediately - 15 Minutes/Day
Simple, Practical & Affordable!
HighBloodPressureHQ.com
101 Clicks | 3.63% CTR | $0.16 CPC
```

The state of the ad campaign, at the time that David contacted me, was similar to many other campaigns I've seen. He was bidding on 600–800 keywords, all of which were in a single ad group. None of the keyword phrases was making use of anything other than Google's broad-match option. David's initial request was to get the minimum cost-per-click of many of his keywords below the $1 and $5 Google was requesting.

Improve Web Site to Increase Keyword Quality Score and Lower Bid Prices

The campaign's overall CTR had been around 0.50%. My immediate goal was to raise that number dramatically. I knew by doing that, I would be able to decrease the minimum bid and our average CPC. The initial cost per click was $0.23. However, David still had hundreds of keywords he wasn't bidding on due to the $1 and $5 minimum-bid requirements. In addition, I recommended that David add content to his Web site so that Google would find his keywords more relevant. He went to work on that while I worked on increasing the CTR.

Add Quotes and Brackets to Every Keyword

First, I created phrase- and exact-match versions for every keyword in the campaign. Those keyword variations often have less competition, which means their bid prices can be lower. Additionally, they often attract better-targeted visitors than the broad-match versions of the same phrases.

Delete Poorly Performing Keywords

Next, in order to quickly raise the campaign's CTR, I needed to delete the keywords that were performing poorly. I deleted phrases that, after 200 or more impressions, had resulted in no sales and had not achieved at least a 0.80% CTR.

Interim Results after Two Weeks

Implementing these strategies helped us increase the campaign's cumulative CTR to 1.02% by the end of the second week. Additionally, we managed to lower our average CPC by nearly 10%, to $0.21, during that period. By the end of the first month, our overall CTR was 1.67%. Google reported our average ad position for the first month as 5.6; indicating that our ads appeared, on average, in fifth or sixth position within Google's sponsored listings.

Segment Keywords into Ad Groups

The next step was to segment the keywords into groups of related phrases. This work was time consuming, but not difficult. I reviewed all of our keywords and identified 18 targeted groups. For example, a person searching for `"hypertension cure"` *may have a very different mindset from someone who searches for* `"lower blood pressure quickly"`, *though both are good prospects for David's product. Segmenting the overall market allowed us to write specific ads targeted to the apparent internal dialog of each person searching for a solution. A valuable side benefit of this exercise was that the resultant shift in perspective from the market as a whole to market segments allowed us to unearth additional search phrases that doubled the size of our keyword list.*

Continued Split-Testing

We had, of course, been split-testing ads all along. One particular ad (the first one displayed above) had consistently out-pulled all contenders. In the new groups, we split-tested that control ad against ones specific to each group's market segment. In about half of the cases, the control ad still won; proving that you never know what will work best until you test. We continue to write market-specific ads and split-test them against the control, however, and new winners emerge each week.

Discouraging Unqualified Traffic

In the interest of increasing sales conversions, we took a few actions that reduced our CTR. For example, as soon as we got the overall CTR above 1%, we introduced several negative keywords (such as "-free"). This combination of forward and backward steps resulted in an overall CTR of 3.88% over the first five months of the campaign. At that point, several of our ad groups had achieved a CTR over 4%; the highest was 4.98%. Dozens of specific keyword phrases garnered double-digit CTR.

Current Results

In summary, over the first five months of this campaign, we increased the CTR by 597% (0.65% to 3.88%), while reducing the average CPC 22% (from $0.23 to $0.18) and maintaining an average ad position just over 5; as low as 3.5 in one ad group. Additionally, at the 5-month mark, no keyword phrase had a minimum bid amount over $0.40. As a result of all this work, David's blood pressure is even lower today than when we started.

You can find an expanded version of this case study at Kelly's Web site, www.ctrexpert.com.

15-Cent Click to $1,700 Customer in Minutes

Mike Stewart of www.internetvideoguy.com doesn't spend hours creating new ads or designing amazing Web sites. He doesn't research hungry markets or spend hours creating long e-mail follow-up sequences. He buys cheap clicks on AdWords on keywords related to recording teleseminars and phone calls. He split-tests his ads but doesn't generate enough impressions to make significant changes very often.

Mike's landing page (at www.teleseminartools.com) features a prominent 2-minute video commercial for a home talk show recording studio priced at $1,695. The video cost almost nothing to make, compared to tens or hundreds of thousands of dollars for television commercial production. But the decreased quality doesn't matter on this site, because the AdWords traffic is so highly qualified. A commercial airing during a break in *The Office* is shown to everyone watching the program; only a tiny percentage of the viewers will be interested in a given product at a given time. That's why commercials on mass media need to be repeated so often. But a commercial on an AdWords landing page can specifically respond to the itch represented by the keyword.

For the low-traffic keyword teleseminars and its variations, Mike generated 134 clicks at $0.15 CPC over a 3-month period, for a total advertising spend of around $20.00. These clicks generated 13 sales totaling more than $22,000 over the same period. Mike cautions that these numbers are possible for two important reasons:

1. The keyword teleseminars generates a customer who is likely to be qualified for the offer.

2. The product for sale lends itself to a video demonstration.

Mike teaches others how to create inexpensive Internet commercials at www.internetvideoguy.com.

Local Search with Video Web Site

One of Mike Stewart's clients is www.carpetdepotdecatur.com, a local carpet store in Decatur, Georgia. The owner, Brad Flack, bids on about 30 keywords in the Atlanta market only, and drives traffic to a Web site that uses video to introduce the store and answer frequently asked questions. The ads are simple, and include the call to action, *watch online video.*

The video on the home page features Brad introducing himself and explaining the benefits and dramatic differences of his store. He guides visitors to click the "Deal of the Week" video, view customer testimonials, and meet the staff. He also invites them to call and shows them where to find the phone number, and demonstrates how to shop on the site. The most significant call to action is for the visitor to view the "Measure Your Home" how-to video.

Customers now come to the store feeling like they already know Brad from viewing several minutes of video. He has stopped running ads in the Yellow Pages because most customers use Google first and some rely on online search exclusively. Because none of his competitors is advertising with Google at this point (and he hopes they don't read this book!), his ad is the only one that prospects see. With no competition, clicks are cheap and his number-one position is guaranteed.

Generating B2B Leads without Cold Calling

Joe DiSorbo of www.webgistix.com uses the Web to generate targeted business-to-business leads for e-commerce companies who want to automate or outsource the packing and shipping of orders. Because his service is a complex business-to-business sale, he uses the Web strictly to generate leads. Joe explains how he went from AdWords zero to hero in 12 months by employing very basic strategies:

Prior to using AdWords, we engaged in the painfully slow process of surfing the Internet, locating a potential target (an existing e-commerce company), finding their contact information on their Web site, and then cold-calling them to pitch our services. We opened an AdWords account in May 2005, made a list of all possible keywords, and got started.

Our first 12 months using the system can be broken into 3 distinct 4-month periods with significant jumps in CTR.

Phase 1 — The Beginning (May 2005 through Aug 2005)

Impressions: 146,028
Clicks: 467
CTR: 0.32%
CPC: $0.71

During the first four months, we established two things:

> *1. People were actually searching online for fulfillment services and clicking our ad.*

> *2. We didn't yet know how to attract and convert enough prospects to make AdWords cost-effective.*

We started with a single campaign that contained a single ad group. That ad group consisted of every related keyword we could think of (broad match only and a single ad). When we ran a new ad, we shut off the original one. We didn't know how much the campaign was going to cost so we limited our daily budget and kept our bid prices low, which gave us a low position. Over that period, our highest CTR was 0.77%.

The good news was that prospects were in fact clicking on our advertisements and coming to our Web site. Some even filled out a form and requested more information. Once we had their information, we could call them back. These calls were much easier to convert to sales than the cold calls we had been making previously.

Phase 2 — The Big Leap (Sept 2005 to Dec 2005)

Impressions: 169,616
Clicks: 2,583
CTR: 1.52% (376% increase over Phase 1)
CPC: $1.62

During the second 4 months our AdWords efforts started to pay off. Beginning in September 2005 our CTR increased to 1.52%. We had significantly more people visiting our Web site and were converting more of them to sales. Over that period we tried various ways to increase our response rates. Three tactics in particular improved our campaigns the most:

1. *We got rid of the poorly performing and non-related keywords. This lowered our overall impressions but improved the connection between keywords and the ad.*

2. *We broke out like words into their own ad group so we could customize each headline for each set of keywords.*

3. *We began split-testing ads.*

Because these changes were working well, we added new keyword groups in November 2005. Impressions rose along with CTR as we applied our newfound skills to the new ad groups.

Phase 3 — Continuous Refinement (Jan 2006 to Apr 2006)

Impressions: 393,021
Clicks: 10,990
CTR: 2.80% (83% Increase over Phase 2, 774% increase over Phase 1)
CPC: $1.23

In January 2006, our CTR took another big leap upward. We had been split-testing vigorously for the past 4 months and refining our ad groups and keywords. The big leap came when we tested a display URL that matched, or was closely related to, the search term the person typed in. Now, both the headline and the display URL were related directly to what the person was searching for.

Up to this point, we had been using our corporate domain, Webgistix.com, only. Once we started using targeted URLs, we again saw a big increase in CTR. We went out and bought all the URLs we could that were related to our industry and started using them in the display URL for our top search terms. These included:

Keyword	*Display URL*
Fulfillment Center	www.FulfillmentCenter.biz
fulfillment costs	www.fulfillmentcosts.biz
kitting	kitting.biz
pack and ship	packandship.info
literature fulfillment	literaturefulfillment.biz
ecommerce fulfillment	ecommercefulfillment.biz

In addition to customized display URLs, we set up Web sites with those URLs to act as landing-page gateways to the main www.webgistix.com *site. We optimized those Web sites for different keywords, creating, in effect, landing sites instead of just landing pages. We kept the corporate logo at the top, but the important text and URL reflected the keyword. The Web site* http:// fulfillmentcenter.biz *is optimized for the keyword* "fulfillment center".

This change increased our Web-site conversion from 1% to 3% instantly, without any split testing.

The overall business result has been 80% sales growth three years in a row.

Understanding and Answering Customer Objections

Jaco Bolle of www.savefuel.ca sells a small generator that can be installed in cars and trucks to add hydrogen gas to the engine for better gas mileage and lower emissions. When he came to me for help in improving his Web site conversion, he faced several marketing challenges:

1. Very few people have heard of supplemental hydrogen.

2. Most people are skeptical when they hear that they can improve their gas mileage by adding hydrogen to their gas tank.

3. People associate hydrogen gas with the *Hindenburg* disaster and are scared to generate it near their vehicle engine.

Through informal market research (talking about the product with everyone we could find and reading posts in online forums dedicated to hydrogen technology and fuel savings), we identified these and other objections that were preventing sales. Then we put together a nine-day e-mail course, titled "Supplemental Hydrogen Secrets Revealed." Each day addresses a different objection head-on — educating and entertaining the reader, building a bond of trust, and moving them closer to buying.

The first e-mail has the subject line, "Hydro-Gen, Iran, and Poison Ivy." It lists the big benefits of hydrogen supplementation, includes several testimonials, and is chatty and engaging. The references to Iran and Poison Ivy in the subject line, which were included to pique curiosity and get the e-mail read, are echoed in this text from the e-mail:

For most of us, saving money and time (fewer fill-ups) is a pretty good motivation all by itself. But in this case, there [are] a couple of very strong "non-selfish" reasons to want to consume less fuel.

Everyone has a different take on world politics, but I've never met anyone who thought that the U.S. should become more dependent on Middle Eastern oil. It's a little crazy to think that we're worried about Iran's nuclear program and that we've been funding that program at the pumps for years.

And I don't know about you, but I'm starting to believe the signs of global warming. There [have] been reports on the news about poison ivy plants growing faster and being itchier as the carbon dioxide levels in the atmosphere rise.

On the third day, we tackled the big objection: safety. An excerpt from the e-mail, titled "The Hindenburg, *Die Hard*, and Sad Toddlers: Is Hydrogen Safe?" follows:

Of course, we get a lot of questions at SaveFuel.ca about the Hindenburg. People want to know, "Is my car going to burst into flames over central New Jersey if I install a Hydro-Gen unit?"

It's a good question. It's the first thing I'd ask before installing anything in my car: Is it safe?

First of all, nothing is without its hazards. Forks, staplers, bicycles, cars, toasters — they all can be misused in dangerous ways. So the real question is, Is the Hydro-Gen safe if used properly?

Here's why the Hydro-Gen is safer than the gasoline or diesel you currently use:

+ + + Hydrogen is less of a fire hazard than gasoline + + +

The Hydro-Gen uses a small amount of electricity to turn water into its two component elements, hydrogen and oxygen. Hydrogen is much less flammable than gasoline. Gasoline bursts into flames at anywhere from 228–501 degrees Celsius (442–933 degrees Fahrenheit), while hydrogen doesn't ignite until 550 degrees Celsius (1,022 degrees Fahrenheit).

All those scenes in the Die Hard *movies where the car flips over and bursts into flames — that's ordinary gasoline, not hydrogen. Now, cars don't actually burst into flames very often in real life, but still — gasoline is far more likely to ignite than hydrogen gas.*

Here's another thing: If you were ever forced to memorize the first row of the periodic table, you'll recall that hydrogen is the first — and therefore lightest — element. How light? Fifteen times lighter than air. Twice as light as helium.

Did you ever give a helium balloon to a small child at the amusement park? And they let go? That balloon really took off, didn't it? Next time you comfort a sad toddler about the loss of their helium balloon, imagine a balloon twice as buoyant in air, filled with hydrogen.

Because it's so light, hydrogen disperses upwards. Quickly. It doesn't stick around and burn, like gasoline does. If you watch a video of the Hindenburg fire, you'll notice something amazing: That giant ship burns hydrogen only for 30 seconds. Rescuers run to the scene almost immediately.

(Check it out yourself in this video: http://tinyurl.com/lue73*)*

Here's a startling fact: 62 out of 97 passengers on the Hindenburg *survived the disaster on May 6, 1937, many of them relatively unharmed. The ones who died either fell, or were burned by dripping diesel fuel.*

Note the chatty yet authoritative tone, the use of story to make the point, and the non-salesy nature of the e-mail. This e-mail ends with a by-the-way call to action: " . . . if this e-mail has just put your mind at ease regarding safety, here's the link to order a Hydro-Gen and get started saving gas and money right away: www.savefuel.ca/oxy-hydrogen."

Another e-mail addresses concerns about the unit voiding a vehicle's warranty or harming the engine. Day 5's installment answers the objection, "This sounds too good to be true. If hydrogen supplementation works, then the big car companies would be using it."

Slowly, the autoresponder sequence answers objections, provides more and more testimonials, explains the technology, and culminates with an ironclad risk-reversal guarantee. Borrowing language from a Robert Collier sales letter of the 1930s, we write, "By ordering, you obligate me, not yourself. If it doesn't work the way I say it will, I insist that you return the Hydro-Gen for a full and prompt refund."

The result of this e-mail sequence, coupled with several other improvements to the site, including tested headlines, the addition of live chat, and live phone operators available 20 hours per day, was a doubling of the site conversion, from roughly 1.75% to 3.5%. Jaco relates that a competitor approached him in despair, asking whether he would consider selling the competitor's product on the www.savefuel.ca Web site.

Making Money in an Impossible Market

David Bullock of www.davidbullock.com believes so strongly in rigorous testing of the sales process that he decided to put his methodology to the test in a nearly impossible situation: buying AdWords clicks for $0.25 and sending the traffic to a Web page promoting an affiliate product that produces $4.25 per unit sale for David. In order to break even in this scenario, David's site needed to produce one sale for every 17 clicks. In other words, if the affiliate site — over which he had no control — could convert a very healthy 5% of its visitors to paying customers, David could not have made money on the front end, even if he had been able to send every single visitor to that site!

His goal for the campaign was a net profit of $30/day, stable and predictable. He gave himself one advantage: He chose an inexpensive product with built-in continuity — an impulse purchase that would lead customers to buy more over time.

During the intense testing phase, David limited his Web site traffic to 100 clicks per day. His conversion at the start of the experiment was 2%: one sale for every 50 visitors to his site.

Task #1: Lowering the bid price

The first task was to lower the bid price. At a quarter a click, there was no way to turn this campaign into a financial success. David employed two strategies: improving the ad CTR and firing underperforming keywords.

He employed Taguchi multivariate testing to find the ads with the highest CTR. Taguchi testing uses matrices to create several ad variations at a time, simulating the actual testing of thousands of ads. This method works only with a very significant traffic stream. If you only get a few hundred impressions per week, Taguchi testing will actually slow you down. From an initial figure of 0.25% in January 2006, David's CTR rose to 0.95% in February, 1.25% in March, and 1.73% in April. It now holds steady at approximately 2.00%, an eightfold improvement.

Second, he tracked his initial list of 335 keywords, and fired words that weren't leading to sales. Ultimately, the campaign contained only 85 keywords. David's CPC is now $0.12, less than half its original cost.

Task #2: Improving Web site conversion

David focused his tests on three elements of his landing page: the headline, the presence or absence of a photograph of the product, and the text on the page. The original headline was "How to Buy X." The eventual winner became, "How to Get X without Any Hidden Harmful Y" (sorry, he's not going to reveal the product or the Web site).

He found that an image of the product improved conversion, and that a long-copy Web page did better than a short-copy Web page. Once the page format was established, David performed Taguchi testing on the first few paragraphs of the copy to establish the right words in the right order.

Now the site sends 50 percent of its AdWords visitors straight to the affiliate site where they can purchase the product. One visitor out of every 24 makes a purchase. His overall conversion rate from click to sale is 4.37%, significantly higher than the breakeven requirement of 3.32%. And because of the continuity, the back-end profits make the site even more lucrative. In April 2007, David spent $109 on AdWords and earned $1,122 in affiliate income. Additionally (he'll be embarrassed for me to reveal), it took over an hour for him to look up all these numbers because he locked down this campaign over a year ago and hasn't touched it since.

A single AdWords campaign to a single Web page selling a product he doesn't make, stock, or ship — and it pays the mortgage month after month. All because David focused on the fundamentals and tested and tracked his results rigorously.

Index